BEYOND THE 'BUT'

A Long Road to India

Alun Person

Copyright © Alun Person 2015
This book is sold subject to the condition that it shall not, by way of trade or otherwise, be lent, resold, hired out, or otherwise circulated without the publisher's prior consent in any form of binding or cover other than that in which it is published and without a similar condition including this condition being imposed on the subsequent publisher.
The moral right of Alun Person has been asserted.
ISBN-13: 978-1507776841
ISBN-10: 1507776845

To my navigator, through land and life.

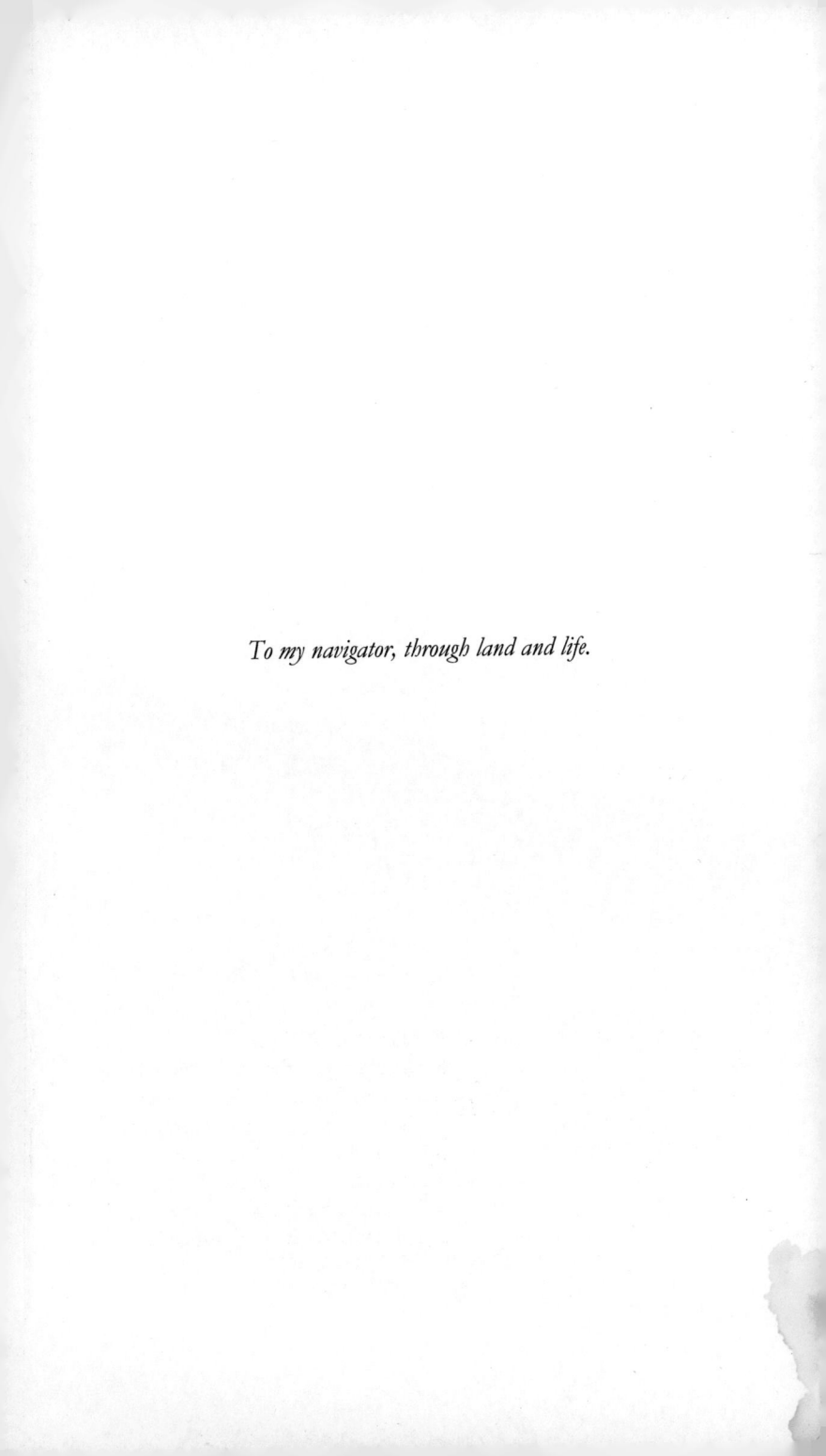

CONTENTS

Chapter 1 England *1*

Chapter 2 France and Belgium *16*

Chapter 3 Amsterdam *24*

Chapter 4 France *31*

Chapter 5 Italy, Croatia, Slovenia and Yugoslavia *55*

Chapter 6 Greece *81*

Chapter 7 Turkey *95*

Chapter 8 Iran *136*

Chapter 9 Afghanistan *290*

Chapter 10 Pakistan *314*

Chapter 11 India *350*

Chapter 12 England *456*

Chapter 13 India *472*

Chapter 14 England *484*

AFGHAN INSURANCE COMPANY

P.O.BOX 329,
GHASI WATT,
KABUL, AFGHANISTAN.

VISITORS TO AFGHANISTAN:

You have just arranged temporary assurance with this Company, and to make your motoring holiday more enjoyable and accident free we would draw your attention to the following points:

1. Horse drawn vehicles and cyclists do not have lights at night and parked vehicles are not often lit.

2. Careful watch at night must be kept for load-carrying animals, man propelled carts and pedestrains.

3. Cyclists never obey "Stop" signs or traffic lights.

4. Lorries and taxis are often driven onto main roads from side turnings without stopping.

5. Each patch of shade is likely to hide a child or an animal.

6. In the event of an accident it is probable that the driver of the vehicle will be detained and in some cases the vehicle as well.

7. In the event of an accident, please inform the Company immediately.

8. No admission, offer, promise or payment shall be made by or on behalf of the Insured.

9. The Insurance Company is only responsible for claims made upon the Insured by Third Party. Traffic fines are the responsibility of the Insured.

10. Finally, the local people expect to be given warning by horn.

<u>We wish you a safe journey</u>!

..../hk

(Back row) Timus, Kakey, Isobel, Alun, Black Bob, Alun Jnr, Fran. (Front row) Glynis, Charlie with baby Mellony. Behind you can just see our bus.

Alun, Isobel, Mellony and Alun Jnr. Stopped for a cup of tea. The place is halfway between Kandahar and Kabul. Long drive, hot day!

Gulf Road Photos

A 'white freightliner' after rolling a few times.

They treat them like toys.

Gulf road boys. They'll grease your truck while you have dinner.

Long road. Gulf route, Ahwaz, Iran 1975.

No breaks left, Gulf Road 1975.

Asleep at the wheel

The docks at Bandar Shapoor, now (2014) Bandar Khomini

Causeway to floating docks Bandar Shapoor, Iran 1975.

This Dutchman didn't make it home. Gulf Road, Iran 1975.

Goa Photos

Sunset, Anjuna Beach, GOA 1975.

Anjuna Beach, 1975.

The fish lady calls at our house.

Bobby's Chai Shop, Anguna Beach, GOA 1976.

Persopolis. Southern Persia (Iran)

Chapter 1

England

The 1970s hit me like an express train. Everything happened for me during that decade. I got married, had children, got involved with LSD, ended up in a psychiatric hospital, went to prison for possession, got divorced, met my lifetime's companion, went travelling and made loads of money.

While recovering in a psychiatric hospital in the city of Wells, Somerset, South West England, from excessive use of LSD. I met a gorgeous, leggy, tall student nurse by the name of Isobel. She had a beautiful mind and a body to die for, a body that was hugged very closely by her green student nurse's uniform. She was nineteen years old, five years younger than me. This was her first time away from the farm that her parents owned over in Upper Langford near Weston-Super-Mare, South West England. She was engaged to a young hardware salesman and her future was planned out by her parents and relatives. To say that the excreta hit the air circulation device, is the polite way of putting it. In her parents eyes, I was everything they loathed and feared. You can't blame them. Here was this hairy, drug using, psychiatric patient, married with two children, and in their eyes, an all-round waste of space. Not only that, a socialist, against their countryside, working class, right wing, Tory-voting world.

We were the 'chalk and cheese' that the proverb talks of. What happened from there, I will tell another time. It would make a good movie. Suffice it to say that Isobel gave up everything to be with me, even being written out of her parents' will. I take comfort in the fact that before Isobel's parents died 30 or so years later in comfortable old age, we were as close as blood relations! They passed on a few years ago knowing that Isobel and I were, and still are, together. Now with three beautiful grandchildren and thirty-five years, or so, under our belts.

By 1973 I was twenty-three years old. I'd cleaned up my act, divorced a wife that I should never have married in the first place, gained custody of my two beautiful kids, Alun and Mellony and was living in the run down, garden suburb of Montpelier, in Bristol, with Isobel. I was working as a truck mechanic or truck driving.

The 1970s as I remember them were not rich. Housing was a big problem; the housing debacle of the 1970s was at its height and the semi-slum landlords were making a killing out of the students or otherwise homeless. Isobel, the kids and I were living in a single room, albeit large, in a three-storey student residence typical of the area. Poorly paid jobs were there if you dug around and kissed as much arse as possible but wages were so low as to just keep you ticking over, especially with a young family. The 'system' offered only stagnation as a future.

There was a thriving 'alternative culture' in Bristol. This

ranged from the black and hippy communities of St Paul's and Montpelier, known locally as 'the Jungle' to the upmarket but just as 'student' and 'alternative', Clifton, known as 'Ponceville'. The cannabis revolution was in full flood and every man and his brother were puffing away. You could get the really nasty stuff like speed, coke and smack etc., but there was no big 'powder' scene in the city at that time. The floods of cartel cocaine and war torn, cheap heroin had yet to arrive on these shores in large quantities. I admit to being well into the subculture and was known as a bit of a cannabis 'buff', someone who was not cheap but the quality of the goods were beyond reproach. I got to know hundreds of people and could move amongst those importing as well as those buying on street level.

Montpelier was full of 'The ragged people' to quote Simon & Garfunkel's 'The Boxer'. All classes, all races, all shapes, colours and characters. It was a good place to be, where nobody judged anyone else, and I don't remember any racially motivated crime or violence, we respected each other and nowhere was barred to either black, white, Irish or Asian. To illustrate how life was then: there was an old run-down cinema just off the Gloucester Road by The Arches, called 'The Scala'. It had been closed for a couple of years until the 'freaks and hairies' moved into the area and started to run late night 'cult' movies like Mick Jagger's *Blow-Up*, Stan Kubrick's *A Clockwork Orange*, and Bogart's *Casablanca* etc., etc.

The Friday night show was very popular. It began at midnight and this particular Friday show was the hilarious 1930s anti-dope film *Reefer Madness*. It was being shown to howls of laughter from the audience. The place usually stunk of various strains of 'the herb' or "erb" as herbal marijuana was known, and various solid hashish types, like medium quality Moroccan or Pakistani Black. Suddenly without warning, the film was interrupted and a disembodied voice with a heavy West Indian accent penetrated the darkness, over the P.A. "Bredren' and frien'. Me got some crucial word, man. Me tell ya frien', 'erbie bin captured by de man. 'Im in 'orfield (Horfield) jail waitin' trial. Bredren! Y'all know 'im give good deal and good quality, 'im never rip-off. We takin' collection on de way out, yu' put in de money, we make 'im free. We now ask two-minute silence to spark up and remember 'erbie."

There followed general nods of agreement and rustling of skins and matches as everyone lit up and thought of Herbie (it was not his real name, just his profession). On went the film. Eventually Herbie was able to hire a good Q.C. and got just two years instead of five for 100 kilos of weed, a lot of dope in those days. Life went on wheeling and dealing, ducking diving and surviving into 1975. All the time I knew there was something better and all it took was a little hunger for adventure and travel. It would be possible to do what my parents could not; opt out of conventional life and go globetrotting. Who wanted to be locked into a dead-end, low paid job and a mortgage designed to enslave you for life, when there was a world out there? Some of which I'd already seen as a serving soldier. In fact it's worth noting, that the first place I got involved with sex and drugs, was in the British Army in Singapore! I was already well into rock 'n' roll!

During my social rounds in Bristol, I had come across a bunch of young people who were squatting in one of the beautiful, multi-floored, Regency properties that were empty at the time in the Clifton area. The owners hadn't returned from their yacht in Monte Carlo and this particular house, and several others in the architecturally important terrace, lay empty while thousands in the city were homeless. The group consisted of Timus (Tim) their leader, and his lady 'Kakey' (Cathy) who was a local to Bristol and had their particular accent – soft and round, to some, moronic, West Country yokel, to others; Black Bob of Pakistani or Indian ancestry, depending which country we were in at the time; Charlie, the artist-with-bad-attitude and Glynis, his slender, shapely partner, with whom I'd already had a casual scene some time ago when Isobel and I were on a break in our relationship (we were on a BREAK!); Syd the 'free-wheeling Franklin' character from *The Fabulous Furry Freak Brothers*; Other Tim and his partner, the petite and perfectly formed Debbie; and lastly, Fran. Fran was a strange and slightly plump young girl with short hennaed hair and an effected shyness that didn't fool me.

They were a strange group. Psychology students would have had a field day studying tribal ways, leaders and followers, the intertwine of relationships, especially as they were fairly loose and open about sleeping with each other! They would survive as a group by working at short, highly paid but dirty or dangerous jobs. Other times they'd sell some weed and sign on the dole. They would give all their money to Timus and live very cheaply indeed until they had enough saved to do what they wanted.

One fateful day in early '75, Isobel, the kids and I returned from the park to find a note pinned to our front door. It was from the group, signed by Glynis. She knew I was an experienced heavy truck mechanic-cum-driver and that was just what they wanted as their plan involved buying a suitable vehicle, converting and driving it, none of which they could do themselves. It seems that they had held a meeting and decided that the UK was not a nice place to be so they wanted to go east. After all, they reasoned, that's where the dope comes from! They had read Jack Kerouac's *On The Road*, also *Easy Rider* and the *Magic Bus Hippie Trail* of the early '70s and wanted some of it.

The note was written on a piece of scrap paper and difficult to decipher. At first I thought it was asking me to 'do a trip' with them. I hadn't done acid for years. I thought it strange but nice of them to offer. I put the note in my pocket and forgot it until a few days later.

Isobel had just got the kids ready for bed when there was a knock on the front door. As was my habit, at the time, I looked out the window to the front door below, to see a sizeable group of people. My initial reaction was that we were being busted by the drug squad, who in those days were even bigger villains than the people they were busting and thought nothing of planting evidence if they couldn't get what they wanted. On second glance I recognised Glynis amongst them. This calmed down the rest of the house and stashes that were poised over the toilet bowl were returned to their containers by trembling hands, with mumbled words of relief.

The group had decided that mass persuasion and plying with good drugs was the way to go. I started to say how nice it was of them to visit and bring such high quality resin, but that I gave up acid years ago. "Did you want me to assess the quality or something?" They looked at each other with puzzled expressions. I picked up on their glances. "Your note said something about doing a trip with you."

Glynis realised what had happened and started laughing. In her broad Kendal accent she said, "Noo yuh daf' booger. D'yu want t' GO on 'trip wi' us?"

"Ohhhhh!" said I, my brain struggling to translate Kendal into English. With dawning realisation, and feeling a bit foolish, "Where to?" I gasped between the guffaws.

Just as my cup of coffee touched my lips, Glynis replied in a now silent room, "India!"

I did the classic coffee-down-the-nose job. When I recovered, I glanced at them each in turn. They appeared to be serious. When I questioned them about money, paperwork etc., they answered my questions and seemed to have done their homework. "You are really serious about this aren't you?" They nodded in as near bright-eyed enthusiasm as the late hour and huge amounts of cannabis consumed would allow.

As I listened, their enthusiasm and confidence impressed me. The excitement grew and it was difficult to maintain a level response. Eventually, late into the night we finished our talking and I promised to go to their squat next day and give them their answer, Isobel and I would have to talk it over between us.

Sleep would be impossible. My mind was racing with the possibilities. Here was the dream I'd always had. To live in a bus and drive it anywhere! As Isobel closed the front door behind them she turned and looked at me. In that instant I knew we were going on a wonderful adventure, the rest was window dressing! We flung our arms around each other in excitement. We barely made it to the bed, ripping each other's clothes off as we went. Adventure is a powerful aphrodisiac!

Next afternoon I rode my old moped through the afternoon traffic of the Gloucester Road, up through Redland, across Blackboy Hill into Clifton. The huge front door opened to my second knock. I walked towards the open stairway. As I got to the bottom step, Glynis appeared at the top of the stairs with most of the group in tow. They perched on the landing and stairs and asked me, "What d'you reckon?"

I paused for effect. "As long as you understand that the driving and upkeep of the bus are down to me and that wherever we go, as far as I'm concerned, my family comes first." I smiled. "That agreed, then yes I'm your new driver."

The place erupted with a big cheer and Black Bob came down the stairs and shook my hand, grinned, and said, "We're going to have some good times, man." I agreed but at the same time I could foresee a possible friction point. I am my own man and there was no way I was going to submit to anyone else's will. I would not be led like the others and to a certain extent was aside from the group.

They in turn were totally reliant on me for the inspection, purchase and preparing of a suitable vehicle and then getting all the paperwork together, then driving to India.

We looked at a number of vehicles over the next month with nothing suitable coming up. One day, in rushed a breathless Syd. "I've just been speaking to a guy who has an old AEC single decker for sale. D'you think it would be any good? He lives up Gloucester way."

I was already grabbing my keys and we all piled into a borrowed van and set off for the place. We surprised him by almost beating him home. And there's me telling everyone not to act too eager!

It was a 40-seater AEC Reliance, the six-cylinder diesel engine, was slung on its side, and mounted halfway down the chassis, toward the back of the bus. It was of 1955 vintage and very clean for its years. The engine had an oil pressure that was good when cold but dropped alarmingly when hot, typical of the AECs of that era. It didn't burn any oil and all in all, was worth the £350 that the owner was asking. I looked closely at the whole bus inside and underneath and decided that it was just what we wanted. Actually I'd wanted it as soon as I saw it. I figured to check as much as possible before leaving, as there sure wasn't going to be any AEC spares for a bus that old where we were going!

The next few weeks were a whirlwind of activity. I would wake up on the bed with a sock half off and would not be able to remember whether I'd fallen asleep getting up or going to bed! For me it was getting all the customs documents together. In those days to take a vehicle into Pakistan, India and Nepal you needed a customs document called a Carnet de Passage. This was a large pad of entry and exit counterfoils that you had to get stamped on the vehicle's entry and exit of the country. It was designed to stop the flood of western vehicles being allowed into the country as tourist vehicles and then sold without paying import duty on them. If you did not get the proper stamps on exit, the issuing authority, in my case the RAC, would be liable for the import duty which would be calculated on double the estimated price of the vehicle. The RAC would only issue this Carnet when a deposit of the new value of the vehicle was in their bank account. This deposit would be refunded at the end of the trip, on presentation of the cleared customs documents from India or Pakistan. We had known nothing about this document!

We were stopped in our tracks. We couldn't come up with the deposit of tens of thousands of pounds that the RAC wanted, to issue a Carnet. We were all gutted and the group meal that night was silent. I told them to leave it with me – I'd dig around a bit, see what I could find out. Next day, feeling as though I was just going through the motions, I went to the RAC office in Whiteladies Road to pick up my international driving licences. While there, I was talking to a chatty counter lady and telling her what I thought of her rip-off organisation. She looked at me with surprise. "Haven't you been to Hamblins the insurance people in London?"

I asked her to explain, she went on to tell me that Hamblins specialised in insuring you for the sum needed by the RAC before issuing the Carnet. This was wonderful news. I could have kissed her, as the premium for the insurance was only £300 a year. A chunk out of the budget but more attainable than twice the new value of the vehicle!

I flew back to report this joyous news and was greeted like a victorious warrior. While I was away Charlie, the artist among us, had decided to paint the bus in stars and stripes with pictures of Hendrix and lions all over it. "I see you have written 'Bust Me' all over it," I said disapprovingly. We all got totally shit-faced that night. It was a wonderful evening full of a sense that if we could overcome that kind of obstacle then we can do anything! I'll draw a veil over the rest of the night's proceedings, but it was VERY friendly, all round!

With most of the paperwork done it only remained for me to get the bus together mechanically while the others got busy building the bunks and cooking area inside the bus. Charlie came into his own on this and was a good carpenter. I decided to renew all the oil and fuel filters and have the injector pump and injectors checked and set up correctly. We all took a test drive over to Tom Day, fuel injection specialists in Keynsham, a firm still trading as I write. When he saw the bus and heard what we intended, he said he would check the pump for free and that he had a new pump on his shelves that he would never use. He asked if we would like to take it with us as a spare. We were dumbfounded and accepted quickly before he could change his mind. This was not the last time we were to come across great generosity from people who were inspired by what we were doing. For instance, the teachers at our children's infants' school were so concerned about the kids' education that they gave us a complete set of books that they would use over the year, at school.

There were so many people who would say, "We think what you are doing is amazing. We'd love to come with you but..." Always the 'but'. We had decided to go beyond the 'but', and we were not playing at it, we were deadly serious.

On the way back from Tom Day's place, we decided to go for a short test drive. Everything went well until we started to climb out of Pensford on the return journey. The road out of the village is steep and narrow, requiring large vehicles to stop and let each other pass. Where did the fuel lift pump, the only part of the fuel system I hadn't renewed, decide to give up? Right on the narrow part going uphill. I managed to reverse back down the hill and got just far enough in to let other vehicles get by. A couple of the group were beginning to get very worried. I assured them that it'd be OK and to their amazement started to pull the access hatches up in the middle of the aisle.

I set about bodging up the lift pump. It was clear that the thing was worn out and I was glad I'd renewed the rest of the system. On inspection of the diaphragm there was a small hole worn in it. That small hole meant no suction and no pressure, which equals no fuel to the rest of the system. Luckily I'd bought a couple of packs of Araldite Rapid Industrial. I mixed up a tiny amount and covered the hole. We waited for the Araldite to harden. After about an hour I had managed to get the pump working enough to get us home. I replaced the hatches, grabbed the cup of tea that had been made for me, and sat in the driving seat. "Should be ok but keep your fingers crossed," I said as I hit the starter button and prayed that the four massive 6 volt batteries, wired in series for 24 volts, would last long enough to crank the engine, to put fuel in the cylinders and to fire up. Over and over went the starter motor. Nothing. I stopped, counted to ten and tried again. Nothing. I looked round at the others – they were looking a bit anxious. As I turned I caught Isobel's eye. She was smiling just slightly and was fully relaxed. As I looked at her I hit the starter button again. Two turns and it spluttered on a couple of cylinders, then it picked up as it got more fuel.

Eventually it ran smooth and over the din of cheering and the engine I heard Glynis say, "See I told you. 'E'se a bloody genius." I must say it felt good to have cracked our first mechanical problem. Isobel's smile got ever so slightly wider!

Next day we went to the local AEC main dealer in Bristol to buy a new lift pump. The spares counter staff were so impressed with our old AEC that they gave us the new pump at half trade price. They also gave us a load of spares left on their shelves that they would never sell. That saved a load of money but there was one thing they didn't have that I wasn't going to leave without. Half shafts. Mountain hill-starts, with the vehicle fully loaded, have been known to snap one or two half shafts in the rear axle, in my experience. Once we left England, there would be no chance of finding new ones. This meant an excursion, in the bus, to a dockside bus breakers in what used to be the Tiger Bay area of Cardiff. It would be the first time we would be using the bus as we would be using it in the months to come.

The yard was a paradise to the bus enthusiast. There were ex-London Transport double deckers, half-cab, AECs and old 'fishtailed' Bedfords, row upon row. Everything that I needed was there. The owner of the yard was an affable, straight Welshman and readily agreed to us parking overnight as we didn't get all I wanted. He locked us in the yard and we set about cleaning up and getting some dinner. The only place with running water was the old toilet block. The girls decided they didn't want to shower in a dirty, draughty, open shower room, and as we had curtains all-round the bus it was decided that water should be heated by the bucketful and strip washes on a plastic sheet, in the back of the bus were the order of the day. We may be hairy travellers but dirty was not our way. We washed, bathed and cleaned the inside of the bus, every day, even in cold water, much to the kids' hatred!

The women and kids decided to go first and after heating a couple of bucketfuls of water I started to put my jacket on and open the door. "Where 'yu going?" asked Black Bob.

"The girls are taking a wash," I said, as if that answered everything.

Cathy appeared round the partition that separated the kitchen/living area from the double bunks area. She had already removed her top in preparation, revealing two larger-than-average breasts of exquisite form. It fair took my breath away but I struggled to hide my reaction. "We are going to be living closely together for a long time so what the fuck? Shut the door you're letting all the heat out," said Cathy without embarrassment of any kind.

I looked at Black Bob, he said, "Don't look at me mate, I just love these tits walking around all day. I don't have a partner at the moment, so it's the only way I get to see any naked crumpet." While talking, he had manoeuvred closer to Cathy and gave her left breast a fondle. She slapped his hand away with a laugh and flounced off down the back of the bus.

I looked around to see everyone laughing. The boys sat down and started skinning up, drinking coffee and talking about the day's progress. As we talked, there at the back of the bus, in full view of us all, were the girls including Isobel, continuing to strip and pouring steaming water into plastic bowls. I tried to act as if this happened every day but inside I was on fire watching my own Isobel, naked as the day she was born, washing the back of the other girls, also naked as the day they were born. The others had been living as a family for a long time and were, to a certain extent, blasé about it all. In the end I gave in and watched openly. Eventually I had to get up and go to the driver's seat on the pretence of doing something to the bus, it was just too much for a young, hetero male to take. Over the coming months we would often be naked and even making love in each other's company, without embarrassment. If the trip was going to go like this, then it was going to be even better than I had anticipated. I came from an all-male household, excluding mother, of course. I wasn't used to naked females that I wasn't having a relationship with. It was a pleasant learning curve for me!

Next day we continued to gather spares and by midday the only thing left to do was to extract a spare wheel from a pile of scrap bus chassis. The heavy bus wheel had to be lifted over an obstacle and Syd, Charley and Timus were heaving away and generally goofing around, despite my warnings that scrapyards are very dangerous places. Just as they got to the top of their lift I looked up to see them about to give the wheel a final shove and let gravity do the rest. "Nooo!" I shouted, but it was too late. They'd forgotten to take into account the fact that the tyre was still inflated. Sure enough it bounced quickly down the yard and straight into the door of a beautifully restored and painted American Dodge Polara owned by one of the lads in the yard. I was livid. There was no way we could not tell the guy we'd just trashed his driver's door.

He took it remarkably calmly, which was a good thing as he was a big Welsh dude. I'd have gone apeshit. When looked at closely it wasn't as bad as it looked. The paint hadn't cracked and although dented, the panel hadn't creased. I spent the rest of the day in the cold, stripping the interior door trim and handles to gain access to the rear of the panel. I applied equal and opposite pressure to that which the runaway tyre had applied, and with a satisfying 'crack' the dent came out without a mark on the paintwork. A quick, intense polish finished it off. It was well dark by the time I finished. I got back to some very guilty faces. I slid the door open and all went silent. They couldn't do enough for me.

"Cup of hot tea Alun?"

"Would you like dinner now or some hot water to clean up first?"

I decided they'd learned their lesson.

"Relax, just be more aware in future. We'll be in some dangerous situations, not helped by the fact that we are well stoned, most of the time, so just be careful."

There was a chorus of "Yeah, right man, he's right y'know. Sorry Alun."

"Don't apologise to me. I just had to slip him a £20 note for his trouble, that's coming out of trip money!"

We spent another night in the yard, reasoning that a few beers could be partaken as we'd had a good mission despite the remodelling of the car door. Next day we drove back to Bristol buzzing in the knowledge that departure was only a week away. I had all the spares I wanted.

Eventually we were ready to go and I arranged to take the bus to the water tower up on the Downs as a departure point. When I arrived I was horrified to see the amounts of luggage they'd brought and promptly told them to dump about half of it. They weren't happy about it but couldn't argue because I had given them all sorts of technical reasons why they couldn't bring all that crap, i.e. overweight means high fuel consumption, working the bus too hard in the heat etc., etc. We packed what was left, still too much, and said goodbye to friends that had come to see us off. The idea was to drive down to The Stonehenge Festival, stay a few days, and leave for the hovercraft in Dover.

We decided that as we were going to the festival we should take a thousand microdot acid tabs and sell them for a quid a hit. This we did and it enabled us to pay for our hovercraft tickets and diesel for the bus. It was a wonderful festival, the sun shone and as we drove away everybody waved. We had attracted attention. This was long before traveller's convoys gave it all a bad name. Not many people lived in buses in those days, let alone drove to India in them.

Chapter 2

France and Belgium

We arrived at Dover Hoverport on a wet and blustery day. The rest of the group went on board the huge hovercraft while I followed the directions to load the heavy bus in the middle of the craft. Cars were being packed around the bus as I climbed the stairs to join the others in the seating saloon. Eventually the engines started and wound up. The craft began to rise on its air cushion.

Slowly we started down the slipway, onto the water of the English Channel. We were on the first steps of what would turn out to be a life altering journey. When would we be seeing these shores again? The crossing was a bit rough. We would hit the tops of the waves, thundering down the bottle neck that is the English Channel, from the North Sea. Each wave top would bring a shudder from the craft but it carried on and forty-five minutes later we had arrived. I drove the bus out from the hovercraft and the wheels touched foreign soil for the first time.

We arrived in France with seven people, two kids, a bus, and just £200 left in the kitty!

The only problem was that Charlie, Glynis and Syd had been late with their passport applications, so they headed for the passport office in Newport and we had to leave them behind as the hovercraft was booked for that specific day. They were camped out in Newport and spending every day hassling the passport office staff mercilessly until they got their passports. They would then travel, public transport, to Dover and we'd pick them up from Calais Hoverport. This meant that we had to hang around Calais and environs for a week or so.

We drove out of Calais as soon as possible that afternoon and stopped in the first large lay-by. By now it was late afternoon so we decided to stay there for the night and got down to preparing dinner. I, of course, was exempt from any of this 'domestic engineering'. Being the only driver and mechanic, it was decided that when I wasn't driving or maintaining, I wasn't required to peel potatoes!

We had all been too worried about French Customs to bring any dope with us. That, and the fact that Charlie had written 'bust me' on the bus with his painted stars and stripes. Charlie and I had fallen out about that. At first I'd asked him why the fuck he had done that and refused to drive it painted like a carnival float. He had to tone it down a bit. As it was, we were getting loads of waves from the French people, believing us to be a touring theatre group of some kind. The French love to show their approval of such things with a wave. The welcome smell of dinner, usually preceded by a pre-dinner spliff at home, would have to be greeted with some wine, the quality of which can be gauged from the fact that it came in a plastic bottle and cost two Francs!

The kids were still in the 'novelty mode', and getting them to go to their bunks was no problem. They were living and sleeping in an old bus and that was the coolest thing. They were also being spoilt rotten by the others and they soon learned the politics of manipulating grown-ups! The windows steamed up with the cooking. All the curtains were closed and with the interior lights on, the atmosphere on board was excited and happy; we planned what to do tomorrow. It was decided to go to the local park in Calais and throw some Frisbee. We'd do some shopping and see what the scene was.

The wine, dinner and a long day's driving took its toll. I mumbled goodnight, and warned not to leave the interior lights on too long or we'd have no battery in the morning. I then staggered to the back, climbed on the double bunk and passed out. Isobel must've undressed and covered me, I didn't make it that far myself. Thus was my first night in France. The others burnt the candles on into the night.

Bit grey the next day but not actually raining. The fuel tank was a bit low so I decided that a fuel transfer routine could now be practised, the exercise being, to transfer red diesel from the forty-gallon barrel that I had installed in the boot, to the main tank. I set the lads to getting the hand pump set up and we took turns to fill the tank.

Driving to Dover I had run the tank deliberately low, in the knowledge that the diesel bowser from the local petroleum products distributor would be on the dockside filling up the tanks of the refrigeration plant on the 'fridge, articulated trucks, that were waiting to board the ferries. This would be red diesel which is tax-free and intended for farm and stationery machinery. As it is tax free, it is illegal to use it on ordinary road going diesels in the UK. It has a red dye that is extremely difficult to get rid of. If you happen to mix some red with its tax paid, legal, white diesel counterpart, the tell-tale red dye will hang around in your tank for a very long time, increasing your chances of being nicked by Customs and Excise, should you be unlucky enough to get a roadside inspection from them. They take a very dim view of anyone using 'cherryade' on the Queen's highway! It was referred to as cherryade as it resembled the soft drink. The French don't give a toss what colour your diesel is! I filled every tank and container with cherryade.

By the time we got to the park, the sun was shining. It had taken much longer to get there as I was still learning to drive on the right. We formed a large circle and started to throw the Frisbee. All of the boys were quite skilled with the device and before long a small group was watching us. I noticed one particular face in the crowd. A young lad about our age, with the soft-eyed, smiling, open face of the dope smoker. I could see he wanted a throw so next time the disc came to me, I waved it at him, indicating that I was going to throw to him. Without hesitation he joined in and we laughed a lot that afternoon. We learned that his name was Claude and he lived in Calais. Claude was blown away when we showed him the bus and invited him on board for a coffee.

"'Ave you le shit?" asked Claude.

"What?" said Black Bob. "We don't have a toilet on board we use the woods."

"Non, non. Le shit you know, shit." Claude made a toking gesture with his fingers.

"Ahhhh," I said, as it hit me that the French still use the old English word for cannabis which was 'shit'. I told Claude that we all loved a smoke but were too paranoid with French customs etc. The memories of the Timothy Davey busts in Turkey and the *Midnight Express* episode had just gone down, again in Turkey. We had agreed before leaving that we would wait until we got to the countries that were a little more relaxed about smoking dope, before we would indulge.

"Ah, le Duane Français," snorted Claude with disgust. "All they are interested in, is stealing from the truck drivers or anyone else who comes through. They are arseholes."

"Yeah," said I. "It's a shame, I'd love a smoke right now." I was never the one for drink but I'd smoke anyone under the table and I was already missing it. Not like you would miss heroin, with the cramps, sweating, running nose, shaking etc. This was milder than craving for a cigarette, but still there.

"Oui, it make me crazy, zat one country you can smoke but three 'undred kilometre sud, zey go mad. It ees just too crazeeey," said Claude.

We all laughed out loud at Claude's drawn out expression, 'too crazeeee'. It became one of the 'sayings of the trip'. From then on everything was described as 'too crazeeee' with our best, exaggerated French accents. Not only that but his statement that dope was freely and cheaply available in Amsterdam had started us toward an adventure that was the precursor for many other incredible happenings as we travelled the vast road to India.

We parked in town that night. In a place that Claude had shown us. As dinner was being cooked, I sat in the driver's seat, people-watching in the dark. I noticed Timus coming down the aisle towards me. He slumped down in the seat opposite and said quietly, "What d'you reckon?" I didn't have to ask what he was talking about. It had already crossed my mind. Timus was the thinker of the group and he recognised that I was the only one he had to talk to to implement any plans. We had a respect for each other. "We've got a week of sitting around here. We might as well go."

"How much money do we have?" I asked.

"Enough for the diesel at three hundred kilometres, at, say, ten to the gallon, we're actually doing more than that. We could buy around half a kilo, sell it by the gram and make around £400 profit with all the bills paid. Claude reckons it would sell here at ten Francs a gram."

"Hmmm," I said.

"Yeah, it's your call," said Timus. You'll be doing the driving across the borders."

I thought some more and after a while I said, "Always wanted to see Amsterdam."

Timus nodded. I said I'd leave him to tell the others. This he did and it was generally agreed that Amsterdam would be a great place to see and we couldn't wait to get started.

We met Claude for coffee and croissants the next morning and told him we were going to meet friends and we would see him here in 5 days' time. We left for Amsterdam that morning sticking to the national routes rather than pay the tolls on the autoroutes which were expensive. As soon as we crossed into Belgium we got onto the autoroutes to save time. I was beginning to relax into driving on the right and the motorway was impressive with big overhead signs saying things like 'Gent', 'Utrecht', 'Antwerp' and 'Masstrict'. I felt like the big international driver as we ploughed on into the night. Just before the city, I stopped in a service area for what was left of the night. Most people had crashed out while I drove, so I just turned out the light, got undressed, and fell asleep.

We stowed away all the overnight gear and drove on toward Amsterdam, now only fifteen miles distant. Before we got too far, I noticed a police car following us. "Looks like we're going to get a pull," I said. "The old bill are behind."

This caused a flurry of action.

"Relax!" I shouted. "We haven't got anything, remember?" It was a reflex action to grab the stash for possible eating at the last moment!

"Shit! Right man, we're clean. They can't do fuck all. I'm going to wind them up a bit," said Charlie and proceeded to wave at them through the back window, but with a smile.

It wasn't long before a couple of others and both the kids were waving at them. I'd been watching them in the mirror. All of a sudden they pulled to the right a little so that they were a clear view in my mirror, switched their blue lights on for an instant and flashed their headlights. I immediately signalled my compliance and we came to a stop on the hard shoulder.

Both the driver and his partner got out and approached my driver's door. They both wore sidearms, something we weren't used to, had smart uniforms with leather jackets and hair down to their shoulders! I was surprised to see how laid-back they were. As they approached, they looked closely at the tyres, lights and general appearance of the bus. To my surprise they actually saluted me!

"This bus is not roadworthy. We can get our technical police here to inspect it."

"I'll tell you something right here and now," I replied with a little indignity. "You can bring any expert you like and I will help you by going over every inch of this vehicle but I can tell you now that this bus is old but in excellent condition. I am a qualified heavy vehicle mechanic and I went over everything before leaving England."

It worked. The one that had spoken said something to his partner in Flemish. There was a curt nod between them and he turned, smiled, saluted again, waved to the kids and departed saying, "Don't smoke the marijuana and drive, it is dangerous, OK?"

"Thanks fellahs, I'll remember that, we don't get that kind of advice from our police." I waved back. They both grinned, got in the car, pulled onto the motorway, and sped by with a blast on their siren and more waving. How nice they had been. Direct but friendly and polite, and they could see I wasn't bullshitting.

Chapter 3

Amsterdam

"What the fuck?" was a very common expression from me in the next few hours as I drove our way into central Amsterdam. It was a nightmare! A very steep learning curve for me! Especially turning left at a major junction. The confusion came from the fact that not only do you have a way for vehicles, but other lanes for trams, which, if there were no trams present, then it was OK to drive along there as well. The tram lane and other vehicle lane were separated by a line of kerb stones so once you entered them you had to go that way till the next junction. The other lane to the right of the carriageways was the bicycle lane which was very busy with bikes. I wasn't used to bike lanes. We didn't have any in Britain at the time. But here in Amsterdam they were everywhere. Not content with the bike lanes they would dart everywhere without too much notice! I needed all my concentration and was very glad that I'd not had anything to smoke that morning, that's for sure! Just to add spice, we had hit the lunchtime rush traffic.

I eventually stumbled onto a large quayside that was big enough to take the bus and plenty to spare. "Don't start leaving the bus yet," I said. "Someone is bound to want us to move on." A number of barges were moored up and a couple of faces appeared at portholes to see what had pulled up. After half an hour or so, a young guy and his lady came over to the bus. "Here we go," I announced as they approached. "You can't park this here I'm calling the police," I mimicked. We had been tainted by some reactions we had received when parking in England. Timus drew the door along and met them at the steps.

In a Dutch accent the guy said, "Hi. Do you want some coffee or some things?"

"Oh!" said a surprised Timus. "That's very kind of you but we have everything on board. Would you like to come aboard and have coffee with us?"

He smiled broadly. "Ya ve come, danka. But first Gina will get the fresh croissant."

Gina disappeared to return with a tray of warm croissant, butter and strawberry jam. Our new friends were Henk and Gina. They lived in a canal barge tied alongside several others in a little canal community, just a block or so from Damm Square and the railway station. They had two children the same age as Alun and Mellony. Both pairs of children had met and were playing like old friends on the quayside.

As we finished the coffee, I remarked to everyone that I was going to catch up on some sleep as I hadn't got too much yesterday. It was a beautiful sunny day and I was sorry I needed to sleep as I wanted to explore the city and try a few different smokes in a few different coffee shops!

"Would you like to smoke before you sleep?" said Henk.

My eyes went just a little wider as I asked excitedly, "Do you have some?" I immediately realised what I had said.

"Ya, dis is Amsterdam. Ve have plenty here!" grinned Henk.

"Sorry. We're not used to such openness when it comes to dope. They don't like it back home. Get quite upset, they do, if we enjoy a quiet smoke."

"Ya," said Henk. "You English take your dope like you take your sex. Wid a huge load of guilt."

It was said with such humour and with the lilt of the Dutch accent, we all wee'd ourselves laughing.

I shared a smoke of some very respectable Moroccan with Henk, got absolutely trollied because I hadn't smoked for a couple of days by now, and went to sleep. The others went to explore the city and I was left in complete peace.

At around seven in the evening I was awoken by the side door sliding open. The place exploded with noise, chatter, and excitement. The kids were telling me what they'd been up to and what they'd seen. Although we had to watch every penny we spent, it had been decided that we should have a nice meal this evening with our new friends and do the business tomorrow, when we'd all be more together. It wasn't long before I was laying in the top double bunk watching dinner being prepared. The curtains were drawn and steam fogged up the windows. After dinner Timus gave me the full SP on what they had been doing towards getting a quarter kilo of very nice Moroccan hash. Henk had taken them to a good friend who said he would bring us 250 grams of some Moroccan. The initial reaction from Timus on hearing that it was Moroccan was disappointment.

"We get that shit over in England. Don't you have anything special from Asia? Some Thai weed or some black Afghani?" said Timus.

"Ya dis I can get but only for smoking. For business you should get Moroccan. This is better for business; the Afghani and Thai weed are so expensive, better to have this just for your own smoking. The Moroccan here is better quality than you get in England." To back this up he gave Timus a decent sized lump to try before he came the next day.

Now in the after dinner full-bellied comfort, the kids had been fed and put to bed in their own closed off area at the front of bus. Their little heads had hardly touched the pillows before they were out like candles! They were loving the excitement and attention. The lump was produced and we all proceeded to skin-up amid much rustling of cigarette papers and scratching of matches. It was decided with well fucked-up grins, that the dope was indeed respectable and we would purchase as much as we could afford.

Henk and Gina gave us advice about travelling the autoroutes with cannabis aboard. The French were hysterical if they found any. They would pour disproportionate manpower on the border crossings and were determined to show those 'useless, long haired hippies' that they wouldn't tolerate drugs in their spotless country. All this said as their alcohol-laden breath caused you to wither! I decided that a special place would have to be found to stash the hash.

The sun streamed in as I got up early and quietly, next morning. I grabbed the camping gas, coffee and water bottle and went outside to the rear of the bus, raised the boot lid and started to make some coffee. It was nice to sit there in the early morning sun. I had parked with the boot facing the water and I watched the waterfowl to-ing and fro-ing, all over the gaff. Coffee made, I decided that the luxury of an early smoke was in order as we wouldn't be driving till tomorrow. I snuck back onto the still snoring bus and got the accoutrement.

I rolled up a single skinner and sat in the sunshine, very pleasantly buzzing, and feeling clever that I'd got us to a foreign city. As I sat on the rim of the boot, I became aware of a gentle rocking of the bus. I laughed to myself as I realised that the boot was directly under the two transverse double bunks at the very back of the bus. The top bunk was inhabited by Timus and Kakey, the bottom empty, awaiting the arrival of Charlie and Glynis. Timus and Kakey were having an early morning session and the bus was rocking. Even so, most of the others were still sleeping, or pretending to be, anyway.

I started to lower the spare wheel which was carried in a cradle under the rear of the bus. It hadn't been moved for a long time and was caked in road dirt and rust. Black Bob had arisen and he started to give me a hand. "Why are you doing this?" he asked.

"Well if we're going to be carrying some hash back to Calais, then it's going to be well stashed. Don't forget, Charlie's paint job cries out for a search in their eyes!"

As it turned out, the paint job was a blessing in disguise. Not only did it attract loads of new friends but it made us so 'uncool' we were, in fact, 'very cool' in respect to getting attention from police and customs officers. The paint job said "Here we are, right in your face, search us if it makes you happy." Not for us, the furtive glances as we scurry from place to place. What's more it worked for the whole trip! The dude with the hash turned up just as the rest had arisen. I gave Kakey a wink as she made some coffee. She grinned and despite her professed, easy attitude, coloured up a little but held my stare. I was sure I had understood that look! We paid the guy and he left quickly, a very busy man apparently. I broke the slabs up into strips and rolled them in polythene and bound them all in insulating tape.

Next I broke the bead on the tyre of the spare wheel and separated one wall of the tyre out from the rim. I inserted the 'sausages' of bound cannabis resin between the inner tube and tyre, and then pushed the tyre wall back on the rim. I snapped the large locking ring back on the rim and left everyone laying around on the barge, basking in the sunshine, while I drove to the service station down by the bridge, to re-inflate the tyre.

Bob helped me reinstall the spare wheel on its cradle and we smeared mud all over it to hide the fact that it had been disturbed. We made a good job of it too. "Don't forget we have a few hundred miles to do before crossing into France, it should be well shitted up by then," I said.

It was decided that we could leave after lunch. That would enable the kids to show me some of the things they'd seen on their earlier outing. It would also give me the chance of sampling Amsterdam café culture as it existed then.

We all got back to the bus just after midday, I was just about to start the engine to move off, when in screeched the guy who'd brought the hash earlier that morning. He came on board and I stopped the engine. "Henk tells me you are looking for something special for yourselves, ya?"

"Yeah, but we spent all our money on the other gear. We only got diesel money to get us back to Calais," said Timus.

"Na, na! Dis is you first time coming in Amsterdam, ve vant you have good memory." With that he produced some of the finest looking Thai weed I'd seen up until then.

He passed us a couple of sticks and a lump of firm black hash. We were gobsmacked, we looked at each other in disbelief. He saw our reactions and took great delight in them.

"That is such a wonderful thing to do," said Kakey. She

gave his arm a little squeeze and a peck on the cheek. "That's from all of us," she laughed. "But let's have a smoke and a coffee before pulling away." She looked at me with an enquiring glance. I nodded.

"No probs. I'd love a taste of that weed before going." I said naïvely.

The kettle was put on and we started skinning up, by the time we said our goodbyes we were fizzing! It was weed the like of which I'd seldom tasted before. Other Tim had made a little piggy of himself and was laying in the back of the bus, puking into a waste-paper bin, as I fought with the rush-hour traffic of Amsterdam, on the wrong side of the road, off my trolley.

I glanced quickly in the interior rear view mirror to see what can only be described as a scene of devastation, with bodies everywhere. The weed was so strong they hadn't made it to their respective bunks and were lying akimbo everywhere. All except Isobel, my navigator, who was sat in the front seat across the aisle, looking rather fragile and prone to collapse, but determined to stay awake for the kids and to guide and map read for me.

Something clicked inside my head and I can remember thinking, *C'mon, you can do this. Keep calm and observe all round and you'll get out without a scratch, or more important, hitting any pedestrians.*

We made it out of the city and I felt well pleased with myself. It was the most difficult driving I'd done so far. I had a feeling many personal records were going to be shattered before this trip was over. How could I have known the driving to come?

Chapter 4

France

We made good time and parked for the night on the Belgian side of the border ready for an early run into Calais and perhaps some news on our missing passengers. We left the autoroute on the Belgian side and went to cross the border on the ordinary roads. To the French border guards, this meant we were sneaking across because we had something to hide. We tried telling them it was because their paeages were too expensive but they still wanted to search the bus.

"Go ahead, look where you like but please hurry as we are meeting friends off the Ferry."

"And where are you coming from?" said one officer.

In my innocence I replied, "Amsterdam."

That was all they needed to start swarming over the

bus. I recalled Henk's 'hysterical' warning but took comfort in the fact that there was no dog present!

Eventually their orgasmic-scale fervour was dissipated when, after an hour's search, they had found not even a roach. As she handed back our passports I asked the female officer, "Shouldn't you be having a post-coital, cigarette by now?"

There was a snigger behind me and one of the officers who spoke better English than her looked intently at the floor as he desperately tried not to laugh. She blazed a look at him and marched off. We drove away quickly.

We drove to the park in Calais and threw some Frisbee while we waited for Claude, whose words had started the Amsterdam sojourn. "My friend say 'e see ze autobus is here. 'E come straight to tell me. Do you 'ave ze shit?" Claude said as we got on the bus.

"Oui, mon ami, je 'ave le shit." We showed him the piece we had. He had a smoke with us and agreed it was good.

"The shit is so good it makes you speak French," he laughed.

"You think that's good, try this." I produced a Thai stick.

Claude gasped and asked, "Is that Buddha Weed?"

"I believe it's called that in some places. We call it Thai sticks in England, it's very rare and potent."

By this time Bob had rolled a single skinner and gave it to Claude to spark up. This he did and took several deep lungfuls without breathing out, before passing it back to Bob. We looked at each other knowingly.

There was the sound of those deep tokes being breathed out slowly from Claude. We didn't hear any more from him as we shared what was left of the joint. All of a sudden Claude blurted, in French, "Jesus fucking H. Christ that is some fine shit man! I don't think I can stand up without my knees buckling." That is a fairly accurate translation. He had gone white and was about to 'white out' – a condition that comes about when, in reaction to THC hitting the bloodstream, blood sugar drops to a low level and one passes out, briefly. The cure is to get sugar into the blood, quickly. Hence the 'munchies'.

We laughed. "Claude. Have a very sweet coffee or just eat a spoon of sugar, it will restore the balance in your bloodstream."

Claude went for the latter and soon stopped shaking as the sugar got into his veins.

Eventually he got to his car, taking with him 100 grams of the Moroccan hash. He would sell it by the gram and return in a few days. *How trusting we are*, I thought. *We don't know him from Adam, yet have just given him a large piece of our resources.* I had his car's licence number but what was I going to do? Tell the police he'd run off with our dope?

That evening we went to a local bar to use their telephone and find out what was happening with our missing passengers. The message was passed that Charlie, Glynis, and Syd had got their papers and were en route to Dover as we spoke and would probably be in Calais late that night. At last! Now, when we'd sold the dope, we could go on.

We drove to the ferry terminal and watched several ships disgorge their passengers but none of them ours. Eventually Glynis was seen coming down a gangway and quite quickly they emerged from the terminal main door. There were whoops of joy and hugs all round. At last we were all together again. As I drove back to the park, Timus and the others brought the newcomers up to date.

"How's the bus behaving, Alun?" shouted Syd.

"Yeah great, man. It's done well so far, only thing is it gets hot easily."

Little did I know that statement would come back to haunt me as the journey progressed.

For the next week we hung around Calais and its park. For the first three days we saw nothing of Claude. Just as we were getting worried we would never see him again, in he came in a flurry.

"Hi Claude. Good holiday?"

"*Je désolé*. I am sorry my friend, everyzing is too crazee! No one 'ave any money. I go everywhere but I only sell 50 grams."

This caused a few uncomfortable glances but we could see Claude was not bullshitting.

"I hope you put a little on the price for yourself, Claude," I said.

"Ah, oui, mon ami, I make a few Francs and I 'ave z' piece for myself but I am like the rabbit, running here and there."

"Well at least you tried," I said.

We had a good dinner that night. Afterwards we told Claude that we would be moving on tomorrow. Claude was disappointed but understood that we had to sell the rest of the dope.

"We've decided to go to Paris to sell the rest."

"Oui, you will 'ave ze best chance zere but you must be very careful! If you go to ze tourist places, that is where ze, 'ow you say? Narks, zey 'ide in ze crowd."

"Yes, it'll be a bit risky but there are ways of reducing that risk."

We started to discuss how we would do it. We would not carry more than 5 grams at a time. The bus would be well away from where we were selling and, if caught, we didn't know each other and we certainly didn't have an old bus parked round the corner.

"You must be fucking joking!"

The words pulled us all up like air brakes! We all turned to see a very un-amused Isobel. "Are you serious?" she asked a now completely silent bus. All the more silent for the fact that not only had Isobel said 'fucking' but she had said it in full earshot of the kids! She was pissed right off, and no mistake!

"I went along with the Amsterdam trip even though I thought it well risky, but selling dope by the gram, to strangers? You don't speak the language. What happens if you get busted? I think you are being stupid. What happens to me, the kids and the bus, then?"

She was talking directly to me but it was uncomfortably clear that she meant everyone there. For the first time Fran chirped in, dropping her annoying, affected, shyness. "I'm really not comfortable with this either."

I wanted badly to say, "And your plan is?" but kept quiet.

I could take a telling off from Isobel but from Fran the 'preener' and general do-nothing-towards-keeping-the-bus-going, not to mention whingeing a fair amount of the time, I was not going to take it quietly. "Look!" I said, a little too forcefully. "OK it is well risky, and we've established I ain't the brain of Britain, but here we find ourselves. What do you suggest?" The last words being spoken to Isobel while boring Fran right in the eyes, challenging her to come up with a plan, rather than just whining criticism. She withered and remained silent. No one else ventured a plan. I sat there fuming.

"Take it easy, Alun. We'll think of something," said Black Bob.

I realised I'd reacted a bit heavily. "Look how about this," I reasoned. "We choose two guys and two girls. They are completely away from the bus and only return when everything is sold. That way if they were followed back to the bus, there would be nothing on it to be captured by the Gendarmerie. Anyway, we must keep a sense of proportion here. We aren't pushing smack or beating old people for their pension money, we're just having a smoke!"

It was agreed that as the only driver and father of kids, I would not be out in the crowds, selling. This placated Isobel somewhat. "I still think you are bloody stupid to do this," she said as we walked outside.

"Every day I took risks back home. It's a bit different here but we'll just have to adapt. We're in it for the long run. What do you want me to do, pack up and go home?"

"Oh do what you want, you usually do anyway." She stormed off to the back of the bus.

We set off for Paris feeling that possibly we'd made a mistake buying the dope, but there was nothing we could do now but to sell it as best we could.

We headed for the one famous place in Paris that we all knew. The Eiffel Tower. We didn't smoke on the drive as we didn't want to eat into the profits, so by the time we arrived underneath the tower it was dark and we were hungry. We decided that we would park right underneath the Tower for the night. The miracle was that for the whole night we weren't told to move on. Looking back I think it was the paintwork. It was assumed we were show people. There legitimately, for some spectacle. We were woken early to a horrendous cacophony of horns. The Paris rush hour was going on around us.

I learned that on leaving the small island that is Britain, the car horn took on new meaning. Gone is the beep-beep of the English open road. Here was the long, angry blare should you transgress. We'd had a good sleep and some breakfast and were feeling a little better. Here we were in Paris, next to London, the most exciting city in the world! Even Isobel, who everybody had been tiptoeing around, was smiling. We discussed over breakfast, where would be the best place to park up and sell the rest of the dope. I suggested we go where the 'ragged people' go. The Montmartre was the artist area and all the street level life that goes along with them, would be there.

Just as we were about to move, a policeman came onto the bottom step and indicated we must leave immediately. I got into the driver's seat and fired up the engine, as the others stowed everything for travelling. Out we went into the morning rush hour Paris. I knew something of the Montmartre area. By funny coincidence, I had started to read a copy of Henri Charrière's book, *Papillon*. The things that the French authorities did to those prisoners in their penal colony just off the coast of South America were inhumane in the extreme. It made me look at the French authorities in a new light and I can remember feeling good that our British system would never do that to a man. I was still very naïve in those days, you understand!

In the next few days we explored Paris, talking to as many people as we could and making connections. Timus, Kakey, Other Tim, Debbie, Charley, and Glynis went out selling what they could but it was slow going. We all learned the French, "Voulez-vous acheter du shit? Dix francs, une gramme." We also learned the expression, "Trés expensive... OK, dix grammes, s'il vous plait." They couldn't resist. It was slow going and we were taking appalling risks. We would move amongst the multinational tourist crowds on the green outside the Notre-Dame at night and sleep late in the back streets of Montmartre, sometimes being moved on by the street traders or patrolling Gendarmes, but generally being left alone. These were the back streets and bars of Charrière's *Papillon*.

Never have I lived a book in such a way and I was caught up in the atmosphere.

"Hey, Anglais!" I heard shouted at me through the driver's window one morning as I read my book. I sat up to see two of the biggest and ugliest French dudes you have ever seen! Ugly, in that there was the odd cauliflower ear and broken nose but set in the typical hard-as-nails French appearance, all at an altitude of six feet or more!

"What the fuck are you doing here?" Before I could reply they were heading for the side door. They came aboard with the clear intent of frightening us – they needn't have bothered. I was scared already.

"What's the problem?" I asked.

"You are ze problem. You are selling dope 'ere on our streets. You don't do that, zis is our territory a' we do all zat 'ere. You are in big fucking trouble." He started towards me. "'Ow much you 'ave?"

I decided from what I'd been reading that being straight with them and that appealing to their sense of street level was the only way of avoiding trouble. It was a risk but what the fuck? "We only have about 150 grams that we bought in Amsterdam. We are going to India but don't have enough money. We just wanted to make a few Francs and then move on. We didn't mean to tread on your toes, man. We'll go right now if that is what you want."

"'Ow is zis 'tread on your toes'?" the large dude said.

"Uh, I mean move in on your act." More creased brows.

"Um, we are sorry to do this in your area. Now that we know, we will stop and move on if that's OK."

They looked at each other and one was about to speak when Mellony appeared round the curtain. She was still half-asleep and her blond hair fell around her shoulders.

Instantly the mood changed.

"Zis is your daughter?"

"Yes that's my little girl. My son is still asleep. That's their mum, there," I said, pointing to Isobel.

"'Ello baybee," said the first guy in a sing song voice, bending right down to her. "'Ow do you like Pari, baybee?"

"It's lovely," she replied in a tiny voice. This delighted them both. As they talked I sat down and motioned them to do the same.

The first guy looked at me a few times, and at Mellony, and said, "I am Jules 'e is Joe. 'E come from jail only this morning, 'e stab a traffic warden for always putting ticket on 'is car."

"Oh. We could do with his services in England, they're a right pain in the arse, little Hitlers," I said without thinking.

Jules turned and translated what I'd said into what sounded like Arabic to me. Joe's stone face cracked into a pearly white grin at the mention of Hitler.

The situation had calmed down and I telepathically asked Isobel to put the kettle on the gas. "Would you like a coffee fellahs?" I asked.

"Non," was the clear reply. "You Anglais don't make good coffee, I prefer schnapps," he said as he pulled out a hip flask.

I took a gamble. "Look here! Coming on our bus and threatening to confiscate our stash is one thing, but to insult our coffee making skills is just too much old man," I said in my best stuffed shirt, arrogant, British accent. It worked. Jules snorted and the atmosphere calmed right down. We spent time telling them what we had been doing to get this far. I think they were impressed and it was clear to them that we were not taking the piss, that we were in fact, just a family moving through, doing the best we could to get by.

As we talked, a Gendarme came up to the driver's window, intent to move us on written all over his face. As I stood to talk to him, Jules grabbed my arm. "Attende," he said, as he moved into view of the officer. "Eh, Claude, you fascist pig! Leave these innocent tourists alone or I'll tell your captain about the women you keep!" He laughed.

"Ahh Jule my friend. I did not realise you were about your foul business. Don't you play any of your scams on them, either." Jules explained that we were just there for a couple of days and that we were alright as we had young children with us. He asked him if he would mind if they parked for a couple of days.

The Gendarme, pleased at his implied importance, touched his peak and said, "Be good," as he walked away.

I was impressed and said so. "Zey want a quiet life just like you and I. Zey know we don't do 'eroin like the Algerian and Turkish immigrant. We don't touch kids," he made a knowing gesture out of the sight of Mellony, "like some sick bastards. We just live, so they tend to respect us, as long as we stay quiet. Now zhat zey know you know me, zey will leave you in peace for a while. We keep them well-greased."

We spent the rest of the afternoon getting to know these truly hard street people of the Montmartre. When Isobel, Fran, and Kakey took the kids out sight-seeing, out came some very decent black hash and we proceeded to do the best we could for our country. We smoked many spliffs and by this time Joe, fresh from the nick was sat silently opposite with an even bigger grin on his, heavily pockmarked face. All of a sudden he stared me in the eye and blurted out a string of Arabic in a very formal way, ending with a curt nod.

"He said English people are arrogant arseholes," Jules translated, "but straight people. He likes you because you are not arrogant. You are willing to learn. Trust me, Englais, from him that is almost a declaration of love!"

We fell about laughing. I caught Joe's eye and nodded slightly. He returned the nod, and it felt good. Even here in a foreign land I could connect with ease. Jules and Joe staggered off the bus, telling us they would return tomorrow. They also cautioned us to beware of police in plain clothes, in the crowd.

"You don't mind?" I shouted as they headed for a nearby bar.

"Non, non, no problem, but be cool. *Bon courage!*" shouted Jules as they disappeared into the bar. Isobel had heard the warning and looked like thunder!

"You cannot go out there again tonight. It's just mad." This started another discussion as to what we could do instead.

"Why don't we go to the South of France?" suggested Timus.

"The coastal resorts are full of tourists," said Other Tim. "It would be a cooler place than here."

"At last," said Isobel. "Someone else, getting real."

Black Bob chimed in. "Yeah let's go down south and see some French crumpet in bikinis. I need t' get me rocks off."

"I'm up for it if that's what's wanted," I said. "We've only got about 100 or so grams left so why not? We've got some diesel money haven't we?"

It was decided to leave the next morning. Jules and Joe turned up looking even more haggard than yesterday and treated us all to breakfast in the bar. Heaping attention on the kids and buying them ice cream. We left them promising to return on the way back and tell our stories.

The trip south was wonderful. A meander down poplar-lined roads of great length. As we crossed into Provence, the temperature had climbed to the point where you start shedding the heavy northern latitude clothes in favour of shorts, T-shirts and sandals. All the windows were open and it was midday heat as we rounded a corner to see a clear river flowing through the deserted valley. I pulled over, well off the road under some trees, to whoops of delight.

"Yeah man, let's go for a swim!" shouted Syd.

"Just what I had in mind. We can do the washing as well."

"The place looks deserted," said Black Bob, "and it looks like we're miles from the nearest village on the map."

"Yeah, with these trees all around it's very secluded," I observed.

We grabbed the washing and the kids and headed down to the river. It was a bit of a scrabble down some undergrowth but eventually we came across a beautiful clearing in the hot sun, shaded by some trees, with rocks just the right height to do the washing.

We took all our clothes off and settled in for some serious sunbathing as the girls, in their birthday suits, did the washing. I had noticed how perfectly formed Debbie had appeared under her clothes. It was wonderful to have my anticipations confirmed as she stood before me, *au naturel*, a memory I will carry with me all my life. Charlie, a well-hung lad, was up on the rocks giving instructions in a loud voice, making sure all the females saw his above average tackle.

Tim, Kakey, and Fran were lying side by side in the sun beside the half-done washing. Kakey and Fran's naked bodies standing out amongst Timus, Syd, and Black Bob, lying naked on the other side. Isobel and the kids were messing around in the water and I was just thinking how nice a smoke would be, when I noticed the water getting very muddy and the bushes began to crack. I saw a flash of uniform through the trees. "Look out!" I shouted, as about ten Gendarmes came crashing into the clearing.

The girls made a grab for towels and anything to cover up from the openly leering, fat and sweating Gendarmes. Isobel had nothing, neither did the kids. As a couple of pigs waddled toward us, stumbling on the rocks because they were so busy staring at Isobel, I shouted, "This is my wife and mother of these children. Turn around while she dresses!"

They looked at each other sheepishly and to my surprise, turned and waited while Isobel dressed the kids and put on my jeans that I had been wearing. I still had my underpants.

"What are you going to wear on top?" I asked her.

"I don't give a shit. Let the lecherous pigs have a good look, maybe their wives will get a good time tonight." She marched off with the kids, defying them to look.

We were herded back to the bus and told we were under arrest for public nudity. I was ordered to follow, in the bus, to their station. It seems a member of the aforementioned public had had to climb out of his car, scrabble down a bank and through some trees, in order to be offended by our nudity. Presumably the pervert had pleasured himself in the bushes before outrage got the better of him and he had to call the police. I put this theory to the Captain of the Gendarmerie to which we were taken. He couldn't stop himself from laughing when he heard this. He lectured us closely and made us sit in the corridor while the rest of the station had afternoon tea.

A door opened to reveal one of the sweaty policemen we had encountered earlier. He was still sweating in the air conditioned station but was now smiling as he carried a tray of coffee, croissants and cold Cokes for the kids. We thanked him and smiled a lot. No point in being churlish, besides we were still packing a little hash and they could get awkward if they wanted.

The captain came to his door and called me in. "You are free to go m'sure, but please, keep on the clothes until you get to the beach, even then you will need something." He made a covering gesture to his genital area.

"Understood. I'm sorry we gave you so much trouble."

He smiled. "I didn't have to ask twice for officers to go and arrest some naked hippies in the river!" he grinned.

"Touché," we laughed.

As we drove away, we swapped stories of how one officer nearly came in his pants, when he crawled through the bushes on his belly, only to look up and see the beautiful naked body of Debbie standing over him! Or how another officer, so intent on staring at Kakey in the buff, did the perfect prat-fall, face down in the water. It was priceless. Like something out of a French version of Keystone Cops. They certainly made themselves look ridiculous that day. What we didn't take into account was that we were in a Catholic country.

On we drove without further incident and arrived in St. Tropez late in the afternoon and found a slightly industrial area not too far from the seafront. We started to get ready for dinner. The police came by very slowly in a patrol car. When they crawled by for a third time, I thought, *Time for some P.R.* I stood at the front as they approached. I waved them down and they pulled up in front of the bus, and rolled down the window.

"Bonjour m'sure." They both nodded.

"Parle-vous Englais? S'il vous plait, m'sure."

"Yes we both speak English." I was impressed. How

many English police officers speak another language, even in the tourist areas?

"I notice you have come by a few times, and I just thought I'd introduce myself to you."

"'Ow many are you?" asked the driver.

"Including my two children, there are thirteen."

"You 'av the children?" the other officer asked.

"Yes." As I turned back to the bus I could see Alun Jnr. sitting in the driver's seat as he often did when we were stopped. "That's my boy, there, driving the bus," I joked.

"Ah, bon. He looks like he was born to it." He smiled. "Please bring all the passports to us now and we will not need to trouble you."

"No problem. I'll collect them and return."

"Bon."

I got back to the bus. "Trouble?" asked Other Tim.

"No, they only want to know who we are and what we're doing here. I'm taking the passports." We had the good sense to install a steel box, bolted to the chassis just under one of the rear access hatches.

"Tell the nosey bastards to fuck off. Fucking pigs." I laughed as I turned but Charlie, who had spat that out, had a face like thunder. I had forgotten his inability to distinguish between a bent drug squad officer and an ordinary policeman. To his anarchist mind they were all pigs. I found it easy at first to take his poison, spawned as it was from bitter experience of being 'fitted up' and sent to prison by a bent drug squad officer then operating out of Bridewell Street station in Bristol. I would have found him amusing even, had he not been a dead ringer for the infamous killer Charles Manson. To cap it off, same first name too. OK, Charlie's features were softer and there was intelligence and compassion in his eyes but when he got like this he was ugly.

"Cool it Charlie, for Christ sake! They're out of their car. They'll hear you," said Other Tim.

"Fuck 'em. They are all a bunch of cunts," said Charlie, too loudly.

"You're a twat Charlie. You'll get us all in trouble," said Other Tim, clearly losing it with him.

"Shut the fuck up, the pair of you!" I hissed, the policeman now nearly on the bottom step of the entrance. "Remember what we have." My eyes bored into Charlie's.

This calmed him a little as it would, in his view, be an even bigger uncool gaff, to jeopardise the stash. The Gendarmes were now on the first and second steps looking into the bus. They said good evening and smiled at the kids but in the ways of the never off duty, their eyes were everywhere. I was glad that the others had made a good job of cleaning up and that we hadn't smoked on the bus for a couple of days.

"Would you like to come in and sit down?" asked Kakey. I had noticed her ability to smile and be nice to strangers and admired it. I also noticed she could be a bit of a madam if she didn't get her way.

"Non merci," said the officer. "We must be quick."

"Sorry about that. I had to get them from the steel box where we keep our valuables."

"Bon! You must not leave the autobus alone at any time. It will be broken into if left alone here," said the Gendarme as he leafed through our passports.

"Where are you going?" asked the second officer.

"We are on our way to India," said Glynis.

"Oh hoh, oo la. Le grand tour," nodded the Gendarme, impressed.

"Alors, merci," said the first officer, handing me the stack of passports. "Bon voyage. Please remember to carry your passports on you, wherever you go."

With a salute they returned to the squad car and were gone. "See!" said Other Tim, looking at Charlie. "There was no reason for that. They just wanted our passports but you could've got us busted."

Without warning, Charlie lunged for Other Tim, who stepped backwards too quickly and went tumbling down the steps into the road with Charlie following in similar flight. Luckily there was nothing coming, otherwise they both would have rolled into the path of some shocked French person quietly driving through the area.

They fought like schoolboys, locked around each other and not really getting anywhere. I would have left them to it but some people crossing at the junction were looking disapprovingly at the fracas.

"That is fucking it, man," I spluttered as I got up. I jumped out the door and grabbed both of them by the collar and used my boot to separate them. I looked at Black Bob for help but he pretended not to see. "I'll bang your fucking heads together. You're frightening my kids!" I must have said it with the conviction I felt, as they both calmed down pretty damn quick. "Thanks Bob," I muttered as I passed him going back in, "you were a great help."

To my surprise he turned shifty and said something about them both being his friends. Bob was about my size and could be intimidating to look at, but a bit of a pussy when it came down to it. I was not so surprised at the conflict. Charlie had an accent similar to the great Harry Corbett of 'Sooty' fame. Sentences punctuated by a very annoying, drawn-out "Riiiiyyght," as he sought conformation that we all understood what he was saying. His slightly bullying way with all who disagreed with him.

This and the lack of a smoke for the last couple of days had put us all on edge. We were beginning to see that the romantic idea of overland to India had its pitfalls in reality.

Personalities were beginning to change as people found that they were now out of their familiar manor. I too was feeling the strain. I'd had to make the point that while eating very little in order to save money, it was disheartening to finish a twelve hour driving day to have a meal big enough for a child. If they wanted me to continue driving then they'd have to increase the food budget. This was deemed a reasonable request as I was doing all the work at the moment. The meals got bigger and better, we even tried horse meat, once! For the next few days Isobel the kids and I, spent as much time in the sun, on the beach as possible. The others strolled the beach talking to tourists and selling the rest of the smoke. By the time we pulled into Nice we only had a few grams for personal use left. The atmosphere was a bit heavy and at dinner, Other Tim suddenly said, "We're going home."

"What?" The word was uttered in unison.

"Yeah, we've got some other things we gotta do and Debbie is starting uni, soon. We'll leave you the money we have left."

I was annoyed but kept quiet. *Is this how it's going to be all the way across?*

"Why don't we all have a smoke?" said Isobel to my surprise, as she very rarely toked on the weed.

"We've sold most of it for more than we expected and it's only a few clicks to the Italian border. Why don't we relax for a couple of days and then Tim and Debbie can still go home if they want to."

"We've only got about ten grams left," said Timus. "We don't want to cross into Italy with anything."

Other Tim and Debbie didn't want to change their

minds and prepared their gear for departure. I took the opportunity and got another load of gear dumped from the roof rack. This time I didn't get any opposition as it was now clear to all, that we wouldn't be needing it.

The other reason I didn't get any opposition was that on the way down, I'd had to drive very carefully. Not to keep the speed down but to keep the revs up. The further south we got, the more I had to watch the temperature gauge. The cooling system was the weak point. The engine was mounted half way back down the chassis but the radiator was right at the front. This meant long water pipes and a long driveshaft for the cooling fan. The long water pipes meant that air locks would build up and stop the water circulating, the temperature would then rise – it was difficult to keep it cool. The only way was to make sure the fan was spinning fast enough and sometimes that meant changing down for a hill, before it was really necessary.

I had spoken to people who know the old AEC before we left. They had warned me of the problems that I might encounter with the cooling system. The only way to cure the problem of air locks, was to fill the cooling system from the lowest point. The method was to use a high-pressure supply, attach it to the lowest drain cock, and then stand by the radiator filler cap and watch as all the air and water gushes out. When all the air pockets have been blown out, shut the cap and then the drain valve and the job is done, simple. It might be difficult to find a high-pressure supply of water but we'd cross that bridge when we came to it. Other Tim and Debbie decided to catch the train back to Calais. We drove them to the station and said our goodbyes. All except Charlie who skulked in the back of the bus. I drew Other Tim aside. "You sure about this, Tim? Don't let him spoil an adventure for you and Debbie."

"If I stay on the bus I'm gonna swing for that mouthy bastard, so it's better we leave now. Besides Debbie does really have to start uni. She would have had to leave at some stage anyway."

Debbie, hearing her name, came over to join us. "I'll tell you something, Alun. Black Bob and Syd are the laziest bastards I've ever come across. Fran is a bit of a drama queen. We've known this lot for over two years and on the whole they are good people if you don't mind overlooking their faults. Don't let them get away with doing nothing. I've noticed that it's only you, Isobel, Kakey and Timus that are doing any of the work. Glynis is under Charlie's influence and is seeing to his needs rather than everyone's."

"Don't worry Debs," I replied. "I've got Charlie's number. He already knows he ain't gonna get anywhere with me, using his usual tactics. Plus I'm too big for him to bully! Anyway, He'll be alright."

I remembered the incident when we drove to a lake in the Mendip Hills. It was a hot day and we all went skinny dipping. Afterwards, in the evening, we sat around a campfire and watched the kids playing at the water's edge.

Suddenly there was a shout. We all looked around to see little Alun fall from the bank, into the water – at that time he still could not swim. Charlie sprang up and jumped into the water as quick as a flash, without any hesitation whatsoever. The water was only waist deep but he couldn't have known that. He grabbed Alun, who had sunk beneath the water, and almost threw him onto the bank. I watched, too far away to get there before Charlie.

"You're a fucking hero, mate. Thank you for what you did, he could've drowned."

"I just saw him go under and jumped."

"Thank God you did."

The truth was that either Timus, Black Bob or myself would have dragged him out but Charlie was like that. Do it, then think about it. I was very glad of this philosophy, this time. "I owe you, big time!" It was this that caused me to bite my tongue already several times when I should've told him he was out of order. We watched Other Tim and Debbie struggle with their luggage. They got halfway down the train and opened a door. They turned, waved, and stepped aboard. I never saw them again.

We all returned to the bus a little subdued. Charlie was still sulking around. "Let's bugger off out of here. I've had enough of hanging around. Are we travelling or camping?" I said with a little more energy than I felt. By now it was late in the evening but we decided it would be a little boost to cross into Italy now.

We set off and before long we arrived at the French side of the border at Ventimiglia, where we had no problems clearing customs. We carried on to the Italian side where we were met by a fat border guard. He pushed past Isobel who had gathered all the passports together and was going to take them to the office. Seeing the passports he grabbed them from her hand without a word.

"Well! You're a rude bastard, aren't you?" I said from the driver's seat, not caring if he understood or not. Isobel flashed me a glance.

"What you say?" said Fat Guard.

You don't have to be so rude, is what I said." I realised I'd spoken before thinking.

"You say more than that." He chose to ignore me from then on.

"Where is the Valium, Valium?" he said twice to emphasise it. He then went down the bus turning over seats and crashing through drawers. Every now and then he would hold a bag or box in the air and say, "Valium, Valium?" We were losing it with him, big time.

"What the fuck is your problem, pal?" spat Black Bob,

who'd lost it completely and was being very aggressive to Fat Guard. Shame he couldn't have been more aggressive with Other Tim and Charlie when they fought.

"Why you tell me fuck off?" said Fat Guard, going towards Black Bob. I was feeling distinctly uneasy as I saw this unstable, fat guard carried a nine millimetre Glock handgun in his holster.

"Excuse me, señor," I said. "He didn't tell YOU, fuck off. He asked what the fuck is happening. You weren't saying fuck off to the officer, were you?" I said, glaring at him.

"No," came the sullen reply.

"Where are we, Dad?" The sleepy blond-haired head of Alun Jnr. came round the partition. Fat Guard calmed right down, looked in my passport and saw the '2 children' attachment.

"Where do you go?" he asked.

"We are going to India, señor," replied Isobel quickly and calmly, taking over the situation. "Could you please be quick as we have all had a long day's travelling and as you can see, you are disturbing my children."

It didn't stop him searching around some more but it was now much less aggressively and noisily. He was about to head for the door when he turned over a seat. It just happened to be the seat where we stored our machete for chopping wood. His beady eyes became more protruding when he discovered the tool. "This is dangerous weapon. You cannot enter Italy with this thing."

We tried to explain that we used this for chopping wood to light cooking fires but he was having none of it. He kept us there for hours as he decided that more offensive weapons would be found in our boot. Sure enough our axe was deemed to be a danger to the Italian nation. "So what are we supposed to do?" I asked, flabbergasted.

"You cannot enter Italy with this things," he said again helpfully.

"So you are saying we have to turn around, go back to the French side to dump our tools. Why can't we just dump them here?" I asked.

"These weapons cannot enter Italy so they cannot be dumped here. You must go back!"

We had no choice but to turn around and drive back to the French side who were surprised to see us and were at a loss to answer our questions as to why the Italians were being such pigs. We described our tormentor. "Ah! We know zis man. 'E'z wife leave 'im. She live wiz ze 'ippy American."

It turned out that his wife had tired of border existence and run off with an American traveller! This answered everything! We returned to the Italian side, bereft of all wood chopping implements. Fat Guard was waiting for our return with relish. He got on and went through the "Valium?" routine again.

We however, had learned our lesson and answered with fixed smiles, "No señor. No Valium."

"You, come." He pointed at me and I walked with him to his office for passport inspection and stamping. As the bus was in my name and passport, I had to have a page full of stamps to signify the correct import or export procedures had been followed. I blessed Isobel's foresight in getting a ninety page passport for me, instead of the more usual forty pages!

As he stamped the documents he said in a decidedly friendly way, "You will be crossing many frontieras, if you are like this every time, you will 'ave trouble."

"But you were very rude to my wife, señor," I said respectfully, "and you kept on about Valium."

"Looking like you do and going where you will be going, you will have many times like this and you must learn the best way to deal with it." I marvelled at his greatly improved English. He looked me straight in the eye.

I realised we'd just been taught a valuable lesson.

"Good journey," he said as I nodded and left. As I walked back to the bus I was annoyed at the loss of equipment and time. However, I was more annoyed because the arsehole was right!

I explained to a very angry Black Bob, what he had said to me. Bob was not in the mood for thinking so I just left him to it. It was dark and we were headed into a new country. We had agreed to stay off the autostradas to save money. We would just get across Italy without spending too much money. We wouldn't be going into Venice as it would just be a tourist trap and expensive. A decision Isobel and I weren't happy with. How many chances would we have to see Venice?

Still we were outnumbered, so gave way as we didn't have too much cash.

Chapter 5
Italy, Croatia, Slovenia and Yugoslavia

After a hundred kilometres or so I pulled up just before a large village somewhere in the mountains. We made a cup of coffee before sleeping. We were a little pissed off still but generally happier now that we were moving on. When dawn broke and we all went outside we realised that there was snow all around us, and in the background, the Italian side of the Alps were still in view, capped with snow. We had parked in a lay-by beside the road. We were all off the bus, looking at the wonderful sight of the mountains when a large Alfa Romeo screeched to a halt as the driver spotted the bus and us.

"'Ello darlings," said a very sleek-looking lady in a

Chanel headscarf. "Ah, *bellissimo bambino*," she said, pinching the kids' cheeks lightly." They smiled back at her which drove her on. "You are English, yes? I 'av the son, 'e live in England in the 'otel."

"He lives in a hotel? That must be expensive for him." I smiled.

"No, no, 'e is the 'ed chef at the Dorchester 'otel in London."

"Wow head chef. That's a very big job. He must be very good."

She preened at this. "Where do you go?"

"We are on our way to India," replied Isobel. This impressed the elegant lady and she asked if we had had breakfast yet. We replied that we had not.

"Ah you must come to my friend's restaurant. He will be cooking the breakfast now."

We explained that we were running on a really tight budget. It was very nice of her to ask but we had to save money. The kids hadn't had so much as an ice cream since we left.

"You cannot come to Italy without trying our wonderful ice cream, especially the bambinos," she smiled at them.

"You follow me in the autobus. We go eat, come! Come! Don't worry about money, he is my friend."

We looked at each other and shrugged. We didn't need asking twice. We drove to a large, shiny restaurant on the main street and sat at a large table while our host had a good morning kiss with her friend and some close conversation about us.

"I have told 'im you are my guests. He will put it all on my account. Now you have cooked breakfast and the bambinos can have ice cream for breakfast."

The kids were dancing up and down at the sight of all the tubs of different ice cream on display. But the best sight for me was the trays of cooked items of a breakfast nature, scrambled eggs, tomatoes, spicy beans of some kind, fresh bread and many other delicious trays all steaming hot in the mountain air and smelling wonderful. The owner loaded up our plates and would hear no protest of, "That's too much."

"Eat, eat my friends you are in Italy now!" he bellowed with a smile of pride.

He finished heaping our plates and dragged up a chair to join us. As we did justice to their hospitality, we talked of our homes and our adventure. We related, to their horror, the events on the border the night before.

"Ah! They are arseholes," remarked the chef. "Here the police live as we do and all they want is a quiet life. On the border, they are different people."

"Well, we were very upset by their treatment. But that has been more than compensated for by your wonderful hospitality this morning. When I remember Italy I will not think of him but will remember this moment."

They both beamed and we continued our breakfast. After more chat our Italian lady stood and announced that she must leave for an important meeting. "Relax my friends, Leave when you are ready, you must have some Coca-Cola for the babies."

After thanking and hugging this wonderful lady she departed as swishily as she arrived. As we finished our breakfast the chef informed us of the identity of our hostess. Apparently she was Señora Rindlfini. Between the 'Señora' and 'Rindlfini' were a couple of titles including 'countess' and several forenames. She was related to the Italian royalty and her family owned most of the land and villages around the area. We felt honoured. What a wonderful experience. It more than compensated for the treatment we had received at the border. We thanked the chef and assured him other travellers would hear of his wonderful establishment and good food. By this time several customers had started their breakfast and the chef made sure each plate came with an explanation of what this bunch of hippies were doing in their mountain village.

Their faces went through the whole range. Smiling in welcome, then serious with distaste as they heard of our treatment, then smiling again as they waved at the kids. When we went out the door, full with soft drinks, crisps, and chocolate for the kids, even the assistant chef came from the kitchen to wave us off.

The whole café came out to wave us goodbye. As we drove back to the main road, spirits were high and we had been restored. I hunkered down for some long distance driving. Cities like Turin, Milan, Verona, Venice, and other names only seen in an atlas so far, came and went. The idea was to get out of expensive Europe as quickly as possible. Then the next target would be Tehran in Iran. We had heard how jobs were plentiful in the oilfields and the Iranians were twenty-five thousand truck drivers short, and although they had the oil wealth, they had to rely on foreigners, mostly American, English and German, to get it out of the ground and onto the world market. The result was that every country in Europe was sending truckloads of equipment and other imports overland to Tehran. Even the Eastern Europeans were trucking down there.

The most memorable was the Bulgarian State Transport. They would travel in convoys of twenty Volvo F88s at a time. If you got in trouble as a petty criminal in Bulgaria, you were given the choice; prison, or become a driver on the State Transport! There were thieves, pimps, drug dealers, and all sorts. We would pass them, all lined up in a lay-by first thing in the morning. Each driver had his engine oil dip stick in his hand ready for the lead driver, a card-carrying party man, who would walk down the line, inspecting them for correct oil levels.

We gave them the nickname 'F troop' after the madcap comedy program of the same name, about a troop of American cavalry, popular in the sixties. Despite their reputations, we were to share some good experiences down the road.

The kilometres rolled on and we were now in some really hot weather. The cooling system shortcomings were becoming more apparent and I was keeping my eye on the temperature gauge closely. So far it was coping but it was marginal. Trieste was the last city in Italy, it used to belong to Yugoslavia as it was called then, but the border was moved in some dispute or other and Trieste became Italian, much to the relief of its citizens, I would imagine, as Yugoslavia was not a nice place in those times, as we were about to find out.

We were ready for more hassle from the border guards and customs, but even though we crossed in the dark, they were not interested and just stamped our passports and didn't even come out of their offices. This was great! We were going to go on now towards Rijeka, but we decided we'd better fill up with diesel just over the border near a town called Kozina.

It was now well towards midnight. There was a service station up ahead but it was on the other side. *No problem*, I thought, *I'll just go on and do a U-turn in and out of the station.* We had changed money at the border so had plenty of dinars to fuel up. We continued in the direction we had been going by doing another U-turn out of the station.

It wasn't long before we were overtaken and flagged down by a very dilapidated police car. If we thought French and Italian police looked intimidating, what approached my driving window was straight out of some cold war film. They looked very heavy and very Soviet.

"Passport," was the only word spoken. The other brick

wall, had drawn a little diagram of the bus crossing a solid white central line to get into the garage. "Verboten! Verboten!" He indicated the diagram. He then wrote a figure of several dinars, equal to a ten-pound fine. They then both retired with my passport, to their car behind.

"We ain't paying those fucking arseholes ten fucking quid!" shouted Charlie.

"I know, but they've got my passport, it's late at night, they know we can't go to their station and complain. We can't do anything. They've got my passport and won't give it back 'til we pay them money." We all moaned a little more but we had no choice but to give into this official highway robbery.

I took the money to them and asked for a receipt and my passport. The driver reached for the money.

"A receipt please, officer."

He scowled but drew a pad from his pocket, filled it out and signed it. I took my papers and stared them in the eye just long enough to say, "Fuck you, you robbing bastards," then walked back to the bus.

As I drove off, Isobel, who had been scrutinising the ticket, said, "This ticket is dated three years ago. We've just been ripped off."

"Nice place this. It feels like Russia," I observed. Not surprising really as Yugoslavia was still a Soviet Satellite State at the time and we were to run up against it again before leaving the country. Oh, yes! I was so disgusted over the treatment by the crooked cops that I drove on to Split, a seaside town with a large waterfront on which we parked for the rest of the night.

When I awoke it was midmorning and beating down with sunshine. The others had sortied into town to do some shopping, leaving Isobel, Kakey, Glynis and the kids to clean the bus and cater to my needs. I was pampered and fed and sat on the sea wall in the hot morning sun. The sea sparkled with the light dancing off it. The air was crisp and smelt wonderful. It was our first sight of the Adriatic, it was beautiful and I couldn't help thinking of the weather back in England, and gloating horribly.

As I sipped on my coffee I heard some exited voices over at the door of the bus. The boys had returned with another big bus. It had parked up behind us and was disgorging passengers. "We met them in town and they wanted to come and see the bus and meet you all," said a breathless, excited Syd. "They're going to Goa for Christmas."

"Goa? I've heard of it but..."

Before I could say more an American accent said, "Wow, love the rig, man!" as he climbed aboard. "You guys come all the way from England? We've just come from Amsterdam, non-stop, man. I am fucked up but we wanna be in Goa for Christmas. It's a gas, everyone who's travelling goes there from all over Asia."

He went on to tell us of the miles and miles of palm-fringed deserted beaches where the travellers go. Clothes are optional as most of the beaches are deserted except for other travellers. It's in the sub tropics and very hot and sunny, not only that but you can live well on five dollars a day.

The other driver and his mate came over for a word. They were Dutch and had just decided one day, to buy the Saviem rear-engined, forty-two seater and go to Goa. They had toured Amsterdam centre with a sign saying 'Goa for Christmas. $200'. Within two days they had enough passengers and money to just go. Unlike us, they had made no preparation at all, preferring to spend their way out of trouble. They had plenty of money from the passengers and could afford it. They were travelling free and without wondering where the next tankful was coming from. I liked what I saw and a light went on in my head.

Thirty-eight passengers at two hundred dollars a time was over seven and a half grand! We were doing it the wrong way! It seemed a massive sum to us who had landed on French soil with two hundred quid. That evening we all sat on the beach and had dinner there, just as the sun went down in a crimson sky. I listened intently to what the driver and his friend were saying as we talked around the fire. They had done the route before and knew a few things.

"How is your rear-engined bus getting on with the heat?" I asked the Dutch driver whose name was Sten.

"I have no problem. The Saviem was made for Mediterranean use so it has a big cooling fan and radiator the size of a dining table." I felt envious and described our problems.

"You should sort that before Turkey. It starts to get murderously hot after that and you won't get far in the desert of Iran. I'd do it in Greece. They have loads of old English trucks and buses still running."

Good idea, I thought. I learned as much as I could from them. They seemed to think working in Iran was a good idea to raise cash.

"You can always teach English. They are desperate to learn because it is the language of business. Some friends of mine did it last year and made loads of money," said Sten.

I knew there was a boom on in Iran. British, Dutch, French, German, even Spanish-registered, American-type trucks and Uncle Tom Cobley were passing us every day. We usually got a loud blast on the air horn as a British truck went by. I was excited by the prospect of working in Iran and making loads of money. I took every opportunity to talk to the truck drivers in the motor camps along the way. They thought we were mad and loved to give the impression that the only people capable of doing such journeys were themselves. A bunch of hippies, in a twenty-year-old bus had no chance. They still liked hanging around the bus because of the women. The truth was, of course, that we were the gutsy ones, and went places with our twenty-year-old bus that put the fear of God into the driver of posh, polished, trucks of the time.

We were told many times that our old bus would never last. Yet many times we passed those same drivers broken down, where the road had shaken the guts out of their Scania, or Volvo. We would drive by, waving and shouting things like, "Sell that foreign crap and buy British!" Their thunderous faces said it all!

As we arose in the early morning after sleeping on the beach, the Dutch bus was almost ready to go. They had just thrown all their gear into a couple of rows of seats at the back. Their method of travel was to do a week or two solid driving, many times one driver would sleep while the other drove. They would stop for a day or so in the large towns in order to clean up and do the laundry. Their passengers were Dutch, French, German, American, Canadian, and a couple of Brits. They slept on the move and figured to be in Goa in four weeks. That was a fast trip. There would be no sightseeing along the way, for them. Their only desire was to see the sun and sandy beaches of Portuguese Goa, and they were going for it.

"Head for the pudding shop in Istanbul. All the travellers go there and leave messages for each other. Be careful though, the place is crawling with narks, Turkish drug squad," advised Sten's co-driver, Pete.

A young English kid and his mother had recently been busted with kilos of hash. His name was Timothy Davey. He and his mother's treatment after arrest caused an international incident between Turkey and Britain, and questions to be asked in the British House of Commons. The Turks behaved like animals and were exposed to the world's gaze. Their appalling human rights record was clear for all to see.

The famous Hollywood film *Midnight Express* told the tale of a stupid young American tourist who taped a couple of kilos of hash to his body to fly back to the States. He was caught and put through all sorts of torture and degradation. Eventually to set an example the leaders in Ankara forced the judge to sentence him to life imprisonment in one of the worst jails in Eastern Europe. For two kilos of hash! It did more to damage the image of Turkey and relations with other countries than serve any perverted sense of justice. Even today in the first years of the twenty-first century, Turkey still has a questionable human rights record and their entry into the EEC is still being denied because of recent history. They tortured people to get confessions and were generally hysterical towards any foreigners caught with tiny amounts of cannabis for personal use, yet turned a blind eye to their own people who were making loads of money dealing in hash or, more often, heroin.

Taxi drivers were selling hash from their cabs in Istanbul, even beat policemen were known to be dealing. Corruption was rife. The desire to bust foreigners was driven, like so many other useless anti-drug schemes at the time, by huge amounts of 'foreign aid' money from America in their corrupt and degenerate 'war against drugs'. They'd have been better off starting war against some of their whiskey distilleries and breweries back in the home country.

Then, like now, both America and Britain were awash with a cheap and legal drug that most people were on. Alcohol. In the year that 180 people overdosed on heroin in Great Britain, 230,000 died from alcohol abuse, a further 150,000 died from the use of nicotine, a most deadly poison. In it's pure form, just sniffing it would kill you! Go Figure!

"If we don't see you there, we'll leave a message and meet you at the Gol-Leh-Shah motor camp in Tehran. Every traveller stays there for a few days – it's on the southern outskirts of Tehran city. I wouldn't stay too long in Istanbul, it's too much paranoia. You'll get ripped off if you stay in Istanbul motor camp." said Sten, as some parting advice.

I noticed Black Bob kissing one of the Yank females from the other bus. It looked like he got lucky. *Good for him*, I thought. *Only trouble is, we'll have to hear about it for the next five hundred kilometres!* We'd made friends with the people on Sten and Pete's bus as only people in new and alien environments, can. We were to rendezvous all along the road across Asia, with these guys. A bond had already formed. We waved them off and got on with our own packing. By contrast with the other bus, everything had its place and was stowed before moving.

The next few days were spent meandering down the Adriatic coast. It was so hot and the sun so bright all of the time. We would stop at lay-bys when it got too hot and swim for a while. We ended up finding a beautiful little fishing quay with a small sandy beach. I managed to fall asleep in the sun after swimming. Luckily, Mellony, my four-year-old daughter, had seen this and thought it a good idea to soak a rag and dab my forehead.

The memory of waking up to a cool wet rag being dabbed on me, and my 4-year-old saying, "Don't burn Daddy," has stayed with me, and will for the rest of my life.

All along the road through Yugoslavia we had been hassled by the police. Most times it would be in order to fine us for some imagined, petty traffic infringement. Mostly it was to get money so they could go the local bar to eat and drink. Their wages were a bit low and erratic. One morning we rounded a mountain bend to see the breathtaking sight of Dubrovnik. The Medieval seaside town was an amazing sight complete with a Spanish galleon tied up at the dockside – it was such a special sight that we stopped to see it. It was times like this that I regretted that we didn't have a camera. It was deemed to be a waste of money to buy films. We decided not to go into the town. We just wanted to get the fuck out of that country.

There is no doubt about it, the authorities were absolutely corrupt, low-life pigs. A typical stop on the road went like this: Round the bend you would come to be confronted by an armed police officer. He would hold up his 'lollipop', a fluorescent disk painted on a circular background, all on a stick, to be waved at drivers to stop. Along with the ubiquitous whistle, of course. He would swagger up to the driver's window and utter the only English word he knew. A word that always brought in some money.

"Tachograph!"

"Ah good morning officer. How are you today?" I would say with a smile.

"Tachograph!" he would say, more sternly.

"Yes it is a beautiful morning, and I'm very well thank you, nice of you to ask."

"Tachograph!" This time with thrusting palm and almost a sneer.

"Well it's been nice to talk to you, but I must get on. Tell you what. Would you like to see my tacho while you're here?"

"Tachograph!" he shouted, like some unaware, trained monkey. At this point I changed completely.

"Never mind the bloody tachograph," I snarled back at him. "How much?" I shouted as I massaged a two hundred dinar note under his nose. He was startled but wrote a receipt and handed it to me. Surprise, surprise, it was for two hundred dinar. I looked at the receipt – its printed date was a year ago.

I handed him the note, screwed up the receipt and threw it on the ground and spat after it. Without a further word, I drove off with the word 'thief' on the air. He didn't follow us and was presumably headed for the nearest bar. "I'm getting really pissed off with this," said Timus. "This has cost us more to cross Yugoslavia than France and Italy put together, and we're only halfway across, so far. If it goes on like this, we're not going make it to Tehran. As it is, we're going to be totally broke by the time we get there."

This news didn't make me feel any better. I was feeling the stress from worrying about money. It was OK for us grown-ups to go hungry for a day or two but I was not going to allow that to happen to the kids, not for a moment. "I'll make it clear, now, that if we run out of money, I will drive to the nearest British Embassy and ask them to repatriate us there and then."

That didn't go down well with the others. The bus and customs documents were attached to my passport and couldn't be transferred without the consent of the RAC in London. In short, a paper nightmare. Especially when you consider that international telephone communication was in its infancy and calls to foreign lands had to be booked hours in advance. If you got a reasonable line it was still difficult, if you got a bad one, it was impossible.

I didn't really care which way it went at that point in time. I'd been doing some serious driving hours and was getting really pissed off at the lazy attitude of Black Bob, Syd and Fran. Charlie was also getting right up my nose with his overbearing attitude with everyone. I'd had to pull him up about it and to tell him to shut the fuck up. He sulked for nine hundred miles, but he shut up. Kakey was another stumbling point. She was now out of her normal surroundings and was no longer able to manipulate the situation. She had tried everything to bring me into her 'sphere of influence' from pleading in a childlike way, to wiggling her beautiful tits at me. She made it obvious to me that if I wanted to have her, all I had to do was take her. I didn't think it a good idea, which got up her nose even more. She was not happy with me because the others were listening to what I said and ignoring her! She was also furious with Syd and Black Bob for deserting her for the girls on the other bus. Even though her relationship with Timus remained unaltered, she would sulk, big time, when we met the other bus down the road somewhere.

It's no wonder Yugoslavia split up into autonomous regions. The people were suppressed in a heavy way. They were bullied into submission and were exploited by all those with a little power. The police were little more than bandits and ripped us blind at every opportunity. But worse was to come.

We pulled in late one night to a small village beside the Adriatic. It was named Podgora. It was undeveloped and still largely a fishing village. We pulled up on a piece of waste ground just before the village and passed out for some badly needed sleep.

After what seemed to be just ten minutes, but must have been longer, as it was just getting light, There was a thunderous banging on the door. I came awake with a start as did most of the others. I pulled on some jeans and Timus and I answered the door. There was a big officious-looking suit who was gesturing wildly, flinging his arms around and shouting. "Guess what? I think he wants us to leave," I said calmly.

"No shit," replied Timus, equally calmly.

Our calmness seemed to wind him up even more.

"Calm down, pal. We have children here. You understand?" I made a gesture to indicate we had children on board. "Your gob is upsetting them." He glared at me, I glared right back.

"Yes, yes, OK we will go but we must get ready, feed the kids and then we will go, understand?" Timus indicated an hour on his watch, it was one hour away.

The loudmouth made a sucking noise on his teeth but turned on his heel and drove off.

By now a small group of villagers had gathered to see the strange travellers. The mythical hippies they had heard about. In contrast to our earlier visitor, these people were friendly and smiling. The men were interested to see our portable fuel pump. And I showed them why I was running the line to the boot. I lifted the lid to reveal a forty gallon drum sitting there. There were various 'ahh's of understanding and discussion of what a useful tool it was.

Three or four cars arrived as I was finishing pumping the diesel into our main tank. I thought it was some more men from the village, there were about ten of them when they had all got out of the cars. One guy started shouting at the villagers. I sensed something was wrong. "Hey, bully boy leave them alone."

He turned and started shouting at me in the same manner. The rest of his thugs started to psychically push Isobel and Fran onto the bus. That was it as far as I was concerned. I had dealt with forced, illegal evictions, before. I had come close to imprisonment for disabling a hired thug, sent round to clear his bosses dilapidated hovel for development.

I was not an ex-covert forces expert but when I was in the Royal Corps of Signals I was attached to special forces as a communications specialist. I could, and still do, send Morse Code at thirty words a minute! There was a wealth of knowledge to be had and I took full advantage of being there! I got permission to attend some courses and took training, unofficially, from the other lads. I was more than equipped to take care of bullying scum.

Thank goodness I was able to show the magistrate that I

was protecting myself and family from immediate threat. He dismissed the charge. "You touch those kids again and I'll break your arm. You understand, you fucking Yugoslavian prick?" I said forcefully removing his hands from Isobel's arm by digging my thumb as hard as possible, into the middle between the four knuckles of the hand. Again, a nerve point, and applied correctly, there is nothing you can do but open your fist. He started to push me towards the bus, shouting in my face and thumping my chest.

"Alun, no!" screamed Isobel but it was too late. The old crimson mist started to fog the eyes. I had already drawn back my hand, about to chop that spot on his lower neck, just where the main nerve routes to the brain. A hit there will fell the largest of thugs.

This was too much for one of the village men. They had been pushed into a group and kept back while the bully boys did their work. They stood there not believing what they were seeing. The villager broke away and grabbed my arm.

"Nah, nah, politzi, politzi," he said frantically, only to be roughly pushed back to the others.

"Shit, they're pigs. Why the fuck didn't they identify themselves?" I asked as we gave up all resistance. No amount of explanation and telling them we didn't know they were police, calmed them. They were out to teach these hippies a lesson. They called for a secure van, flung all of us males in the back and confiscated our passports. They left crying kids, traumatised women, and villagers aghast.

The villagers could do nothing. They had to live under these fascist pigs, all of the time. They were told to return to their houses. The pigs drove us into the local town of Markarska, some ten miles back up the road. They then locked us in a rooftop room above the courthouse, with wooden floors and locked shutters at the windows. Towards evening the policeman I nearly trollied arrived and brought blankets.

"Hey. What's going on, why are we here. What have you done with our families?"

"Men here, women at autobus," he said with a snarl.

"Tomorrow, you," he said pointing at me, "court, trial, jail understand?" He crossed his hands as if in handcuffs.

"What the fuck for?" I exclaimed, now getting very worried.

"Ah fuck, fuck, fuck," he mimicked. "You fucking Yugoslavian prick," he quoted. "That's big problem for you. Insulting the Yugoslavian nation and resisting arrest."

"We didn't know you were police. We were going anyway and we didn't resist arrest as soon as we knew who you were."

"Trial, tomorrow."

"Do we get fed?" asked Black Bob as he started out the door.

"We no fucking hotel, black bastard," he said with a mock American accent. He locked the door.

"What a charmer," said Timus, turning to Black Bob.

Black Bob shrugged it off. "I've eaten bigger racist arseholes than him for breakfast."

"Well, we are right in the shit, or rather I am. He seems to have it in for me. Do you really think they'll put me in jail for parking in the wrong place?" I was having visions of being forgotten in some shithole of a jail on the outskirts of Belgrade somewhere. I don't mind admitting it, I was scared. I tried to pass it off and we swapped jokes about our situation.

I was worried about the women and children. But, in a moment of calm, I remembered how level-headed Isobel was, how strong she was and that she had already shown these qualities on the journey so far. I went to sleep a little easier.

At first light we were herded downstairs and shown the disgusting, smelly, area that served as a shower. It had one outlet with no shower head and a stream of cold water rushing out. "I think they want us to shower," said Timus.

True to form, Black Bob and Syd started clowning around as they stripped for a welcome shower. The sun was up and it was getting warm, anyway. Despite my fear, I couldn't help laughing at the antics of the others. They had turned it into a very noisy, confused situation with the guard dumbfounded and unsure of what to do. Eventually, we were herded, in frustration, back to our rooftop cell. The policeman I nearly clouted opened the door. "You, fuck, prick," he said. "Come." He indicated me out of the door.

I was taken downstairs to the courthouse, sat in an office, and told to wait.

In came an official of the court with an interpreter.

"You are charged with insulting the Yugoslav nation and resisting arrest," he said in good English with what sounded to me, like a little sympathy in his voice. With his eyes he was telling me to say little by darting his gaze at the disinterested guard.

"What will happen?" I asked worriedly. "Will I go to jail?"

"No," he said easily, so as not to call attention from the guard. "They want to teach you a lesson for questioning their authority. Keep that worried look on your face, it'll help."

"What will happen, then?" I repeated with great relief.

"They will fine you some money. You have money?" he asked.

"Yes, a little, but it's back at the bus with the women."

"OK, I can drive there and bring your wife to pay the fine. You can pay for my petrol, yes?"

"No problem. Thank you so much." I was amazed at his kind attitude after the times we'd just gone through. He left to return in five minutes with another man in tow who had all our passports in his hand.

"Come," said the interpreter, and we were whisked into a plush office with a big desk with a big chair and an odious little man who'd already started talking as he eyed our passports. I understood none of it. Eventually the proclamation came to an end and I was dismissed with a couple of waves of downward pointing magisterial fingers, as if dismissing me with a nasty smell under his nose!

"What?" I asked, as I was led back into the other office.

"Fined 2500 dinars for insulting the Yugoslav peoples and nation. Nothing about resisting arrest."

"That's about sixty quid." I was alarmed at being fined so much out of our limited cash.

"It could have been worse. Keep quiet for now. There may be one or two who understand some English, I will fetch your wife. Which one is wife?" he asked.

Of course, I thought. *Her passport name is different to mine.* I showed him which was her passport. He took it and returned the others to me.

"Give to your friends. You must go back to the room. As soon as the fine is paid, you can go."

He stayed for a while and talked to us. He told us how awful it was to live under lowlife fascists, such as their police force.

"Don't blame the villagers. They took risks of reprisals to talk to you."

"We don't blame them at all," said Syd. "Please tell them we know this, if you get a chance, when you pick

Isobel up."

"OK, I go now." He nodded. "I'll be as quick as I can."

"Thanks so much, man. This is so good of you," we all chorused.

"No problem." He half smiled as the guard locked the door.

"Sixty fucking quid," lamented Timus. "That's a chunk out the kitty. "We've been set right up and ripped off, just for parking on some waste ground with a rubbish tip in one corner."

I explained that we would be out in a couple of hours and that we would work out what to do then.

After what seemed like hours but was, in fact, one, we were led downstairs to a waiting Isobel and local taxi. We hugged as I asked if they were all alright. I turned and summoned all the hatred I could muster as I glared at the copper I nearly bashed. He was stood at the top of the steps watching us leave. Isobel told us what had happened after we were taken away. Despite being scared to help us, the villagers had filled a sack with food and drinks for the little'uns and had approached the tip as if to discard a sackful of rubbish.

Seeing nobody around, they diverted to the bus at the last minute, deposited the sack on the steps and departed, swiftly. Later, under cover of darkness, two women came onto the bus and comforted the kids, and told of the oppressed life they lead.

"They are lovely people actually. They hugged and kissed us and said sorry so many times before they left. They said we must go to their house for dinner before we leave. Can you believe that? With all the fuss that could cause. I get the impression that they'll only be pushed so far," observed Isobel.

We all arrived at the bus to much fuss, hugs and kisses.

We related the story of where we spent the night.

"We've had a shit time since we got to this rotten country," said Glynis.

"It'd be great to get that money back somehow," said Charlie

It was agreed that we would think of something. In the meantime we had been invited to dinner at the largest house in the village, so we washed and changed into some clean gear and set off at a discreet distance from the village ladies who led the way. Suddenly they disappeared. As we reached the same point, we were whisked into the courtyard and the gates locked immediately.

As we stepped onto the huge veranda, most of the village people seemed to be there. They gave us a wonderful, smiling welcome. It looked as if most of the food in the village was laid out on a long table, as well. There was fresh spicy fish, asparagus, tasty big tomatoes which looked perfect, without so much as a blemish, potatoes sliced and fried with spices and poppy seeds, and ice cream for the kids that we all ended up finishing!

It was wonderful. The evening sun was at just the right angle and bathed us all in a golden light. We drank cold beers and laughed so much with those lovely people. The Navajo people of North America had the perfect expression to describe people such as these. They were simply 'real people'. A higher accolade you could not wish for.

We managed to rise early after our wonderful night out and said our goodbyes to our hosts of the night before. They waved us off with gusto. In later times, on other journeys, fate allowed us to call into the same village many times. Each time we were treated like visiting royalty and the tale was told again, to howls of laughter. We were still determined to get back at the authorities but no sensible plan came to mind. On and on I drove. We just wanted to get out of that shit country as soon as possible. The whole episode had dragged us right down.

As night fell it became bearably cooler as we started to climb up the hairpin bends in the foothills that we had to climb to get to Titograd and on to the Greek border at Skopje. We knew the Greek people were basically English people, with a funny way of speaking. I couldn't get there fast enough. Just as we started to climb it was becoming dark. We came across a huge sign proclaiming, in English and Cyrillic script. 'Road upgrade', it boasted. Such-and-such a province doing this, government-sponsored that. Blah-de-blah.

It was a huge project. "Must be costing the government loads of money..." DING! A light went on in my brain. "Whoaaaaa!" I shouted suddenly, after a hundred kilometres deep in thought and therefore, silence! I hit the brakes big time and virtually skidded to a halt.

"Wassup?" spat Charlie, who was nearly launched through the front screen.

I looked around to faces that said, "What the fuck is up?"

I pulled off the road into the woods. We were completely out of sight of the road. It didn't matter as I hadn't seen another vehicle for hours. It wasn't suitable roads for bigger vehicles so there were no trucks either. I waited till the engine stopped. "Did you see all that plant?" I asked.

"What plants?" asked Kakey, bemused.

"No. Construction plant, I'm talking about those bulldozers down there. There's loads of them spread out all the way down the works."

They still looked puzzled.

"What do they all run on? What have we just emptied a barrel of into the main tank?"

"Shiiiiiit!" exclaimed Charlie in his drawn out way, as it hit him. "Diesel!" he shouted.

"Exactly!" I said, glad we were reading from the same script. The others still looked a bit baffled.

"We park here until late. We break out the containers and we drain every earthmover of diesel, until we can take no more! It's sponsored by the government. It says so clearly, in English."

Luckily, I had drained the forty gallon barrel into the tank and now we had used most of that as well. We would have had to buy diesel very soon anyway.

It was agreed that I would wait with the bus, women, and children, to assist with filling the barrel from their containers and getting ready to make a speedy getaway and try to cross the border before morning. It wasn't long before the boys returned, looking dejected.

"All the bloody tanks have hefty locks. Not only that but the barrels of diesel have been trapped under the hydraulic arms in such a way that you can't unscrew the caps," said Timus.

"OK, this is what you do," I said, inspired. "You go in the boot, you takeout our twenty ton, hydraulic jack..."

"Lift the boom," exploded Charlie, ahead of me again and already heading for the boot. "Jack up the boom, roll out the barrel to such a position that the filler cap is at the highest point and the diesel will almost syphon itself."

They stepped off into the darkness and were soon staggering back under the weight of full containers, which I quickly pumped into our barrel in the boot. Several journeys later we were full in the main tank, and had forty-five gallons in the barrel. We even filled the transporting containers – we couldn't get another drop in. We certainly got our money back, and then some!

I had cautioned them against spilling any diesel. It

stinks and hangs around for ages. It was decided to wash up before moving on. There were still no other vehicles so we didn't have to hide. It was a beautiful clear night and warm enough to still be wearing shorts and to wash outside. I gave Charlie the keys to the boot after I'd cleaned up so that they could go on washing while I ran up the bus engine. I left instructions to lock the boot. The boys got back on board and I pulled out to a deserted, dark road. We climbed a couple of hairpin bends when little Mellony asked for a toilet stop.

I pulled the bus in. As Isobel and Mellony got back on board, I switched the interior lights on and happened to glance at the hooks where we hung all he keys.

"Where are the boot keys, Charlie?"

"On the hook, man."

"No they're not, I'm looking at the hook and it's empty."

As if to doubt my word he emerged from behind the partition and stared blankly at the empty hook, willing them to be there.

"What did you do with them after you locked the boot?" I said, knowing the answer.

"I put them on the bumper to wash my hands," he said slowly, as if wrenching the picture from his brain. "Fuck! They will have fallen off between there and here."

I went absolutely apeshit at him. All the frustration and stress that had built up in me, came out. "You fucking dickwad Charlie. You're so fucking busy browbeating everyone else, you can't cover your own fucking act. Well this time you can clear up your own fuck up."

"Waddya mean?" he challenged.

"I mean, if you think I'm trying to turn, in the dark, on a narrow mountain road and taking the bus back down into an area that we've just pinched gallons of diesel from, you got a big re-think coming. It wouldn't take long for even these fuckers to put two and two together. They don't worry about little things like evidence."

"What can we do then?" asked Timus, looking worried.

"Charlie, you get the bike down from the roof rack and pedal down there."

"You're joking. It'll take hours. Anyway there's room to turn around."

"Do I look like I'm fucking joking you stupid cunt?" I shook the keys. "Here you go. You turn it. Just give me a minute to get Isobel, kids and our gear off as I'd hate to lose it all down the cliff."

He said nothing. Just swallowed his anger and I knew it would return at some stage. *This is going to come to blows somewhere along the line*, I thought. I really hoped it wouldn't as I was genuinely grateful to him for his selfless action, when young Alun fell in the water. He also knew about Glynis and I. That was before him, but I think there was still some resentment there. She probably told him what a wonderful lover I was, to spite him when they were having a row, one time. On second thoughts I doubt that was true. He was a well-hung lad and from all the moaning and gasps we heard when lying in our bunks, Glynis liked his technique just fine, thank you very much!

Charlie unstrapped the Moulton bicycle from the roof rack and peddled off down the hill in complete darkness. He took our only working torch.

We sat around brewing tea. A couple of cars went passed but took absolutely no notice of us. Two and a half hours later Charlie returned absolutely shagged out. "They were on the ground just passed the lay-by we were in. I had to walk on the way back up, it was just too steep," panted Charlie.

"Get a cup of tea. I'll put the bike back up," I offered.

By the time Charlie got back I had been dozing in the driver's seat and felt like shit, let alone driving for the rest of the night. We pulled off for what turned out to be a marathon run into Skopje and across the border in the early hours. All the way, I was watching the temperature gauge like a hawk. Several times I had to pull up and run the engine fast, to cool the radiator down. This wasn't good, the engine was running hot, so therefore the oil would be thinner and the running pressure, dangerously low.

Chapter 6

Greece

There was only one border guard on each side. The Yugoslav guard stamped our passports without getting on the bus, which was just as well, as only Syd, Isobel and myself were awake. He then waved us through and settled back to sleep. On the Greek side, they hardly woke up to stamp our passports. They just weren't interested. After all what would we be smuggling from England? You can bet they would crawl all over us on the way back. I don't know what time it was when I eventually pulled up just twenty km inside Greece, somewhere around ten in the morning. The sun was in a clear blue sky and hot already.

I looked for some trees and drove the bus between them in the shade. Without a word, I shrugged off my clothes and lay naked on the bunk and was soon in a deep sleep. When I awoke it was early evening. Isobel, Kakey, and Glynis were cooking and Black Bob was playing with the kids. He looked up and saw me coming, bleary-eyed, down the aisle.

"That was a drive and a half," he remarked, smiling.

"Yeah, it was a bitch but it's nothing to what's coming. And it's only going to get hotter, which is what's bothering me."

'Bothering me' was a big understatement. I was now very worried about the bus and this cooling problem. The bus had performed well, so far with no problems, but overheating had to be put right before we hit the really hot Middle East.

The other source of stress was money. We just about had enough to get us to Tehran where we planned to park up for a couple of months and try to earn enough money to get us to India and beyond. But we were going to have to spend more to sort this problem.

At evening dinner I got everyone's attention. "I don't know if you noticed last night, I had to stop quite a few times."

"Yes. I woke up a couple of times and you were running the engine up," said Black Bob

"That's unusual. You can normally let a bomb off beside him and still he doesn't wake," said Kakey.

"Is it the cooling problems again?" asked Syd.

"'Fraid so. It's now getting serious and I'm afraid we're going to have to spend some money on the problem."

That got everyone's attention. "How much?" asked Timus.

"I can't say but what I have in mind is to visit a Greek scrap yard. They have loads of old Fords and other old British motors. We can find a radiator from a bus or truck and we can probably get an electric fan to cool it. I can plumb it in but it's going to mean hanging around for a day or two while I fit it."

"How much have we got left?" I asked Timus.

"If, and I mean If, we are doing around ten to the gallon, we have enough to get us across Turkey into Iran. If diesel gets cheaper in Turkey we should be OK, but it's going to be tight on everything else. I won't allow the young'ns to go hungry." The rest seemed to be willing to get to Tehran, hungry and broke.

"They won't be hungry," said Fran, as she checked her newly hennaed hair in the mirror.

"Perhaps they won't if we spend money on food rather than fucking henna to put in your hair," I said as sarcastically as I could.

I'd learned that Fran had thrown a tearful wobbler because she wanted to buy this henna to do her hair. Behind mine and Isobel's back, they had given her the equivalent of two days' food rations to buy this crap. When I heard that fact I reacted in a predictable manner and from then on it was open warfare towards Fran and her attitude, and conflict with the others for giving her the money.

"Only cost a couple of quid Alun, don't be a mean booger," said Glynis.

"It ain't that, Glynis. It's the principal. We've been buying nothing. Not even ice creams or drinks for the kids. I've been driving for days and all she does is preen herself up. Can't you see that she's a fucking selfish, lazy bitch?" All the frustration was about to flow.

"C'mon, man," started Black Bob.

"And you and Syd ain't a lot better, Bob so just give me a fucking break will you?"

"Waddya mean?" they chorused.

"How come, when I ain't driving, the people I don't

see doing the potatoes or cleaning the bus or doing any work at all, is you three?"

"Calm down," said Syd a little weakly.

"I'll calm down when you get off your fat arse and share a bit of the work. The other day I came off driving for twelve hours and peeled the potatoes, while you and Bob discussed the merits and de-merits of Superman over The Flash and lay around smoking. And if I see her combing her hair and preening in a mirror again, I'll put a hammer through it.

"Hey Fran," I taunted. "How come you spent so much time tarting yourself up but then hide when we have company or a group photo is being taken."

"Alun!" snapped Isobel.

I knew I'd gone too far. Fran was now in tears, Black Bob and Syd were in shock, and everyone else was quiet as they recognised truth in what I was saying. Too late I realised that the stress of keeping the engine cool, feeding the family and getting us all across Asia in one piece was beginning to tell on me. Add to this the fact that we hadn't had a smoke since we left France. We were all well ragged at the edges! Before I could say anymore, I stormed out the door and slid it closed behind me.

The sun was down and it was getting dark but the air was full of an interesting smell of food and flowers. It was a warm, balmy night. The ground was warm and the rocks held the heat, reminding me of the problems of heat dissipation. Soon Isobel was beside me with a coffee in her hand. "Well, you've upset Fran. She's playing it for all she's worth."

"Do you know what she said to me the other day? She said she thought I could avoid some of these potholes in the road. She accused me of doing it on purpose! She's fuckin' lost it, big time! She sits around doing nothing when was the last time she helped at the border with the paperwork, or took a turn map reading? When did she last help with the dinner?"

"I don't think she can cope with the situation. You lot getting arrested freaked her out. You're only going to freak her more."

I knew what she was saying was right and I felt a bit of a bully. "OK, I'll be back in in a second."

"Dinner's almost ready anyway, and the kids want to tell you what they've been doing today before they go to sleep."

I sat around a little longer until I was certain that I had calmed down and then went back aboard. I sat calmly and ate dinner. I was damned if I was going to apologise so I just kept quiet. I spent some time with the kids but I was still tired, so I announced I was going to crash out again. I slept for another six hours. When I surfaced it was just getting light. I quietly made a cup of coffee and went outside to sit on a rock. We had stopped under some trees at the side of the road. Now that it was light I could see we had parked not far from a small town. People were driving into the town to work or go to the shops. Occasionally, someone would spot our GB sticker and wave or toot the horn.

Just as I was thinking of going back to the bus to rest my waving arm, a car pulled up with a smiling man aged about thirty-five or so. "Hey man, good coming. What do you want?"

I realised that was bad English for 'Welcome, is there anything you need?'

"Just arrived last night. We stop for sleeping." I fell into broken English myself.

We talked for a while and I realised I could use his local knowledge to deal with the overheating problem.

Explaining the problem and what I wanted to do about it would be a challenge. The guy's name was Demi and he liked English music and English people.

"French, people OK, German people..." He made a face as if he had a bad smell under his nose. "They come. They drive in car, make beep, beep and drive fast right through. Don't stop. Go only to beach," complained Demi. "English, Dutch, Italian they come. Eat in restaurant, drink in bar, make petrol at service area, go to local market and shop."

"C'mon Demi. The Germans are OK. They live in the same weather as I. We never see the sun like this. You can't blame them for wanting to get to the beach quickly."

"Yes." He spotted the box full of cassettes by the player. We had pooled all our cassettes and I had fitted an old Dansette mono cassette player and wired it into the old P.A. system of the bus. Hardly Hi-Fi but it was better than no sounds at all. We ended up with more albums than we could ever play even if we played them end to end, all the way to India. I realised we had currency here as Demi was lovingly reading the labels in English. He then launched into a broken version of 'It's a Long Way to Tipperary'.

"Shhh, Demi, please." I made a gesture indicating that people were sleeping on the bus.

"How many you have?" he asked, now in a whisper.

"Eleven including two kids." He looked impressed. "Demi, I have a problem with the Engine. I need to find..." How would I describe a scrap yard? "I need to find a garage... a service area for the autobus." He looked at me, puzzled. "I have a problem with the motor," I said, lifting the floor hatch. He could see the engine. I then took him to the front, knelt down and indicated the radiator. He still looked a bit unsure but before I could say anything he was heading for his car.

"I come here after one hour. I have uncle with motor shop," he said, and drove off.

Timus was the first to wake and he came to sit in the front with me. "Did I hear you talking to someone?"

"Yes, a local guy stopped to talk. I thought we could use his help, he did offer. His English wasn't that good but he reckons his uncle has a car shop. The other thing is, he seemed really keen on our music. Reckons he can't get any new stuff here. I thought we might be able to swap some cassettes for some bits to do the cooling."

Timus nodded and looked at the scene before us. Everything was now really foreign. The cigarettes were different, as were the milk cartons washing powder, everything was there but different. Road signs, the way roads were laid out and lanes marked. Large vehicles were expected to pull over and drive along the hard shoulder when flashed at from cars behind, enabling them to overtake with more room. All this added up to give the impression that we were now in a foreign land.

"Well at least we got to Greece, I always wanted to see Greece." He fell silent for a while. "God, I'd kill for a smoke."

"You ain't fucking kidding, mate, me too but y'know how the song goes, 'the Greeks don't want no freaks'"

We both laughed at the mention of the old Eagles track.

"I'm sorry about last night, Timus, but I'd just had enough of them three. Charlie's a pain in the arse but at least he mucks in and does stuff, now and again."

"Even Kakey is getting fed up with their laziness so I shouldn't dwell on it. I don't know what the fuck is going on with Fran."

By this time Glynis and Isobel had organised a wash down area at the back of the bus and were taking advantage of the stop time. The kids were receiving a good scrub also.

"How about this. When Demi returns we get him to take us to a scrap yard. We tell him we'll swap music for parts, that way we won't be using the cash."

"We really need this stuff Alun?"

"I gotta do something. It's getting hotter every day. If I could just get a high pressure water hose, I might be able to get all the air out of the system. The main problem is, of course, that it's twenty years old. It was built for an English climate. I doubt if the cooling system was ever pushed hard in its whole working life. I reckon giving it more cooling area will help."

"What happens if we go on as we are?" asked Black Bob, who'd now joined us.

"The first thing will be boiling the water in the radiator. That'll cause a hose to split and we will be surrounded in steam. But the worst would be the possibility of a ring picking up."

"A what?" asked Timus. I forgot I was talking to people who had no idea what went on under an engine cover.

"When an engine overheats, one effect is to lower the oil pressure and the bits of metal that tend to break down first are the piston rings. The friction of them going up and down with no oil melts the wall of the cylinder and actually pulls off the surface metal. That snaps the rings and so it cascades into a big bang with oil and engine bits all over the road. And I'm not exaggerating!"

"Eyhhchk, that don't sound good," said Syd, who understood these things a little better than the others.

"It'll stop us dead. There will be no way to repair it here, we just couldn't afford it. I'll have to get the Greek customs to see that it's scrap and clear it from my passport before I leave the country or I'll be liable for the import duty."

Everyone was now up and listening to the discussion.

"We really don't have any choice. We've got to fix this or we're not going to make it to India. If we can, we'll trade some cassettes for parts but even if we have to spend money, it's got to be done. Believe me this heat is nothing to what we're going to get."

"How come this wasn't taken care of before we left?" asked Fran with a glare. Not missing the chance to get back at me. I totally blanked her.

"If it's got to be done then we'll just have to get over it," chimed in Kakey. Fran saw she had no allies and sulked to the back.

Just as we started lunch, Demi returned with his uncle in the passenger seat. Uncle was a large jovial man who spoke good English. They both came aboard and we introduced each other. "Demi tells me you have a problem with the engine," said Uncle.

"Yes, it's the cooling system actually." I went on to describe the problem.

"We sometimes use an extra header tank over here but most of the British trucks can cope with the extra heat. Sometimes they have deeper fans to move more air. What do you intend to do?"

"We don't use the internal heater system, so I thought I'd route the heater water through another radiator mounted to the side of the chassis, then back into the system," I explained.

"Good idea, will the water pump be strong enough?" asked Uncle.

"That's the million dollar question." At least I was dealing with somebody who understood the situation. I decided to go with a separate radiator, electric fan, and some rubber hose to plumb it in with.

"We don't have a lot of money, that's the other problem. Demi was saying he liked our music. We have many tapes we can swap for parts for the bus, or maybe there's something else we have you may like."

Uncle turned to Demi and spoke in Greek. I saw Demi's eyes widen just a little and he said something enthusiastically.

"Have you got Levis?"

"Levi denim jeans?" I asked. "Yes we have a few pairs. We packed them away when it started to get hot coming through Italy."

"I very much like Levi jeans," spluttered Demi.

"Well my friend, you have a deal. We will have these parts and you will have Levi jeans and some music, but please remember we have little money. We hope to make it to Tehran and find some work. We have heard from other travellers that there is lots of money to be made."

"We can go now to my workshop. I have many broken trucks and cars, we will find something. "Hello baby," he said, as little Alun came from their sleeping area. He patted Alun's hair. Alun smiled in a sleepy way. I'd already explained to him how Greek people had mostly dark hair and found his blond locks irresistible. He tolerated it with a smile but I knew that smile would wear thin before we got where we were going. We got ourselves together and drove off behind Demi and Uncle. We went into the industrial area of the town, eventually we pulled into a yard full of scrap vehicles.

"Yes! This is just what we need." I was out of the bus and looking around for the bits.

Uncle invited everyone into his air conditioned office which was large. It had a Coca-Cola machine, straight out of the fifties. I think it would have made a couple of thousand pounds at some of the trendy antique parlours in West London. In the other corner was a BEL-AMI jukebox in full working order complete with Greek records and one or two old and very noisy rock 'n' roll ones. It was a thing of great beauty with chrome and coloured panels. I looked in the back to see an old but perfect valve stereo amplifier, its valves glowing. I pushed a few buttons and everything came to life with clicks, bangs, and whirls. Eventually a Greek rock band ground out an appalling, but wonderfully Hi-Fi, sound.

"Ah, you like the old jukebox," said Uncle with a grin like only a Greek man can. All white teeth and olive-skinned. I remember thinking, *How the hell do we Brits get a look in? There's all these handsome Mediterranean types, with their swarthy good looks and flawless, white teeth.* Young Demi was not without admirers. I'll name no names, but noses were put out, is all I'm saying.

"Yes, I'm an engineer. I just love anything mechanical or electronic."

"Ah! Come," said Uncle, and made for the rear door of the workshop with me close on his heels. We walked into an Aladdin's cave. Down one dusty wall was a row of about ten old jukeboxes, in various states but I could see, were complete. My eyes would have been fixed on the jukeboxes were it not for several old American cars, again in various states, filling the rest of the garage. There was a fifties Cadillac, a Studabaker, and a Ford Thunderbird of about 1965 vintage.

"Wow! I love these old American motors. The fifties and early sixties models were wonderful, over the top pieces of automotive art."

Uncle preened and smiled. He had found someone who didn't think his garage was full of junk, as his wife was convinced.

"I must take your address. When I return, we can do

some good business," I said.

Uncle's eyes widened ever so slightly. "When do you return?"

"About a year or so. I'm making lots of contacts as we go and I'm learning a lot. I'd like to buy all of your cars and jukeboxes but I just don't have the money right now."

"You can sell them in England?" he asked with interest.

"I have contacts in England. I could sell them all in one lot."

"How much is worth in England."

"Ah! That's the question. You have to sell to the right people. I couldn't say but there would be a good profit for us both."

Uncle smiled and gave me his business card.

We spent a couple of days parked up while I selected an old truck radiator, a few pipes, and an electric fan from a Saviem pick-up truck. I used Uncle's workshop facilities and we had a pleasurable time fitting the new stuff to the bus's cooling system.

The kids were spoilt rotten. Ice cream and pop and days in the sun. The next door neighbours had a couple of donkeys and the kids spent hours riding and brushing them down, feeding and watering them. Eventually I finished the work. We had a wonderful evening meal with our friends, and promised them we would send them a picture postcard when we arrived.

We all rose early, and said our goodbyes before the sun was fully up. I was anxious to see how the new cooling modifications would cope in the midday heat. I had my sights set on getting to Thessalonika. On and on went the road through lines of trees with their trunks painted white, and lines of whitewashed stones marking the edge of the road. Every now and then a car or truck would come by with an arm waving out the window and blaring on the horn. We stopped in a few roadside truck stops but never bought any of the delicious-looking trays of different dishes – stuffed peppers and aubergine, it looked, and smelt, wonderful.

Days went by. Hot and dry. We were away from the coast and missing our swims. During one stop out in the middle of nowhere, I fixed up an outside shower made from an old plastic barrel with a hose that hung out over the back of the bus. I would back up to a rock face or some bushes and an al fresco group shower would be taken. The routine, to save water went: wet down, lather up, rinse off and do it quick. It was great fun, all of us trying to stand as close together as possible to rinse off. I heard a muffled shriek from Isobel.

"Bob will you please turn around a little bit and point it that way?" Bob looked like a dirty old man with a happy face as he turned a little.

"Don't point it this way, you dirty booger," squealed Glynis, closely inspecting the offending piece of Bob's anatomy.

We laughed like schoolkids. I don't know if any locals saw us, or what they would have thought but we didn't get a repetition of the French episode!

We passed Thessalonika, stopping only on the outskirts to buy vegetables and other needed items. It was now getting so hot in the daytime that we decided to have a couple of hours' break around midday every day to make it a bit easier on the bus and us. The new cooling bits were helping and just keeping the temperature level but it still took careful driving. The daytime temperature would climb into the high nineties. The tarmac would be on the point of melting and would make a singing sound as we drove along.

To this day the smell of diesel, tarmac, and the sound of those rolling tyres fires up my blood. Strange but there it is. On and on we went without any problems. There were fields and fields of tobacco all along the road and each house had its own drying racks in the back garden. Through Xanthi, Rodop, Alexandropolis, and finally early one morning we crossed into Turkey on the T.C. Edrine crossing.

Chapter 7

Turkey

This was it. This was the dreaded Turkey. We were so paranoid about this country and we weren't in a hurry to repeat our experiences in Yugoslavia, so we decided to head to the Black Sea instead of the direct route through the centre and passing close to Ankara.

We were well pleased to have made it this far but decided to stay as little as possible. We had arranged to meet our friends on the Dutch bus in the motor camp just before Istanbul City. It was on the main highway and you couldn't miss it. It was full of trucks from every European country you could name, including the East Europeans.

The place was a toilet. They kept the trucks and the tourist vehicles apart but it was still a shit-hole and we didn't want to stay longer than needed. We learned that the Dutch bus was around somewhere but not here at the moment. It was decided that Isobel the kids and I would go to the pudding shop opposite the St. Sofia mosque, the famous Icon of Istanbul with its stunning dome and minarets.

The pudding shop featured in the starting scenes of the film *Midnight Express*. The Turks were still stinging from the international condemnation that the film's showing at the Cannes film festival had provoked. That, and the fact that they had allowed Billy Heyes to escape, to the world's ridicule.

The Turks viewed every longhair as a drug carrier and they were itching for revenge. We were not going to give them a chance – we would carry nothing and smoke with nobody. Isobel, the kids, and I walked in an made our way to the wall where everyone left messages. Sure enough a message had been left to say they were in the city and would be leaving that morning, and if we missed them we were to go to the Gol-Leh-Shah motor camp on the outskirts of Tehran city.

Just as we were reading this we heard a shout. "Alun! Isobel!" We both turned to see a smiling Sten coming toward us. We shook hands and hugged, it was really good to see them.

"We were just about to leave, man. Where are you staying?"

"We in that shit-hole motor camp on the main road in from Greece. We are only staying there overnight. We're leaving first thing tomorrow morning."

"Come on let's not stay here," said Sten. "The place is crawling with plain clothes police. The bus is over by the mosque. Let's go."

We got to the bus to be greeted by the other passengers. They were pleased to see us and readily agreed to go back to the motor camp to see the others. The two girls that had struck up a relationship with Syd and Black

Bob were very enthusiastic on the idea and were smiling broadly.

Sten had slipped into the driver's seat and had started the engine. I was surprised by the lack of engine noise. The engine was rear mounted and very quiet. The suspension was much softer than ours as well. I wasn't sure whether that was good or bad, thinking of the roads to come, or rather, the lack of them!

We arrived in the motor camp with air horn blaring. Sten parked at a right angle to our bus forming a nice area facing the sun. Unfortunately we were facing the truck park section as well and I could see several drivers enjoying the sight of scantily clad females. We ignored them and got together to cook dinner over an open fire.

While the cooking was going on I decided to go round to the truck park and see if there were any British trucks there. As I walked around the ranks of trucks I noticed I was almost ankle deep in a fine sand. It was blowing everywhere. Trucks going in and out would travel at a crawl for fear of stirring up the dust and getting lynched by the other drivers. Eventually I came across a British registered Volvo, F88. The driver, a large Brummie, who looked rather like 'Fat Freddie' only, unlike the idiot cartoon character, this guy was sharp as a razor.

As I approached the driver was looking in his food locker, underneath the trailer.

"How's it going, mate?" I said. He was very surprised to hear his native tongue.

"Are you English?"

"Yeah I'm driving that old AEC in the tourist camp, name's Alun." I held out my hand.

"Arthur." He responded with a nice firm handshake.

"I'd noticed the old bus. I used to drive an AEC. Where are you going?" he asked.

"We're going over to India."

"India!?" He looked gobsmacked. "In that? You gotta be kidding."

"Do you mind?" I asked with mock indignation. "That'll go anywhere your fancy Volvo will go. Alright so it won't pull so much weight but it'll get there."

"How old is it?"

"Nineteen fifty-five. It's done twenty or more years commercial work, now we're taking it on a twelve thousand mile, round trip. It's built like a brick shithouse!"

"Have you had dinner?" I asked.

"No I was just looking in the locker."

"Come on round and have dinner with us. We've just met up with our friends from Holland. They've got a bus as well. We are having a massive cook-up so you'll be welcome and you can pay for your supper by letting me pick your brains about the road and all that stuff. The other bus has done the trip before a few times but I'd like to hear your experiences as well."

"OK, I'll just lock up and we can go round."

As we walked I learned that Arthur was going down to the oil fields south of Iran's second city of Isfahan. He came from Dudley and had been doing this for a year or so.

We got to the buses and I introduced Arthur to everyone, and asked for another place to be set for dinner. After we'd eaten, Sten, Timus, Black bob, Isobel, and Charlie, sat and listened to some of Arthur's stories. He told us of the infamous mountain pass known as Tiere Pass in Eastern Turkey. There was no road surface except a bulldozed, hardened mud road big enough to let two cars pass but not two trucks or buses. Passing places for big vehicles had been blasted out of the rock face, but if you met another vehicle one of you had to back up.

"The approach to the pass is very steep with loose surface. If you stop you will never start up again. It really is that steep, and once you lose traction that's it, you are highly unlikely to get going again without a push or pull and you are blocking the pass! The local youth know you cannot stop and stand on the rocks above you. They have rocks in their hands and are making a smoking sign at you. If you don't throw out a couple of packets of cigarettes they will smash your windscreen and there is nothing you can do about it! If you go over in the winter it's a real bottle job. I've been in a situation where I've had all the brakes on and I'm still sliding! Make sure you follow the local bus through."

"Why's that?" I asked curiously.

"Because the bulldozer will come out for the bus but he won't come for the TIRs."

TIR stood for Transports International Routier. It was a general term given to most international trucks but actually referred to the type of customs document they were using.

"Last winter I watched as a truck and trailer went over the side. The driver had managed to stop before going down the cliff edge but he was blocking the pass. Every time the driver tried to move, he would just slide it nearer the edge. Eventually the bulldozer arrived and started to hitch steel cables to the truck with the idea of pulling it sideways, back onto the road."

"Go on," I urged. He had our complete attention.

"Well the bulldozer started pulling, there was black smoke roaring from the exhaust. There was this giant twang as one of the steel cables breaks. It was old and rusty, just like most of the equipment they've got out here. They are like dangerous children when it comes to driving and machinery. You wait till you get further in Turkey. They play games with trucks as if they were toys. You see some gory accidents. Anyway, I digress, There were another two cables attached and if the bulldozer had just kept the throttle open and stayed with it he could have pulled the truck back on the road. But this guy had no desire to meet his maker, whether there were virgins waiting for him in paradise or not, he wanted none of it."

"Don't like these people much do you, Arthur," said Timus.

"The people I deal with are all lowlife bandits, from customs, border guards, to the corrupt police, they're all on the take and see us as fair game for cartons of Marlboro and money. The ordinary people are OK but I don't get much chance to meet them. What you were telling me about what happened to you in Yugo is common. They're bandits. It don't matter which country. They see all these foreign trucks coming through their manor and they practice a modern form of highway robbery. There's nothing you can do, that's why I try and do Yugo in one hit. Travel as much as possible at night when the bastards are asleep."

"But what about your tacho?" I asked.

"Once I leave Italy, I don't bother putting one in. If you get stopped, you're gonna pay anyway and they don't really know what a tacho is."

"Ain't that the truth. You pay with cartons of Marlboro here. They are all on the take," said Sten.

"Masters at it," confirmed Arthur.

"So what happened to the truck?" asked Kakey.

"Oh! Yeah, it went over the cliff and took the bulldozer with it. You can still see the wreck lying in bits at the bottom. The load scattered everywhere but nobody can get down to salvage anything. Nobody was hurt, the driver jumped out as soon as he saw the dozer driver exit at a rate of knots."

"If I were you, I would go round the military road. Because you can bet there will be a long queue of trucks at the border crossing with Iran," said Arthur.

"Military road?" That got my attention.

"Yeah, there's a road used by mostly military and local traffic. It goes right up alongside the Soviet border. You can see the goon towers, chain link fence and razor wire about twenty foot high. It runs right along to the Black Sea. You'll see a sign for Mount Ararat but it says clearly that TIRs are forbidden to use it," said Sten.

I was getting the distinct impression that Sten and Arthur were trying to outdo each other with dramatic stories, still, I just had to take it all in and do it the best way I could. I was confident I could handle anything. The confidence of tender years! These guys had done the route before and it was all good knowledge but nothing they could say would make me turn around, so I listened closely. "We usually go the truck route because we are classed as tourists and we can go down the line of trucks to the head of the queue. There is usually about a ten-kilometre tail back of trucks but it's the most direct route. The military road goes around the foot of Mount Ararat, it's right on the Turk-Iran border. You have to go around it to Bazargan border crossing but you end up at the same crossing," said Sten.

"But they don't mind tourists using it?" I asked.

"No. You might get a pull by the army or police but it's only because they're so twitchy near the Russian border. Once they see you are tourists, you're on your way," said Arthur.

"I reckon that's the way we should go," I said, looking at the others for confirmation. They nodded enthusiastically.

"I'd love to see Ararat." Isobel was excited at seeing the

resting place of Noah's Ark.

People were falling asleep around the fire and it was getting late, but I still had many questions for Sten and Arthur.

"We are heading for Tehran. We've just about got enough money to get us there, d'you reckon we'll be able to get some work there?"

"I know a few people who've worked there, mostly in the oilfields. I do know that there is a shortage of truck drivers there. Somebody reckoned they're twenty-five thousand drivers short in the country," said Arthur.

"Some friends of mine worked as teachers of English. They only wanted British passport holders, it has to be your native tongue. They were paid well," said Sten.

"I should think you should be able to make some money if you are prepared to work. Actually, I've just thought, you could do what we call an 'internal'. There's a two week wait to tip at Tehran Customs area. Every truck that comes into Iran, must clear their load there before delivering in the country. The place is huge with hundreds of trucks from all over Europe. The Iranians are importing millions of dollars' worth of equipment. They got oil money coming out their arses, only trouble is, they can do none of it themselves. They've had to bring in the Americans, Brits and Germans to get it out of the ground and move it onto the international oil market." Arthur was showing a keen understanding of the country and I was impressed.

"Anyway, what you do is get together with other drivers. One of you stays at the customs area to tip the trailers. The others take their units and beg, borrow or hire a trailer and go down to the docks at Bandar Shahpur or Bandar Abbas, on the Persian Gulf. You load whatever they have, and bring it back to Tehran. Takes about a week and it's £500 in cash, in your hand, in dollars or sterling.

You all chip in to pay the guy who stayed behind and tips the trailers and Bob's yer uncle. The docks are so desperate to move the imports that they are buying like crazy with their oil dollars and diesel is piss cheap."

"What are they importing, Arthur?" I asked

"You gotta see it to believe it. They are bringing in shiploads of trucks, earthmoving equipment, heavy oilfield equipment, steel-stock, fruit and other cold store stuff. You name it, there's tons of it on the docks down there and the ships are backed-up, at anchor down the Gulf as far as you can see."

"Sounds like that's the place for me. I'm a qualified heavy vehicle mechanic."

"Ah! You should find work easily then. When you get to Tehran, come to the Gol-Leh-Shah motor camp. All the truck drivers that don't stay at the customs yard, take their units there. It costs them, but at least there's a restaurant of sorts and a swimming pool, not to mention all the tourist girls hanging out round the pool." Arthur grinned at Isobel in a way that caused me to make a mental note not to leave her alone with him!

"Yeah, that's where we'll be staying, too," said Sten as he rose from the fire. "Anyway, Isobel, Arthur, nice to meet you. Alun my friend we will be leaving early and you are going up to the Black Sea so the next time we meet will be Tehran. We will stay at the Gol-Leh-Shah too." He gave us all a hug and disappeared into his bus.

I must admit I admired the way Arthur worked. There was a sophistication about him. He spoke a little of the languages of the countries he moved through and was far more aware than any truck driver I'd ever come across in Blighty. I must admit the sound of becoming an international truck driver stirred my blood.

They were a special breed, the international truck

drivers of the time. No motorways or autoroutes. Once you pass Istanbul the roads start to deteriorate into compacted dirt roads that shake the guts out of any vehicle. Every driver I spoke to recommended stashing a machete or large tyre iron in a handy place in the door pocket! These guys have to deal with corrupt border guards, night-time bandits, corrupt local agents and police etc. Then they have to deal with any truck, mechanical, and document problems. There were no credit cards or mobile phones then. You carried your money in cash. If you were lucky you had an agent along the way when funds got low.

The other way of topping up funds was to sell a litre of your blood to the local blood bank run by the Red Crescent, the Turkish equivalent of the Red Cross.

A litre of best claret went for one hundred and eight Turkish lira (at the time about 45 pounds sterling) plus a voucher for the restaurant round the corner. The theory being that you must eat a good meal after donating blood. I was very worried about the hygiene aspect but needn't have worried as it was all from sterile packs and a clean environment. We all trickled back onto the bus looking a little drained, but it was more from the withering noon heat than loss of blood. We caned the meal vouchers for as much as possible and had a wonderful local-style meal. Black Bob, Isobel and myself started to have a few rakis, a drink similar to Pernod, tasting like aniseed with a kick like a mule, with a couple of Turkish army guys on leave. They kept telling us that they "Very much liked Englis' people. Very good soldier and very good footballer." After a single drink, I felt I was not fit to drive but as we were hanging out here for an hour or two it would be OK and the effect would wear off.

Unknown to me Kakey was on the bus waiting to depart as she was not having as good a time as the rest of us. She wanted to go because one of the soldiers had pinched her arse and she'd reacted badly. She made the mistake of marching in and demanding that we leave now. She had reached tantrum state. Her rude interruption had killed the good time we were having with the two Turkish lads. Being slightly tipsy, I stood and grabbed the keys of the bus and said, "The only way the bus is going anywhere right now is if you drive it," and flung the keys dramatically, at her feet. "And if you so much as start the engine you'll be looking for another driver, right now," I followed up.

Her face like thunder, she spun on her heel and flounced out like some diva. Unfortunately for her the lads didn't need to understand much English and just collapsed in guffaws of laughter as we all did seconds later.

Eventually we moved on but Kakey didn't speak to me for days. I waited till one morning when all the others were off the bus and trapped her as she got out of bed. I pushed myself into her body and felt her naked breasts pushing into my bare chest. She was surprised but automatically ground her crotch against me. I leaned even further in, grabbing her round backside and whispering in her ear, "I know you want some of this," as I gave her a little thrust with the somewhat swollen bulge in my jeans, "and it's for fucking sure I want some of it too, but I just can't without Isobel's permission and not with the kids so nearby." Her increased breathing rate and closed eyes told me my words and method were working.

"But be sure that if you ever talk to me like that again in front of others I'll get you when you least expect it and give you the fucking of your life. You won't be able to walk for a week. Is that clear?" I asked, staring her in the eye and totally dominating her. She gasped and thrust back. I had long ago discovered that talking to her like this with complete dominance drove her wild and I swear I felt her stagger in orgasm. She was certainly panting and very flushed when we eventually stepped apart.

I ran my hands down from her shoulders, over her

breasts and ended cupping her backside. "So are we friends again? Now that you know I'd give you one at the drop of a hat?"

She wasn't expecting that, and closed her eyes and snorted in laughter. "Yes but I'll get you yet," and she was gone, leaving me to contemplate what that would be like.

If you had to make a telephone call back home, then it could delay you for a couple of days as you had to book the call hours in advance, and you had to go to a major PTT office in one of the larger cities to make it. Not only that but you had to break the fundamental law; NEVER leave the truck on its own.

Isobel, Arthur, and I talked well into the night.

"You going up to the Black Sea, then?" asked Arthur.

"Yeah. We're all paranoid about the dope situation in Turkey, with all that *Midnight Express* crap going on."

"Whatever you do, don't buy anything here. The dealers will flog it to you and then get the police to bust you. The dealer gets his dope back and the Turks can tell the Americans 'Look what good boys we're being. We're busting people for dope, can we have another 20 million dollars in overseas aid please?'" laughed Arthur.

"That's why we're staying as far from Ankara as possible and it will tie in nicely with going round the military road."

"Once you get into Iran, It's a little less paranoid but be very careful. The nearer you get to the Afghan or Paki border, you'll see it growing alongside the road anyway."

This got my attention and my imagination ran wild at the thought of free weed. Some of my fantasies were about to come true.

"In the land of grey and pink.

Where only boy scouts stop to think.

We'll pick our fill of pump weed.

And smoke it 'till we bleed.

That's all we'll need."

The words from the song ran through my head a few times! Arthur got up to go back to the truck. "See you in Tehran. Mind how you go, the road gets worse from here." As a parting shot to Isobel, "See you by the pool, Isobel. I can't wait to see your bikini." He winked.

"Oi, you cheeky git," I smiled.

"No. Just a lonely and sex-starved old trucker."

"You're a what, fucker?" I retorted.

"See ya Al." We could hear his laugh as he departed.

"Thanks Arthur," and he was gone.

Next morning I was awoken around nine thirty by the sound of Sten and the other bus departing. They couldn't resist tooting the horn in farewell. This was a mistake as an answering horn from another vehicle sounded musically. Next came the air horns of the trucks, and before you knew it a cacophony of horns were going off everywhere!

"That'll be sleeping over with, then," I said a little testily. Actually it was getting hot already, too hot to lie in bed. I slumped into the driver's seat as the others got up. I waited for some coffee to be brewed.

"Coffee, Alun?" asked a dressing gowned Glynis.

"Yes please. Why is your delightful naked body on display Glynis?"

She looked down at her thin, short dressing gown. It had fallen open as she handed me my cup. "Seen it all before haven't you?" If Isobel could have seen the look on Glynis' face she'd have not been amused. "Anyway, it's my strip wash day."

"Oh, steam up the bus time again," I said, making a

mental note not to go anywhere until Glynis finished her strip wash!

The time came to pay the bill and depart. The manager of the camp was trying to get more money than agreed and I was losing patience. I sent Isobel to deal with him and she returned some time later with a brass souvenir and a paid bill.

"How much did that cost?" I asked, surprised that Isobel would waste money in our position.

"A squeeze on the arse."

"What?!" I exploded out of the seat.

"It's OK I've dealt with it. I went apeshit at him and threatened to call the police."

"What happened?"

"He went white as if he didn't realise he'd done wrong and asked me to please choose a gift, as a peace offering."

"Dirty old bastard. We're going to have to watch this from now on."

"How d'you mean?" asked Glynis.

"All the females are going to have to cover up more in public. Shorts are out and I reckon it'd be good if the blokes don't wear shorts either. As it is, we must wear shirts all the time."

"These people dress their women, literally, head to foot in a black shawl and yet don't mind feeling up our women," observed Syd.

"Yeah, from what I can make of it, they see our women as 'easy' because they don't cover from head to foot and are treated as equals by us men."

"Sounds like they've got a good thing going to me," chimed in Black Bob. "In future you girls walk thirteen paces behind."

This earned him a swift kick in unison from Fran and Kakey. Earlier, I had asked Black Bob and Charlie to stow away some of the gear we'd used the night before. I noticed with irritation that it hadn't been done and, on past form, would be left for me. I decide to make a point by not starting the bus.

"Whassup Alun?" asked Timus, noting my annoyance.

"I asked Bob and Charlie to stash that gear up on the roof rack, I see I was wasting my breath."

"C'mon man I forgot," spluttered Black Bob.

"You didn't forget Bob, you were too busy posing in front of the girls on the other bus."

"Well you can't blame a bloke for getting his rocks off," joked Bob, trying to get out of it.

"No I don't blame you for that but this is your bus and it comes first," I said.

"What makes you so special?" spat Charlie, unable to contain himself any longer.

"How do you mean?" I asked. He didn't reply.

"I'm doing twelve hours a day and then more hours in the night so we can struggle to Tehran before running out of money. I check the water, oil, lights, and fuel and loads of other things every day. How many times have you come and helped me pump fuel or pack the boot away in the mornings or peel potatoes or do the washing up or the fire lighting? Need I go on? I do it myself and do you know what I hear as I'm doing it? Your whingeing overbearing gob, telling everyone else what to do and what not to do Charlie. That's what I hear. And yet you can't do a simple job like put away the gear when I asked you."

"You ain't the boss," he spat again.

"Oh for fuck's sake, I fucking give up with you Charlie. You might intimidate the others but it ain't gonna work with me 'cause I'll just punch your fucking lights out."

I realised that I had stood up from the driver's seat and was advancing towards Charlie. I was annoyed that I'd let him wind me up, so I diverted to the outside of the bus before I did something I'd regret later. It wasn't long before I heard the door slide open. I turned to see Charlie, Bob and Timus start to pack away the gear onto the roof rack. I went back aboard. "Shame I've got to come down heavy just to get shit done."

I waited till they all got back on the bus. "We are about to do the longest drive we've yet done. Turkey is a vast country and this is going to be a long, long drive. I don't want to see the same people doing all the work and the others doing fuck all. It'll get on my tits, I know it will. Am I being so unreasonable?"

Nobody had anything else to say so I started the engine. "We'll cross the Bosphoros Bridge before we diesel up, we'll be into some serious driving after that so everyone, do what you gotta do 'cos I don't want to keep stopping, if I ain't being too bossy." I glared at Charlie. I pulled out of the motor camp. The manager was hiding and we didn't see him. We drove down by the Sultan Ahmat right past the Blue Mosque which was dominating the skyline.

The city was heaving with traffic of all kinds with very little regard to road rules. Eventually with some slick map reading and directions by Isobel, it wasn't too painful. We managed not to hit anything, mainly down to the new philosophy of driving. If you show any fear whatsoever, they will take advantage and carve you up. Drive like one possessed and beat them at their own game. They also had an annoying habit of overtaking going up mountain roads. If something comes the other way unexpectedly the driver's mate leans his arm out the window in a frantic up and down movement to indicate they need to pull in quickly. This they then do and Allah protect the poor sod they pull in on. We're talking forty-four ton American, Peterbuilt, Kenworth or Mack trucks here. Finally we reached the bridge over the Bosphorus.

"We're about to cross from Europe into Asia in case anyone's interested," shouted Timus.

"Yeah man, I am," I said, feeling pleased that at least we'd made it to the fabled Constantinople, as Istanbul used to be known in the Byzantine Empire.

We crossed and continued towards the town of Gebze and filled up in a small service station on the road. Diesel had dropped down to almost half the price that it was at home. A small group gathered to watch us and were very friendly.

We continued on towards Zonguldak on the Black Sea coast. It was about three in the afternoon and we were just coming into a small village with tall crops growing each side of the road. I suddenly realised what those crops were.

"Dope!" I cried. It was a reflex action! Everyone crowded forwards to look out the windscreen.

"Wow!" cried Syd. "Stop."

"OK keep calm, let's pull up for a break a minute and think about this," said Timus.

I didn't need telling twice. We pulled off onto some waste ground just where the village started. We stared at the scene in front of us in silence. There were twelve-foot tall plants everywhere. Fields and fields of it as far as the eye could see!

We hadn't had a smoke for so long now, the sight of all that weed was just too much for us.

"It's gettin' on a bit. Why don't we have an early dinner, hang around till it gets dark and we can creep in and cut a few plants down. Nobody will even know we have any," suggested Black Bob.

We didn't need much persuasion. We decided that as the ground we were parked on was clear, why not throw some Frisbee? We formed a large circle and started to throw the disc around. It didn't take long for a couple of kids from the village to see us and came over. They loved it, and their squeals of delight brought some of the adults out from the houses. A couple of farmers tried their hands at throwing but made a complete mess of it. They giggled like schoolgirls and watched fascinated, as the disc floated between us experts.

It wasn't long before a tray of coffee and glasses was produced. It was the first time I tried coffee, Turkish style. It came in a small glass tumbler. The bottom of the glass had a fine coffee sludge. The thing was not to drink down to the sludge and to disturb it as little as possible. It was strong. Full of rich flavour and aroma and when you had one, you knew you'd had it a couple of moments later, when the intense caffeine hit your bloodstream! Great for long driving sessions.

We decided to move on a little bit and wait for dark. If we stayed there we would get no chance as most of the village wanted to see the hippies and their strange flying disk. We talked for some time with some of the farmers. As much as you can talk when neither understands the others language. We drove away after a couple of hours and drove just beyond the village. It was almost dark by now so we wouldn't have to wait long.

Charlie and Syd volunteered to grab a couple of plants and I'd have the engine running ready to make a speedy getaway. We sat in the dark with the lights and the engine off. We could hear Charlie and Syd crashing around like elephants in a cane field. Next thing you know the door slides open and in comes this huge plant followed by Charlie then another two huge plants followed by Syd.

"Sure you've got enough there, Syd?" I smiled.

"It's like Christmas in a free department store," was Syd's descriptive comment.

"Get them down the back by the rear floor hatch. If we get stopped dump them out through there," I suggested.

We drove on for miles while the boys tried to strip and dry the leaves. All the time I watched my rear view mirror for any following vehicles, feeling very paranoid. The truth of it was, that we didn't see another car all night. I stopped when I thought we'd put enough distance between us and the village. We rolled up some spliffs and stuffed a pipe and an impromptu chillum made from a drinks can.

We smoked and smoked the un-cured weed. It tasted awful but, we reasoned it'd be worth it in a minute! We waited and waited. Nothing!

We smoked a load more, made tea with it, ate it, did everything we could think of... Absolutely nothing, zero. Zilch! We were very disappointed and couldn't understand why we weren't getting hideously stoned. What had happened, of course, in our ignorance, we had just raided a hemp plantation!

These plants were grown only for their fibre. Hemp rope helped to keep the British Navy afloat during the wind driven ship days. That's why they were twelve-foot tall with one central stalk. They were grown for the fibre. These plants contain only two per cent Tetrohydrocannabinol (THC – the bit that gets you stoned!). It doesn't matter that apart from the single central stalk, these plants and leaves are identical to their THC producing cousins. Their cousins contain up to twenty-six percent THC! We were bitterly disappointed but saw the funny side of it. We cleared the bus up and moved on into the night. We were on deserted roads and when I'd had enough I just pulled over and slept. Next morning it was overcast and drizzling rain. A change from the high temperatures of the more southern areas. We put our Blighty clothes back on and hit the road as soon as morning tea was made.

"Hang on to your teas I'm pulling onto the road." I didn't want to wait while breakfast was being made. Isobel and the others would get breakfast on the move. Sometimes I'd stop and eat it while sat in the driver's seat. Most times I'd eat on the move.

The track was wide and had been pounded hard by countless trucks and buses. Every now and again we would be passed by an articulated Mack or Kenworth truck. The drivers were like kids with new toys. They did the most horrifyingly dangerous stunts with these trucks and there were scenes of carnage all along the major routes through Turkey.

The trucks passed us at full speed with no regard for the potholes or rough surface. Their axles would smash into the chassis when they hit a hole at eighty kilometres an hour. It was painful to watch. There were many wrecked cars and trucks along the dirt road we were travelling. We started to climb into the mountains and despite the rain, the views were spectacular. Just as we were climbing up towards the pass we came up against the back end of what looked to be, a long queue of trucks. There were many people milling around and they turned to look at us when we pulled up.

"I don't know what the fuck is going on here. I'll see what I can find out." I was glad of the chance to stretch the legs. "Come with me Isobel, please."

We walked over to the nearest group and after much gesticulation and sign language we got the message that there was a bad landslide up ahead because of the rain, and the road was totally blocked. The bulldozer was coming out but wouldn't be there until the day after tomorrow. I sent Isobel back to the bus with the news.

"I'll just see if I can find out what's going on." I

wandered down the line of trucks. Most drivers were cooking up dinner and sitting around in groups. They all returned my nod as I walked by. I came to one group and as I passed I heard one of the group ask me something.

"Allemagne, Allemagne?" They seemed to be asking me a question. I didn't know it at the time but they were asking if I was German.

I placed my hand on my heart and nodded, as I'd seen them doing. They all got up and shook my hand. Doing the hand on heart bit was very respectful. Couple that with my slight dipping of the head, it was just right. Apparently the more you dip your head, the lower down the pecking order you are. My slight nod meant that I was superior. Nothing like having an inflated view of yourself.

"Excuse me but I don't understand," I said.

"Ah! Englaise," said a large and very swarthy driver. "Bobby Charlton, Rock 'n' roll, Piccadilly Circus," he said with glee. "Come my friend, sit, eat, drink tea. After tea, we smoke."

"What?" I asked as calmly as I could. There was a big leer on the face of Swarthy Man. "Hashish?" I asked, pointing at the pipe, although, it didn't look like any hash pipe I'd seen before. It had an elegant and delicate, turned stem about nine inches long with a tiny, blue decorated enamelled bowl. It was a thing of beauty and seemed out of place in Swarthy Man's hands. One of the other drivers pointed at the pipe and said something in Turkish. He repeated it a couple of times but I didn't understand.

"Opium, Opium." Swarthy Man grinned. "Today working, working. Tonight eat, drink, smoke, smoke." He grinned.

I learned that it was the custom out here, to finish a day's work with a couple of bowls of the sticky black goo that is the extract of the seed case of *Papaver somniferum*, otherwise known as the white opium poppy. I had tried opium when in Singapore but I'd tried to smoke it like cannabis. All I got was the very acrid smell and that was about all. I didn't know at the time that you have to prepare it properly by baking in a flame until slightly crisp.

"Driver, you?" asked Swarthy Man, pointing at me.

"Yes I have autobus," and I pointed back down the line. This seemed to impress the other drivers sat around the fire. "I have nine, I drew in the dirt a figure nine, friends, Kameraden, and two kinder." I indicated children with my hands. The mixture of French, German and English words seemed to be working. They were surprised to learn that I had my wife and children with me. "We come from Bristol in Inglistan." I learned that Inglistan was the Asian word for England. Most of the countries out east ended in 'stan'.

"Huh?" Swarthy Man screwed up his face.

"Mon ville, mon citie, Bristol." I drew a crude British Isles in the dirt and indicated the city in the south west.

"Ah. Work, you?" he asked.

"I'm a truck and bulldozer mechanic. Uh, mechanic for the gross, Caterpillar und Das Kraft Wagen."

Swarthy Man translated to the other drivers and I swear they were even more impressed. Out here, in what was still a wild country, anyone with practical skills like an engineer was treated with great respect and his skill valued by the community. These drivers were the real people of Turkey. We were well off the tourist routes, such as they were at that time and these people were not tainted by the tourist trade. I was warming to their ways.

"Alun." I turned to see Isobel approaching with Alun Jnr. and Mellony. I stood up to greet the kids and introduced them.

"Mine Frau, Isobel und mine kinder Alun, same as me,

und Mellony." To a man they stood and shook hands with Isobel and the young'uns. They were fascinated with the blond-haired kids and were busy giving them locally made sweets and bottles of Fanta orange from their ice boxes.

"Look Dad," said Mellony as she showed me what they'd given her. It looked like a pink pretzel in syrup and was syrup-sweet.

The Turks loved their sugar and would drink their tea whilst sucking on a cube of sugar. They would never add the sugar before drinking. Both tea and coffee were drunk from glass tumblers and the tea was always without milk, clear and golden in colour and easy to get addicted to! As we'd found in Greece, the Turks loved their tobacco. I had discovered a brand in Greece that came in a flat box of twenty. They were aromatic and strong, but didn't make you hack your guts up. The Turkish Tobacco was even better. Every village of size had its own brand in Turkey. Here, we were in the region of Sinop and the cigarettes came in a simple white, American-style, paper pack with the area's logo printed on the pack. The tobacco was first class. The finest stuff you'd buy from Harrods or some of the specialist hand-rolled cigarette houses in London, perhaps with your family's crest on each cigarette. You had to smoke them reasonably quickly as the heat would dry out the tobacco and it would fall out of the paper tube, virtually, in dust and by then, very harsh on the throat.

"Dinner's ready, I've been despatched to fetch you."

"OK I'm going to invite this lot to come and see the bus. "Mine freund, I am going to the autobus now. Essen," I said, patting my belly. When you finish essen, you come, autobus ok? You come autobus und smoking, drink coffee, OK?"

"Ya ya we come." He translated my invite to the others and they quickly nodded.

When I got back to the bus I noticed that some other

trucks had pulled up behind us and the drivers were talking to Timus and Black Bob. More drivers were cooking up around fires and the place was beginning to resemble a pop festival.

"I've just been talking to some drivers up there. They think they're going to be here a while. It's a big slide."

"These guys have been telling us of a dirt road, ten kilometres back down the road that ends up on the coast around Sinop," said Black Bob. "Sounds good. Only trouble is, the bus has taken a pounding on these dirt roads. It seems to be taking it ok but it's a hell of a shaking. The dirt road diversion will be worse I suspect but what can we do? We can't sit here and run out of food and money," I said.

"Let's get dinner before it gets cold," said Timus.

As we turned to go to the bus, Black Bob grabbed my arm. "Alun, one of these guys might have some dope, I reckon."

"I've been talking to some drivers up ahead and I know for sure that they have some opium. I saw his pipe!"

"Whu-hu. We could all do with a relax. D'you reckon we can get some?"

"I invited them to come and see the bus later on, so I reckon there's every chance. I bloody hope so. I'd murder for a smoke right now."

"Yeah, not many," agreed Bob. I was impressed how Black Bob could switch to whatever drug was available at the time. Alcohol, cannabis, coke etc., etc. I was more a one drug man and that was weed, weed, and more weed. Even with Black Bob's prodigious and conspicuous consumption, he couldn't keep up with me when it came to cannabis!

We had dinner, a singularly unexciting affair, particularly after seeing what the other drivers were cooking up. They had some kind of stuffed peppers and potatoes in spicy sauce and it smelt delicious. Still mustn't grumble, at least we have something. I made a mental note many miles ago, to never do this journey on a budget again. My mind returned to Sten and his bus and the seven odd grand he had made.

As we cleared up after dinner, Swarthy Driver and two friends showed up. I showed them around the bus and pulled up the hatch to show them the engine. They noticed my modifications to the cooling system.

"In Englistan it is cold." I wrapped my arms around myself in the gesture of being cold. "Here it's very hot." I fanned myself with my hand. I pointed to the original radiator at the front and said, "Problem, kaput!" They understood immediately. These guys weren't just drivers, they had to do their own fixing when they broke down.

"You make this, Englis'?" They looked impressed.

"Yes," I replied.

"Tea?" asked Isobel. "What about these guys. Do you think they'd like one. Take them outside with the others, I'm just about to put the kids to bed."

We sat around the fire and drank tea, English-style with milk, which was a source of amusement to our Turkish visitors. They told us it was possible to bypass the landslide but it would be over a very rough dirt road. I asked how wide the track was and I gathered that they had driven their trucks over it. They were all driving six or eight-wheel Ford D-types. If they could get them down the track then I'd get the bus down there.

Eventually, out came the opium pipe. Timus, Syd, and Black Bob decided they'd have a pull or two but I declined. I didn't want to be muzzy-headed from the opium, especially with this landslide situation – I'd need my wits about me. The one good thing about smoking marijuana is that I never get any kind of hangover and am always in control. Not so with opium. It's more a total body and mind dream.

I made a few gentle inquiries about hashish but none of the drivers had any. We talked for a while about what we should do. We'd wait for the bulldozer tomorrow.

I said goodnight to them all and had an early night. I woke at some point to hear Black Bob heaving his guts up around the back of the bus. One of the first things that happens after smoking opium, is to throw up. It's usually without the retching and gasping that accompanies spewing. You simply deposited the contents of your stomach, effortlessly, on the ground, or whatever you happened to be near. You usually got two seconds warning and there was nothing you could do to stop it.

I woke next morning to a scene of devastation. Bodies lying akimbo. Isobel was already up and getting some breakfast for the kids and a coffee for me. The mountains could be crumbling beneath us but everything would have to wait until I'd had my caffeine 'injection'. Anything could be handled once I'd had my 'kick-start'. It's a terrible thing to be addicted to such a drug!

It was still overcast and drizzling but reasonably warm, considering we were in the mountains.

"Bad news," said Isobel. While I was laying in, one of the drivers from last night returned to tell us that the bulldozer would not be showing up today, due to another slide further down the valley. By now the others were stirring, splashing cold water on their faces and getting some tea.

I broke the news to them. "We're going to have to go back and take the dirt road."

"Isn't that going to shake the shit out of the bus?" asked Charlie, who was wide awake because, to my surprise, he didn't touch the opium.

"Yeah, too right it is. The only thing we can do is to slow right down or we're going to break a spring or shake the body off the chassis. This old girl wasn't built for off-road driving. She's taken a pounding so far but there is worse to come. It's going to be an ordeal at fifteen or twenty miles an hour for two hundred and fifty miles!"

We finished getting ourselves together and while the rest, including Charlie, got on with stowing stuff on the roof rack, I wandered up to Swarthy Driver's truck to say goodbye. I had observed that it was the custom amongst Turkish men, that when you came across a bunch of your mates, or an unusual scene, you would extend your right hand, palm upward, fingers spread, and shake it slightly from side to side, shaking your head and screwing up the brow, as if to say, "What's going on here?" If you are respected, then the breakfast, the beer, or whatever was being consumed at the time, was waved back with nods as if to say, "Come, join us." If you were ignored, you were a twat.

I decide to try it and went through the ritual, holding out my palm.

Automatically, there was nod from all the drivers and food and glasses of tea were waved at me. I felt really cool and international! I'd connected with these drivers of, what was still, a wild frontier.

He and his mates were staying put till the bulldozer arrived and thought I was brave to attempt the dirt road diversion. I can remember thinking, *Well if you can get these six and eight wheel Fords down there, then I'll bloody well get this bus through.* Ah! The bravado of youth!

"Gut Risen! Und viel gluck!" shouted Swarthy Driver. As I walked away I heard him add "Insha'Allah," which was Arabic for 'God willing'. We were to hear this expression many times. It was used as we use 'God willing' but for some reason, this time it put the fear of God in me. I must admit, if only to myself at the time, I was scared at the prospect of taking a heavy vehicle along mountain tracks that had been loosened by rain! I can actually remember thinking, *It'll be something to tell the grandchildren!*

We started the engine and I ran it up gently while Timus went behind to ask the odd truck or two to move so that we could turn around. I had to make a three thousand point turn on that mountain road and made everyone get off the bus and stand back while I did it.

"Timus you go to the back please, and stand where you can see my driver's mirror, that way I'll see you. OK? Isobel at the nearside front, please. I'm going to need every inch! And watch for rocks on the overhanging bodywork. The trouble is," I said, as they disappeared down the steps, "it's gonna be in full view of a dozen Turkish truck drivers. They'll be watching to see if I'm any good."

"Get on. You'll do it alright," smiled Isobel. It was everything to me to have her confidence in my abilities.

"Timus! Watch the swing of the arse end. I don't want to smash it against the rock-face as I crank it round hard." That got a thumbs-up from Timus in my mirror.

I pulled forward on full lock. The boot corner missed the rock-face by an inch or two with Timus right there in my mirror watching progress very closely.

Forward, very slowly with Isobel crouching down watching the front wheels.

"Stop!" she shouted, stood, and raised her palm. I raised my eyebrows, she didn't need any words. She raised her thumb and index finger to indicate about two inches to go to the edge of a hundred foot drop without so much as a kerb between me and the drop! I sat there for a moment, staring out into mid-air, and it flashed through my mind,

I'm actually over the precipice, as the driving position is well forward of the front wheels. I swear I felt the old sphincter muscle twitch a little.

As I needed every bit of room possible, I cranked round the steering, full lock, the other way. I had to do this before moving at all, otherwise I'd lose valuable space. There was no power steering on the old AEC and my arms and shoulders ached and I was running in sweat with a knot of fear, only just under control.

I shoved the stick into reverse gear and let off the handbrake, to my relief, we moved back on reverse lock. I got back with Timus' guidance and actually gently touched the rock with the rear bar. Off I went with the steering thing again and so it went on until after a multi-point turn, I was able to pull right round, on full lock, with Isobel watching as my front wheel ran in an arc, right along the edge of the precipice. I pulled up and sat there for a moment as I wasn't sure if my legs would support me.

There was applause and shouts from the Turkish drivers and I gave them my 'Royal' wave to big grins and an 'insha'Allah' here and there.

"Well done, Alun," said Black Bob with a grin and bloodshot eyes. I noticed a couple of the others looking a bit fragile. I can remember thinking how they were going to enjoy the dirt track.

We moved off to a couple of air horns and much waving. I can remember thinking how resilient these guys were, and how different it was to driving in England. You don't have to wait for many landslides on the M4! We got to the diversion. There were no signs but it was pretty obvious from the mud tracks coming from that direction, plus I'd just seen a truck go down that way. I started to turn but braked when I saw what we were going onto. "Jesus. Look at that." It was potholes all the way, filled with water and deeply rutted.

"Well, we got no choice. I'll try and keep out of the ruts. Hold on tight kids, we're going to shake from side to side, watch out for stuff flying out the overhead racks."

I stuck it in crawler gear and drove on. The back slid around and the front wheels slid into grooves but we continued to keep traction. Eventually we climbed out of the ruts and water, onto a very rough but reasonably level track, bulldozed and graded. There were bad potholes here and there without any warning. It was impossible and dangerous to do any more than fifteen miles an hour. As we came through a group of rocks we could see the track joined a road through a large village. At the junction stood a young man with a very old man on sticks. The custom was, when wanting a lift, not to use the thumb as we did back home but to wave down and then indicate with the hand that you want to travel down the road. The young man started to wave us down so I started to slow down. As we got close he realised we weren't the regular traffic and his jaw dropped when he realised we were strangers.

We pulled up and Timus slid the door open. The young guy looked at me and asked something. I just indicated forward and said, "Sinop, Sinop." By this time Isobel produced the map and confirmed we were going through his village some thirty kilometres ahead.

"Yes. Come," indicated Timus. The old guy didn't need asking twice. He nearly danced up the steps. He smiled and patted the kids and nodded to us all and sat down, right as you like.

His eyes gleamed as he looked around. The young guy was awestruck. He'd never seen foreigners, let alone scantily-clad English girls. Any woman not covered was scantily clad to him. The old guy pulled out a paper bag of sweets and offered them to the kids. I looked quickly inside and nodded to them to take one if they wanted. They were pure concentrated sugar. Those Turks, they loved their sugar!

We drove on at a really slow pace. The dirt road was a little less prone to losing an axle down a pothole but the surface was rough. Eventually we arrived in the village of our passengers.

We stopped long enough to have a coffee with Old Guy's brother and wife. Old Guy's brother spoke good English. It turned out that Old Guy was an ex operative of SOE (Special Operations Executive. The British Intelligence organisation, during the war). He was so angry at the Nazis, he worked for the British in SOE, behind the enemy lines. It caused all sorts of friction in the village and divisions that were to surface again when Yugoslavia broke up. I don't care what anyone says, to go against all your peers, in your homeland, because you know what they are doing is wrong, takes lots of bottle.

I decide to just drive until we got to the coast road. By my reckoning we had another 200km at 20mph, to do before we got there. My kidneys were going to be shaken out! I drove all night and most of the others stayed with me. They couldn't get much sleep anyway, they were getting bounced off the bunks. The kids were on a temporary bed on the floor and oblivious to it all. The bus was taking a real pounding and it seemed to go on and on into the night.

About four in the morning, we came to the outskirts of a small town called Karabuk where at last the dirt track joined a tarmac road albeit patched and rutted. We were able to make better time and before long, hit the coast road of the Black Sea at Bartin.

We'd passed Sinop and came across a patch of land right on the beach. I pulled up and parked. I got undressed along with the others and we crashed out for what was left of the night. We decided, next day, to rest and clean the mud and dust of the dirt road, out of the bus. While the others got on with cleaning. I donned my overalls and started to get out the oil and filters I'd brought from

England. I was going to change the oil in the engine and gearbox and top-up the rear axle, plus a general inspection for any damage. The sun was shining and I was glad to be in the shade, underneath the bus. The others were making a thorough job of cleaning, even the beds were turned out into the sunshine.

A police car stopped to see what we were doing but they didn't get out of the car. Black Bob gave them a wave but they just pulled on. I finished the oil change and grabbed the washing up liquid and headed for the sea. We were well below sea level here and there was a strange quality about the sea, clear but dark. It made fine bath water and it wasn't long before I was shining clean again. There was nobody in sight so I just stripped right off and de-greased.

As I walked back to the bus, Isobel came toward me. I could tell she wasn't happy.

"I was putting the bed back in the bus. I went outside for the duvet, when I got back Charlie had taken our mattress and wouldn't put it back. He said it was his turn. I think he's losing it under the strain."

I started off toward the bus but she caught my arm. "Alun! Don't. You're only gonna make it worse."

"When we were putting all the stuff in the bus to leave, did we or did we not agree, that as I'd need to sleep properly to be awake and alert to drive, I would have the only sprung mattress to come aboard. Everyone, including Charlie readily agreed. Right, or not?"

"Leave it. You're just gonna make it worse."

"The fuck I will. It's OK but I ain't letting this go, OK?" I headed for the door, determined not to let him wind me up.

Kakey met me on the steps and just shook her head to say, "What can we do?"

"What the fuck are you doing Charlie. Where's my mattress?" I asked, looking at my naked bunk.

"I've got it and I'm having a turn at it." He shouted at me, right from the off. Isobel was right, he was out of control. I had seen these stress related symptoms before. Take a person out of their normal environment and heavy insecurities manifest themselves in aggression.

I reminded him of our agreement. He just went apeshit. Telling me how he'd worked hard for hours in the DHSS offices getting money, and other incoherent arguments all delivered at the top of his voice with his face about an inch from mine. I looked at Glynis and shrugged as I dug two stiff fingers into his diaphragm.

It had the desired effect, which was to wind him and back him off me. I turned and said to the others, "Did you agree with this?"

"Didn't know anything about it till just now," said Black Bob.

"Well I ain't having any more to say to him because I'll tear him a new arsehole as soon as look at him. If you want me to continue to drive, you'd better have a word with him. I'm going outside to light the fire." I stormed outside and slid the door to as hard as I could.

Isobel looked at me. "That's another hundred miles of sulking," she said.

"Well, I ain't taking that from him. I only winded him anyway, just to make him shut up. I ain't going to be spoken to like that by him, especially since I'm doing all the work at the moment."

Timus came out to give a hand getting some firewood, there was plenty of driftwood on the beach and it wasn't long before a ring of firelight spread from the camp fire. I was just getting dusk and the tranquil scene contrasted with the friction now on the bus.

"How the fuck have you lived with him for so long?" I asked Timus. "You're a thinking type, how do you put up with his bullying?"

"We just ignore him, though he's not usually this bad. He is the type to hold a grudge."

"That was all before him," I said. Referring to the one night stand Glynis and I had.

"Keep it in yer pants, next time," said Isobel, only half joking.

"We have convinced him to put the mattress back."

"Sulk city for the next day or two then."

Pans of vegetables and tomatoes were now being brought out by the girls and we all did a little peeling and chopping.

We had a good meal and the activity had dispersed the bad energy a little. Isobel was just putting the sleepy little'uns to bed, when a car pulled up just on the road opposite the bus. I got up and walked toward the bus. Two young men got out of the car, I heard loud rock music as their doors opened.

"Hey man!" one of them shouted. "What you doing?"

"Is there a problem? We are only parking overnight."

"Problem, what problem?" asked the car driver in reasonably good English.

"You have not come to tell us there is a problem parking here. Will the police tell us to move?" I was choosing my words carefully to help with understanding.

"What? Police, parking, fuck man what you talk? Relax, fucking police, I tell them fuck off no problem!" He spoke with contempt but with a smile.

Just as my nose started to raise a red flag and set off a very loud electric bell ringing in my head, his pal leaned around with a leer and passed him a large spliff of some very spicy smelling hash. I couldn't help it, when I smelt it I gave out a loud sigh and put my nose over the fumes. Without hesitation he handed it to me for a puff. I hesitated and looked round. Nobody could see me, I was behind the bus.

I wanted to, so badly but I just said, "No, police, big problem." I made the gesture to indicate handcuffs, putting my wrists together.

"No. Fuck police," he said forcefully, and gave me the spliff. "Relax, no problem."

I just couldn't resist temptation any longer. I filled my lungs with the spicy, black-green Turkish hash mixed with local tobacco. The tobacco made me cough but before long I felt the relaxing, effect wash over me. I felt the tension drain through me as if I were a lightning rod conducting all the high tension to ground.

"That is very nice hashish, my friend," I said with a big grin on my face. I felt a little guilty that I'd broken our agreement not to have any dealings with local dealers who would grass us up to the police for a reward. The young Turks were grinning and looking at the bus.

"Come, drink coffee by the fire," I invited them.

We walked over and waved to everyone. "These guys wanted to see the bus and wanted a quiet place to have a spliff," I said pointedly.

Normally that would have instantly got everyone's attention but even Black Bob was reluctant to talk openly to the newcomers.

"Too many police here," said Syd, as they offered the smoke to him. Nobody else would take it and the lads could see we were too paranoid. After a while they could see we were not going to buy any, and they left. I fell asleep by the fire and woke up in the morning with a blanket over me. It was a sunny morning, but I still felt tired.

I didn't want to hang around too long. Yesterday's scene had left me determined to leave the bus when we get to Tehran. I'd find some work and Isobel the kids and I would continue on our own. We packed up and were ready to move fairly quickly, aided by my walking around with no attempt to be quiet. Charlie kept well away from me but Glynis was outside on her own.

"I'm sorry about yesterday Glynis but he's just gone off on one. What's the matter with him. Is he alright?"

"Noo 'e'se not 'imself, a bit oopset, you know."

"Is it 'cos of you and me?"

"Noo don't worry 'e'll settle down."

"Well I hope so because I foresee trouble if he doesn't calm down. What effect does he think it's having on the kids? I ain't gonna stand for that. I ain't got a problem with him it's just the way he's behaving."

"'E'll calm down, I'll see to it."

I sat in the driver's seat. Everyone was almost ready so I ran up the engine which usually had the effect of speeding everyone up. I watched the oil gauge closely. I had run the engine after the oil change to check for leaks but extra care would be good for a while. I was watching the water temperature closely anyway.

We left our overnight parking place and drove along the coast road towards Sampson and Trabzon. I was aiming to get as far as Mount Ararat and spend the night on the foothills. Every village that we went through had it's own cottage industry. Growing tobacco. Every area that wasn't growing vegetables had trestles full of leaves drying in the sun. When I opened my side window, the warm moist air was full of the scent of the world's second favourite dangerous drug.

I suddenly remembered what the different feeling was that I'd noticed when driving towards the Black Sea. We were now well below sea level and you could feel the difference in atmospheric pressure. The bus brakes were not operated by air, as is the way with modern commercial and passenger vehicles. They operated by a mixture of vacuum and hydraulic fluid. The vacuum pump and system were only just up to the job. The problem was wear. Over the years the ability of the pump to pull a good vacuum, diminishes. It was interesting to note on the mountain passes, how the vacuum struggled up to twenty-four inches of mercury on the gauge, while now we were below sea level it was showing nearly thirty inches of mercury. Almost the theoretical, but never attainable, perfect vacuum!

On we went and made good time. We left the coast road and headed through the snow-capped mountains past the ancient city of Kars. Not long past Kars we came across the turning for the military road. Sure enough, it had a huge red circle with a silhouette of an articulated truck, with a diagonal line through it and the initials underneath read 'T.I.R.'

Above this sign was another indicating Mount Ararat. We turned onto the military road. After about half an hour a military Jeep with four soldiers of the Turkish Army, swung in front of us and waved us down. An officer got out of the passenger seat and approached the bus. He had a big smile on his face, so it didn't feel heavy.

"Guten Tag, meine freunds," he saluted as he came aboard.

"Guten Tag, mine herr, Ich bin ein Englander."

"English. Ah I have brother in England in Manchester. He is builder. I go there next year to visit him."

"Well I hope you have a good time as we have here in Turkey." I figured a little arse kissing wouldn't go amiss.

While he was talking and pinching the kids' cheeks and patting their hair, he was walking around having a look. When he decided we were just hippy tourists, he started out the door.

"When you stop for the night, stay away from the wire," he said, indicating the twelve-foot chain link fence topped with razor wire. "There are sensors in the ground and we will have alarm. I don't want to be out here tonight."

"I was hoping to park nearer the mountain. Are there places to park?"

"Ah you will have no problem there." He waved and was gone from the door. He swung into the seat and they all waved as they shot off like something out of an American war movie.

"Wow," said Timus. "That was a bit..." He struggled for the word.

"Flash?" I suggested.

"Yeah, did you notice the uniforms? High quality and they looked much smarter and better equipped than the other Turkish Army we've seen."

"Must be some elite border guards. That's the Armenian border there and that is Soviet territory." I studied the communist scenery and noted how identical the land looked either side of the wire.

As I studied the vast plains and mountains it became obvious how absurd man's attempt to isolate one from another, was. The fence became ridiculous. We ran alongside it about two hundred yards to our left. Every now and then there would be an observation post but no sign of life. All of a sudden the fence paled to insignificance as we rounded the rocky corner to see the stunning sight of the snow-capped Mount Ararat. "Shit! Will you look at that?" I gasped. I stopped the bus right there in the road. Everybody crowded forward including the kids, who sat on the dash looking at the sight before us. I felt regret that we couldn't afford a camera and film.

I suddenly realised we'd been silent, staring at the mountain. I looked around and realised we were sharing a special moment experiencing this wonderful sight. As if a film were restarting we came back to awareness. "I'd better get going or we're going to have a Tonka Truck up our arse.

'Tonka Truck' was the name we'd given the six-wheel tippers, made by Volvo, that were everywhere. They were bright yellow and resembled the famous toy trucks of the same name. Needless to say they were driven as if they, indeed, were toys. In the most dangerous possible way but, to paraphrase the expression; I hadn't seen anything, yet.

We stopped on the western approach to Ararat and started to get the dinner. We had our meal and sat around talking. Fran remarked how relaxed it felt after the last couple of days. I took my cue. "Well I hope so, because if I have to subject the kids to a heavy scene again I'm leaving the bus."

That took even Isobel by surprise and it got everyone's attention.

"I really don't want to do that but I ain't driving like I am, and getting shit from you Charlie and watching others doing fuck all." I could feel myself about to unlock the flow. Charlie was staring straight into the fire. "I don't know what it is you've got against me Charlie, but now's your chance. We're sat here quiet, let's hear it. I can tell you now, I've got no problem with you, especially, but don't expect me to stay quiet when I see people not doing their fair share of the work. I'm driving around twelve hours a day and I'm looking after the bus, what more do you want me to do? So what is it?"

"I don't have a problem. I guess we're all a bit grumpy without a smoke."

"That wasn't 'grumpy' Charlie," I said as gently as I could. "It was like you hated my guts, mate." To my utter surprise, he got up and offered his hand to me. I readily accepted it and we shook hands. There was a general relaxing and exhaling.

"You weren't really going to leave, were you?" said Kakey.

"Nah, we're going to India, man! All of us!" There were laughs and whoops and spirits were up.

If someone from the rocks above had observed us they would have seen a vehicle and its passengers, in the middle of nowhere, a long way from home, but feeling at home round a camp fire, with each other. The bus had a real good rocking that night!

I was up just as it was getting light. I made a coffee and went outside in just a pair of shorts. I sat on the rocks and before long I was silently joined by Isobel Glynis and Charlie.

The sun came blazing over Mount Ararat and lit the tops of the mountains. It was a stunning spectacle. I realised the sun had risen like this over this vista for several thousand years. I found myself staring at the upper part of the mountain and wondering if Noah's Ark really did come to rest up there. After a while somebody moved and it broke the spell of the mountain.

"What's for breakfast? I'm starving!"

"How much diesel have you got Alun?" asked Timus as we walked back to the bus.

"About three quarters of a tank. Should be enough to get us across the border. The barrel is empty, though. How much money have we got left?"

"About ninety quid," said Timus.

"Shit! By the time we fill up, we ain't gonna have

anything left to live on."

"Yes we will," said Isobel. "I have been buying extra every time we went shopping and stashing it away. I did it so's we'd have something to fall back on, plus the kids aren't going hungry. Now we're so close, we can use that to fall back on," she announced in such a way that said "I ain't taking any questions on this." Nor did she get any.

"Didn't Arthur say the diesel was cheaper in Iran?" asked Black Bob.

"Yeah, with that and the food stash we should get to Tehran with about a week's food, should be enough," said Timus, with more optimism than the situation demanded.

"Shall we go to Iran, then?" I asked. I sat in the driver's seat and ran up the engine. We pulled onto the road. Before long it curved south toward the border at Bazargan.

We made good time through the mountains and started to descend to the valley floor. As we came round the last bend before the flat I could see the road running up to the border crossing across the desert floor. I could see the road but I couldn't believe what I was seeing.

Chapter 8

Iran

The crossing consisted of a large arch leading into a huge courtyard. From the customs office on the Turkish side, vehicles were exiting into Iran, through the arch at the other end of the courtyard. After clearing Iranian Customs. The border fell right across the centre of the courtyard. The courtyard was full of parked trucks going in and coming out. It was a scene of complete chaos, with trucks trying to get through and trucks coming the other way and nobody giving way. To give way over here was ten times more a macho thing than it was at home.

I then looked the other way to see a queue of trucks of every nationality, snaking back as far as the eye could see, which was about fifteen miles! "Looks like we're going to be here a few days!" said Syd, but I'd spotted another way. As we approached the road junction I noticed a dirt track running parallel to the main road. I remembered what Sten, from the other bus, had said.

"Because we are tourists, we go down the outside of the trucks."

I didn't have much choice as the trucks were nose to tail across the junction. I approached the dirt track. It was single track but I reasoned there'd be no traffic the other way because the road going into Turkey was clear. I turned onto the dirt road and could see it snaked off toward the crossing. As I went along the dirt road a few horns went off here and there and when we went past the Hungarian state transport, a right cacophony went off. As I got further down towards the crossing I spotted Arthur's F88 Volvo. I slowed down and pulled up, he leaned out of the cab window and we all waved.

"I thought you'd be in Tehran by now."

"Not with this lot. I've been here four days, I should get through tomorrow."

"Christ. Is it always like this?"

"Pretty much. Did you come round the military road?"

"Yeah we got stopped by Audi Murphy and John Wayne in a Jeep," I joked.

"Yes. That's the border guards, special unit like our S.A.S only nowhere near as good."

"Are they gonna give us any hassle, driving down the outside?"

"No. All the tourist cars and vans do it. The local bus goes down here."

"OK well I hope you don't have to stay here much longer. We'll see you in the motor camp, Arthur.

"Yeah, cheers, drive careful, it's even madder from here."

We moved on to a fanfare of horns. We passed a few other British trucks. I gave them some horn and the others waved. That got another fanfare from them and wild waving. They were all suffering from the loneliness of cab fever, and were disproportionally happy to see their fellow countrymen.

As we got close to the arch, a guard came onto the track and waved us on. He had seen us coming, and had bullied the trucks to make a narrow access to the courtyard for us. He waved at the kids as we went by. I pulled up in one clear corner.

"I should make some tea or something. This is going to take a while," I said, as I got all the passports together and headed for the office. When I got there it was packed with drivers, all shouting to the harassed staff behind the counter. It was absolute bedlam.

All of a sudden one of the guys behind the counter delivered a ringing slap to one of the drivers. He continued to verbally harangue the poor driver, punctuated by the odd slap. It brought the level of noise down. The driver could do nothing in retaliation, despite being a large-looking dude. He had to earn his living across this border and it depended on the good will of the border guards. Suffice it to say, had it been repeated in England, then the slapper would have his hand broken, guard or not!

The slappy guard look right at me and said something. I didn't understand and hesitated.

"Tourist?" he asked. I looked totally different form the dark, swarthy Mediterranean appearance of the Turks.

"Yes sir," I replied. He swaggered a little and he was flattered to be called 'sir' in front of all the other drivers. I noted the effect and worked a few more 'sir's in here and there. He held up my passport to a nearly silent office and said something. It was open on the page that carried the bus stamp along with all the others I'd gained so far.

"I tell them, this is what a long distance driver from England looks like."

I looked around the room to see shaved, black-haired heads nodding at me. I smiled in return.

"We are going to India," I said. This was translated and murmurs went around the office.

The officer stamped our passports and passed them all back to me. As I exited the office the bedlam started again. I crossed the courtyard and across the border in the centre. The Iranian customs office on this side was a contrast to the Turkish office. Smart, uniformed officers in a large air-conditioned office were dealing with the drivers quickly and rubber stamps, carrying, to me, indecipherable symbols but looking cool in the passport, were being thumped up and down by bored officers.

A tray of clear brown tea in glasses and a big bowl of sugar lumps was being carried in by a young boy of about ten. He had a cold pack with three bottles of Coke, which I learned later cost, at the time, the equivalent of two and a half pence a bottle. The oil money certainly showed in the frontier post, the first impression overland travellers got of Iran.

There was a life-sized picture of The Shah, descending as if from the clouds, with back lighting and doves flying.

"Phalve Raza Shah, leader of Iran." I turned to see a smart Iranian army officer, who if their shoulder pips mean the same as they do in the UK, was a captain.

"Very impressive," I remarked. "Is he a good leader?"

The captain stiffened slightly. "He is a modern leader. He takes the Iranian people and educates them and brings western technology. We sell much oil. We have all the petroleum products, you will see, our roads are all tarmacked. To make the legendary Persian rugs you must make ten thousand knots to the square foot. The only people whose hands are small enough are young children. They worked in bad conditions in poor light. The Shah forbids them to be employed like this and ruled they must all be educated."

"He sounds like a good man."

"Oh yes very good." I noticed the captain's eyes flick around the office. I could have sworn he looked a little nervous.

"You speak excellent English," I said.

"Yes, thank you. I was educated in America and returned for military service which is compulsory in Iran. Now, my friend," he leaned in close to me. "Do you like a Coca-Cola?"

Without waiting he barked an order to the boy who brought a cold Coke and opened it with a flourish. He handed it to me with a young smile that showed a thousand Arabic generations in its appearance, to my western eyes.

"Shukrea," said the captain. That meant 'thank you', though, he explained, as Iran had close ties with France in the past, "'Merci' is understood by all and many here speak French."

Just as we were talking Isobel arrived with a handful of stamped passports. I introduced her and the captain asked if she would like a Coke.

"Not for me thank you, but I would love to take one for the kids. They have been waiting in the hot bus."

Again without a word he called the boy and not only were two cold ones produced but straws as well.

"Thank you very much." Isobel smiled sweetly and turned and headed for the bus. The captain had a good look at her departing back and bottom, but saluted politely.

"Ahem," I coughed. He jerked back from his little fantasy and I can remember thinking, *I guess these guys' women are covered from head to toe as well as the Turkish women.* The mere sight of the shape of a female body under comparatively tight western clothing was irresistible to the males.

"Have you any music cassettes or Levi jeans for sale?" The question was unexpected.

"Yes we have some cassettes for sale on the bus. Please come and look."

After meeting and ogling all the girls, he had a quick look through our music and wanted the Rolling Stones tapes. We told him five pounds each and he seemed happy with this. He waved us goodbye as we exited the arch and into Iran proper. Just down the road, about 300 yards, was a large, well-used, petrol station. The truck fuel pumps were back separate from the normal pumps. The truck pumps were dented and battered and had been repaired many times yet were not that old. The concrete kerbs were deeply scarred and stained with tyre black where they'd been swiped many times. There were shiny Macks, Whites, Kenworths and International Harvester 'Transtars'. I had not seen so many new American trucks before. They were lined up down the road.

We pulled onto the pump and I asked the young lad assistant to fill the tank. As he did so I unlocked the boot and opened the barrel. When he finished on the main tank I got him to stretch the hose and pump another forty gallons into the empty barrel. He gave me a written bill which I gave to Timus to pay. While he did that, Isobel picked up the bill and studied it.

"How many gallons did you have?"

"It was only marked in litres, and we had seven hundred."

She looked again at the bill. "He just charged us thirty pounds for one hundred and forty gallons!" said Isobel, disbelief written all over her face.

"That's what I thought," confirmed Timus.

"Let's get out of here before he realises his mistake."

I got into the driving seat and waved as casually as I could to the truck drivers who were watching us. I looked back to see the young lad busily pumping fuel into the cars behind us. We were already forgotten.

I drove out onto the road and headed off into Iran. The road was smooth and long. We drove through heat and mountains. It was epic country, long black ribbons of tarmac disappearing into the mountains some two hundred and fifty miles distant.

There were hundreds of large trucks running up and down and a whole separate world was built around them. You could stop your truck and have tea in a modern equivalent of a 'Caravanserai', while the enterprising young boys greased your truck for you. There were tyre shops and battery shops, both of which would have given health and safety inspectors a heart attack. The battery shop had young lads of ten and upwards stripping old batteries of their lead, merely flushing the acid into the ground with water. They were not using gloves and had just an apron to protect them.

We filled the main tank in a service station and discovered that the boy in the last station had not made a mistake and diesel was about five pence a litre! We carried on, driving in the dark, passing Tabriz, day after day of intense heat and semi desert, and running for Tehran city before the money ran out completely.

I swam into consciousness to find everybody up and about, doing stuff and talking to the young lads that had gathered. I had pulled up in the dark under some trees that

I thought were in the middle of nowhere. It was very hot and I could hear the slapping sounds of a truck's tyres approaching down the road. You could hear it for miles, then as it passed, the Doppler effect would progressively lower the note as the truck receded. The smell of the hot tarmac and diesel, amongst other things, will always remind me of Iran.

"Salam wh'aley coom. Vat is your name?" asked one of the youths as I exited the stuffy bus.

"Alun is my name."

"Ah, Alain Delon," he replied. The only same name they knew was the French film star who I'd never heard of at the time. "Vere do you come from?" The questions came in a regular form. They were trying out their English and weren't really interested in your response as long as they got one.

We even heard the phrase, "Hello, what is your name? Where do you come from? Send me some details."

We creased up when we heard this. It was straight off the back of some Superman comic. Everything was modelled on the American way of life but with mosques and mud-walled homes on the outskirts of the city. The oil dollars hadn't gotten everywhere, that's for sure.

I was handed a coffee and I realised I was more exhausted than I thought. Still, I could rest up in Tehran and let the others take some strain. I dipped the engine oil and had a general look round the bus. It was standing up to some serious driving with admirable guts.

I started the engine and the others came back aboard. "We are about a hundred and fifty kilometres away from Tehran. We should get there around nine or ten tonight. How much have we got left, Timus?"

"If we don't need to fill up again we will arrive with fifty quid or so."

"No, we have enough diesel. What shall I do? Drive to the city centre and job hunt from there?"

It was agreed that we'd try and find a decent place near the centre and look for work from there. I had been given a few leads on truck driving jobs but they were all in the city.

"If you can handle the shit-fight of the driving. I've noticed it's even worse here than Turkey," said Timus.

"I think we'll stand a better chance in town." said Charlie. He was hoping to use his artistic skills to earn some money. I was a little sceptical, but glad he was positive.

Black Bob seemed to think that being black would disqualify him from getting a job. I didn't agree but as one of us would have to stay with the bus and look after the kids during the day, I said nothing.

"OK I'll do me best, we are gonna have to get our act together quickly if we ain't gonna run out of money," I said as I let the handbrake off and we waved to the youths we'd been talking to and they returned the waves enthusiastically.

Out onto the road, we followed a British truck. As we hit the hills, he had to change down the box and we overtook him with a wave. I could see in my mirror the surprise on his face that a bunch of hippies had driven what he'd just driven, and in a twenty-five-year-old bus!

We eventually arrived in Tehran city after getting lost in the suburbs, to the surprise of the locals. Headed for the centre, we came across a wide boulevard with side streets that were big and would take the bus without causing a traffic problem. Driving in the city was insane, there's no other word for it. If there was a space and it was in front of where they were, they would go for it, even if it was a pavement or a grass bank.

The taxis were unbelievable. They were, in fact

nineteen-seventies Hillman Hunters. They were shipped out from England in parts, in a wooden crate, and put together in factories in Iran with a 'Made in Iran' sticker attached. They were bright orange in colour and the method of use was to stand at the junctions of roads that were laid out on the grid system. When a taxi slowed down you had to shout your destination and if he was going that way he would stop. It didn't matter how many he had in the cab! I have seen one passenger on the right of the driver and him steering with very restricted movements as there were another two to his left! Then he had five in the back. These were right-hand drive of course.

The journey never cost more than ten rials, also known as a 'tomen', hence the packing them in. I soon learned that 'musta rheem' meant 'straight on' and would usually get a ride straight away. You could always get another going cross-town, anyway.

We pulled right up one of the side streets and parked well out of the way. Nobody bothered us as we cooked dinner and had an early night. We awoke to the sound of heavy traffic and lots of people. I walked down the side road to see a wide boulevard, busy with the throng of a large city, the boulevard went on as far as the eye could see, lined each side with huge glass and concrete buildings.

I felt a lift of spirit. Surely we'd be able to find work here. This was a modern city. The boulevard was alive with shops and restaurants and department stores. All the big names were there including all the French perfumes and western clothing manufacturers. I was surprised as I know the Koran forbids the use of make-up.

We finished breakfast and I decided to go to the addresses I had, and see if there was any work going on. The first place was German engineering firm. They said they had nothing at the moment but would be taking on oilfield workers next month. I left my details with them and told them I would call next month or they could send me a letter care of Post Restante at the main PTT, Tehran. It had become a habit now to check the Post Restante, a very handy system where your post will wait for you at the next main post office or PTT.

The second firm, known as The Income Company had a very plush office on Ferdowsi Avenue. I had been given the address by an American truck driver. We met him in Turkey at a roadside transport restaurant. He was with two young drivers and they each had a Mack tractor unit and were taking them down to Tehran from Rotterdam, presumably where they were imported from the States. They still had US plates on them. Something struck me as not quite right, nothing sinister but something I couldn't put my finger on.

My reception at their offices just confirmed that something was amiss. I was greeted by a corporate 'robot', politely enough, but obviously my arrival had upset something.

"Where did you obtain this address?" he smiled.

I told him the story and he disappeared to take instructions. I heard some very mumbled talking and it sounded as if someone was getting a real dressing down. Eventually Robot reappeared looking extremely embarrassed but under control.

"Thank you for coming but I'm afraid we're not hiring at this time."

"What do you do?" I asked casually.

He looked shifty. "Er, we're a trading company." He smiled unconvincingly. I realised I wasn't going to get any farther so I left, feeling a bit strange and a little deflated that I'd turned up nothing, and walked miles as I didn't want to waste money on taxis. Silly really, as you never paid more than ten rials but when you get into the no spending habit, it's hard to get out of it. Especially when in the back of your mind you know you have a family that must not go hungry.

By the time I got back to the bus the others were returning. The only ones left on the bus were Black Bob, Syd and Fran, who was busy combing her hair in the mirror. I resisted the temptation to rip the mirror off the wall and smash it in the road.

"Where have you and Syd been today?" asked Kakey.

Neither of them answered. I looked at them.

"Did you hear what the question was, Syd and Fran?"

"Hey! Lay off man," said Syd.

"Yeah I'll lay off when you get off your fuckin' lazy arse and do something to help. What have you been doing?

"I've been really tired today and I went back to sleep. I just wanted to feel together before I go walking around."

"What about you Fran?"

"I had nobody to go out with. I didn't want to go out alone," she said pathetically.

"So how come Glynis, Isobel and Kakey can get it together to go with Timus and Charlie to find work to keep us going, but you can't?" Fran was showing stress from being away from all she was familiar with. I recognised this and decided that giving her a hard time was not going to help. She was a hopeless case and seemed oblivious to the resentment she was gaining. Syd was a different case. He was just plain lazy.

"How can you sit around doing fuck all, when our survival on this trip depends on getting money and feeding ourselves?"

"Gimme a break. We've only just arrived."

"Yes I know. I drove you here, remember? I'm the one

who keeps the bus going but I can get up and walk miles round a hot fucking city."

"Let's get some dinner," said Isobel calmly. "At least we've had a result."

"Really?"

"Yep. We bumped into this Iranian guy in a fancy suit. He gave us his card and told us he ran a company called, wait for it, 'The PooY-esh Language School'. Isobel passed me his card. "He asked us if we were staying long and said he was desperate for English teachers. He has a contract with the Iranian Army to teach all its officers. The only qualification needed was a British passport."

I turned to Syd and spread my palms upward as if to say, "Ta-daa. That's how it's done so how come you can't?" Only I didn't need words. Syd now wore a very black face, so dark that he would've hit me, had I been smaller.

"Yes you can look at me like that Syd. It isn't you that will have to get repatriated. It isn't you that will therefore be liable for the payment of the Carnet de Passage because I'll have to leave the bus behind, it'll be ME, so don't give me any bollocks, cause I'm tired of seeing you and Fran doing fuck all." Black Bob would have been included in this bar the fact that he had taken responsibility for the security of the bus and the kids and seemed to be taking it seriously. It changed his attitude, overnight. Syd stormed towards the door.

"Syd. We're just going to do the dinner," said Isobel.

"I'm going for a fucking walk cause we ain't in a fucking prison," he snarled at her.

"Okey dokey," Isobel said sweetly, mocking him.

He picked up on it and went to say something nasty but he caught my eye, saying without words, "You fucking dare attack her," and thought better of it. "It's alright he won't go far, it's dinnertime soon," I said, as loud as my speaking voice would allow. I hoped it dripped in sarcasm.

As the evening wore on, I learned what had happened with the Iranian guy, Mr Gillani. He had told them that it was not good to stay where we were and there was a good tourist camp called The Gol-Leh-Shah. He said he has contacts there. The other thing he said was to stay away from the Amir Kabir Hotel. It's where all the freaks and travellers go, and there was loads of drug dealing and rip-offs, going on there.

"Drug dealing! Oh dear!" I said with mock concern. "Can he take all of us, what's he paying?" I enquired, not relishing the idea of teaching English, mainly because of my poor education caused by ill health as a boy, plus being a thicko, that is!

"He reckons ten dollars and hour, paid in dollars not rials, which is pretty good. The only trouble is, it's in Isfahan," said Timus.

"Where's that?" I asked.

"It's about 400km south, it's the second city of Iran." Timus had done his homework.

"There's loads of Americans from Bell Helicopters down there and it's nearer the oilfields!" said Charlie. "Are you up for driving down there if we get the work?"

"I can't see why not. I gotta tell you though I ain't terrifically excited about teaching English. I don't speak it that good myself anyway."

"You can do it. I'll help you," offered Isobel with her A-levels in English. I didn't share her confidence.

"We have a couple of days until our interviews, so why don't we go to the motor camp tomorrow," suggested Kakey. Clearly they had all been talking about it and were excited.

We spent the rest of the evening talking to the young lads that had gathered. The atmosphere was relaxed and we were swapping stories of life and football. They knew all about Chelsea and Tottenham Hotspur etc. Not being a football fan I couldn't give much information so I kept a little quiet. At one point I asked for a light from one of the lads. Seeing that I wasn't too interested in football he started to explain the etiquette of cigarette lighting. As the cigarette is lit for you in cupped hands, you must tap the hand of the lighter with your index finger and mutter, "Hceesh," or something sounding like that. Most times it was just abbreviated to a tap and nod.

While we were on the subject, I asked him to explain another thing I'd noticed. Instead of saying 'no' in answer to a question, they would make a noise like a 'tut'. At the same time tilt the head up and back. The lad, who spoke broken American English, Explained how sometimes even the 'tut' was missing and a barely perceptible rising of the head would be used, especially if you were upper class.

The young lads couldn't help gaping a little at our females. They don't see women except under a black veil. There were many women wearing make-up and western clothing but they tended to be older, married and rich. Many student types were trying to wear ordinary jeans and T-shirts of a very modest type. Sometimes you would see a compromise of a young girl wearing an all-encompassing headscarf but with sweater and jeans. The combination was not unattractive. They would usually don a dark all-encompassing veil when they were off campus.

Isobel and the others girls had taken to wearing long skirts and long sleeved T-shirts, but even so they still went in where they went in, and round where they were round! They all drew the line at wearing the head scarves and walking thirteen paces behind their men, though. The nightlife of Tehran was active and it seemed we were in a bit of an unsafe area. A couple of capable looking guys said we'd be alright for tonight. They'd be around to keep an eye on us but tomorrow they were out of town.

I left the others and fell into a deep sleep. I awoke to a mixture of birdsong and early morning traffic noise. I decided to grab a coffee and walk down to the boulevard. I stumbled off the bus to see two of our acquaintances from last night, hanging out by a doorway further up the side road, drinking steaming tea from glasses. They both waved and I raised my mug in return.

I watched Iranian city life go by for a few minutes. There were trucks, buses, minibuses, hundreds of cars motorbikes, horse-drawn carts, even handcarts. It was absolute chaos with a cacophony of horns blaring, with no rules as far as I could see. Junctions would be blocked for hours because nobody would give way. Large American trucks would literally tangle themselves around other trucks and cars and would be locked for hours, each nudging forward on his particular course and to hell with everyone else, and if there was a gap ahead, go for it. It was an extremely immature and dangerous attitude towards using vehicles. It's hardly surprising that we came up with the saying 'you can't go from camels to cars without horses in between!'

We later became convinced that when two Iranian guys go to the truck showroom, they are first shown where the horn was, then the 'go' pedal, then the high beam, headlights. Job done, truck sold!

They were so desperate to move the goods out of the backed-up ports, it was easy for any person with a half decent plan to get finance from the bank to buy a truck and trailer. Usually a couple of guys, perhaps brothers or cousins or just friends, would buy a truck between them. There was no HGV test, you just bought the licence. They would then run it non-stop, twenty-four hours, up and down from Tehran to the Gulf ports. One would sleep, the other would drive. They would pull up in a desert lay-by and drain the sump oil directly into the sand, fill with clean oil and a new filter and off they would go. Some of the larger lay-bys were badly polluted with sump oil and used filters. The oil would spread up the road on the truck's tyres, contrasting sharply with the sun-bleached sand and surroundings. Often they'd get the enterprising kids in the towns, who owned their own grease guns, to do a lubrication job while the drivers had a meal.

Because there was no regulation of the trucking world, the accident rate was appalling. One transport yard we passed had about thirty International Transtar truck units, all lined up on one side. They looked impressive with their chrome exhaust stacks and spacious cabs, nicely painted. Opposite them were all the wrecks they'd towed back in. There must have been an equal number of smashed up units, some so bad they were unrecognisable. I can remember thinking that someone had money to burn! It wasn't until later I was to learn the money came from 'overseas aid and grants' from the Americans, hoping to continue their profitable relationship with the Shah.

Hard as it is to believe, in light of recent world events, but at that time the Iranians aspired to the American way of life and thought it, and the goods, a very good thing indeed. There were Yank-mobiles and Mercs everywhere, the living standard here in the city was high. I was to learn that it wasn't like that all over the country.

I got back to the bus to see Isobel and the kids having breakfast. The others were tidying up. It was then that Syd decided to try and surprise us. "I won't be coming to the motor camp with you. I met an English bloke last night and he says he can give me a job. I'm going to work in the oilfield."

I was hoping that my pleasure at this news was not showing on my face. It was hardly a surprise. How the hell he expected to work in the tough surroundings of the oil fields, God alone knows, especially with zero experience.

He grabbed his bag and with a half smile, was gone out the door. We never saw him again.

We drove to the southern part of the city, trying to find the Gazvin road. Where that entered the city, was where the Gol-Leh-Shah motor camping was.

"Down there, Dad!" shouted Alun Jnr. as we sailed by a road junction.

"What makes you think it was down there?"

"I saw the camping sign, like a tent."

"You sure?" I was surprised to see that Alun was learning to read the road signs. I drove on to the next junction and turned. Sure enough he was right and we all heaped praise on him and he beamed.

"Well spotted," I said, impressed. He beamed even more.

Just about two miles down on the right was the motor camp. An enormous area completely walled all round with an entrance gate and arch. There was a restaurant beside the gate office, and on the next lot was a truck servicing bay with two inspection pits and a truck wash. Inside the camp large individual parking bays were laid out, with shrubbery dividing each bay. There was also a large swimming pool that looked well kept. It seemed popular as well.

We decided that it was a little expensive for us and it would be cheaper to park just outside and use the facilities in the camp. Plenty of trucks and tourist vehicles were going in and out, not much attention was paid to foot traffic, besides the more tourists that were there, the more it appeared this was the place to be.

There were trucks from all over Europe. They had arrived at the customs clearance centre on the eastern edge of Tehran to be told of a two week wait for clearance of their load. They would drop the trailer in the customs parking area, a massive dust-laden area, where if you moved at more than five miles an hour, you risked a lynching from the other drivers because of the choking dust that would be kicked up. Drivers would all park with their countrymen and little enclaves would spring up. Swedes, here, Danish, over there, Brits, French, Spanish, here. It was a dangerous place because of all the backed-up trucks and roaming packs of dogs at night-time. Drivers had been attacked when getting up in the middle of the night for a pee. Not only that but tilt covers, the tarpaulin that covers the skeleton of the upper part of the trailer, were being sliced by night-time bandits and parts of the load stolen. It didn't happen very often because when caught, their right hand would be cut off! The guards that patrolled the customs area took no prisoners, and had been known to shoot at intruders. It didn't pay to wander far from the truck after dark.

Many truck drivers didn't want to stay in such conditions, so took their tractor units to the campsite where they could eat and keep clean, plus the added bonus of seeing the girls around the pool. Many a liaison was struck up between a bankrupt female traveller wanting a ride back to Europe, and a lonely truck driver.

There was a large sign in French, English, German and Italian, asking females not to leave the pool area in bikinis or other swimming attire, and to make sure they are unseen by anyone outside the camp. It was also a rule that Iranians were not allowed into the camp unless employed there. Needless to say the waiting list for a job there was lengthy!

We settled in our parking area and as the day wore on, in came Sten and his bus. We were pleased to see each other and before long we were invited to dinner, later on. They had been shopping and were going to have dinner al fresco, round the fire.

I was messing around tidying up the debris that had accumulated on the dash when I saw Black Bob ambling toward the bus. "Hey Alun," he leered through eyes like piss holes in snow. "I just had a smoke of some fucking wicked Afghani. I only got a few tokes while passing it round but I'm fucking shit-faced!"

"You don't have to tell me that, I can see it. You look trollied. Have you got any?" I asked with widening eyes.

"Nah, it was their last bit but one of their passengers stayed behind in town, to pick some up and he'll be back in a taxi, in time for dinner."

"Shit hot, man!" I blurted.

I couldn't wait. Here, now, would be our first taste of the legendary 'Afghani Black' as it should be. Unadulterated and fresh. I counted the hours with a growing thrill. I had missed my smoke more than I cared to admit.

The hour rolled round and we gathered around the fire and started making the meal for all of us. Halfway through the proceedings everything went tits-up, as the guy arrived with the dope. He had several large lumps and passed me one to make a smoke with. It was sticky, and black with a brown interior that looked like a waxy, coarse substance, but solid.

The fragrance released when warmed slightly by a lighter before crumbling into the joint, was exotic and promising. I lit up and inhaled the pungent smoke. I knew from experience to not overdo it. A couple of pulls, wait a while. A couple more and pass it on. Round it goes until it returns to you by which time you know where you are and adjust your intake accordingly.

By the time it got back to me I could hardly co-ordinate my fingers and arm to arrive at the proffered spliff! In short, I was shit-faced! A right mess! It was so strong! It had hit me like a wonderful, velvet sledgehammer in the back of the neck! I could feel the tension of the past weeks drain out of me. I savoured the feeling of relaxed contentment.

With a big smile on my face, I returned to helping with the meal. We had a wonderful evening and we all laughed a lot, helped no end by the relaxing effect of the smoke. We swapped stories and experiences. Halfway through the evening, there was a loud blast on an air horn. We looked around to see Arthur, the Brit truck driver we'd met in Istanbul, signing in.

He parked in a vacant bay just down the row from us and joined us at the fire with a large bottle of schnapps in tow. "That's it. That's me for the next two weeks."

"Don't you have to check on your trailer?" I asked.

"They put a paper up each week with the loads they are gonna tip that week, so I only have to go over there once a week. I've seen my agent and just picked up some cash. So I'm set up. They can take as long as they like, which they usually do, it's bloody chaos over there."

"Are you gonna do an internal?"

"Nah, I don't need to. I get paid alright and you can make a bit of money with this and that, along the way. Talking of which, have you lot got work yet?"

I explained how we had work as English teachers and how I didn't like the idea much but we desperately needed the money.

"Didn't you want to drive or something?"

"Yes but I haven't had any luck. I went to a couple of places but they didn't have any work."

I told Arthur of my experiences at The Income Company. "I bet that was a front business for 'The Firm'."

"Waddya mean?"

"The Americans are here in force and so is the CIA. They are paranoid that the Russians could make a lunge for the oilfields of the Gulf. They have little establishments like that all over the place."

What Arthur said made a whole lot of sense to me, and I laughed to think of their surprise when this limey walked in, asking for a job!

"I saw an old friend of mine at the customs yard," said Arthur. "He works for Pars International Containers. He got a three year contract with them as a transport manager. He used to have his own motors and a little firm in Kent but he went through the hoop, and ended up taking the ex-pat route."

"He runs a couple of trucks of his own, on the side, up and down to the gulf ports. He asked me if I'd do an internal for him and offered five hundred quid for it. I said I wasn't interested but then I thought of you."

"Excellent. Where does he live? I'll go and see him tomorrow."

"No need. He's coming here tomorrow evening. The company he works for are so short of drivers that they've imported about fifty drivers from South Korea. They don't have enough room in the transport compound so they've billeted a couple of dozen here in the camp but there's some kind of fiddle going on and Jensen, that's the guy's name. Unusual, ain't it. Just like the cars. Jensen has to come here with some of the company big-wigs and sort it out. You can have a word with him then."

It sounded good and I was excited about the possible job. I don't remember passing out but all the tiredness of the road overtook me and I fell asleep by the fire and woke up there covered in a blanket. The smells around me were of wood fires and kebabs. The sun was up but low and people were just making for work in the city. The national bus fleet, known as TBT, consisted of all new Mercedes Benz, and they went everywhere. The roads were generally very good and would disappear into the mountains on the horizon. Just occasionally there'd be a road works. No signs to warn you, no lights at night, just a trail off the road into the desert until the blockage was passed, then back onto the tarmac with a bump. The other favourite to come across at night was the end of the tarmac. Again, no warnings, the tarmac would just end for some works or other! You'd hit dirt road for a couple of miles.

I went out to the bus to be greeted by Isobel who informed me that they were all going into town to check the Post Restante at the central PTT and get some supplies. I said that I was going to hang out by the bus and do some sunbathing. They all managed to catch the local bus into town, kids and all. I wondered about that as it was already a very hot day but many of the shops and offices were air conditioned.

I set a camping chair in the shade of the bus and watched life go by. I saw many British units go by each with a nod or a thumbs-up when they saw the GB plate. One guy drove a Scania 110 and had the name 'Simontour' emblazoned on the top along with a row of massive Cibie spotlights that lit up the whole forward area when switched on! He had hair down to his waist.

Another couple of brothers had a Dodge truck and were called 'Twin Tee's Transport'. One driver came over to me and said hello. His name was Dave out of the East End of London. He was a typical East End lad who owned his own Volvo F88 and trailer. He was on general haulage sub-contracting to a firm called 'Cantrell's Transport'. They were notorious back in Blighty as a couple of their drivers had been busted with large amounts of cannabis at Dover. It was a regular perk apparently, to bring a bit back and flog it around town but then it got really popular and everyone started doing it, and customs got very busy! Dave said he played it clean as there were plenty of other legal ways to make a few 'sov's'. I told him I was going to see this bloke Jensen tonight about doing some driving.

"Jensen Potter? I know Jensen, he'll see you alright. He works for Pars International Containers. They've got this massive compound out on the Saveh road. They run Macks and Mercedes. They're owned by the state."

"He wants someone to do an internal for him," I said.

"That's a decent run. You go down to Bandar Shahpur or Bandar Abbas on the Gulf, load up whatever they give you and bring it back to Tehran. £500 in your bin and you c'n do it in a week, two days to get down there, a day to get loaded and a couple'a days back. 'E'll pay you in US dollars or sterling if yu' wan' it."

"I don't speak any of the language. It's going to be difficult isn't it?"

"They speak a bit of English. French is well understood. Used to be French territory or summat."

Dave said he would return and give me a few tips and meet the others later, but now he was off for lunch and then a relax round the pool. I learned later that his nickname was 'Dave the Arab' because of his almost 'Rasta'-type hair and black beard and his Bedouin-like ways, across Asia. It was ironic really as Dave was Jewish. As it turned out, we would meet up again many times and places in the future. It was early evening when Isobel the kids and all the others returned. They had had a good day but all the women had suffered from being pinched on the arse by the Muslim men who cover their own women head to foot. They think they can take liberties with western women whom they consider 'loose' because they do not cover their heads or bodies, act as equals, and don't walk five paces behind their husbands.

Evening came and Dave returned to the bus and I introduced him to everyone. As time went on I noticed he had zoomed in on Isobel and was using all his East End

Cockney charm to make her laugh, which she was doing. I can remember thinking I'd have to watch this guy!

Arthur came over, he and Dave were old acquaintances and swapped a few quick details of what they were both up to.

"Alun. Jensen and some other brass from Pars have arrived, they're just sorting something with the owner, so now is the time to catch him," said Arthur.

"Right. Let's go." I grabbed my shirt and headed with Arthur to the courtyard outside the offices. When we got there some serious shit was going down with lots of gesticulations and words flying back and forth.

Arthur caught Jensen's eye and he sidled over to have a quick word. Jensen was about six-foot-six high and about the same across the shoulders. A real giant of a man, built like the proverbial out-house. You could easily see him as an East End villain. He glanced toward me as Arthur pointed me out. He raised his hand to me and I nodded back. He wrote a number and gave it to Arthur then turned back to the problem in hand.

"He can't talk now he's got to sort out the problem with the Korean drivers staying here but he's given me his office number over at the compound. Give him a ring tomorrow and he'll send his car over for you."

"No shit," I said, impressed.

"Well he is their transport manager. Perks of the job," said Arthur. We went back and spent the evening getting trollied on hash and schnapps and reading all the letters from home. Nan and Grampy were missing their grandchildren but were thrilled to get the postcards we sent from Greece and glad to know we were all doing well and that the bus was still going. I must admit to a little homesickness at that point.

Dave, Isobel, and I seemed to gyrate off to our own

little corner and were busy listening to advice from Dave about driving down south. "The British Embassy advise all tourists not to drive the Gulf Road, but if they must, then do not drive at night."

"Wow is it that bad?" I asked, wondering now what I'd let myself in for. After all, while I had been driving buses and trucks before I'd never actually driven a full blown articulated 30-tonner before but I was young and full of confidence and there was really no doubt in my mind that if Dave and Arthur and all the other Brit drivers could do it, then so could I.

"If you can drive here from England, you'll have no trouble providing you keep it together and be aware," said Dave.

"I've got to take the bus and the others down to Isfahan. They're going to teach English to army officers."

Next morning I called Jensen on the camp payphone. I got straight through. "Can I speak to Jensen Potter please?" There was a grunt and some muffled voices.

"That you Alun?" asked a very cockney accent.

"Yeah, Jensen it's me. Can you see me now?"

"Sure. It's only a couple'a clicks from the camp, come over now and we'll 'ave some lunch in the canteen 'ere. Wait outside the camp entrance and I'll send me driver. 'E'll be in a black GMC pick-up wiv red wheels and loads'a chrome. Yu' can't miss it."

"Sounds like it," I quipped. He laughed.

"Yeah they love the old chrome over 'ere it's all flash pal, all flash."

"Alright Jensen I'll wait for him and see you in a tick."

"Alright sun." He ended with the Cockney short name for 'sunshine'.

I got back to the bus and told Isobel I was going to see

Jensen about the job.

"How are we going to work it then?" asked Charlie.

"I'll drive the bus to the motor camp in Isfahan and come back on the TBT bus."

"Where are you going to stay when you come back?" asked Glynis.

"Arthur has said I can take his bottom bunk for a couple of days till I get my own motor."

I sensed that all were not happy losing their driver.

"If we do this for about eight weeks we'll have enough money not to have to worry anymore. I can make five hundred a week."

The prospect of all that money calmed a few fears and all I had to do now was convince Isobel that I didn't mind being in Tehran while they were in Isfahan and that I would be careful. I met the driver who looked like something out of *The Blues Brothers* and we headed off for the transport yard in the outlandish, chrome-laden Ford pick-up. We arrived after a short chaotic trip with the driver blaring on the horn all the way. I was shown into Jensen's office. He wasn't there at my arrival. He was in conference with 'the colonel'. The colonel was appointed by the government and ran the whole operation.

After a while Jensen came in with a big smile on his face. "Alright sun?" he said and extended his hand. "Come'n 'ave a look round."

We walked around the compound. It was massive. There were rows of forward control, Macks, some cab-over Kenworths and row on row of International Harvester 'Transtar Eagles' .There were also some 'Jimmy huffers', GMCs that were air start. I'd never come across an air start truck before, it sounded like a giant Black & Decker until it fired and black smoke poured from the exhaust stacks. Over against the far wall were about thirty wrecked tractor units.

"Jesus! They like trashing them over here don't they."

"That's nufing, you should 'ear some of the stories behind that lot. They're just like kids 'ere. They drive these like dodgem cars. Their motto is 'never give way'. Some of the accidents are just, blood 'n' guts, carnage."

We went to the dormitory block which contained the canteen. As we walked into the canteen there was a load murmur of conversation from the South Koreans eating their lunch.

"You can have egg and chips or Korean gimshee. I'd be careful with that stuff. It'll give you severe 'ring sting' next morning.

"I'll give it a try. I like the spicy stuff," I grinned.

"On your head be it."

"I think it'll be my arse, actually." We laughed. I was already warming to Jensen, probably as I was born and spent the first sixteen years in the East End of London and he reminded me of it. I still consider myself a Londoner, though I've now spent more of my life, away from the place of my birth.

The Korean drivers were a little surprised to see their transport manager having lunch with another westerner. They smiled and bowed a lot and Jensen played it to the hilt. The affable boss character. "They're so short of drivers 'ere they bring these blokes over, teach'm 'ow t'drive a truck and send'm off down to the Gulf ports and run 'm twenty-four seven. They work for three months and then take all their wages home. The Iranians treat them like shit, so I got a few things like running money and one day off a week, now they 'fink the sun shines outa me arse."

We both looked around and received smiles and bows. I tucked into the gimshee to find it consisted of spicy cabbage and potatoes. It was tasty but burning hot spice. I wasn't going to admit that it felt like two forks had been stabbed into my tongue, and continued to eat. I broke into a sweat! I looked up to see several faces full of expectation that I would spit out the burning mouthful, when I didn't, there were mumbles of admiration and lots of grinning and pointing at the meal with their chopsticks. I grinned back feeling good that I'd connected with these drivers from a very different culture than me. Their first encounter with English men was Jensen, then me.

Egg and chips piled high and not looking quite right arrived for Jensen. "I 'ad to show'm 'ow t' do this and I taught'm about 'bubble and squeak' and proper English tea."

"Hard being an ex-pat then?" I asked.

"Nah, it's just that working 'ere is like the middle ages. They got all this oil money and they don't know what to do wiv it. They got money coming out their arses and they're importing all the western goods and equipment as fast as they can. They can't get the oil onto the market themselves so the Americans are doing it for 'm. There's a lot of the country don't like what the Shah is doin', westernisin' the country."

"It's a mad but wonderful place, I've never seen driving like it. Absolutely insane things to do to a truck," I said.

"So d'you think you'll be ok to do an internal for me?" Jensen came to the point over a mug of tea, English style.

"I reckon so. What's the deal? What motor will it be?"

"I get £2000 for every load I can get t' Tehran, it costs about £250 to £300 diesel and runnin' money. £500 in cash is yours and the rest for me. As many runs as you can do will mean more for us both, it's as simple as that."

"Motor?"

"You'll have my F88 that I brought out from England

when I took up this job. It's a good clean motor but it's 'ad 'n 'ard time on the roads commin' out 'ere."

"Tell me about it."

"Yeah. Arthur said you got an old bus, AEC or somthin'?"

"A '55 AEC Reliance. It's had the shit shaken out of it but it's held together well."

"Them AECs don't break. What're the rest of your group doin'?"

"They're teaching English to the army in Isfahan. I'll have to drive the bus there and catch the TBT back. It'll only take a couple of days."

"That's OK as it 'appens. I'll get the truck greased and serviced, cleaned up and polished."

"OK, I'll be back in three days then, nice to meet you Jensen," I stuck out my hand and we shook on the deal.

"I gotta meeting with the colonel, so I'll have to run. My driver will take you back. See you in a couple of days then."

"Yeah, couple days." I waved at a disappearing Jensen.

The driver took me back to the camp. I got to the bus to find the others had adopted a local Iranian guy. His name was Rajeef and he had a pocket full of some dynamite black Afghani.

"Raj needed somewhere to skin up," said Bob with a grin.

"Well, one has to be polite," I replied.

Turned out that Raj lived just behind the motor camp and made a few rials by selling hash to the tourists. He was selling it at a higher price than you would find in the city but was still piss cheap compared to western prices. In 1975 black hash of reasonable quality was around £12 an ounce. Here in Tehran, a country that shared a border with Afghanistan in the East, an ounce would cost around 75p! We were all thrilled by this fact and would often speculate what we could sell it for, back in Blighty.

It was Raj that first showed us how hash was smoked in Iran. They would carefully remove the tobacco from a Winston or Marlboro cigarette. This was done by rolling the cigarette between the thumb and first digit. The ambient heat caused the tobacco to dry quickly and this aided its evacuation from the paper. You discard part of the tobacco and mix in an equal amount of hash. You then, and this is where the skill came in, kept the mix in your palm while scooping with the now empty paper tube of the cigarette. The final crumbs were sucked in. Once the joint was finished you gave a little twist to the paper to stop the mixture from falling out. Then the tip must be removed. Don't want to filter anything out! Roll a piece of card and replace the filter and there you have it. Known by us to this day as 'doing a Farsi', when you run out of skins. Iran had no cigarette papers whatsoever, and had no idea what we were talking about!

Raj entertained us all by emptying three cigarettes and sticking one between each finger of his right hand. He then filled them all at the same time, from the pile of mixture in his left hand! By now, we had rigged up a cloth between us and the wall, to give a little shade. It was so hot on board the bus. A table had been put outside and we had our own little camping area where we could light a cooking fire. Most evenings, Dave, Arthur and Sten would hang out with us and smoke and chat. "We're leaving the day after tomorrow," said Sten. "We are going to do a bit of carpet shopping in Meshad and cross into Afghanistan. Some of our passengers want to pick up some Lapis Lazuli in Herat so we're going to stay there for a couple of weeks."

"Yeah we're off as well tomorrow. I've got to take the

bus down to Isfahan and then I'm coming back on the TBT to do a bit of driving for Jensen."

"You got the job then?" asked Dave.

"Yes I'm looking forward to it."

"I'm not," piped up Isobel. "I'm going to be without my man."

"What with all them handsome Iranian army officers to wine and dine you? They'll be like bees round honey," said Dave with a grin.

"Oi! I got my eye on you. You been on the road for too long!"

"Well I did come on the bus earlier on and found Isobel having a strip wash. Purely by plan, I mean accident, of course." We all laughed.

"Took my breath away," grinned Dave.

"And did you cover your eyes and stammer an apology? No you stood there gaping!" teased Isobel, going slightly pink. I thought for the second time I'd have to keep my eye on them as I think there was a mutual attraction there.

We said our goodbyes to Sten and his passengers and promised to look them up when we got to Goa. We promised also to get there before Christmas. Bob was a bit subdued to be leaving his new found friend on Sten's bus and, for a moment, I thought he might continue on with them.

The drive down to Isfahan was exciting to say the least. Many road conditions were encountered but all in all, a good drive. It was very hot and bright during the day and even on the move the temperature was climbing into the eighties. All the windows and roof vents were open to maximum and there was a good airflow through the bus. Trouble is, that airflow was hot enough to boil a kettle!

We arrived in the evening when it was pleasantly warm. This motor camp was not so large but was full of tourists. Some in cars, others in VW microbuses or Ford Transits. It's here we first bumped into 'Rotel Tours'. They were a German firm that ran around the Middle and Far East, towing a trailer, the same size as the forty seat Mercedes bus. The trailer had bunks for forty two people, and resembled a pigeon carrying trailer. To complete the impression the whole of the side lifted up when parked, to allow ladder access to each tier of bunks. It all looked claustrophobic.

Seeing as how most of the people on the Rotel Bus were rich and elderly Germans, they got the nickname 'Geriatric Tours'. I hope the poor driver was paid well, as he not only had to drive but do the shopping and cooking. Rather him than me. We, of course, were not spoken to by these people. They parked in the opposite corner of the yard, as far away from us and the other travellers as possible. We were beneath contempt for them, a decision they came to regret, as we passed them one day in the middle of nowhere. The driver had his head in the engine bay and some very hot passengers sat in the shade of the bus, suddenly without air-conditioning. This time they decided to wave and stood up as we approached. We passed them without, acknowledgement, knowing that the driver had the money to do whatever needed to be done.

We settled in and parked by the pool. We had attracted some attention and the others were already meeting people while I backed the bus into place. We paid three weeks in advance. I felt a little better knowing that at least the bus would be safe. Black Bob was going to be looking after the bus and kids during the day while the others were at work. The Iranians were not ready to be taught by a black person so there was not much choice for him, however not having to go to work every day, hang around the camp, drink tea and chat up the tourists, was fine by him.

As I left for the bus next morning. I kissed my family goodbye and gave Black Bob another lecture about child minding. I told the kids to behave and to do as Bob told them and look after their mother. "I'll be back in a while, I have to go to earn some money," I told the kids as I said goodbye.

"When are you coming back, Daddy?" asked Mellony.

"I'll be back next week, don't worry."

That seemed to be acceptable and there were no worries.

"We're going to the swimming pool Daddy," said Mellony, already forgetting that I was going.

Alun was fine, he just said, "When are you coming back, Dad?"

"I'll be back at the end of next week, alright young'un? I'll bring you a present back." He hugged me and then returned to his sister who was now shedding clothes ready to get in the pool. I admit I had to choke back a tear or two. I was going to miss those kids, but it had to be done. We needed money to carry on.

"Look after them and if Black Bob doesn't do his job properly, call me at Jensen's office number and I'll be back, and fuck the job, we'll fly home if there's any problem."

"Oh go on, it'll be alright, you'll handle it OK, so will I." Isobel and I walked down to the main boulevard to catch the Tehran bus. It was already at the stop and taking on passengers and strapping down bundles on the roof rack. It was a new Mercedes with air conditioning. Each bus had a young lad as courier and his job was to issue ice cold Cokes whenever needed by the passengers. It was all in the ticket price. It was early and the low, dusty sun had its own quality. Early morning in hot countries is something special to those of us from more northern latitudes.

I felt bad about leaving my family and I confess that when it came to it, I nearly got off the bus before it pulled out. I just had to remind myself that we had to have money. I waved as the bus pulled out for the six hour drive to Tehran. I reminded myself that at least I didn't have to worry about the kids. Isobel was more than capable of dealing with any problems that arose. Even Black Bob was showing that he was taking his responsibilities seriously, so I could relax and enjoy the adventure I was about to embark upon. I watched the road and noted the traffic and the way it all worked. Everything down the Gulf Road was for trucks. A whole cottage industry was spread along the town roads. I figured, *If these guys can drive it, I'll manage!*

It wasn't long before the road lulled me to sleep. I awoke some time later to see the young courier leaning over me to close the sun shades over the window. I nodded my thanks and he gave me a white teeth smile and flipped a pack of Marlboro for my convenience. I was amused to think how curtains on a public bus seemed funny. They were a total necessity in this glaringly hot land.

Eventually we pulled into the bus station on the outskirts of Tehran city, and I found a small restaurant and had some chello kebab, which was the main diet. Boiled rice heaped over a bar of kebab meat. Each grain of rice was separate and not boiled like pudding rice. A large knob of butter on the top, and a green salad with deep red tomatoes made a tasty meal. It was cheap, around ten pence, with loads of fruit to follow – pomegranates, honey melons, and sweet grapes. There were small lemons and limes to squeeze into your black tea. Tea was taken without milk of course, in a sherry-type glass with sugar cubes piled one on top of the other so that they protruded above the surface of the tea! No wonder dental work was needed by so many.

I thought I'd try the experience of using the taxi system to get to the customs truck parking area. I stood with a small group on the corner of an avenue, and waited. I watched as a taxi, with four people in it already, slowed to listen to the destinations being shouted to him. One of my fellow waiters shouted a destination but he wasn't going that way so didn't stop completely. As soon as he heard a destination that he was going past, he would give a little toot on the horn and stop to allow another passenger to be shoehorned into the cab. In this way, you could get across the city by waiting at junctions for north to south cabs or east to west. It never cost more than ten rials, known locally as as 'yec toman' ('yec' is Pharsi for 'one'). Just like we used to call two old shillings, 'two bob'. By the time I arrived at the customs parking area it was dark. Luckily I could see the Brit drivers all parked together and I spotted Arthur's unit.

I started to walk towards him and was surprised that my feet sank at least nine inches in to very fine power dust. It was everywhere, even the truck wheels failed to disperse the stuff, helped by the fact that nobody went over five miles an hour. Goodness knows what it would be like when it rained. I hoped, silently, I'd never see that. I knocked on Arthur's door. His curtains were pulled but his light was still on. The curtain flipped aside and the face broke into a grin as he recognised me.

"Alright sun, made it ok then!"

"Yeah, left'm all parked up in the motor camp. Them TBT's are a bit swish aren't they."

"That's another government run concern. Transport is the business to be in, that or oil. Anyway, wha's yer plan?"

Arthur had been doing his paperwork. He put it all away and tidied the top bunk as we talked. "Be careful if you have to go out in the night, there's packs of dogs around. Don't know how come they're here, the Muslims think they're 'unclean' but I wouldn't stray too far from the motor. The other important question is, got any hash left?"

"I have indeed. I always try to keep a little with me. I don't drink much but I love a smoke. I thought you were a drinking man," I said. "I've taken a liking to having a smoke and then going to sleep. You just get so much more relaxed. If I have a drink I wake up early!"

"I'm going to have to see Jensen tomorrow, I don't have any money left, he's going to have to give me a sub. I hope the motor's ready as I don't want to impose on you any longer than needed."

"No trouble, sun. Jensen'll see yu' ok. Dave's coming over tomorrow morning to check the tip list, 'e'll give you a lift to see Jensen. 'E loves runnin' around in 'is unit."

We spent another hour or so smoking and talking and I picked up as many tips as I could. I climbed in the top bunk and tried desperately not to vent the gas that I felt building up in my belly. Rule number one; no farting in your mate's cab!

I awoke to the sound of moving trucks. I pulled on my shorts and as gently as possible, I tried not to shake the cab too much as Arthur was still noisily, knocking out 'zed's. I wandered over to the small café and ordered tea and a bowl of steaming soup. The bread was unleavened and fresh out of the stone oven. I watched the baker and his boy assistant making the bread. The dough would be stretched out pizza crust style. Then it was laid on a large padded end of a long wooden pole. The young lad would place the rolled out dough on the hot oven wall. It would stick to the walls of the mud and fire brick oven until cooked. It would then be removed and added to the pile. People arrived and waited as their order was baked and then took their order away wrapped in a tea towel or newspaper.

There was a loud honk on an air horn. I looked around to see Dave grinning at me. "Alright Al?"

"Hi Dave. Gonna have a tea?"

"Yeah, get'm in, I'll just park up."

I got the teas in and Dave arrived.

"Got 'ere OK then."

"Yeah. Came up on the TBT. Real comfort with the air-conditioning and soft suspension, bit different to our leaf spring set-up on the AEC."

"Where's Arthur?" asked Dave.

"He's still sleeping, he had a smoke last night and he sank into a deep sleep. He said you might be into taking me over to pick up my unit if it's ready."

"No problem, it's almost on the way back to the motor camp. It'll be good to see Jensen, I ain't seen him since he left Kent."

I grabbed my stuff from Arthur's cab. He was just stirring.

"Arthur, thanks for the stay, Dave's arrived and he's gonna take me to pick up my motor."

Arthur yawned, loudly. "Wassa time, Al? Fuck that was a good sleep," he said, stretching and sitting up. I reached into my pocket and brought out the lump of Afghani. I broke it in half and put it in his glove compartment.

"There you are, half what I've got."

"Ahh! Diamond! Cheers Al."

"Least I can do, mate. Thanks for putting me up. I'll see you later, if the road don't get me."

"Alun!" he called, so sharply it spun me round to face him.

"Seriously, it's fuckin' carnage down that road. Keep yuh wits about yuh or you WILL end up dead. Keep yuh concentration and yer more than capable but lose it for an instant and you'll be in the shit. Remember this ain't England or Europe or even Turkey. This is THE Gulf Road and apart from the basics, it's a world of its own."

I reached in and took his outstretched hand and shook it. "Thanks Arthur. Don't know what's gonna happen but yuh gotta try ain't yuh?"

"I admire yer bottle, be lucky."

I realised then, that moment would stay in my mind for many years, even now I remember that moment between us. Dave was waiting with his motor ticking over. I threw my bag into the bunk and climbed in to the passenger seat, donned the sunglasses and we headed out into the early morning mayhem that is rush hour traffic in Tehran city.

Dave was a steady driver but even so, we ended up several times driving on the bank, the central reservation and even followed a line of vehicles that decided they weren't going to wait for the snarl-up to clear up ahead. Instead they just spilled into the fast lane of the opposite carriageway and drove toward a gap that was past the obstruction. Cars and buses were swerving violently coming the other way, but it was 'the will of Allah' that nobody collided with each other.

"Jesus, Dave. These fuckers are insane. Is it always like this?"

"Pretty much all the time. It's a macho thing, they think it's an insult to their manhood, to give way."

"But this is fucking insanity. It's gone beyond a joke, these fuckers are going to kill each other," I repeated. I was beginning to wonder about this. Driving is one thing but fending off suicidal drivers is another. We made it to the yard and I could see the blue and white Volvo F88 standing over by the pumps. It was coupled to a red 'tilt' trailer. The huge tarpaulin cover was folded and tied down to the front of the frame. We walked into Jesen's office –

he was sat behind his desk looking like a fish out of water.

"'Ello Dave, long time no see."

"'Ow you doin' Jensen? I ain't seen you since you left to come out here. 'Ow's it working out?"

"Not too bad but you gotta watch these fuckers. They don't mind breaking a contract."

"Alright Alun?" He turned and we shook hands.

"Yeah. I'm a day early I know but I've left all we had, back with the others. I'm broke and need somewhere to crash."

"That's not a problem the truck is ready and I'll give you some expenses. You can head off today if you like."

"Yes I might as well, that's what I'm here for."

Dave and Jensen chatted for a while, while I got my stuff into the cab. I gave it an inspection. Inside was clean and tidy but the outside had taken a battering and all of the plastic trim had fallen off, including the large moulding around the radiator. Everything else worked as it should and the paintwork was still in good nick.

"Right! I've gotta run," said Dave. "I've got to tip in a little place outside Isfahan."

"Thanks Dave. If you go into Isfahan give my love to my family. See you later mate."

"Go steady and be careful." And Dave was gone.

"The batteries on this're a bit down, if you can, park on a slope."

He must have seen my look of concern. He added quickly, "Don't worry I've given you enough to get you out of most problems. All you gotta do is use the same gumption that got you out 'ere. It ain't a drive down the M4 but I'm tellin' yuh now, you'll love it. I've put a couple of maps in, and a few tapes for the stereo. I've gotta go now, I spend more time at meetings than anythin' else. Drives me to sleep. Anyway, I've written me 'ome number and the office 'ere and they are in the map tray on top, along wiv the directions for what to do and where to go when you get to the docks."

"OK Jensen I'll see you in a week or so then."

"Keep in touch when you're near a phone. Be lucky." And with that, he was striding across the yard toward the administrative building. At least he had confidence in me.

Well there I was. There was no putting it off any longer. I climbed into the driver's seat and studied the map. I wrote a little list of the towns that I should pass through. I started the engine and let it warm up. I pulled out of the compound. This was the first time I'd taken an articulated truck out onto the road. I'd driven all sizes of bus and many smaller, rigids, but this was actually the first time with an artic. Talk about baptism of fire!

I turned onto the Qom road and settled down in the truck. It drove nicely and was clean inside. Jensen had boasted to me how he had clean sheets in his bunk every night, as he drove out from England. The road was a long and black tarmac ribbon in a sun-bleached landscape. Roadhouses and filling stations were spaced out along the route and, as I was now off the usual tourist, or international truckers', routes, I caused some attention when a British truck pulled up for a cup of tea.

I passed many plots of land given over to vegetable growing. In amongst the carrots and spuds were the odd marijuana plants. To my eye they stood out like beacons and I promised myself that if I ran out of Afghani hash, I'd chop one of these glistening, female plants and smoke it! I was loving this. It was everything I'd expected in a foreign, Arab country. Hot sun, very different culture, and very different people. I drove on with all the windows open, dressed in just a pair of shorts and sandals. I kept a long-sleeved T-shirt for when I got out of the cab. The terrain stayed flat and bright, and I went through towns and villages feeling like I was getting further and further into a land I didn't know and leaving everything familiar behind.

The road, and the nature of the traffic on it, demanded full attention and then some! Most of their other vehicles were trucks interspersed with buses and minibuses. If anything, the driving was worse in a different way, out here on the open road. I was concentrating so hard that I hadn't noticed how low the sun had got. I had come about two hundred clicks and it would soon be dark. I remembered the advice about avoiding driving the Gulf Road at night and decided, for tonight at least, to stop in the next small town about seventy clicks further on.

The road went right through the little town. The streets were very quiet. I pulled up just down from the only shop that had a light outside. I walked back to the shop and asked for a couple of Cokes. The shopkeeper was so surprised to see a European, he looked out the door to the opposite carriageway parked, and then he understood.

"Allmagne? Allmagne?"

"No. I'm English. Je suis Anglais."

"Ah! Englistan." He asked a question in Pharsi but from his hand gesture I realised he was asking where I was going.

"Bandar Shahpur. I'm going to the docks," I said with a smile.

The shopkeeper translated for his two pals and they nodded and smiled back. I paid two 'toman' for the Cokes and noticed that everyone was tucking in to a communal dish of what looked and smelt like spicy aubergine and rice.

The shopkeeper noticed my glance at the pot and being a Muslim immediately offered me some. I was the stranger, the traveller in their midst and their religion demanded that they give shelter and sustenance to a stranger. I smelled the dinner and it had reminded me I hadn't eaten at all since a meagre breakfast.

"I would love some. Thank you very much." I put my hand on my heart as I'd seen them doing to each other, and nodded to indicate my pleasure at being invited. Immediately they started to shuffle round and a box was put upright for me to sit on. The shopkeeper handed me a plate of cold, long grain rice. He gave me a serving spoon and an ordinary one. I noticed spoons were the choice for most things.

The meal was wonderful, the cold rice contrasting deliciously with the hot spicy sauce and aubergines. I finished a large plateful and had to insist that I had no more, as I was bursting. The youngest of the three disappeared to return with a tray of tea. The teapot was silver and the cups a surprisingly delicate china with glazed blue and green patterning. Also on the tray was a soft pack of Winston cigarettes. The shopkeeper opened them and passed the pack round.

The youngest got busy emptying the tobacco from three cigarettes simultaneously. *Is he doing what I think he's doing?* The lad caught my eye and grinned the biggest grin I'd seen for a long time. "Hashish?" I asked, nodding toward him. He nodded back. Just one nod. I learned later that a single nod meant you had some to smoke or sell.

"Wow. I don't believe this, a wonderful meal and now this!" I said aloud.

Every fantasy I'd had about being in a strange land and offered strong, local hash, was coming true and I took a moment to savour that fact. I beamed and must have looked how I felt as they broke into laughs all round.

The evening was balmy, with a clear, star filled sky. The odd car went by but the streets were empty. We smoked the hash and I found it was a little better than mine, so mine stayed in my pocket! I sat with the three men. We didn't have too many words in common but we had communicated. It crossed my mind how the scenery and company may well be different but the activity is the same!

Fatigue suddenly caught up with me. I thanked my host profusely and shook hands all round. I wandered back to the truck, climbed aboard and unrolled my sleeping bag, though I doubt if I'd need any covering as it was so warm.

Suddenly, without warning the peace of the night was shattered. There was an enormous BOOM! The sound was so intense that it rocked the cab and reverberated round the area. "Shit! That's a tyre gone off." Thoughts of the roadside tyre shops flashed through my mind as I climbed back out the cab and started to inspect the tyres on the trailer. Nothing!

I looked at the tyres on the unit, all OK there, so what the hell was it? The guys were still sat around outside the shop talking and laughing. Surely they must've heard it. I just couldn't fathom where this enormous explosion came from. It was all quiet now and I was tired, so I started to climb back into the cab when, BOOM! There was another loud explosion. So loud that it was impossible to tell where it was coming from. I stood there absolutely dumbstruck. "What the fuck is going on?"

I walked back towards the shop. I staggered in, to their surprise. "What the hell was that explosion?" My words made no sense to them but they could see I was alarmed.

"Boom, boom." I exploded with my hands. "What was that?" I spread my hands to say 'what was that?'

"Ahh," said the storekeeper and indicated me to follow him. He led me across the road behind the trees that lined the highway. There, amongst a cloud of smoke that hung in the trees, was a large cannon! There were a few people gathered around it, one of them looked like a mullah, a religious leader.

"Ramadan, Ramadan," he said twice, pointing at the cannon. I must have looked puzzled as he went on. "Ramadan start, BOOM," he said. "Ramadan finish, boom!" He mimed.

"Oh, bloody hell! I understand, yes I understand, boom, start, boom finish."

I was gobsmacked and relieved at the same time. I started laughing and so did the shopkeeper – he could see I was relieved. No wonder they were tucking into the meal. During Ramadan they can only eat after sunset and before sunrise. Their daylight hours are spent fasting. I bade them all good night, all the time laughing to myself. I climbed back into the cab and decided to have another smoke before going to sleep.

As I lay there savouring the calming effect of the hash and drifting off to sleep, the phrase 'stranger in a strange land' kept going over and over in my mind. I curled up in my sleeping bag in that bunk and felt very, very alone.

I awoke to find the sun just painting the tops of trees and houses. I wandered back up to the shop which was still open. The shopkeeper was now alone and dozing in his chair. I attempted a local greeting, "Salam wh'aley koom." (Peace be upon you.)

"Wh'aley koom salam," (upon you be peace) came the reply. I bought some munchies for the road and had a couple of glasses of sweet, golden coloured tea with him.

"I know you don't understand me but I want to thank you so much for your hospitality, thank you." I gave him a packet of John Player Specials that I'd been saving. I blagged them off a Brit driver who was going home. In those days, JPSs were in a very impressive shiny, black card pack. The embossed gold lettering finished off the luxurious appearance and all sealed in cellophane. He had never seen them before and was very pleased with the gift.

He stood to shake my hand, followed by hand on heart with a little nod of the head. I did the same and turned to go, not knowing that I'd visit that little shop every time I passed on the way to the Gulf. Just one of the many friends I made down that road.

I left the town behind and after about two hundred kilometres I started to climb into the foothills of a low mountain range. I decided to pull in and get some diesel. I filled both tanks, about eighty gallons, which cost me all of twelve pounds sterling! Filling up was a real novelty! As I climbed toward the pass I saw several twisted wrecks of trucks some domestic and some international. The first wreck I came across was a Dutch registered artic. It was completely on its side, tractor and trailer still together. The cab part was badly damaged and hanging over a very steep ditch. There was no windscreen left and signs that the cab had been looted were everywhere.

I wondered how this had happened and what had become of the driver. I was determined that this was not going to happen to me. As I got up to the level part of the pass I saw another wrecked truck. This one had gone into the ditch and struck the high banking that lined the road at that point. It had hit the bank so hard that the trailer had broken free by ripping the 'fifth wheel', the device that couples the trailer to the cab unit, right off the chassis, and the inertia had sent the trailer forward crushing part of the cab. There were signs of carnage that I won't go into, let's just say that they don't have the wonderful paramedics we have in England, nor do they have the people whose job it is to clear up the gore after an accident. The scene was disturbing in the extreme and underlined the fact that if you are a truck driver out here, you are on your own. Even the law was nowhere to be seen and very loosely applied, if you have enough money for bribes, that is.

I carried on but feeling shocked at what I'd just seen.

The road surface was excellent and well laid. It was one of the benefits of having oil. Tarmacadam is a by-product and the Iranians lost no time in spreading it onto their roads.

I was going gently downhill now, the road became winding and several bends were shrouded by the rock face that lined the road. I came round a gentle, sloping bend doing about forty miles an hour. The sight that greeted me as I rounded the bend, sent about a gallon of adrenalin straight into my bloodstream.

The road had just disappeared. Where there was once tarmac there was now rough rock. It had been exposed because the intense sun had melted the tarmac. The bed of the road was showing because there had been no compacting of the surface before laying the tarmac. The tarmac itself had just melted and rippled in the intense sunshine. Other trucks had just continued to drive over, or round it until it had been churned and deeply rutted, just as if it was mud! There was no warning whatsoever. The local trucks knew it was there and could take action but I, a stranger, had no chance. There comes a time in every driver's life when you have the bowel-emptying feeling that you are going to crash and there's very little you can do about it except watch in a slowed-down version of reality.

I hit the brakes but it was way too late. The front wheels just hammered into the chassis. Their springs and shock absorbers unable to cope with such a huge jolt. The cab just exploded with everything going into the air, including me. I was just bouncing totally out of control. Somewhere, somehow, I recognised that the tractor unit was being overtaken by its rear end. The trailer was pushing me into a 'jack-knife'. That condition, feared by every driver of articulated vehicles, where the cab cannot slow the weight of the trailer. The trailer pushes on, with the effect of snapping the cab around like the blade of a jack-knife and smashing it into the side of the trailer, usually killing the driver, depending which direction the cab is swung round. From somewhere, to this day, I know not from where, I remembered the instruction, "If you feel the truck jack-knifing, pull the 'dead man's handle." This was really the handbrake lever but an extra feature on all modern trucks meant that if you pulled the lever to just before locking it on, all the air would be channelled to the trailer wheels only. This had the same effect of throwing a heavy anchor out behind the truck. It locks the trailer wheels only and therefore tends to 'snap' the vehicle straight and drag it to a stop, rather than the front axle's brakes trying to hold the weight back from the front. It worked! I was snapped back straight just as I hit a smooth patch of ground. The brakes bit and started to bring me to a bouncing halt. The trailer swung wildly and a huge shower of dust went into the air as the rear axles hit the dusty roadside. I came to rest at an angle of about forty-five degrees to the trailer with the cab in the middle of the road.

I just sat there in the swirling dust and smoke from tortured tyres. My heart was racing and I was trembling violently. I don't know how long I was sat there but suddenly there was a blast on an air horn. I looked round to see a couple of large trucks coming up the other way.

They had stopped so as to give me room to crash without involving them. I moved into gear and dragged the trailer back onto the tarmac. As the first truck passed I swear the hooded face of death stared back at me from behind the wheel! It was just the shock of course, but I swear, that's how it felt.

I pulled on, shaking, but determined that I wasn't going to crack in front of these drivers. I stopped around the bend in a lay-by. I got out of the cab on shaky legs and started to look for any damage. Apart from some scuffs on the tyre walls and chips out of one wheel rim, I could find no damage. All the air lines were ok and the truck was holding its air brake pressure, so I seemed to be undamaged, physically that is! The walk round had brought me back under control. I climbed into the cab and lit a cigarette. By the time I had finished it, I was ready to pull off again, this time I would take nothing for granted. Lesson number one: you cannot go into a corner assuming that the road continues on, in an uninterrupted fashion. Anything could be round the corner!

This is, of course, true of any road in England but you get some warning there. Here there was none. 'Insha'Allah' (it is the will of God) and no point in putting up signs, was the philosophy here. I had driven a few kilometres and was now back under control and not shaking, I rounded a couple of hairpin bends with rock walls on either side of the wide road. Travelling very slowly now, as it's easy to build up speed without noticing it, when coming down hill. I was letting the engine hold me back, in low gear and just dabbing the brakes As I came round the next left hand hairpin, a sight greeted me that I shall never forget.

Many of the trucks running up and down the route were Mercedes, six-wheeled chassis. The body-builders had equipped them with high sided, wooden, beds for melon-carrying. One of these trucks, overloaded up to the hilt with melons, had gone into the corner too fast. His top-heavy load had gone over when he had to break unexpectedly for a Mercedes taxi coming the other way, also grossly overloaded with a family and other passengers. The truck had just ploughed into the rock face taking the taxi and another following car with it. The cab was just flattened, the high sided bed had detached from its chassis under the force of impact and smashed to pulp the load of red melons. It was a scene of utter carnage. Blood and body bits mixed with the red of the melons and dead and injured were hanging out of twisted metal. As I passed very slowly I spotted two dead bodies just being covered by others who had stopped. I couldn't help it. I stared at this scene with horror. I nearly freaked, there and then, when I realised I could be driving over body parts right now. I wanted to throw up.

I don't know how but I kept driving. Heart thumping and hands shaking, I carried on down round the next two hairpins, and there was a lay-by. I've never been more relieved to see a lay-by in my life. I pulled in, put on the parking brake and stopped the engine. I was in 'post-event traumatic stress', I know that now. I had to get out of that cab before I lost it completely, I was almost giving way to hysteria over what I'd just seen. I managed to lower myself from the cab. I had to use my arms as my legs didn't seem to be working. As my feet touched the ground I went over backwards into the sand. My knees had just given way and refused to support me. I had to lift myself with my arms, turn and prop myself in a squatting position with my back to the wheel. There I sat for a full half an hour, trying to pull myself together and get my shaking legs to work!

I got myself together eventually and pulled on for another couple of hundred kilometres, very cautiously indeed! I was now in the foothills that led down to the plains and desert that I must cross before reaching the Gulf port. I stopped at another filling station to top up the diesel and buy something for dinner. I didn't feel like eating at all, but you have to eat something. I pulled off the road on a hill overlooking the country I was about to cross. I could see for hundreds of miles. I parked so that the truck was between me and the road.

I gathered some wood together and made a fire. By this time it was getting dusk and I could see the road with headlights and the towns and villages like sparkling jewels in a desert. On the horizon hung the pall of black smoke from the Gulf oil refineries. I went to the food locker on the trailer and found it well messed up from being bounced off the road earlier. Nothing was broken though and I decided some local cheese and tomatoes mixed with a green salad made from spinach and some other peppery greens that were popular but, as yet, I hadn't learned the name of. All this was rolled up into a 'barbari' bread.

This bread was slightly risen and the same shape as the flat chapatti-style local bread. It was cooked in the same mud ovens twice a day. I had queued with the locals while waiting for the first batch, much to their surprise and amusement. I finished off two of these rolls and downed a couple of mugs of coffee with UHT milk.

The night was beautiful with a carpet of brilliant stars in a clear sky. It was still warm and the rocks around me ensured that the temperature would never get down as low as night time temperatures down on the desert floor.

I got my sleeping bag, money and passport out of the cab. I laid the bag by the fire and made a 'Farsi', emptying out the tobacco, mixing it with some hash, and then refilling it. I was getting quite skilled at this and thought I'd never use Rizla cigarette papers again. As I smoked, I put in order the day's events. I realised that I was in a situation that could overtake me and I felt a little panic rise in me again. All of a sudden I jumped up out of the sleeping bag. "I don't give a shit about this fucking road. It ain't getting me!" I shouted at the desert and, copying *Papillon* as he floated across shark-leaden waters on a sack of coconuts, tied together with grass, "I'm still here, you bastards and you ain't gonna beat me." I even shook my fist in a most dramatic way. The gesture seemed to fill me with new life, like I'd just been born again. By God I felt alive!

I slept well under the circumstances and woke just as it was getting light. It was cold but I managed to kick the fire back to life and get some water on for a cup of coffee.

I had an eight-track cartridge tape of the Moody Blues so I put it on. It lifted me a bit and I was determined to get to the docks and back to Tehran and see the family again. I will not be beaten. It's funny how a sound or smell can take you, instantly back to the time you experienced them.

To this day, when I hear the Moody Blues I swear I can smell the desert, the tarmac and the diesel.

I found that the next town was some five hundred and fifty kilometres distant. There would be the odd filling station and truck-stop but there wasn't much between here and there. I dipped the oil and checked the fuel, tyres and brake lines between cab and trailer. Everything seemed ok so I climbed in and turned the keys to start. Nothing!

Nothing but a dull thud from a sick starter motor that was connected to dying batteries. I'd been driving for a couple of straight days now and if those batteries weren't fully charged by now, then they never would be. They were finished, big time! This was probably happening because all of a sudden they were being asked to work hard.

I immediately glanced at the air gauges. The air tanks were full, thank goodness. It meant that I had enough air to blow the brakes off. This is a feature of all modern trucks, you had springs of two ton force pressing the brakes 'on', on each wheel. These springs had to be blown off by air pressure, before the truck would move. Hence you had the 'fail safe' situation. If for any reason you lost your air pressure, while driving, the springs would force the brakes to operate and bring you to a halt. Not only did I have enough air but there was enough of a slope toward the road to get a run and maybe 'bump start' it. I put it in second gear and knew that I'd only get one chance at this so I'd better get it right. I let off the parking brake and it slowly started to roll forward. I let it build up speed till the last moment. I let the clutch out and it started after half a turn of the motor. I hit the brakes and clutch simultaneously and bounced to a halt half a meter from the road! I pulled onto the road and drove for the next couple of hours.

I eventually came to a village where the road just ended. It was dust for several miles without any signs or directions. I came to a point where the road forked. The tyre marks gave no clue as there was an equal amount right and left. I sat with my map. It had place names in English as well as Pharsi. I sat there looking at the only signpost, I tried to match up the squiggles on the sign, to the squiggles on my map! I was sure I had to keep right here.

"Where are you going?" The accent was heavy but, yes! That was English! I looked around to see a smiling local young man in jeans and sweatshirt with a baseball cap.

"I'm going to Bandar Shahpur to the docks. Dezful, Ahwas, Khorramshahr, down that way."

"You must go to the right here. When you pass five hundred kilometre, you will see many oil drums, very high in air. You must go right here, it will take you to the Dezful Road, the normal road is damaged in many places, it's better to go through the desert."

"Is it safe for the truck?" I asked.

"Yes. All trucks go that way, no problem."

"Your English is excellent, where did you learn?"

He smiled at my words but they weren't flattery, he was good. "I work for an American Drilling Company and I learned English as a boy." It seemed the Americans were spreading their version of the English language wherever they went.

"Thank you for your help, I must go on." I leaned out the cab and shook his hand. I saw him wave in my mirror.

The dirt road led out into the desert. The sand was compacted and hard, pounded down by truck wheels. All I had to do was follow the tracks. A couple of Mack trucks came, snorting, the other way. Their load was forty-foot long steel pipes bound for the oilfields and probably made in the UK They were loaded to about sixty tons, to my eye. Way over what we were allowed in the UK but within the design weight of the trucks. Because of their weight they were sinking deeper into the sand than me. I was empty.

Their engines were growling and their exhaust stacks belched black smoke behind them. The drivers gave me a curt nod as they passed. I nodded back.

This desert driving was a bit of a pain as there was no way I could drive faster than thirty-five miles an hour and the truck was taking a pounding. It was no good, there was nothing for it but to slow right down. To hell with being delayed. Both the truck and I had to stay together if we were to finish the job. I slowed down and for the next four hours I drove as carefully as possible. A couple of times following trucks would come past at full tilt. One white Freightliner came past me at about fifty-five miles an hour. He hit a few ruts in the road and I remember seeing his front and rear axles doing things that they were never meant for. The double drive axles at the rear of the tractor unit smashed into the chassis. At one point the cab was airborne. I'd never seen trucks driven with such dangerous insanity.

I pressed on until darkness. I was not far north of Abbadan. One more day's driving should do it, provided there were no cock-ups down the road. I pulled in at a roadside truck stop. I walked in and all eyes turned to me. *Oh well, brazen it out.* I pulled myself tall and walked in like I owned the place. As I approached the bar I got a few nods. The TV in the corner was making a horrible noise that would have been local music, except that the poor speaker was badly distorted and couldn't cope. It didn't seem to matter to anybody as they were drinking, talking and being generally loud.

With great difficulty I ordered some dinner and a tea. I went out the back to the toilets and wished I hadn't bothered. It was unbelievable. The toilets consisted of the typical closet you'd find east of Istanbul. A large ceramic slab, akin to a shower basin, but with a keyhole shaped hole for you to do the business. There were foot pads each side of the hole and you simply squatted and got on with it. Afterwards, there was no toilet paper but a plastic container and a tap. You held the water behind you and tipped a little, this was done with the right hand. With the left hand you washed the area. That is why, when in a Muslim country, you never eat with the left hand, no matter how much it had been washed, and you never, never, offer your left hand to shake hands It would be considered a gross insult! Primitive, yes, but if done properly, could be much cleaner than using paper.

The state of the toilets I won't go into, in detail. Suffice it to say I nearly didn't eat. However, you have to live and I was starving. *Besides if the locals can eat it I guess I'll survive, just don't think about the state of the kitchens!*

As it turned out, the meal was tasty, the bread fresh, and the spoon and glasses were clean. I leaned back in my chair and was about to light up when a voice asked, "Ver are you g'wing?" I turned to see two young Iranians. One had a pack of Winstons cigarettes and was offering me one. I took it and put the end to the lit match he was holding. I tapped his hand and said, "Kheesh."

This brought big smiles and, "Kheesh, kheesh."

"You are Iranian man," said the cigarette offerer.

"Thank you." I then ran through the few words of Pharsi I'd learned. 'Salam wh'aley coomb' (greeting), 'Hood'afes' (goodbye), 'Shoukrea' (thank you), 'Musta rheem' (straight on), 'garshuk' (spoon), 'Tocklamorg' (egg), etc. The piece de resistance; 'Yek, doh, say, char, pange, shiesh, haft, hasht (careful with that one!), ack, nooh, dah (one, two, three... etc.)'.

They were very impressed and asked what I was doing. I told them I was going to Bandar Shahpur for a load and they seemed impressed and the guy that spoke English translated for his mates. "Ah. Sugar, sugar," said one of the mates holding up cubes from the bowl on the table.

I was tempted to reply, "Ah, honey, honey," but I doubted they knew the old Archies song.

"They will load you with sugar or bananas?"

"Bananas in boxes, in carton like this?" I made a shape with my hands.

"Bali. Yes in carton. Big danger, Bandar Shahpur. Not good place, many bandit. Do not park there in night. You sleeping, bandit come."

Just as I was digesting that little pearl of information, a wrinkled and tanned old man came up to the table he was dressed in some kind of heavy wool trousers with a large woollen shawl reaching to his knees. He wore leather sandals. He had a long staff which he leaned on, in a way that said he'd been doing it this way since he could walk. He greeted the men sat with me and they respectfully greeted him. He pointed toward me and smiled while he talked. When he finished, he gave me a little bow with his hand across his chest. I looked at the young men questioningly, holding out my hand palm up and shaking my head from side to side. "He want you take sheep Ahwaz."

"What? Why?"

"Very poor man. Have no money, farmer no money for truck. Walk with sheep."

"He will walk to Ahwaz?" Some two hundred kilometres to the south and my last stop before Bandar Shahpur. I looked at the man, he seemed to be a poor shepherd.

"How many sheep?" They asked him and if I heard right it was around eighty.

"He have eighty sheep and will fit in truck." He'd obviously done this before and knew how many sheep he could get in an artic.

"Yes OK but we leave as soon as he loads the sheep." They told him this and he was so pleased he grabbed my hand with his and shook hard.

The young drivers were very pleased that I had said yes. "You make open truck. He will put sheep here."

I realised he had singled me out because I had an enclosed trailer. Most of all the other trucks were flat-beds and totally useless for containing sheep. We all went out to my truck and I dropped the tail board of the trailer. I wasn't sure how he would get the sheep in there but that was up to him.

"Volvo good yes?" asked one of the drivers.

"Yes very strong."

"I drive Mack conventional," he said proudly. A 'conventional' being an American term for a truck with a bonnet that you lift to get to the engine, rather than the type where the front is flat, these they call 'cab-overs' because you have to tilt the whole cab forward to get to the engine. Cab-overs were a bit rare in Iran so far. They preferred a motor sticking out in front of them as in the conventional. The way they drove, it could be a good thing to have a huge engine in front. To take the smash!

"Too many gear-sticks in a Mack," I said, miming the action needed to change from low gearbox range to high range which, to be done effectively, needed two hands on either of the two gear levers. As we started back into the café I noticed the shepherd had gathered a few assistants and they had a few planks with them. I waved my hand toward the trailer to say carry on. We went back inside and word had spread that I was taking the shepherd to Ahwaz and I wasn't allowed to pay for a thing. Tea, Cokes and everything else was paid for and I never saw a bill before we left. I had shown charity and kindness to a stranger and here, that was a respectable thing to do.

We drove off down the road with the sheep huddled together. The shepherd sat in the passenger seat, smiling broadly. He didn't speak a word of English but we communicated in other ways. At one point he took what looked like a child's wax crayon, out of his robe. It was brown in colour and had a label wrapped around the centre. I mimed not understanding, he made motions as if smoking on a pipe, he grinned and nodded. This got my interest and I said the word, "Hashish?" He 'tutted' and threw his head back, which meant 'no'.

I put it to my nose, the unmistakeable, acrid smell of opium. "Opium?" I asked.

"Opium, opium." It was the same name in any language. He grinned a fairly toothless grin. He broke the brown stick in half and passed it to me. I noticed the label contained the coat of arms of Iran. A lion standing, holding a large broadsword vertically in its paw. I learned later that the government issued these sticks of opium along with the meagre old age pension. I thanked him very much. He'd given me half of what he had but I doubted that I'd ever smoke it. *I'll take it back for Black Bob, he'll appreciate it.*

We travelled on in the heat of the afternoon, every window and the roof-light open. The tarmac was running in waves down the hills where the sun had softened it. I came around some rocks to be greeted by the sight of a Mack truck on its side along the side of the road. The driver and his mate had escaped through the windscreen aperture, and were sat having their lunch in the shade of the rocks with a black cloud over them. The other trucks just drove around the wreck and a little detour into the sand was being hammered down by traffic. I carried on for a hundred or so kilometres and stopped at a truck stop to fill up and eat something. As I got out the cab I noticed that the shepherd was staying put. I looked at him and waved to the café.

"C'mon let's eat something and have tea." I did all the motions with my hands. He shook his head and grabbed his shawl. If I was reading him right he was saying he was not dressed for this place and had no money anyway. This was not the time for tact. I showed him some money and said, "No problem. You are my guest." I put my hand on my chest. "You understand?" I realised he didn't, of course, so I just smiled and repeated, "Come, come."

He got down and I locked the cab, we went inside and sure enough, all eyes turned at the sight of a westerner with a local shepherd in tow. What kind of sight I made to them, I can only guess at. I wore only cut-off denim shorts, not very short but I had only seen one or two men in Tehran wearing shorts. It was considered low cast to wear them but I didn't give a shit, I just wanted to stay as cool as possible in the desert heat. I wore a shirt, of course and a pair of plastic flip-flops.

The waiter came over and was staring at the shepherd and me with equal surprise. I motioned to the shepherd to tell the waiter what he wanted. He made a detailed order and before I could order, the waiter turned to go. I went to tell him he'd forgotten me, when the shepherd grabbed my arm and said something. He tapped his place on the table then mine, and he sipped from an imaginary glass. I realised he had ordered for both of us, including the teas. I looked at his weather-beaten wrinkled old face and wondered what sort of life he'd had. It was sure different to my privileged upbringing, even if mine was in a relatively poor, East End family. At least we had the National Health and a Social Security system. Here you worked or starved. I warmed to this man. There was no bullshit about him. We had a great meal beginning with some spicy bean soup with loads of barbari bread followed by 'chello mourge' which was chicken and boiled rice with green peppers and a dish of black olives. With a pot of tea and bowl of sugar lumps, it cost me all of two pounds, fifty pence including a pack of Winstons!

I looked at my map as we dined. I realised we'd made good progress. I could drop the sheep in Ahwaz and make the port before midnight. I remembered Jensen telling me that they load, day and night, until the particular ship is completely unloaded.

I decided that I would drive in the dark and get to the port. I still had the battery problem to overcome and better to do it there, than in the middle of the desert! I managed to get the waiter to tell me how many kilometres to the port. It was about two hundred and fifty. I also asked the shepherd to indicate on the map where he wanted dropping. He looked at me, puzzled.

I called the waiter over again and with great difficulty and much laughing, I asked him to find out where the sheep were to be dropped and point to it on the map. The shepherd couldn't read or write and I felt embarrassed at showing him up, but he was not. He'd had no education other than how to count sheep and use pebbles to remember how many in the herd. By now a little group of curious drivers had crowded round the table and were discussing, animatedly, what it was that the stranger wanted. There was no other way than to go outside and show them the sheep. This I did and the whole group, and now a couple of waiters as well, came out into the truck park.

I mimed unloading the sheep then pointed to Ahwaz on the map and spread my hands, as if asking a question.

"Le marché, marché, dans le centre-ville," said one driver. He spoke good French, far better than me, in fact.

"Ah! Moisure, s'il vous plait, indicate le point de decharge dan le carta."

"Oui, dans le centre-ville. Gross aire du animaux, no problem pour le camion," he said.

"Thank you so much," I said, and gave a little nod

toward the crowd with my hand across my chest. They all smiled and nodded back.

"Where are you going, English?" shouted a voice from the back of the group. A large man in Levis and sneakers came forward and extended his hand. His name was Ronni, a nickname given to him by the Americans at Bell Helicopters in Isfahan, for whom he worked, running wooden crates of helicopter parts imported into the country through Bandar Shapoor. He drove a vintage Kenworth, with chrome stacks and wheel trims. It looked like a classic American truck out of some early sixties road movie! Unfortunately, he was headed north this time, otherwise I would have followed him to the docks and used him as interpreter. Nevertheless, I figured that a half hour's investment in a cup of tea with him would be a good idea. I asked him to tell the shepherd that I was going to have a cup of tea and I'd be out soon and then I would take him to the sheep market in Ahwaz. He said he would check over his sheep and then come inside.

"So how do I get to the loading area at the docks?" I asked Ronni.

"Simple. Just go as far as you can on the main drag. You'll see a huge area on your right full of brand new truck units and Caterpillar 'dozers and stuff. There's row on row waiting to be shipped into the country, only they haven't got enough people to move it, so there it sits, rotting away in the sea air! When you see the second area like this you will see a big fountain in the square. The main dock's office is right there, you can't miss it, just follow other drivers because they all report there.

"How long will I have to wait to load?"

"They'll load you as soon as you arrive if you want but I expect you'll have to wait in line. There's usually a queue of about twenty trucks waiting. It won't take too long, they work day and night."

"OK sounds alright. The other problem I've got is my batteries. They aren't holding their charge and I have to park on a slope overnight."

"That sounds like big problem for you," said Ronni. "You don't want to get caught in the desert like that. Do you have money?"

"Yeah, some. How much will it cost for new batteries do you reckon?"

"You can get re-built batteries for about three thousand rials, the pair. Or brand new ones will cost about five thousand," said Ronni.

I did some quick mental calculations and worked out that I could afford that, and I'd be glad to pay it just to get rid of the nagging uncertainty about being able to start the engine every time.

"When you are loaded, go to this place in Ahwaz." Ronni handed me a piece of paper with the address of an auto electricians place. It was written in English and Pharsi. Ronni had also written a little intro to his mate, the electrician. "I tell him you are friend of me. He will look after you, especial." (Every English word that began with 'S' was pronounced as 'es', i.e. 'E'student', 'e'speak', 'e'straight' etc., etc.)

"Thanks, I think I've got enough for that. It'll be a weight off my mind."

"To drive this road without a first class truck is asking for trouble, English."

How right he was. I decided to spend the money and Jensen would have to pay for it. You can't run a truck with duff batteries, it was stupid. I chatted with Ronni for another glass of tea and picked up some good information. Forewarned is forearmed!

Eventually I got back on the road, headed for Ahwaz sheep market. As we got close to the city, the shepherd saw some of his friends alongside the road. He pointed, animatedly to the air horn chain just above my right shoulder and made the motion of pulling the chain. I grabbed the chain and yanked it hard. There was a loud blast from above the cab, loud enough to wake the dead. It even made me jump, and I was expecting it!

I slowed a little and the shepherd shouted something in Pharsi and the walkers turned and waved. The shepherd asked me to stop, which I did and several of his friends and relations climbed onto the trailer. We drove into the sheep market like a carnival float, with people hanging off the truck, shouting and greeting everyone they knew. A couple of six-wheel rigids were quickly shifted out of the way so that I could back onto the unloading bay ,which was a concrete pier protected by many old tyres hung along its length.

I didn't make too bad a job of getting the trailer where I wanted it, seeing as how this was the first time I'd done it in anger. When all the fuss of unloading the sheep was dying down the shepherd came over to me with a young lad in tow. He said something to the lad who turned to me and spoke with broken English. "He want you come house. Eat, sleep."

"That's very kind but I must go to Bandar Shapoor before dark."

"My uncle say, you save him much money and much problem for his feet." The shepherd grabbed my hand and shook it like mad. He couldn't thank me enough. He reached into his shawl and from somewhere, drew out a small, beautifully decorated opium pipe. He gave it to me and I examined it closely. It really was a work of art. The delicate blue enamel contrasting with white lattice work , all edged in thin gold wire.

"It's beautiful," I said passing it back to him.

"No, no!" said the young lad. "He gives you this."

I was gobsmacked! "I can't take this from him."

"He want you have this. When you smoke you think of him." He looked at me and I knew if I refused it any further he would be offended.

"It's beautiful. I'll keep it until I see him again. OK? Thank you so much."

They all smiled at this. I climbed into the cab, put it in gear and moved off with a blast on the air horn. I heard many versions of 'goodbye' as I pulled out of the marketplace.

I still have that opium pipe tucked away in a box somewhere for my grandchildren to find, perhaps, when I'm gone. I wonder if hearing the story will move them to travel? It's the only life and highly addictive as, even after all these years, the urge for travel and adventure, is even stronger.

Let's see. A life of going in and out the factory gate for forty years, or something new every day? No competition!

I knocked off the last couple of hundred clicks as it got dark. It was easy to find the docks, the road went directly to the port gates and sure enough, the parking areas for the imported trucks and oilfield equipment were vast. There were row on row, not five or ten rows, but hundreds of rows that were about twenty vehicles deep, of brand new Mack, White, Kenworth, Peterbuilt, and Volvos. Lines and lines of Scania fire tenders, Mercedes buses, and specialist oilfield drilling vehicles. Many of the brand new trucks still had factory inspection stickers in their windscreens.

It really was an amazing sight and I had to pull over to let it sink in. As I looked, I could see the rows of trucks nearest the road had been vandalised. There were broken windscreens, flat, brand new tyres and smashed headlamps. It was painful to look at, even some of the large glass screens on the Caterpillar earth movers were smashed, and everything, and I mean everything, was covered with a thick layer of dust. Brand new equipment and heavy dust just don't look right together. I'd never seen quantities of trucks and equipment like this. There were acres and acres as far as the eye could see out into the desert. I couldn't see the full extent as the sun was well down and the last remnants of light were nearly gone. I was truly amazed. I can remember thinking that at least they wouldn't have trouble with rust, it was so dry here.

I pulled on down through the dock gates and parked right outside the large office complex. I found the despatch office which was a large, open space area with complete chaos going on inside. Fans were spinning, top speed, overhead and it was a hubbub of noise with paper everywhere. After their surprise at seeing me, I managed to make myself understood, with the help of twenty or so local truck drivers.

"I am loading for Tehran," I said as clearly as possible. "Je charge le camion pour Tehran."

It took an hour or so to sort the paperwork out, so I told them I would return in one hour to pick up the papers, meanwhile I just wanted to get out of the stifling office building with its faint whiff of sweat and open sewers.

I had noted as I drove in, that there was a communal wash place over by the fountain which was flowing invitingly. All I wanted to do at that point was duck my head under it and wash off the dirt and sweat of the last few days. It was dark and there was a place you could stand behind to have a scrub down so I locked the cab, sauntered over and stood under the clear cool water – it was wonderful. I went behind the wall and shed the shorts as well. I was soaping up when I noticed a bunch of men watching me and giggling like school girls. Even in the company of other men, in a washroom environment, they never went naked. I just carried on, if they wanted to act like children because of their oppressive, religious upbringing, I wasn't going to let it bother me, I was going to be clean and fresh in this dirty, heavily polluted area of the Gulf.

I felt wonderful as I walked back to the cab, clean and cool. I ordered a tea from a young boy who made a few rials by running around the parked trucks and labourers. By now many trucks had gathered and it looked as if it was going to be a free-for-all when the ship unloading started. I sauntered back to the office well inside the hour. I thought I'd be fairly well up the queue. By a happy coincidence, just as I walked in the room, the clerks were just handing out loading papers. The man that I dealt with earlier handed me a form, filled out and printed in Pharsi. He waved me to follow the bunch of drivers who had also decided to come to the office early.

We started to run down the stairs, a sense of urgency now in the air. The feeling was heightened by the appearance of, not so early drivers, running upstairs. The scene now resembled early film of the Le Mans twenty-four hour race where the drivers have to run for their cars and pull away as quick as possible. This time it was with trucks!

It was absolute mayhem within minutes. Dust and scrabbling trucks, headlights everywhere, no order no restraint, no view to safety. It was a repeat of the attitude out on the road. I figured the only way to get anywhere was to drive exactly as they do, only even more so! I had left the engine running all the time, not something I'd normally do. Diesels don't like ticking over for repeated long terms. Not only does it tend to overheat but it gums up the piston rings with sludge and varnish which, in turn causes it to burn excess oil, loss of compression etc., etc.

I drove like one possessed and forced my way into the queue not too far from the front. There was much snarling and fist shaking which I countered with laughing at them. They just couldn't keep a straight face at this hairy foreigner, poking fun at them, not only that but to admit to being angered by another was to totally uncool in Iranian macho society.

Only once, was I ever about to strike in self-defence. It was in a fuel stop. A driver tried to jump in before me and didn't like it when I stopped him from doing so. I had reached the point where the red mist had fallen down my eyes. I stood in front of his truck and gesticulated to him to fuck off and kiss my arse.

He took exception to this, of course. This foreigner challenging him in front of his countrymen, definitely not on, he couldn't back down. He got out his cab and I saw he was about the same size as me. Everything I'd been taught in the army, went through my mind. To fell any sized man, a simple chop to the nerve that runs up the side of the neck and he will go down like a sack of shit. The other thing I recalled was the words of a Special Forces instructor I'd had the privilege of meeting. "Doesn't matter how big or small you are, the first thing to do is to run at your opponent, screaming and shouting and making as much noise as possible. Just as in nature, make yourself appear as big as possible. I guarantee you that, whoever your opponent, he will be startled by this huge, screaming maniac running at him."

I ran straight at the driver before he could take too many steps! I don't know what I was thinking. Truth was, I wasn't thinking about anything but dropping this twat who was threatening violence to me. I had it in mind to hit that nerve and hope he went down. I figured if I could hold off his blows long enough to get in close and drop him. I hadn't figured what his mates would do if that happened but logic wasn't strong at that point.

I saw his eyes widen and he deflated, turned on his heel and actually ran for his cab. I felt elated and stood in front of his cab and raged at him. "You wanna kill me?" I shouted and thumped my chest like some demented gorilla. "Wait till we get on the road you can try with your truck, you camel shagging motherfucker. I'll rip out yer lungs and gob down yer fuckin' neck."

You'll gather from this that I was 'gone'! I threw every insult that I could think of, then in inspiration, I held my little finger in a position that mimicked a small penis and began masturbating the finger and pointing at him. This had two effects. One, it dissipated my fury. Two, it caused every driver within my sight to fall about in steering wheel-slapping mirth. They couldn't help giggling like schoolgirls at any reference to anything remotely sexual. My opponent took a little heart from this and saved a little face by the fact that he'd got me angry. I felt a hand gently on my arm. I turned very quickly to see the pump attendant who jumped physically as I turned.

"Mister, mister," he said, pointing at the pumps. I realised that our confrontation had blocked one line of pumps.

By now, my anger had subsided so I decided to indicate that I was only pissed off with that driver and not everyone else. "Excuse me," I said with a little nod and my hand on my heart. "This man is an idiot," I said, patting my backside and pointing to him. He was staying quiet behind his wheel. As we walked back to the pumps I placed my hand on the attendant's shoulder and said, "No problem, mister, no problem."

I sat in the restaurant glaring in post-anger fallout. I was happy that come to it, I was prepared to defend myself but deeply disturbed that I'd been driven to contemplate using a move that if over-applied could have killed, or, under-applied would leave me open for further attack.

In the restaurant I suddenly realised that several tables were watching me. As I looked up they nodded at me so I returned a little nod, not ready yet to give way to a smile. I noticed a few drivers tapped my table as they went by. I looked at one guy and made the gesture of questioning him. He drew his left hand up his arse and pointed toward my opponent driver who was skulking with a couple of his mates in the corner. I gathered from this that the other guy wasn't too popular around here anyway.

Apart from this episode I usually adopted the local habit of laughing at anyone who got angry.

Back to the docks. I was pretty certain that the Mack I was following was driven by one of the guys in the office, whom I was told to follow, but I couldn't be sure. We headed along the quayside, nose to tail. It was very slow going and now totally dark. I had turned on the lights which immediately renewed my resolve to get the electrics sorted, because they were useless! They were working but very dim. When you revved the engine they became bright – classic symptom of knackered batteries. An hour or so went by. We were now nose to tail and getting nowhere. Suddenly there was activity in front and engines were starting. We started moving, I had to follow there was nowhere else to go. Is this the right queue? Should I be following blindly? These doubts, and others, paled to insignificance when I realised we were now driving out on a causeway made of railway timbers over steel frames, just like a pier at the seaside, only this went on for a mile and a half out into the water!

The causeway was about as wide as a country lane. There were no edge markings nor anything to stop you putting a wheel over the side! My bottle was getting decidedly shattered and I decided to lean out the window to check the position. I wished I hadn't done so. I looked down to see the dark and boiling water some twenty feet below! Strips of sleepers were missing, here and there, and we were driving over this!

By now, we were about a mile out and I was very scared. I had to sit there and calm myself down, keep reminding myself that if they could do it, so could I, but I sure wished I hadn't had that smoke of hash an hour ago! "If these guys can do it, I can do it, after all, it's not as if there are any corners. It's just a matter of sitting tight and keeping the wheels straight and follow closely the guy in front." So went the mantra. There were no lights along the causeway, another reason to stick to the guy in front. My lights were useless.

By now it was well past midnight and there was no sign of where we were going, so there I sat, in a line of vehicles suspended above the water by, it seemed, sheer will power and over a mile out to sea. Will the causeway take the weight of hundreds of nose to tail trucks? Everything will be alright, insha'Allah! I nodded off as the throbbing engines around me went nowhere.

I was jolted awake by an air horn from behind. I was startled and for a few moments couldn't remember what I was doing there. I got it together and noticed that the truck in front had moved a few hundred yards. I couldn't see bugger all in front so I had to steer by looking out the window at the edge of the boards. I again swore to get those batteries fixed.

A couple more hours went by and I could now see where we were going. A massive floating pontoon with big cranes and floodlights. The whole area was the size of four football pitches and several ships were moored along the four sides. Many trucks were being loaded straight off the ships, by hundreds of labourers. Groups of loaders were sat around having tea while others worked and even more, slept in make shift shelters in one corner of the pontoon. These workers would stay on the pontoon day and night until there were no more ships to unload, which rarely happened, seeing as how ships of all nations and super tankers, waiting to come into the p ort and unload, were backed up all the way down the Persian Gulf.

I could see that, once loaded, you had to do a U-turn and drive back to shore on another causeway. By the time

I was being loaded, it was about two in the morning. The man in charge of loading spoke a little English. "Mister, you must pay men. They have little wages. You pay OK?" It was normal to pay the labourers a good tip. It ensured a lack of problems when loading. I didn't know this at the time and thought the guy was trying to get money from me. If it really was for the blokes doing the work then it was worth being remembered as the generous Englishman.

"No problem," I said. "I will give it to them myself. How much do they get for a truck?"

"You must give two hundred to each man and two hundred to me." I looked at him and he back at me. I judged there was no malice there and a few quid would make everyone's life easier.

I went to the trailer and gave each man three hundred rials and after their surprise at seeing me, they gratefully took the money. They were dressed in shorts and T-shirts. They had rough sacks used like a hood to protect their backs, heads and shoulders. They were covered in sugar and other dust of other cargos. There were no washing facilities out here.

I went back to see the man in charge. "I am having trouble with my batteries. I cannot stop the engine or I will not be able to start it again. If you can let me stay where I am, I can leave the engine running while I sleep until it is light. Is that OK?" I asked, as I slid a five hundred rial note out of my wallet. And I'd like a pot of tea from the boy at first light OK?"

"No problem m'sure." He grinned a toothy grin as he took the note. "You go cabin, sleep. We make banana in back do everything, m'sure, no problem."

Well that seemed to work, I thought to myself, as I headed for the cab and the bunk. I was really tired and I doubted I'd get much sleep with the engine ticking over, but I was going to try.

After what seemed like two seconds I awoke to a hammering on the passenger door.

"What?" I shouted.

"Mister, mister, tea," came a small voice from outside. I started to say I wanted tea at dawn but as I stuck my head out of the curtains I saw that the first rays of the sun were showing to the east.

The shock on the boy's face when I opened the door was funny to see. Where was the steering wheel? He was looking around with wide eyes. I pointed to the other side and waved my arm for him to go round. I wriggled into the driver's seat and opened the door. The boy had obviously not seen a right-hand drive truck before and he was fascinated. I let him climb up and have a look around. He passed me a tray of tea in a chrome teapot. It was steaming hot with a bowlful of cubes. He climbed into the passenger seat and rolled down the window. He spoke, importantly, to his friends who were now equally as fascinated that there was no steering wheel there.

As I fought myself fully awake I watched the scene outside. The tea-boy had climbed down, waved me goodbye and plied his trade with a fresh tray of tea made from a samovar, boiling away in the camp area. Sacks of sugar were being unloaded onto trucks. I was glad my load wasn't sugar. It was messy, sticky stuff and although in sacks, it got everywhere! The last thing you needed in this heat was more stickiness. I watched as labourers got up, and started to work. Another day in hell as far as I was concerned. Just living and working on that pontoon day in, day out, competing with others just to get poorly paid work. I felt with all my senses, how lucky I was.

I noted that the engine temperature had risen quite a bit because of the hours it had been idling. It had used a bit of fuel too but at approximately twenty pence per litre, it wasn't too important. While I was inspecting the load, the loading boss came across.

"All OK English, good sleeping?" he asked.

"A few more hours sleep would be good, but I must go soon. Do you have my paper?"

"Bali, I make sign here. You take office they give paper for cold store in Tehran." He held out the papers.

"What is your name?" I asked him.

"My name is Mohamed Rafni. I am loading boss, pontoon number three," he said proudly.

"My name is Alun. I will see you again Mohamed Rafni. Insha'Allah."

"Insha'Allah, Alun Dillon," he grinned.

I turned and waved to the other loaders, now taking a break. They all waved back and I felt that they would remember me next time.

I pulled a U-turn on the dock and headed for the exit causeway. There were many trucks waiting to be loaded but not so many on the exit causeway. It was in the same condition as the entry one and at one point my front tyre was caught in a rut formed by a missing timber. I just kept going, holding the steering wheel for all I was worth, and felt the truck trying to steer out of the rut but not having much success. I gunned the engine and at last it came out of the rut and normal steering resumed but not before the inertia of coming out of it sent me nearer the edge than I wanted to be. When I leaned out the window I saw only water!

With my heart in my mouth, I edged back into what I thought to be the middle of the wooden deck. I had no look-down mirror on the passenger side. This mirror shows you your front, near side, wheel and is needed for idiot car drivers that come in on your blind side and attempt to muscle their way in, thinking that you have seen them and will be forced to let them through. That, and brain-dead bike riders, who come up on your inside at traffic lights and junctions, expecting you to see them through the steel of the cab. With my heart hammering I drove on and managed to get back into the centre of the causeway. After a mile or so like this, I turned onto the dockside, never more glad to be on solid ground!

As I was able to drive a little faster around the docks, I noticed the weight of the trailer. It was well loaded to about thirty-eight to forty tons I guessed. As we got paid by weight as well as mileage, I didn't care too much. The Gross Design Train Weight was sixty tons, and I was nowhere near that.

I pulled up outside the office. As I locked the cab, I noticed a very large load moving out the dock gates. It was a double drive, Mack conventional. It was a top-of-the-line, heavy tractor unit. It looked stunning, with its huge chrome front bumper, chrome exhaust stacks and a front grill a mile wide. It was coupled to a special length, low loader trailer. The load on the back was a steel bridge structure about twenty feet high, and about forty-five feet long. I guessed it weighed around a hundred tons. It was secured by three steel cables with turn-buckles and shackles to each side of the trailer. It was a massive load by anybody's standards and the huge twin turbo, V12 engine made a beautiful roar of power as the driver stepped on the 'loud' pedal. He had everyone looking at him and he made the most of it with all the revolving beacons and flashing red lights, he and his mate were loving it.

He took the first corner with reckless abandon, trying to keep up the inertia. I was sure I saw the steel structure sway and move. I can remember thinking I'd have used a few load chains as well as just three steel cables and I'd be doing it a bit slower, that was a serious toy they had there. It never occurred to me that they had stepped right off the mountain farm and into some of the biggest road transport vehicles then available, with zero training and no licences!

I got inside the still chaotic office. The fans were at top speed and all the windows open.

"Hey English!" I looked round to see a middle aged man in white shirt and Dr Kissinger glasses. He waved me over. "I have your papers here." He spoke excellent English.

"Thank you. Your English is excellent, where did you learn?"

"I went to the London School of Economics. I had a flat in New Cross for about seven years then I moved to Gloucester for a couple of years. When the boom started here I took a job for British ex-pats and here I am. Here they consider me an ex-pat Brit and pay me higher wages but I was born in Ahwaz and now I live here again."

"Well you certainly have the right job," I said, looking around the sumptuous office with the air conditioner in the window.

"Yes I'm actually in charge of the whole docks, nothing goes out that gate without my say-so," he grinned.

"I suppose that was your roller parked outside the door," I joked.

"Actually, that and the yellow Maserati parked down the row."

He was serious and I suddenly realised that fact.

"Wow! You must be doing very well indeed. I don't blame you, I'd get a few cars myself."

"What would you have?" he asked.

"I'd start with an original Ford GT40, an Aston Martin DB6 Zagatto, a 'Boss' Mustang 350, à la 'Bullit.'"

"That's about a million pounds' worth so far, if you can find them."

We talked for an hour or so about cars and life in Iran.

He didn't like the way the religious Mullahs were gaining influence in the southern part of the country.

"I suppose you'll be visiting the brothel at Ahwaz on your way back?"

"You're joking. I've never paid for it in my life," I boasted.

"Besides I thought that wouldn't be allowed in a Moslem country."

"There are many things not allowed but we are far from Tehran, here. There is lots of money to be made and many ways to spend it."

I had noticed a walled off complex of buildings just south of Ahwaz and wondered why so many men were walking down the highway towards it at about four in the afternoon.

The complex was in the middle of nowhere but there were many cars parked there. It turns out that about twelve women of differing nationalities, Armenian, Russian, Turkish, African, but no Iranian, keep the local males serviced on an industrial scale. The males rarely see females, except under cover of a black veil, so all that pent up sexual frustration could be relieved, with a high turn around rate! It seemed all the males from Ahwaz city were headed that way.

"When I come back here again is there anything I can bring you from Tehran?" I thought a little greasing the palm wouldn't hurt.

"Scotch, preferably single malt Glefidich or Jack Daniels, you can buy it here but it is forbidden, so it's expensive and probably watered down."

"No problem. I've got a contact in the American Embassy, P.X. supply corps, they get everything there." I said goodbye, feeling that I'd made a friend of the docks manager.

I decided to push on and get a few miles down. I filled up with diesel at the station just outside the gates. The next stop would be Ahwaz auto electrician to sort those batteries once and for all. I arrived at the electricians around midday. He set to work removing the old batteries and when he had them disconnected he applied the Pharsi equivalent of a heavy discharge tester, i.e. a piece of heavy cable to slap across the terminals – you wouldn't find much heavier a test than that. There were sparks and crackling, as batteries don't take this punishment for very long before the electrolyte begins to gas and boil, a sure sign that the batteries are useless. The electrician showed me some new batteries and some that had been reconditioned. We walked into the workshop and I watched in horror as the young lads emptied old batteries of their electrolyte. This electrolyte consisted of a mix of sulphuric acid and water and could eat away at anything it touched, including human skin.

The boys wore no protective clothing and it was almost impossible not to get splashes of acid over everything. I often think of those lads working away with only a vague idea of what sulphuric acid could do to their skin. I wonder if they are now disfigured because of their early work. Halfway through the repairs the electrician came to me with a very worn out alternator that he had removed. This is the generator that recharges the batteries when the engine is turning.

"Problem, mister. Kaput," he said, as he handed me the offending part. I put the alternator to my nose and sure enough the smell of overheated insulation was tell-tale. The electrician showed me four brand new, Exide batteries and showed me two alternators. One was brand new and the other rebuilt. I was having none of the rebuilt stuff and told him to fit all new equipment. I just about had enough money to cover this but it meant I would have little money for diesel. There was no way I was going any farther without everything working properly so I would have to get Jensen to send me some more money, somehow. How, I wasn't too sure at that moment but I'd do it somehow.

I paid the electrician. It cost me all of two hundred quid for two brand new batteries and a new alternator, all fitted for me, while I drank lemon tea in the shade. It would've been more like five hundred in the UK The best bit was when we came to tally up the bill. I was surprised and fascinated when he brought out an abacus and started to flip beads back and forth. He did the calculations as quick as an electronic calculator of the time. They were in their infancy and still quite bulky.

Within seconds he arrived at the total which I counted over to him. I then went into the workshop and gave each worker a one hundred rial note which had the effect of giving them a week's wages, as a tip. "Buy gloves. This is dangerous. You must not touch this water." I pointed to the cells of a battery. "You must buy gloves, aprons and proper boots," I said to the electrician.

"No problem," he said, indicating buckets and tubs of filthy water placed around the workshop. These were presumably the Middle Eastern equivalent of the emergency showers installed at chemical works in the UK. If you accidentally got splashed with acid you dashed to the nearest outlet, pulled the red handle and would be instantly, dowsed with a thousand gallons of water, to dilute the chemical before it could do any harm.

I realised as I spoke that I was telling them what they already knew. They'd managed so far, before I came along and they'd continue after I'd gone but did they know that sulphuric acid can eat away under the skin, even after washing? Years later, deformations of the outer epidermis would result. It is not hard to imagine what a tiny speck of bubble could do to your eye! They were filling cells from large brown bottles of acid with no protection at all. Nightmare stuff. I still shudder at the thought of what could happen under those conditions.

I spent the next few hours stopping the engine at every opportunity just to be able to start it without any problems. I switched on the headlights and couldn't wait until nightfall to see how good they were. I was just driving into the mountains thinking I'd stop at a town called Andimeshk. It looked quite large on the map and would therefore have a decent PTT office from which to call Jensen to tell him I needed more money. I knew that Korean drivers from the yard were up and down the road and maybe it'd be possible...

I suddenly came across another surreal scene of complete carnage. I was already in low gear as I was coming down a gentle mountain slope. To my left was a drop of many hundred feet to my right, a rock face of gargantuan proportions. The road had been blasted out of the side of the mountain. They had also tunnelled through solid rock where necessary, forming short tunnels here and there along the route. Unfortunately the driver of the large bridge section that I had seen leaving the docks, earlier, had failed to take into account that his load was higher than the rock roof and had slammed the steelwork into the roof of the first of these tunnel sections, at around 60kph. Why would it even enter his head? There was no training, even for the biggest of trucks. You simply got in and drove, even if your last mode of transport was a donkey!

Hitting the roof at about fifty miles an hour had thrown both the driver and his mate through the windscreen and up against the rocks like flies against a windscreen. They lay dead in broken and leaking heaps in the road. The trailer had ripped its way free from the cab and taken out a large Mercedes car as it carried on toward the precipice. The steel beam had snapped the steel cables like cotton and had fallen across the rear end of a bus. On its way, it had gouged a trench a couple of feet deep, wiping out a couple of cars as it went.

It hadn't long happened and I was the first on the scene. I remember that unreal quality of huge objects being thrown where they shouldn't be. The dust and smoke and fractured rock were still falling around squealing metal as I arrived. There was screaming and crying as it was realised what had happened. I pulled over to the side well before the site of the accident and well in view of all vehicles coming down the road. I left all the lights on and the hazard lights flashing (thank God I'd had the batteries done).

I approached the body of both the driver and his mate. I won't go into detail but it was obvious that they were dead and no mistake! I looked around to see the saloon car was full of injured people and it was now on fire.

To this day, I remember the look of terror on the young girl's face as she tried to open the door from the inside. Most of the people inside were injured and semi-conscious. She was covered in blood from her mother who'd been sat beside her in the car.

I can remember thinking that the flames were coming from under the mangled bonnet. At *least there's time to get them out before it gets to the tank at the rear.* I lunged for the rear door handle and with superhuman strength, borne of panic, I wrenched the door open. The people fell out and it was then I could see why the girl was covered in blood. An artery was severed in her mother's arm and claret was leaking everywhere. I remembered from the first aid training in the army that you must apply pressure to where the artery crosses the bone i.e. the 'pressure point'. I grabbed the mother under the arm that was broken and smashed, and squeezed as hard as I dared. The sight of all that blood was less of a shock after what I'd seen in the last couple of days but even so, I had to breathe deeply and force myself to concentrate. It worked like a tap! The blood stopped, much to my amazement. Thank you British Army training!

There were moans coming from the front seat and the young girl, now out of the car was screaming and pointing at the fire which had grown bigger. I grabbed the girl as best I could and made to drag her mother away from the car. She understood and began to tug at her mother's unconscious body. We got her away from the car and I calmed her down by shouting into her face.

She stopped her hysteria and watched as I showed her how to apply pressure to her mum's arm. As I ran back to the car I noticed some other cars and trucks had arrived. "Mister! Mister!" I shouted at the top of my lungs. I must have looked like the walking injured as I was well splattered in blood. Several men came from the cars toward me and then saw the blazing car. By now I'd managed to get the front door open and was dragging the driver and his passenger out. They were injured but conscious. Between us we pulled the rest of the passengers out of the car and away from the burning fuel. I remembered the bus had been crushed and pre pared for the worst as I ran, now on pure adrenalin, to the entrance. The driver, it turned out had just dropped most of his passengers at the last town. It was a company bus running the workers home and, insha'Allah, was almost empty except for the last few passengers, sat at the front. There were a few injuries from being thrown around but no one died on that bus. Talk about luck! I went back to see how the young girl and her mother were doing. Her mum was now conscious and in severe pain, and screaming loudly. The girl calmed her down a bit and held on to the pressure point. At least the claret had been stopped. This woman had to get to a hospital soon or she would die that was for sure.

I looked around and there in the queue was a large American-style pick-up. I ran up to the guy driving it who looked like he was in shock himself. "Mister! You must come." I waved him to drive forward. He sat there wide eyed and didn't move. I went up to him and grabbed his shoulder and shook him. It worked. "You must drive this woman to the hospital in Ahwaz or she will die do you understand me? Hospital! Ahwaz, Ahwaz fast, danger d'mort. Vite, vite or she will die." He understood and helped me load the woman and another couple of seriously injured into the back.

"Keep pressure here," I said to the girl, not knowing if she understood. By now the pick-up driver was out of his shock and translating what I was saying to the girl. "Keep pressure here until the doctors says it's OK to let go. To the pick-up driver I said, "Send the ambulances out here as soon as you can if you pass on the road, tell them there is dead and injured here. Tell them to hurry. Now go mister." They drove away and I turned to see some of the other men covering the truck driver and his mate with a shroud. The rest of the car passengers were being treated and I noticed at least a couple of open fractures to arms and legs.

By now the car was burning, fiercely spewing black smoke upwards. All of a sudden there was a *whump* as the fuel caught and blew the tank apart and actually caused me to stumble backwards. I heard the wail of an ambulance in the distance and remember thinking how quickly they had got here. They had been called out from a local area nearby, by chance. They had met the pick-up and one of the crew transferred and accompanied them to the hospital while the ambulance came hell-for-leather to us. As they arrived they were shocked to see a bloodied European directing them to the most seriously injured. They soon forgot their surprise and got to work on the injured.

Unless you have seen the chaos that comes from an emergency in a country like Iran, you cannot appreciate the hysteria that accompanies them. Headless chickens doesn't begin to describe it! I can remember seeing that the medics were on the scene. I walked back to the truck and felt that I must have grown up quick as I could still use my legs! I sat on the tarmac and leaned against the bumper of the truck, I must have passed out as the next thing I remember was a medic lifting me up to the sitting position. "I'm OK I just passed out. Je suis d'accord, no problem." I took a few deep breaths and felt better. Somebody gave me a Coke and I felt better for it as the sugar got into my blood.

"You are good man. Save life of driver and passenger and mother."

"I was first here," I spluttered, and went into a detailed story of how it all came about. I must have talked for ten minutes, babbling as the shock came out.

"Mister you must take truck to Ahwaz, go to hospital," said one of the medics.

"No, I'm fine," I insisted.

I sat in the cab and somebody brought some tea and a pile of sugar cubes. I waited and watched as the mess in front of me was cleared. I don't know how long I sat there in a daze but I suddenly realised that other trucks were manoeuvring around me. This would have brought a cacophony of air horns normally. I got the distinct impression that they didn't want to disturb me.

Eventually I pulled away. As I steered between the wreckage I caught sight of one of the local women. She had stopped what she was doing and placed her arm and hand to her heart and nodded to me, her eyes shining. As I slowly progressed, to my wonder, other men and women did the same thing. I will never forget the looks on their faces and it's one of those moments that will stay with me all of my life. I have tended to forget the horrific side of that night but the fact that I had the opportunity to show that the 'infidel' could be a decent person, is still clear in my memory.

God knows how long I drove into the night. When I did pull up it was beside a large road bridge across a river. I just fell into the bunk, didn't even bother to remove the blood-splattered clothes. I fell into a deep sleep and will gloss over the visions and dreams, borne of sheer horror and exhaustion.

I awoke in the stifling heat to realise I'd parked right beside a wide river running with melted snow from up in the mountains. It was irresistible, that beautiful clear water and the oppressive heat of the semi-desert. I fell out of the cab, shedding clothes as I went. I kept my underpants on – didn't want to frighten the natives, but the only people around were a couple of taxi drivers washing their cabs at the waters edge, nevertheless they were quite curious to see an English truck with the driver hopping and tumbling, as I fled to the water.

I dived in. The wonderful cool water cleared my brain in double quick time I didn't want to surface. I wanted to stay there in the cool where none of last night really happened. I swam to some low rocks and lay partly submerged and stretched out in the sun.

I had taken the soap to the riverside so I swam back feeling alive an in reality again. I washed vigorously as if to scrub away the scenes of yesterday. I sat at the water's edge and brewed up some coffee. I had some bread and cheese which made a great breakfast, after which I made a smoke with some of the hash I'd brought. I realised I'd not smoked for a couple of days, hardly having time to relax, keeping my full wits about me till I was a little less pushed.

It was a wonderful Afghani smoke, bought from a dealer on 'Queen Elizabeth Boulevard' in Tehran city. The boulevard was wide with a central grassed area which formed the banks of a large central water course running the whole length of the road, which was about 2km. The dealer would drive up one carriageway dropping off bits of hash to the lower minions who would sell it to the public. He'd then drive down the other side doing the same.

After the smoke I felt so much more relaxed and

started thinking about moving on. It was then I discovered how much money I had left. I'd spent so much on getting the batteries done that I didn't have enough money to get back to Tehran. I decided to drive to the town of Andimeshk and park outside the PTT office. I could make a call to Jensen from there and it was a good building to rendezvous with one of the Korean drivers who ran up and down to the Gulf ports from Jensen's yard. I arrived outside the PTT in the late afternoon sunshine and managed to book a call to Jensen in the yard and arranged for him to send a thousand rials, about one hundred pounds at the time.

"You sure that's enough, sun?" I heard Jensen shout down the terrible line. "Tell yer what, I'll send two thousand just in case. Alright sun? Just sit tight. You've done really well, just sit there and the driver will find you. He'll be there in two days. Well done mate..." There was a click followed by a dead line. I started to complain but then realised I didn't need to say anything else. I went back out to the truck and started my wait for more money to arrive.

As it turned out, it was to be a very pleasant stay in a town that was very different to the ones I was used to. I'd just finished another smoke when this local lad walked by. "'Ello mister." And then the inevitable, "Vat is your naim?" He obviously didn't expect a reply as he kept walking.

"Hi. My name is Alun. I come from England," I replied quickly. He spun on his heel and came over to talk to me with a big toothy, Arab grin.

"I very little speak English. Learn at school."

"Man Pharsi neece," I replied (I don't speak Pharsi).

He grinned his toothy grin and said, "You speak good Pharsi."

"Haily mam noon." (Polite form of 'thank you'). We

laughed as he struggled on in English and I used what little I'd learned of Pharsi.

"Where is driver?" he asked. From where he stood, he could not see the steering wheel and it turned out he'd never seen a right-hand drive vehicle.

"I am the driver." I replied. He wrinkled his brow. "Come round to the other door." I waved my arm to indicate to him to use what he thought was the driver's door. He opened it and was most shocked to see me sat at the wheel over the other side. His eyes were wide, like a kid's, as he climbed into the passenger seat.

"Ver are you from?" he asked again.

"England, Inglistan."

"Ah, Inglistan. All trucks like this in Inglistan, like this?" he asked, indicating the driver's position.

"Yes. And we drive on the other side of the road."

He looked shocked and asked, "Why you drive on other side? Make big crash!"

"No you don't understand." I started laughing. "We ALL drive on other side there." By the time the last words came out I was wetting myself laughing.

He realised his mistake and started laughing as well.

As we sat talking well into the early evening darkness, I learned that his name was Najeeb and he loved western music and indeed, had a haircut and appearance of Jimi Hendrix. He lived with his mother and five sisters in a rather nice, airy, top floor flat. He didn't mention much about his father, I was to learn why that evening when he took me round to meet his family.

I walked into the main room and was shown some large cushions to sit on. The walls were marble and so cool in the evening heat outside. His sisters, all stunning with their flawless white teeth and jet black hair, fussed about us like humming birds, giggling and talking all the while. I noticed a large picture frame hanging underneath a black lace garland. The picture was turned to the wall.

"What is that?" I asked and pointed to the back-to-front picture, with a smile.

He glanced nervously sideways at his mother and sisters, "Is my father."

"But why turn around the picture?"

"My father is dead and that is what we do when man of family is dead." He made a gesture upward with his eyes. I suddenly realised that I was making a faux pas and all the sisters were silent as they understood from my gestures, what I was talking about.

"Najeeb. I am so sorry. Please tell your mother and sisters that I'm sorry for their loss."

This he did and I watched their faces. His mother turned and addressed me straight on. Najeeb translated the story of how their father had been a truck driver and had been killed in his Mack truck on the very same Gulf Road that ran past the town of Andimeshk.

My blood ran a little cold and I could imagine, very easily, what must have happened to him. As Mother finished speaking, the girls, who had been silent up to now, gave a little titter.

"Mother said it is an honour to give food and have the foreigner from the accident."

The sisters chattered suddenly there was a few gasps and stares at me.

"What are they saying, Najeeb?"

"They are talking big accident."

"You heard about that?" I was surprised.

"Everybody heard. Trucks tell at truck-stop. Factory

workers from autobus tell."

I was surprised, but then everything comes from that road. It was a lifeline of information to the outside world. Mother made another short statement.

"Mother say good to have man in house again." I looked at the sisters that ranged from twelve to twenty. The twenty-year-old was a true Arabian beauty.

I asked why none of his sisters wore the veil and wore make-up.

"Veil is for old people, old people, old in the head, you understand?"

"Yes, please tell your sisters that I think they are very beautiful." He did and they all smiled and laughed. I on the other hand, let my imagination run away with me and I'm sure Mother could read my thoughts. She had a twinkle in her eye.

For the next couple of days Najeeb and I hung around and smoked loads of hash. We hung out under the street lamp in the evenings and at night. We'd get so wrecked that we'd just go to sleep wherever we were. I would usually make it to my bunk in the cab, Najeeb and a couple of his mates would climb on the sacks in the back and just crash in the hot Gulf nights. I got to know these friendly lads quite well while I waited for money to arrive. I often look back to that town and wonder if those lads made it through the Iran/Iraq conflict that lasted almost eight years and killed so many young Iraqis and Iranians.

Some days later I awoke in the hot morning sun to the sound of an air handbrake being applied on a truck that had pulled up opposite me. I recognised the Korean driver and the white Mercedes truck. "I think you are looking for me, yes?"

"You name Alun, I see you help with my friend when hurt foot."

"Oh yes I remember. How is he?" He'd dropped a heavy towing bar on his foot and broken some bones. I put him in my cab and took him to hospital.

"He OK now walk not good but he drive, get pay to send to his family," he smiled.

"I'm glad to hear that. I think you have some money for me, my friend. You have done me a big favour." I didn't know how much he understood but I spoke clearly and a little slowly using as simple words as possible. Unfortunately I'd not learned any Korean except the obvious things like hello, please, and thank you. I told him I would sign a delivery note to say I'd received the cash and he handed me the envelope that contained around two hundred pounds in rials, which considering the price of diesel, was enough to get me to England and back, let alone the thousand or so miles back to Tehran. I took Najeeb and the lads to the local restaurant and bought us all a good breakfast of spicy thick bean soup and fresh barbari bread, just out of the clay oven and delicious.

As we all drank Cokes from bottles with the word 'Coke' in Arabic script, I said my goodbyes and promised to call in the next time I came down to the Gulf. I waved goodbye as I moved off and threaded my way into the insanity that was the Gulf Road.

I had been driving for an hour or so. It was a flawless morning and the sun was getting up in the sky. I decided to treat myself to a slap-up lunch and fuel up the truck. I pulled into a small town called Dezful. It was busy with people going about their business and a faint dusty haze hung in the air lit by the low angle rays of the morning sun. I came down the main street to a big service station and pulled onto the pumps. As I filled the tank I noticed an American truck pulling onto the pump opposite me. The number plate was in Arabic but the country name was in English, it said 'Kuwait'.

It was a magnificent vehicle with all the accessories – chrome exhaust stacks, a big air conditioning unit on the back of the cab, roof airflow deflector, and a paint job that must have taken weeks to apply. It was green metal flake with what appeared to be a coat-of-arms and the name of the company in Arabic on the doors. It also had very tinted windows to keep out the glare of the sun. It was a most impressive truck with trailer to match.

I don't know who I was expecting to be driving it but I got a surprise when the driver jumped out of the cab. He was dressed in full 'Lawrence of Arabia' costume complete with head gear. He had a long-ish beard which was streaked with henna. To all intent and purpose he looked as if he'd just come out of the desert on a camel, only this 'camel' was a $100,000 dollar Kenworth conventional. I noticed he had a few other western bits and pieces, for instance a gold Rolex watch and a chunky gold chain around his neck.

After he stuck the nozzle into his tank and put it on auto stop, he looked around. Ignoring the local drivers he spotted my British number plate and my right hand drive. He looked at me and gave a small nod, I nodded back and this brought a smile full of white teeth in a black beard. *Nothing ventured, nothing gained*, I thought. I walked over to him and tried a greeting. "Salam wh'aley coom," I said and stretched out my hand. He shook my hand and asked in French where I was from. "I am from South West England, my home city is Bristol."

"Ah Englasi, Bristol City football. I know of this city. Why you come here, Englasi?"

"I am travelling across Asia to India with my friends and family but I needed to earn some money to carry on the journey. That is why I am driving the Gulf Road."

"Do you drink tea?" he asked.

"My friend." I smiled. "I am English, of course I drink

tea."

"Come English, we go drink tea together."

"What about the trucks?" I asked.

He turned and shouted to a group of young lads who came running over wide-eyed and almost bowing in awe. He gave them instructions in Pharsi and they set about following them, double quick time.

"These boys will look after truck and will grease it and clean the windows while we have breakfast." He gave more instructions to a couple of lads with grease guns over their shoulders and they dived under the trucks and started greasing all the lubrication points.

We walked to the restaurant attached to the station and when we opened the door the whole place went silent. The owner came out of his office when he saw us and all but grovelled at the feet of my new friend. I found out later that his family name, amongst others, was 'Saudi'. Mohamad Hafeza Salim Bin Saudi was his full name but he told me his western friends called him 'Sal'. It turned out that he was a minor royal in the ruling family in Kuwait and loved nothing more than to drive the beautiful truck to carry luxury items back to Kuwait. The load he had this time included a Ferrari, a Maserati, and a huge air conditioning unit, "And many big screen TVs and stereos just to fill the space." I asked to see the cars but unfortunately the trailer doors were sealed with a customs seal and could only be opened by a very senior customs officer in Iran. That act alone, would cause a serious diplomatic incident between the two countries, so that officer better be sure that there was something wrong inside!

Sal and I talked for a couple of hours and drank loads of tea. I related to him what life was like in England and he told me of his days in the desert as a young man. His family were hereditary rulers of Kuwait for many centuries.

"Where do you go from here?" he asked.

"Back to Tehran and then down to Isfahan where my family and friends are waiting for me to drive them all to India. We are looking forward to Afghanistan."

"Ah Afghanistan. It is a wild and backward country. I sometimes go there to our embassy in Kabul city. I take equipment and sometimes I bring a little something back to Kuwait city, something I think you would like, English." He grinned a huge grin and made the mime of smoking a chillum.

"Do you mean hashish?" I asked in surprise.

"Yes. Very good quality hashish. Many of the men in my family smoke because we cannot drink alcohol. We aren't supposed to smoke hashish either, but it is less of a sin. You will like Afghanistan, English, good people and fierce fighters."

I was suddenly doubly sorry that he couldn't open the trailer as I would like to have tasted his hashish. "Don't you keep a piece for yourself in the cab?" I asked in hope.

"For me, I don't smoke it, nor cigarettes, but sometimes my cousins and I take our hunting birds and everyone gets into our Chevy pick-ups and we race into the desert. We put up the tents and get very drunk for a few days, have a good time, then back home. There would be big trouble if we were caught so we go sometimes one hundred kilometres into desert."

"This is what we call a piss-up in English."

"What you talk piss-up? You piss into the air. Ah! A competition to see who can piss highest?" he said with a crease in his brow.

"No it's nothing to do with pissing. It's what we call being drunk. Pissed."

"Ah I understand. An English word that should only

be used among men? Do you have trouble for hashish?"

"Yes in England I am in big trouble if I am caught with hashish. Maybe go to jail."

"But jail is for thieves and murderers," he said in surprise. "They send you to jail for this?"

"They are very sad people in my country. They would rather send me to jail than protect an old lady from being beaten by robbers for her money. A child could be taken from the streets by sick bastards but the police will still put more effort into sending me to jail for having a quiet smoke than they would finding the child."

The last statement shocked Sal visibly. "My friend you have big problem there, I think."

Eventually we had to leave. Sal was going south to the docks from where I had just come. He paid the boys with a handful on notes. Their eyes widened as he doled out one hundred rial notes to each boy, more than they would make in a whole week.

"I have paid them for both trucks. Do not give them more, they have much money today."

As he climbed into his cab he asked where I was staying in Tehran.

"I park at the Gol-Leh-Shah tourist camp on the south side of the city, on the Qom road. If you get a chance, come and meet my family."

"Yes I must pass Tehran in the next week. I will stop and find you there. We always look for truck mechanic and drivers in Kuwait, most of my family can only drive camels," he grinned.

"You come Kuwait city where is the British embassy. I live in apartment not far from there, ask for Sal Bin Saudi, everybody know me."

"Thank you Sal I might just do that. Go steady my

friend and watch out for bandits."

"I have no problem with bandits. Last week I shoot one in the leg." He flipped back his robe to reveal what looked like a Colt hand gun strapped to his waist.

While I covered my surprise he fired up the big diesel engine with a roar and black smoke out of the two stacks. "Good luck English. I'll see you in Tehran in a few days."

"Go safely Sal. It was good to meet you."

With another toothy grin he pulled off the pumps and out of the station. He slowed to get round the entrance and then with a roar of diesel and air horn he was gone. Seldom in my life was I so impressed by anyone. *What a wonderfully romantic life he must lead*, I thought to myself, with images of that beautiful truck crossing deserts and mountains to places where only four-wheeled, local Bedford J types had gone before. I ached to be like that. I sincerely hoped I would meet this modern day Bedouin again.

Heading to the hills now in the heat of the day, the trip was going well and despite being loaded well over the twenty tons, the Volvo was purring. Remembering the tarmac that had rippled, I was on the long decent out of the mountains using the gearbox and engine to slow me right down to an average of five miles an hour. An occasional dab on the brakes as the speed went over twenty miles an hour. Loads of exhaust, brake, and second gear, kept my downhill speed to around ten miles an hour, more than fast enough on a one-in-five slope with twenty tons trying to push me on.

All of a sudden there was a blast of air horns as a fully loaded Mack came by, at a rate of knots. An arm was being waved out the passenger window. "Hey! English, where you go? C'mon let's go." He came past me at about forty miles an hour. As he passed I realised he was coasting down the hill, out of gear! I couldn't believe it. He was loaded with about forty tons of large diameter steel piping and he was out of gear and using just his brakes to slow at the bends As he passed on down the hill I could smell the tell-tale odour of burning brake linings in his wake.

When brake linings overheat you get what is known as 'brake fade' where your brake linings get so hot they lose grip on the brake drums and hey presto, at the bottom of long slopes you find you have little, or no, braking and it's very hard to stop no matter how hard you press the pedal. *He ain't gonna live long like that!* I remember thinking.

Eventually I reached the bottom of the slope and started out along the desert road to be greeted with the sight of a Mack truck, upside down with its wheels in the air. The cab had been crushed and mangled, the load of twenty-foot long pipe sections had broken free of the trailer, demolished a house, and now lay across the desert like matchsticks tipped out of their box. Another scene of carnage. My 'ain't gonna live long' prophecy was almost instantly realised.

I slowed as I passed to avoid the usual headless chicken onlookers. I should have stopped to help but I'd just had enough of the sight of horrific injuries and I kept going. To this day I can still get stressed about that!

I drove on until late afternoon across long desert roads. As I came to the outskirts of another town I heard a large bang, more like 'whump' really. I felt the trailer twitch a little and realised I'd just had a puncture on the rear of the two trailer axles. More stress. Where was I going to find a tyre repair shop? It could be miles away.

I pulled my thoughts together. I jumped out of the cab as I did I noticed a few houses back off, the road and a few workshop-looking places. I didn't see anything that looked like a tyre shop, just a few guys sitting around the entrance to a house was the only sign of life apart from the traffic rolling on noisily.

I looked at the spare wheel carrier on the unit, yes, there was a spare, albeit covered in mud and desert crud, but if I had a jack anywhere I'd have a go at changing it. I wasn't too optimistic looking at the wheel nuts, they looked tight, as if they'd been put on with a compressed air wrench. I had to empty everything out of the cab onto the roadside. The tools were stowed right underneath the bottom bunk in a special locker. Eventually, and with much swearing and muttering to myself I opened the locker. The sweat was literally running down my face into my eyes, making them sting, and I had to stop regularly to wipe it away. I found the jack and, hallelujah! There was a wheel brace of sorts.

The wheel brace that was supplied with the vehicle was basically a bit 'Mickey Mouse' in that it was made to unscrew mostly new and correctly tightened wheel nuts, not like these, tightened by years of vibration, rust and over tightening by careless use of the aforementioned, air wrench. The other problem with manufacturer supplied tools is that they are usually made of inferior quality steel and the nut receptacles become rounded off because the poor quality metal is soft enough to spread like butter! This particular one had definitely seen better days. I still wasn't put off. I threw the jack and brace out of the cab and set to work on the wheel nuts of the trailer. After about an hour I managed to get all the nuts off and dragged the deflated tyre and rim off the axle. This gave me a bit of a boost as all I had to do was take the spare off the cradle at the back of the unit and fit it to the axle. I was already drenched in sweat. This was no job for a hot desert afternoon. I crouched, heart thumping and breathing deeply, underneath the trailer out of the sun until I had calmed and cooled down a little.

The spare was mounted under the rear chassis cross member of the unit. It therefore gets all the dirt from the road and as it's mounted low down, can also be damaged by rough road conditions. When I crawled under to see how difficult it would be, my heart sank. The nuts were caked in a concrete-hard crust and had probably never been turned since the truck was new. I cursed Volvo for not putting the spare in a more accessible place. I took the wheel wrench and began chipping away at the crud around the threads. Eventually about an hour later I had beaten it all off, cleaned off the threads off the bolts, and was ready to start undoing the retaining nuts. It was in every sense a 'shit fight' getting those nuts undone but with liberal application of some engine oil, I managed to move them all and wind the winch that lowered the heavy tyre and rim to the ground.

I stood for a moment, feeling good that I had got it off. All I had to do now was pick up the wheel and roll to the back of the trailer. This I did but it was heavy and the effort to get it there nearly made me pass out in the heat. The only shade was underneath the trailer. I grabbed my water bottle and dowsed the back of my neck. It felt wonderful and I waited for my heart rate to slow and my breath to return. Refreshed somewhat, I came out into the sunshine again. I checked the position of the sun and noted I still had about an hour of daylight left. I might get it done and be able to do a few hours in the dark, but fate was not to be so kind.

As I started to offer up the wheel to the axle it was clear that it was not going to fit. In an instant I realised that the wheel only fitted the unit and that the trailer wheels were a totally different size. They looked similar but only when about to fit it would you notice the difference. There was a cradle for a spare on the rear of the trailer, but it was empty.

I was gutted like I've never been gutted before. I leaned with my forearm against the trailer, rested my head on it, and wallowed in despair. I don't mind admitting it I was close to a rage of frustration. If I'd been thinking rationally

I would have been calm as I know I have the ability to get myself out of any situation but the heat, the dust, the desert landscape, the carnage of the last few days all conspired to sap my strength.

"Monsieur." A soft hand on my shoulder. I turned to see one of the men I had seen earlier outside one of the nearby houses. "Monsieur." The rest was Pharsi and I didn't get a word but it was clear that he wanted me to go with him. He all but led me by the arm to the large room in the house, where he and the other men I'd seen were sat on the carpet around a huge spread of green veg of some kind, a huge pot of what appeared to be mutton stew with potatoes, and more green beans of a different kind. It looked, smelled, and tasted delicious. There was a large pot of cold, boiled rice, each grain perfectly cooked without the gloopy starch of pudding rice, and several pots of sauces. Rice was eaten cold here as with most Asian countries we visited. There was also a large pile of barbari bread, still hot from the oven, covered in a spotless white tea towel.

As soon as they saw me they all budged over and made space for me to sit with much encouragement from them. "Sit, sit. Eat everything here." He thrust a barbari at me and grinned as he tucked into the steaming pot of stew.

I was so deeply touched to be treated in this way, the true meaning of Islam was on show. I don't know the correct form of words but the Holy Koran teaches that all disciples should offer water, food, and shelter, to travellers. Not just a teaching but considered as important as the Christian's commandments.

This they had certainly done for me and, as luck would have it, the guy who told me to 'sit, sit' also spoke a little more English and some German, again from working in the oil industry. After an excellent meal and several glasses of sweet green tea with endless sugar lumps, I thanked them as sincerely as I could through the 'sit, sit' guy. When

I need to think of something good, as has been the case since all the Islamic extremists kicked off, I think of those kind people who took care of a stranger in distress.

It didn't end there either. After a good night's sleep, around seven thirty in the morning I was awakened by a tap on the passenger's door. I looked out to see a young man grinning and pointing to my punctured wheel that I had leaned against the truck. He also gaped when he saw my steering wheel on the right.

"He will take to shop, town. You give one hundred rials he will take and repair OK?" The 'sit, sit' man said as he walked up to me. I was surprised and delighted that I was going to get help with my puncture. We loaded the wheel into the pick-up and headed off to town. While the boys at the tyre shop got on with repairing it, my friend and I went to the local restaurant to have breakfast. A westerner with a local caused quite a stir in this place. It was well off the road and probably had never had a European there before.

My new friend announced who I was and my predicament. There were nods and smiles at me and I was encouraged to sit and a plate of chello kebab was placed in front of me along with some tea in a small ornate silver teapot. The kebab was freshly cooked and placed on a bed of cold rice with a large slice of salted butter. There was a side dish of minty-smelling bean stew and loads of fresh barbari bread still warm from the ovens.

I felt joyous at the hospitality these relatively poor people were giving me. I felt I had to stand up and speak. I put my hand on my heart and said thank you in English, then in French and then I tried it in Pharsi. "Shukreah, shukreah, my friends thank you so much for this."

This produced large smiles all round and as I sat down I could feel, for the second time in as many days, tears not too far away but this time because their simple kindness had moved me beyond words. They could see I was moved and smiled even more. As we finished eating a boy from the tyre shop came in to announce that the repair was done. I said goodbye to all in the restaurant and thanked them again. I had to physically stop my new friend from paying the bill. I insisted on paying and eventually he allowed me to.

We loaded the wheel into the pick-up and returned to the truck where we both re-fitted it. We went to a well by the houses and had a wash – the cold water was refreshing in the morning heat. I passed by the house where I had eaten last night and the men were sitting drinking tea. I thanked them again with the help of the 'sit, sit' man.

"My friends I must go now to Tehran. I don't have words to thank you. I wish you all good health and good luck may you be rewarded in paradise for your kindness to a traveller." The last bit was a little bit over the top but it got a good reaction.

I jumped in the cab, fired up the engine and with a blast on the air horn and much waving, I pulled out into the traffic knowing I'd never forget these days. To make up the time I'd lost I decided to drive on into the night. If I thought daytime driving was crazy I found night driving completely illogical. Headlights would be on full beam and only dipped at the last moment if at all. The only way I could get them to dip their headlight was to literally drive at them, flashing my lights up and down quickly. I took some appalling risks because I was so frustrated at their night driving technique. The trucks they were driving were new American types with very bright halogen lights. We used to joke that when they went to the showroom to buy their trucks the salesman would show them first where the accelerator was, and second the horn! They never bothered to show the brakes or the dip switch! We had a saying, 'you can't go from camels to cars without horses in between'. However it was easy to get a bank loan and buy a new tuck. The two drivers would run twenty four hours a day, no training, no HGV licence, no idea how to drive a truck of that size. They would drive them like cars and be lucky to be alive in three months' time. But this was the Gulf Road, you had to play them at their own game and see who blinked first, or stay away.

The rest of the journey back to Tehran was uneventful for me. When I pulled up at the tourist motor camp, I phoned Jensen. "Back alright then sun, well done. Wadd'ya reckon?"

"Bloody mayhem and carnage," I replied.

Jensen laughed. "You did it, that's the main thing. Where are you tipping?"

"It's a cold store in the Tact-e-Jamshid area of the city."

"That's easy enough just head for the Meshad road out of the city and you'll see the cold store, it's a massive place, you can't miss it. Don't forget to get paid before you leave."

"OK Jensen, I'll ring when I've tipped and drop round the yard in the unit."

"Well done. I've got another run for you as soon as you've caught up."

"See you tomorrow."

I was glad I'd done well enough for him to want me to continue driving for him but I was missing my family, big time. I started early to the cold store which was just as well, as one of the main road junctions was locked solid with cars and trucks. I'd never seen the like of it before. Large trucks were tangled up around each other across the junction Not one of them would give way an inch. Cars and buses were in the mix and totally jammed into the mess. This would stop the traffic flow for hours at a time, sometimes all day.

If you stopped at a junction in a line of traffic, the car behind would drive round the grass to get in front. If there was a space on the bank or central reservation, a car or truck would get as far into that space as possible even if it meant driving on an angle that threatened to tip over the vehicle. In short; if there was a space in front, then go for it, regardless of what you have to drive over, or through.

I eventually got to the cold store. I remembered Jensen's advice. "Pull yer rear view mirrors in, don't worry what's behind, let them sort themselves out." That's exactly what I did.

As I was driving back along a dual carriageway toward Jensen's yard, I noticed another F88 Volvo. It was a UK registered left hand drive. As it pulled alongside me I could see it was Dave. Because it was left-hand drive, Dave and I were side by side and had a chat as the other drivers on the road hooted as they tried to get by.

"Alright sun?" Dave grinned as he handed me a 40mph spliff. "Fuck'm. Let'm wait," he said, as we travelled along side by side.

Eventually the lanes increased to three lanes and angry drivers were driving past shouting or waving their fists. We just threw our heads back and laughed our bollocks off at them. When I took the money round, in cash, Jensen paid me straight off. "Fancy doin' another?"

"I dunno mate. It was real blood and guts. I gotta be honest all I want right now is to see my family and just be with them for a while. I suppose it's shock."

"Tell yer what. Do another run and on the way down, divert to Isfahan and bring your missus and kids back. They can stay at the flat with us while you're down there. Normally I wouldn't say that a four hundred kilometre detour was ok, but with diesel at two and a half pence a litre, it don't really make a difference."

That sounded good to me. I hung around for a day or two and then set off for Isfahan. I arrived around ten in the evening and parked outside the campsite. Isobel had already crashed out. I was greeted with genuine pleasure by all but Fran. Isobel leaned out from the bunk and squeezed my hand as she came fully awake. The kids woke up and I went to see them and give them a hug. "You can't begin to understand how good it is to see you and yer mum and to know you are all alright."

"Where you bin Dad?" asked Mellony.

"Driving a truck. I'll show it to you tomorrow." The fact that I'd still be here tomorrow had registered.

"Have you been a long way away Dad?" asked Alun and for some absurd reason, I almost burst into tears, but I controlled it.

"Yes I've been a long long way and seen some things. I'll tell you all about it in the morning, now it's late and I haven't said hello to your mum yet." I gave them both a big hug and kiss and they went back to sleep almost immediately.

Isobel had put her night shirt on and announced that tonight she and I would be sleeping in the truck. There were various remarks, mainly of encouragement and leers from the boys.

"Isobel do you know that your nightshirt is completely transparent?" enquired Bob with a big smile.

"It is a bit..." said Timus, desperately trying, but failing, to avert his eyes.

"Now ask me if I give a shit." She sniffed and tossed her head back. She reached for me and pulled me physically off the bus. I barely had time to say goodnight. "I hope that bunk is big enough for two," she said with breathlessness.

"Well one and a half really I suppose. We can always

stack up, one on top of the other."

"I don't care who's on top."

The effect of her being all over me was overpowering and when we eventually got to the truck we didn't get a lot of sleep and the noise was a bit, well, noisy.

"It's the heat," she said between bouts. "It makes me randy. It's the sun shining on that gland on top of my scalp."

"Hmm, more like one of them Omar Sharif types you've been teaching English."

"Well I had to give him an all-round education."

I looked at her in surprise. "You mean you..." I stopped there and we both laughed. I never, to this day, asked her any further questions about that though I've often wondered. What was good for the goose was fine for the gander. What a promiscuous lot we were back then!

Next morning Isobel had arranged to go to the souk with Black Bob, Kakey and Glynis. However, I learned later that Glynis had got the kids up early and brought them and a tray of the local version of croissants and jam, to the truck with the idea of having breakfast together.

"I saw 'troock shaking like 'DT's so I thought t'me sen, souks out today then! I diverted kids' attention and we 'ad breakfast round t'pool. Boot I ad t'answer soom questions from little'uns and do it wi'out laughin'."

We did eventually go to the souk that day to buy a gold ring for Isobel. I had contributed four times the money that all of them put together had earned at the language school so I wasn't having any discussion about it. It was happening.

We found a gold band made of tightly twisted gold wire and a mounting of gold containing a large red ruby. It was fabulous and would have cost a fortune back in the UK but after really haggling, we got it for a few hundred pounds. It had to be altered and I watched fascinated as the shopkeeper lit the wick of a spirit burner shaped like a watering can with a wick in the spout. He then took a small metal tube in his mouth and blew the flame onto a small sliver of gold that was positioned across the cut in the band. It didn't take long for the gold to melt into the two cut ends and, voilà, it was done! Isobel was happy with her new ring. She liked to collect antique and quality jewellery.

When we got back to the bus we started to get dinner together. I announced that seeing as how I was earning four times what they were, I was going to take Isobel and the kids back to Tehran with me. "You're leaving the bus?" asked Glynis rather sharply.

"No! Of course not, it's just that I want my wife and kids with me. We didn't take on this journey to be apart. We'll carry on with our plan but, it's just that the family come with me. When I've done this next trip, that'll take us well into a grand in the kitty. When you have finished your contract with the school, just call me at the campsite or Jensen's number over at Pars' yard. Me and the family'll be back down on the TBT the next day." That seemed to placate the others and we had a good meal round the fire and successfully disturbed the Rotel Tour group who, we suspected, were tut-tutting, as we smoked and laughed.

Next morning Isobel, the kids and I were all packed up and installed in the Volvo. We pulled away to waves and calls to "Be careful!" Everyone came out including the Bell Helicopters lads who were already getting trollied on beers. Everyone came out, except Fran. We made good time with Isobel laying on the bunk and the kids on the passenger seat. They were in hysterics, laughing at the shocked faces of the occupants of the vehicles we overtook when they looked up to see just two kids where the driver should be. Especially as I'd told Alun Jnr to sit up as if he was driving.

He pretended to hold the steering wheel – it looked hilarious. It was hot, even with all the windows and roof lights open. There was no air conditioning on British trucks then.

I took Isobel and the kids in to meet the shopkeeper where the cannon had gone off. He gave the kids Cokes and Isobel and I would not be allowed go until we had accepted a meal with him and his family. We all sat on a plush carpet with cushions. The kids played with a puppy from next door. The shopkeeper had invited his neighbours in for a pot of tea with the foreigners. It was relaxed and they were treating us like visiting royalty.

Eventually we drove on, with me pointing out where so-and-so had happened on the first trip and telling them what I'd seen. I was ready for it this time but Isobel was drawing out the stories as if I was in therapy. It did help to get it out.

We decided to stop just before Andimeshk and have an early dinner, the kids were tired and hungry by now but still pulling faces at the drivers we passed. I pulled in out of the desert onto a double row of truck diesel pumps. The young kid at the pumps, gave us the double take when he saw the right-hand drive Volvo with its British number plate. I told the attendant to fill the tank and mimed that we were going in for a meal. He would come with the bill when he'd finished filling me up.

The rather large restaurant was full with drivers and bus passengers. The hubbub was loud but it died when Isobel, the kids and I walked in like we owned the place. To see western females was unheard of here let alone kids. When I looked around, many of the drivers sat at tables, nodded to me as I caught their eye, I nodded and smiled back.

The rest of the journey was punctuated by various overnight stops here and there to meet friends I'd made on the way down, first time. Without exception, we were given every hospitality you could think of. So many times since, I have thought to myself that if just the real people of each land, could just get together with each other, without politics or religion there would be no conflict. People were basically good to each other, until greed and ruthless ambition, start to rear their ugly heads.

We pressed on for the next day or two trying to make up some of the time we had lost when we called into friends I'd made on the first trip. Often, they would insist that the kids need to rest properly overnight and we should stay the night as well. Our new friends really loved having the kids around and they doted on them. The Iranians are very big on families and get together at the drop of a hat, so all the relations would get called round to come and meet the English tourists and their children, with blond hair! It was a wonderful journey and full of this kind of hospitality. Without fail we always had to promise that we'd call in every time we passed.

Eventually we arrived in the docks. I made straight for the docks office and sought out the Manager. He was very pleased to see us and the bottles of Jack Daniels I'd got the Bell Helicopters guys to donate. We sat in his air-conditioned office and sipped tea and Cokes and we were shown photos of all his cars and family, in that order. He offered to pay for the J.D. which I of course dismissed with the right mixture of 'thanks-for-offering', but dismissed with a slight upward tilt of the head, as unimportant. As was the Iranian way.

It was a very pleasant afternoon and we ended up on the balcony outside his office, through huge French windows. He told us many of the truly amazing stories of smuggling, bribery and the general to-ing and fro-ing of everyday life of the port.

"Where do you eat tonight?" he asked.

"Haven't thought about it yet. I expect we'll cook

something up. I have a food locker, water and a cooker, that's enough for Isobel to whip up a banquet." I smiled at her.

"Ah you must come to the docks canteen. It's huge and has good food and is clean. I will telephone them and you will be my guests," he stated with a manner that was final.

"That's very kind of you," said Isobel.

"And we have ice cream for the little ones." That got their attention! He turned to me quietly and said behind a hand, "And I will have something special for you Alun, which I think you will like."

My interest was piqued and my eyes widened slightly. "Something to smoke, perhaps?" I asked with a grin.

"Yes! I thought you would like that!"

"Too right my friend. I will really look forward to that but I'd better sort out a load first and get cleaned up."

"Don't worry about the load. It can all be arranged and you and your lovely wife and children can relax in the cool of the canteen. There is a bathroom and showers there for the management and a special area for us to have dinner later. Plenty of place to park the truck and you can lock it and leave it. Everybody will know you are my guest and if anyone touches it, they will lose a hand."

I turned, expecting him to be smiling at his jokey, over-the-top, response. He was deadly serious. Once again I was starkly reminded of the frontier lifestyle of this wild country.

When we arrived at the canteen it turned out to be quite a wild place full of merchant seamen from all over the world, including a bunch of British crew from a tanker moored in the Gulf and waiting for a docking and unloading time. They told us that there were ships backed all the way down the Persian Gulf. Certain crews were allowed ashore for a couple of days in rotation so as not to put too much of a strain on the meagre facilities.

We sat and swapped stories for an hour or so, until one of the canteen staff came over and spoke to us in good English. "You are guest of the manager. Would you like to come through to the manager's room now?"

"Amazing what a couple of bottles of Jack Daniels can do for you," I said as an aside, as we followed the waiter through the door. We went onto the outside terrace in the lowering blast of the sun and sea air. There was only one table laid out sumptuously with pomegranates and other fruit, Cokes in ice and the two bottles of J.D. discreetly hidden behind a huge chromium samovar, steaming away in the corner. After having a Coke for the kids, one of the waiters came to our table. He was about 25 and spoke good English.

"The manager asked me to tell you that he will be late. He has been held up with some business." As an afterthought the waiter added, "There is a nice clean shower and toilet you can use. It is only for the manager, so very clean," he emphasised.

"I'd love a shower right now," said Isobel. "The kids could do with one as well. Why don't we get the kit and have a good clean-up. You don't know when we'll get the chance again for a few days."

"Yeah, why not?"

I walked back to the truck and got all the washing stuff and some clean clothes. When I returned to the restaurant, Isobel was in conversation with the waiter who saw me coming and walked off. "What was he talking about?"

"Oh he was just asking how old I was and do I have any sisters or brothers 'n' stuff."

"Hmm."

We found our way to the beautifully tiled and decorated shower room, about the size of a standard living room! Isobel and the kids had got undressed first and were enjoying the gallons of hot water. Just as I was about to join them, a slight movement across the big frosted glass window caught my eye. Just as I began to ask myself what were people doing out there, I spotted a large extractor fan in the opposite wall, at about head height. Sure enough the dirty little shits were lining up to have a gawp at Isobel in the nude. However, all they got was a much phlegm as I could muster, right in the face.

I heard a cry and bushes being broken as they retreated in sheer panic. I got a good look at them. And right there with them was... the waiter.

I finished my shower under tight control. I was seething. The waiter and his dirty, sex starved, little perverts, had set us up. I came out of the shower like a bull out of a pen. By this time the young men were back at their table in the far corner with their heads down pretending they weren't there.

I started for the table, anger had taken over. The waiter came up to me and put a hand out to stop me. I shoved him over the table and marched up to the nearest youth and gave him a resounding smack round the head. The shock made him scream and his pals went white and were mumbling something at me over and over again. I made a gesture of masturbating my little finger (a gesture becoming more and more useful).

Isobel tells me that I was about to slap him again, when the waiter begged me to stop.

"This is my wife and mother of my children, you camel shaggin' pervert! MY WIFE!" I shouted in his face.

Just then the doors burst open and in walked Petri. "Alun what is going on?" He said with alarm. Seeing me addressed as a friend by the docks manager, 'God' to them, made them as white as a sheet. I noticed the reaction.

"It's these little wankers." The last word was spat in

their face.

I told Petri what had happened. As I did so his face got darker and darker and seeing this, I thought the waiter was going to shit himself there and then! Petri issued some curt orders and they were marched out.

"Isobel I am so sorry. We get these scum that hang around the docks getting involved in all sorts of crime a corruption. They are like rats and scurry around. They know the docks area well. Every now and then we have a clear out of these people, but they always come back."

"It's alright Petri," said Isobel. They are just horny young lads who've probably never seen a western female."

"It's the disrespect to a wife and mother. Just about as low as you can get in the Islamic world."

"Quite," I said.

"Besides, I have seen how you dress. You may wear western clothes but you cover your arms and head. You show respect, so must they, and behave like civilized people, not backward animals." Petri really was angry that his guests had been treated so.

I learned that they had been marched outside and given a good slapping and kicked off the docks with instructions not to be seen there again on pain of loss of limb! The waiter was also sacked and banished from the docks. On the whole, I wish I hadn't complained now. There was no way in Iranian society that Petri could've overlooked such disrespect. Punishment had to be very hard and very public.

Despite the fuss, we had a wonderful meal with Petri. All the time waited on by white-coated waiters who knew the 'boss' was well pissed off. They were extra respectful and eager to please. Isobel decided that she would have an early night and thanked Petri for his hospitality. He stood and said goodnight and apologised again. He also said goodnight to the kids. He then issued a curt order in Farsi, to the dock's policeman who was always nearby, with instructions to escort the lady and her children back to the truck. They were given in such a manner, that it was understood that if anything happened to her or the kids, he would be imprisoned.

Petri told me later what he had said and that they were used to him threatening all sorts of murder and decimation to whole generations of the miscreant's family if he transgressed. "They leave me alone for a day or so then it's back to normal, but this is different."

"Now Alun, come we smoke some of this." He plonked a sizeable chunk of top quality, black Afghani hash down on the table. He then brought out a pack of Winstons and started to empty them out.

"Is that alright in here?" I knew we were in a country that doesn't put smoking hash very high up the crime league, it's still against the law, especially for foreigners.

"What about the police?" I looked around through sheer force of habit.

"Here on these docks, I am the police," he said with a grin. "And believe me we have far more serious problems than smoking a bit of hash."

"Like what?" I asked, intrigued.

"Everything from arms smuggling to heroin and people smuggling. We stopped a container bound for France, last year. Inside we found fourteen people. Dead!"

"Oh Christ," I blurted.

"Yeah, the arsehole who took their money sealed them in and didn't think that the container was airtight! They suffocated before the container was even loaded. We only found them because the container had been left out in the sun and we opened it to see if there had been any heat damage. It was the smell when we opened the doors!"

"Oh Christ," I said again, "those poor people, Jesus, God in heaven." I was horrified.

Just last month we found 10 kilos of heroin on a ship about to leave. It had come down from the poppy fields of Afghanistan, by truck. Probably the same truck that brought this hashişh," he said with irony.

"What happened to it?" I asked casually.

"There is no way you could keep that kind of find quiet," he said with a slight grin.

"There was a token, public bonfire by the customs people, of what looked to be packs of powder but it didn't smell like heroin when it was burning. I think it was resold by them. That's the way it is here, meanwhile the men arrested were publicly flogged and lucky not to lose a limb. They are now looking at life imprisonment for this."

"Wow. Heavy." I was stunned at his tale.

"Yes. It all comes through here and I know about everything." He leaned back luxuriously and took a deep lungful of fine Afghan hash.

"Such a responsibility. No wonder you have a roller. They must be paying you very well."

"Oh yes of course. It's a highly paid job with benefits." He glanced at me with very stoned eyes. "Mind you, I draw the line. No heroin, no arms shipments and no people smuggling. The people who work for me know my limits and keep it well within them."

"Shit! That's some fine hash there, Petri," I said, as I realised I'd been hanging on his every word, in intense concentration.

"A truck driver friend of mine delivers to the Afghan border sometimes and he always brings me back a slab of their finest Mazar-i-Sharif, hash. That's what you are smoking right now."

"Some of the best hash I have smoked… so far!" I said with a giggle and rather wobbly eyes! We both laughed and drank and smoked well into the night. Finally, Petri stood up and said he had to go to bed, and it would be a good idea if I did too. He would put me at the head of the queue but it meant getting up at silly-o'clock in the morning.

"When it gets light is when they will start unloading, so be here just before."

"What will I be loading?" I asked. By now we were at the truck.

"Sugar! Goodnight Alun, see you tomorrow!"

"Thank you so much for a wonderful evening, Petri." And at the same time I thought to myself, *Great! That sticky shit is all I need!*

"No problem my friend." He wobbled off with two policemen following respectfully, behind. When they drew level with me, they both saluted.

"Goodnight fellas." I nodded to them and climbed into the cab.

Isobel was on the bunk and Alun and Mellony were curled up in the passenger footwell, which was just big enough for the two of them. I shed my clothes and lay beside Isobel in a contented stupor. I fell asleep immediately, in the warmth of a balmy, Gulf night.

Next morning early I sauntered over to the offices. Petri came over to greet me with a smirk. "Good morning Alun."

"Salam wh'aley coom," I said. "You look a little fragile."

"More problems to plague my life, I have been on the phone most of the night."

"Ah, it's tough at the top." That got a smile.

"I have your loading papers, but there is a little problem. Do you have your trailer cover with you?"

"Yes I have my tilt cover with me, why?"

"Some of the bags are small and could fall out. The sacks are a bit the worse for wear, and we'll have to put you on the weighbridge to make sure you have a full load."

"Great! Is this how you look after your driver friends who bring you nice presents?" I said with a grin.

"The next load is paper, which is a good clean load, but you just happen to be here at the wrong time."

"No problems, I'm just winding you up. I'll take anything as long as I get paid."

"If you could buy another truck and run the two down here you could make lots of money. Iran is short of 35 thousand truck drivers. That's why you see all that Caterpillar, plant and all the trucks lined up, outside the docks."

"Yes I saw that, very impressive."

"All that stuff has been bought with oil money. Trouble is there aren't enough drivers to move it, so there it sits."

"Yes and it's getting vandalised as well. I saw several broken windscreens and flat tyres."

"The locals started pinching bits here and there. It got so bad that the police chief issued a threat to shoot on sight, any looters! Not only that, but all the western goods are taking up huge storage space in our sheds. We have ordered all this stuff but no transport to move it."

"Wow. Yes I can see why these drivers run non-stop. They must be cashing in. Anyway, Petri, I'd better get in the queue. Do I have to go out on that bloody rickety causeway again. Frightened the crap out of me last time! I'm glad it'll be daylight this time," I said.

"Yes I'm afraid it's pontoon number three, same as last time."

"Ah well it'll be OK I'm sure. Imsha'Allah," I laughed. "I'll see you next time."

We shook hands and he gave me a warning to be especially careful on the way back. There was no 'Le Mans' start this time and I just sauntered into the queue waiting to drive out to the pontoon. When I got to the loading position, the loading chief was the same one as before. I made a big greeting and it was grins all round. "Salam wh'aley coom, Mohamed Rafni."

"Wh'aley coom salam, Allain Dillon," he said with a big grin. "You still live!"

"Yes many of your truck drivers try to kill me with their trucks, but I'm still here."

"Who try to kill you?" he said with concern.

"Your truck drivers! They are crazy people!" I tapped my temple. "They drive big trucks but think they still drive camels." I grinned.

"Ahh! Yes. Too much smoking the ---" I didn't catch the word he used but he went on, "make them think they are flying man."

"Flying man?" I asked, puzzled.

"Bali. Red, blue here big 'es'." He pointed to his chest.

"Superman!" I exclaimed as the penny dropped.

"Bali. E'Superman. Him."

"Yes I understand now Mohamed, I understand what you mean. You are correct."

"When first come, I speak 'You still live', huh?"

"Hanoum (Wife. Married woman.) Allain Dillon?" He had caught sight of Isobel in the passenger seat.

"Yes that's Isobel, my wife. Come Mohamed, say hello."

He was reluctant to come with me. "Allain, no good. Here," he pointed to the ground, "for Hanoum."

"I have my children here, also come meet."

"Children here?"

"Dans la cabine."

"No. Here dirt, hot, workmen, and many bad things." He pointed at the cranes and loads.

"Mohamed all I see is men working and trying to stay alive and give food to their families. For me it shows great dignity."

"Dignity?" He parroted with a frown.

"Ahh um," I struggled. I adopted a noble pose with straight back and proud chest.

"A man! A man! Un homme!" I said with my chin raised and chest out. I pointed to the guys working.

"Ahh." He understood.

"In my country, woman, man, same." I put my two index fingers together, extended upwards, to indicate both were equal. "Come say hello to my wife."

He came with me and I introduced him to Isobel. He was clearly not at ease shaking hands and addressing another man's wife. To cap it all, she, to him, was only partially dressed. Even though Isobel was wearing a headscarf and fully sleeved top. What she definitely wasn't wearing, was the burqa. A head to toe, black cover with just a slot for the eyes! He saw the two kids and was all smiles.

"I brought you something." I had noticed many of his men, and he himself, liked to smoke a thin kind of cigar. I had got a couple of packs of quite good quality Virginian cigars from my contacts in the American PX corps. They were in Isfahan, supplying Bell Helicopters with supply services. In fact it was another way of getting CIA agents into the country and keeping an eye on the Gulf ports.

I handed one box to Mohamed and gave one box to a group of loaders who loaded me last time. They were received well with big smiles and much bowing.

"Mohamed!" I shouted over to him. He had been so delighted with his box of cigars, that he'd put down his clipboard and wandered over to the waters edge, lighting and savouring the aroma, as he went. "Mohamed. When your men have finished their cigars, I must load quickly. You understand? Après la fumar, l'homme charge la camion vite, s'il vous plait?" I struggled along with appalling French.

"No problem Allain Dillon, no problem, thank you, thank you." He waved the box of cigars.

"That went down well, then," said Isobel.

"Yes I gave a few rials over the top last time so's they'd remember me and I'd get loaded quick."

"Looks like you are remembered all around the area. I'm glad there are no women around here to hero worship you."

Foolishly, I told her about the walled in brothel just south of Ahwaz. "It reminded me of the place that Pinocchio goes to when he gets corrupted and drinks beer, plays pool and starts to grow donkey ears..." I trailed off, suddenly aware of her stare.

"How do you know? You been inside?" she asked with a smirk.

"No, no, no. Huh! Are you kidding? I've never paid for it in my life. And I certainly ain't gonna share that experience with most of the male population of Ahwaz!"

We were loaded in no time flat and our papers were waiting in the dock's managers office when I arrived. Because most of the bags of sugar were in good, undamaged, condition, I was able to avoid having to put on the tilt cover. A huge, heavy-gauge, plastic covering that goes right over the trailer, front to back. It weighs a ton and would have taken all afternoon to put it on. Not only that but the steelwork has to be put in place to support it, all in the hot sun!

I reached the office.

"The manager asked me to tell you he will see you next time, insha'Allah. He is in meeting with big boss," said a young office worker.

I looked over to Petri's office to see two uniformed officers of the Iranian Army, talking to him. He saw me and I waved my papers at him and put my arm across my chest with a small nod. Things must have been fairly relaxed in the office as he took time to wave back.

The haul back to Tehran was as eventful as the last, with wrecks here and there and some nasty scenes that I did my best to not let the kids see but like a TV screen, it happens right there in front of you. We called into Andimeshk to see Najeeb and his mum and sisters. They were absolutely smitten with Isobel and the kids. I hardly saw them for the couple of days we stayed. They were off being shown the bazaars and markets and local sights. All the time the kids were being doted upon, with Cokes and Fantas and sweets.

Because we'd stopped for a couple of days, I had some time to make up. We drove all day and long into the night. When I got really tired, we pulled off the road. It was a beautifully warm, Gulf night and, because we were well away from any street lights or towns, the sky was crammed full of sparkling stars. Stars like I'd never seen before.

Isobel and I climbed in the back, under the stars with our mattress and sleeping bag on the sugar bags. The kids were zonko in the bunk. All the windows were open and it was very warm. We took full advantage of being alone and made love underneath the stars with the warmth, sounds and fragrances of the desert, all around us. Jasmine and pomegranate and some cactus flowers, wafting on the air.

At the first crack of light to the east, it was a different story. Night-time temperature had dropped way down. But it was a stunning dawn, that is when Isobel and I had to cuddle together because of the cold, and naturally took full advantage of being alone, again!

A quick brew up and some breakfast and a freezing but refreshing jerry can shower behind the trailer for us all, much to the kids disgust! But by the time we'd finished the sun was well over the horizon and it was lovely to just stand there bollock-naked, and dry off in its rays.

By the time we were ready to pull off, I had a mug of coffee in my hand and a 'Farsi' to have a smoke on, as I drove. I wanted to get moving now and was impatient to be underway.

The smoke set me up nicely and we didn't stop until I was forced to by low fuel.

"We'll eat here as well. It'll be a long old slog through the mountains, with this load, but if we time it right, I'll be able to do it in daylight."

Isobel wore her sunglasses, a headscarf and fairly loose clothing and held on tightly to the kids. It was a big truck stop with TBT buses and many trucks. The place was huge and many of the bus passengers were in their as well, so Isobel and the kids weren't the only women and children there. We had a great dinner and I spent some time talking to a TBT bus driver who had worked and driven in England. He was amused to hear my description of the Gulf Road!

I replenished the water carriers. By the time we'd had our meal, one of the young lads from the pumps, brought my keys and a bill, in Farsi, he brought it to our table. It was for four hundred, and change. I gave him a five hundred note and said, "Shukran," as I waved him away, indicating that I didn't expect change.

"Shukran, shukran mister." He smiled a row of dazzling white teeth, first at me, then Isobel.

We bought enough supplies to be able to cook a meal, some ice for the cold box, with melon, pomegranates, some local strong cheese, a pile of barbari bread and a few Fantas.

We were halfway between Dezful and Arak and one way or another I wanted to be in Tehran, some five hundred kilometres distant, tomorrow afternoon. We pushed on through the mountains. I pointed out places where incidents had taken place. It all seemed like a nightmare again as we came across more scenes of carnage. I wasn't going to stop this time, because of the kids, but there were one or two situations where Isobel would not pass by.

We drove on through Arack on the Qom road. Qom is the second holiest city in Iran so I was glad we were going through in darkness. They can get a bit touchy when 'infidels' get too close. I stopped for a few hours rest just north of Qom. Isobel and the kids were fast asleep when I pulled up, so I let the engine idle for a while to get rid of the heat build-up in the engine.

Any truck driver knows that to stop an engine just like that, is asking for trouble when the engine has been working hard. The engine should be allowed to run lightly, before switching off, to get rid of the high temperatures.

I slept for a couple of hours in the driver's seat. By the time I set off for Tehran the first rays of light were just cracking to the East. *Pretty soon we'll be driving in that direction, going even farther East*, I thought to myself. It really felt that now we had loads more money than we'd left England with, it would be less stressful, worrying where the next meal was coming from. The engine overheating was still a worry but now that we had money, it just wasn't that stressful. I knew I could get over any mechanical problems if we had a bit of money for what was needed. We arrived outside Pars International Containers yard late afternoon to be met by a beaming Jensen.

"Got here then sun. Well done. Tell yer what. Park this in the yard, you can tip tomorrow. You and the Mrs 'n' kids can come home with me to our apartment."

That sounded great. Showers, clean beds and a private swimming pool. The apartment was in the Amir Abad area, a fairly up-market area at the time and close to the Queen Elizabeth 2nd Boulevard, where some of the finest hash I'd ever tasted could be bought for next to nothing.

"So wha's yer plans?" Asked Jensen as we drove through rush hour Tehran round the giant Shahyad monument, a huge concrete tripod to the west of the city. An impressive piece of textured concrete sculpture about a couple of hundred feet high, on a massive roundabout.

"We're going on to India just as soon as we can finish up here. We'll go down in a few days to pick up the bus and the others and head for Meshad and across the border into Afghanistan."

"Yeah I fink it's time we moved on as well. I fink the bastards'r gonna stiff me for a month's salary."

"I don't suppose there's a lot you can do about it," I said.

"Nah not much. I reckon it's all goin' tits-up soon, anyway, so now's the time to move on. There's all sorts of crap goin' down at the moment. There was riotin' in town yesterday an' soldiers and tanks, everywhere."

"That bad, was it? Glad we're moving on then." I didn't pay much attention to politics in those days but it was obvious that Iran was heading for some really bad times. The Four Horsemen of the Apocalypse were about to ride across Iran, big time!

It seemed that the religious mullahs were angered by the anti-Islamic ways of the Shah. They felt that he was 'westernising' the country too much. They were losing control of the people and they wanted to take it back to the middle ages. Ayatollah Khomeini was waiting in exile, in Paris. "I tell you what. I ain't lettin' the bastards stiff me. I've got this plan, if you fancy hangin' round for a few days and 'elpin me, I'd really 'preciate it and I'd bung you a drink."

"What you got in mind?" I asked.

Jensen went on to tell me that many transport and engineering firms from Europe had really gone for it when the boom in Iran started. They would set up local transport yards for themselves on the edge of Tehran city. Here they would keep, for instance, several trailers, a workshop with spares, and recovery equipment and vehicles. They had made loads of money during the boom years but now that political and social stability were beginning to crumble, they either pulled out of the country or went bankrupt back home, because the Iranians didn't pay their bills. The Iranians could see what was coming, and thought, *To hell with the foreigners, what can they do about it?*

This meant that the trailers and other equipment were just abandoned and sat around in these yards with nobody to claim them. By this time, law and order were breaking down, so nobody gave a toss about all this equipment left behind.

"I'm gonna 'ave one'a them 'reefers' (refrigerated) trailers away from that Dutch firm, out on the Saveh road. They've gone through the 'oop back in cloggie land, so some slippery little A-rab will end up pinchin' that lot. If you fancy getting under one'a them 'fridges and bringin' it back 'ere, I'm gonna spray paint it an drag it back to Blighty."

"What? With no papers?"

"Nah, 'oo gives a shit about papers? I'll just blag me way across. There's always some corrupt customs man that'll take a few quid and wave us through. I could really do with some help though. Waddya reckon?"

"I don't see why not. Which motor are you taking back to England?" I asked.

"I'm gonna sell that one you are driving. I got a local who wants to buy it. If I take that one back to England they're gonna impound it 'cos I went bankrupt and should've 'anded it over to the receivers."

That left him with a big problem. The other truck, an F89 Volvo, he'd bought from an English driver. His firm had gone bust back home, and he'd just been abandoned! It meant that the driver had no money and no back-up. Jensen gave him a few hundred quid and a ticket home which the driver gladly accepted, and passed the truck over to Jensen. This happened many times as the country declined into religious civil war. Nobody paid their bills and many European firms went bust because of it.

"Only one problem. The motor in the F89 is shot. It burns loads'a oil and 'as a bit of a nasty knock in the engine. I don't fink it'd make it back."

I could see he was in a bit of a pickle. He needed something to get home in, and something to drive and work with, once he got home. We continued dinner and were out on the back balcony, having a 'Farsi' when I suddenly had an idea. I remembered seeing a wreck of an F89 just as I came out of the mountains north of Khoramshah. It was just another wreck, one of many on that road. I had stopped one time and had a look at it. The windows were all smashed and anything of value had been ripped out. The wing mirrors and front wheels had been taken but the engine and gearbox were still in it. The number plates were gone but I think it was German registered.

"I've just had a really daft idea," I blurted out, only half seriously.

"I know where there is a wrecked F89. All we got to do is drag the fucker back here and swap the engines, and Robert's the avuncular relation!"

"Wha'?" came the bleary-eyed response, rapidly turning into serious concentration.

"Bob's yer uncle. Yeah why the fuck not?" I enthused, warming to the idea.

"Well for a start it'd cost loads of wonga to get the engine changed and take months. Y'know what this lot's like for deadlines, it's the 'will of Allah'."

"Well I suppose I could stick around long enough to do that. It shouldn't take more than a week. But you'd have to pay me."

"You?" Jensen looked at me, surprised.

"Oh. Didn't I tell you? I'm a fully qualified heavy vehicle mechanic. I started an apprenticeship when I left school. Then the army took over the apprenticeship when I joined up, and I finished it off in the army. City & Guilds part 1 and 2, I'll have you know," I said with mock pride.

"No you fuckin' didn't tell me that! Are you serious?" asked Jensen, getting more enthusiastic by the second.

"Deadly serious. As long as you can give me some space and the use of some tools and an engine crane and a few heavy jacks, we're in business."

"They've got all that kit over at the yard. Everything you could need but we wouldn't be able to do it in the yard. They'd probably use it as an excuse not to pay me."

"Well that ain't a problem. That big concrete foundation opposite the entrance will do." It was the floor of an abandoned project opposite the transport yard. It was strong, flat and just across the road. "But before we get carried away, let's think about this. When I stopped one time to have a look at the wreck the engine and transmission looked complete but there was no front wheels. What do you think would be the best way to get it back? We could take a flat-bed trailer and carry it home but how would we load it up? Have you got a recovery truck? We could give it a suspended tow, we wouldn't have to worry about missing front wheels then. Mind you, it's a helluva distance for a suspended tow!"

While I had been thinking out loud, Jensen had come up with a way to do it.

"No way, could I get away wiv' takin' the wrecker for a couple'a days. We gotta do this a bit on the QT, if you get my meaning. 'Ow 'bout this; we take a couple of wheels, and an 'A' frame, and tow the fucker back!" said Jensen, with a definite gleam in his eye.

"Let's see, we'll need a couple of twenty ton bottle jacks, wheel brace, better bring all the tools as well, a piece, about five foot long of scaffold pipe to wind up the wheel nuts. Oh! And a set of wheel nuts for each side. Whoever stole the wheels took the wheel nuts as well. We'll need the 'A' frame of course, and all its fittings."

While I was listing, Jensen was writing it all out. "I'll organise all that t'morrer and we could set off the next day at sparrah's fart. Waddya reckon?"

"Well if you're willing to take the chance it's still there. Yes let's do it!" I said enthusiastically.

"Ah blindin' sun! Fanks a miwyon sun, ah blindin', blindin'." Jensen was beside himself with relief. "You don't know what shit this will get me out of."

"Well. Camionaire oblige." I cringed at my own attempt at a pun. "It's an adventure if nothing else. You gotta pay me though," I smiled.

"'Ow abaht a monkey now, an' a monkey back in

Blighty? I'd give it y'all nah but I gotta geddit back, and I'll need all the all the wonga I can get."

"Yeah. I'll go for that."

"Ah, ha ha, blindin', sun. We'd better get some sleep. We got some shit to get togever t'morrah." He was actually rubbing his hands together in relief.

"Yeah 'night Jensen." I remember drifting off to sleep in a proper double bed, with clean sheets, and looking forward to going out and pulling this wreck out of the desert.

Next day we got everything together and loaded it into the ailing F89. I remember thinking that it should last long enough to pull the wreck back in. Just carry a couple of gallons of engine oil. The running oil pressure was OK but it was burning a bit. Which was ok because a gallon of oil was cheaper than Evian bottled water!

We blagged a tilt trailer to carry all the kit and by late afternoon we were ready to go. I'd cleared an area on the concrete slab in readiness to take the wrecked Volvo F89. While we were clearing the concrete an incident at the gate caught our attention.

The gate and barrier were manned twenty-four hours. One of the Iranian guard captains was a real obnoxious, pig of a man, He was huge and a bully to match. However he went too far with one of the Korean drivers, this day.

The Korean guy was half his size and just wanted to return to his quarters inside the compound. It escalated into lots of shouting by the guard captain, right in the Korean guy's face. I don't know the details but the guard captain lost it when the Korean didn't understand what he was shouting about and put his hands around the Korean guy's throat for some reason, and tried to fling him out into the road.

Quick as a flash the Korean guy jumped out of his clutches and caught his attacker with a sharp finger jab just under the bully's left eye. This had the unfortunate effect of popping the guard's eyeball out of its socket. It looked extremely painful and indeed the guard screamed in pain while trying to press his eyeball back in place.

"That was very considerate of him."

"What!?" I asked incredulously.

"Well that Korean geezer is a taekwondo expert wiv some black belt or summfin'. 'E teaches a class amongst the other drivers 'cos the Iranians treat'm like shit. Anyway, if 'ed wan'ed 'e coulda sent his eye rollin' dahn the road. 'E's sayin' touch me again and I'll blind yer. Like I said, very considerate of 'im to give such a warnin'."

As we watched the guard captain was being loaded into a taxi to go the hospital. We learned later that the doctors were able to re-insert his eye but the muscle damage and bruising were going to take a long time to heal. It was still touch and go that he might lose the use of that eye. The Korean driver wasted no time in contacting his embassy, who came on the scene very quickly. This avoided arrest but he was still sent home to avoid prosecution by the Iranians.

We left before sun-up next morning. Jensen did the first stint of driving while I dozed in the passenger seat. We stopped for lunch and we had a cold box with us so it wasn't too bad, comfort wise. By the time we arrived at the wreck it was mid-afternoon. The temperature was around 40°C, as I pulled off the road, and into the huge lay-by where the wreck was parked. The change of engine note and rough road, woke Jensen from his noisy snoring. He was sweating and looked very red. "It's still 'ere then." He was rapidly waking up and grabbed a Fanta out of the cold box.

"Yeah but it's a bit hot out there still. Shall we just wait an hour or so? It'll be in the shade of the rocks by then."

"Good idea sun. But let's just 'ave a quick butchers a minute."

We got out and had a good inspection of it, but the sun was still strong and we just ended up sitting in the shade of the rocks.

"I'm gonn' 'ave anuver Coke. You want one, sun?"

"Nah they're just full of sugar. You end up thirstier. I know you're gonna laugh but I'm gonna brew up, and have a nice puff, and lay in the shade here till the truck's in the shade. We won't get sunstroke that way!"

"Fuckin' 'ippies." Jensen grinned. He didn't smoke dope except after he'd had a few drinks, then he'd get shit-faced. When sober he'd forget all this and pretend to condemn drugs.

"Fuckin' 'ippocrites." I countered, using as many 'glottal stops' as possible, I lapsed back into Cockney when I was around him. I'd got to like and admire Jensen and was glad I'd taken the decision to help him out.

I made a cup of tea and even had some UHT milk from the cold box. I made up a smoke but didn't get far down it before falling asleep in the shade of the rocks. I was awoken with another cup of tea a couple of hours later. The partly-smoked spliff was missing.

"What happened to that smoke?" I asked absently, scratching myself awake.

"I thought I'd better get rid of it. It'd gone out in your 'and and you were asleep, so I thought better 'ad..." he trailed off sheepishly.

"You smoked it yourself, you toerag. I can tell 'cos you have eyes like piss holes in snow!"

"Guilty I'm afraid. I got a little bored while you were knockin' aht 'Z's."

"Thought so. It's all over yer face. Tell yer what

though, you don't need me to tell you, this next bit is a bit dangerous. If we don't do it properly we'll end up losing fingers or summat," I said seriously, as I made up and smoked another Farsi to have with my tea. "Tell you something else as well. That unit clamped to the back of the trailer is going to travel like a pig," I said after weighing it up.

"We can rope the steering wheel and the 'A' frame will keep it fairly straight. We ain't in any hurry, we'll just take it easy."

"Yeah, guess so, but it's going to be a bit cumbersome. It looks like most of the engine, transmission and rear axle are untouched, though."

We worked hard in the next couple of hours installing the 'A' frame and getting the front wheels fitted. We had to jack up in stages and fit the wheels. Although in the shade, it was still heavy work and we were both sweating buckets. It was just getting dark as I crawled out from underneath the truck. I had been winding off the brakes. As we would have no air pressure on the wreck, the brakes would not be blown off, so they would have to be virtually dismantled before they would release their grip. This meant there were now no brakes on the wreck, but as there would be no driver, it didn't really matter. I just prayed that the wreck would follow us smoothly!

I was well overheated and covered in dirt so I took a 'jerry-can shower' which was very refreshing.

"I'm shagged. This 'eat has taken it out'a me. Shall we get a few hours' sleep? We can kick off really early if yu' like," said Jensen.

"Yeah let's just have a couple of hours and I'll be good to go," I said, with more enthusiasm than I really felt.

I took the top bunk and fell asleep immediately. Next thing I know it was getting light to the east and Jensen had the engine running. I tumbled out of the bunk into the passenger's seat.

"I've 'ad a check rahnd, everything's lookin' good. I thought we'd press on and 'ave some breakfast in abaht an hour. Alright wiv you sun?"

"Yeah, yeah, sure. I can never eat first thing. I'll be hungry by then."

"Right 'ere we go then. Better keep an eye on it, see how it's following."

Jensen eased off very carefully without any dramas. You could feel the pull of the wreck but all in all, it looked fine. We took it in turns again to drive and we stopped frequently to check everything. It was all holding together but did have a tendency to swing to the left and right. This was because the rope holding the steering wheel would go slack over the miles of bumping and jerking. Had we been doing it this way in the UK, we'd have very soon got a pull from the police and rightly, charged with an insecure or dangerous load.

Here, it didn't matter. There were no police and you just got on with it. The suicidal Iranian truck drivers gave the 'crazy English' a wide birth, with possibly the odd horn sounded and a wave of the up-turned palm to say, "Why are you bothering with a wreck like that?"

The journey back to Tehran was awful. We couldn't go too fast and we had to keep an eye constantly to our rear where the wreck was swinging around like a drunken sailor. Not only that but the F89 we were driving was pumping out black smoke. We stopped and I secured the steering, this time with some metal butchery that stopped the steering from moving! To this day, I remember what happened next! It was late afternoon as we arrived on the outskirts of Tehran. Desert driving with the wreck in tow was one thing, there you had plenty of room, but here on the edge of town there were people walking alongside the road. Ox carts, bicycles, cars, and motorbikes.

I was driving at the time and was watching an oncoming bus on my side of the road. We were both doing about thirty miles an hour but he wanted to get round an obstruction on his side of the road, before me. I had no choice but to brake rather heavily which had the effect of catapulting the wreck from the middle of the road, to the edge, Missing by a fraction, an old guy carrying a sack of something over his shoulder. He'd been intent on getting where he was going, and was not aware of the wreck approaching him until the last minute. He gave a strangled cry and leapt like a gazelle into the ditch, in one go!

The wreck missed him but it had been a close thing. We drove on, quickly! Can you imagine what would have followed if we had struck and killed him?

We managed to get it to the concrete and I spent the next week swapping over the engines and gearboxes. Jensen had given me his car to commute in, while he took taxis on the firm's account. It was good getting to know where the Volvo agents were and buying bits. Always the bill was added up on an abacus.

I felt I knew Tehran city quite well now. But getting parts often took hours because of the traffic snarl-ups at road junctions. Traffic lights were considered 'advisory' or just plain ignored, causing chaos. I finished swapping over the engines and was pleased to find that it had been worth the effort. It had taken me four days. The wreck's engine, clutch and gearbox were perfect. It ran nicely with good oil pressure and not burning oil. Jensen was impressed, I'd made one real good truck, from two iffy ones.

"Bloody 'ell what c'n you do wiv a workshop, then?"

"Anything you can think of, given the tools and bits. Which reminds me, what about this fridge trailer?"

"Yeah I bin finkin' abaht that. Let's go and 'ave a

butchers."

We jumped into the company pick-up and headed off down to where the Dutch company had abandoned all its equipment when it went bankrupt. The place was overgrown with a rusty padlock and chain around the gates. We could see four fridge trailers and a couple of tractor units, both of them UNICs. There was also a long wheelbase Land Rover that had been kitted out like a mobile workshop. It was not very old and it was sad to see such vehicles rotting away.

I selected the trailer I would take and it looked to be the best of them. Next day I tested out the F89 with its new motor by going for a 100km drive down the Saveh Road. On the way back just as it had got dark, I pulled up at the gates to the Dutch compound. I cut the rusty chain with ease and flung the gates open.

Nobody on the road took a blind bit of notice as I coupled up to my selected trailer. I connected the air and electrical lines to the trailer and noted the brakes being blown off on the trailer, indicating that all was working. I pulled out of the yard and stopped to shut the gates. No point in advertising! I drove directly to a spot behind Jensen's transport yard. It was shaded and a little hidden. Jensen arrived with a portable spray painting compressor and started to spray it in his colours. Within a day it looked a completely different trailer. The small fridge motor on the front was in good condition and started up without problem and within an hour, it had started to pull the temperature in the trailer down, indicating that the fridge was working OK.

When everything was finished Jensen paid me off. I helped him load all his belongings into the trailer and a few days later he, and his family, set off for the drive home to England with no papers for either the tractor unit or trailer. I can only imagine the problems he must have faced at every border. I hope he made it home OK. I never heard of him again until much later in life. I heard that he had taken another ex-pat post as transport consultant to the Ghanaian government. I did hear he was spotted driving around London in a Rolls Royce. Whether that was true or not, I guess I'll never

Isobel the kids and I took a room at the tourist camp after seeing Jensen off. Dave the Arab turned up early next morning to ask me to do him a favour. "You can ride a motorbike?" he asked.

"Yes of course. Why?"

"There's these two German guys I met yesterday. They just come across from Kabul. They found these old Harley Davidson bikes in an old building in one of the villages, must've been leftover from the war or something 'cos they're really early ones. Y'know the type with running boards and gear change on the tank?"

Dave went on to tell me how the two German lads had bought them intending to ride them back to Germany and sell them to a collector, for a fortune. Trouble was, one of the lads had been struck down with hepatitis by drinking from a less-than-clean well. They had enough money to buy the drugs needed and had been treated by their embassy's doctor, but he just didn't feel well enough to ride all the way to Germany. They had the good Idea to hang out at the tourist camp, reasoning that there would be a truck going home that might have some space. That's when they bumped into Dave.

"All we gotta do is go over the Amir Kabir Hotel, ride their bikes back to the customs yard. I've already set up the forklift driver to load them on for me and the lads are gonna to pay me, up front, to drop'm off on the way back. Sweet."

"But ain't that gonna put you out of your way a bit?"

"Nah. I'll just take a return load from 'ere, for

Germany. I'll easy get a load back to England from there, no problem," he grinned.

I admired the way he would just alter course and go with the flow. It was his own motor and he only had himself to worry about and could go where he pleased.

I left Isobel at the TBT bus stop with the kids. They were going into town, to the main post office to check the Post Restante, to see if there were any letters from home. I had arranged to meet them outside the main post office at four in the afternoon. Dave and I jumped into his unit and he drove like one possessed. He used the tractor unit like a Mini! When you are not pulling a trailer, and it's just the unit, acceleration and power are phenomenal, and you have brakes that will stop you far quicker than anything else on the road. Believe me, with no trailer to hold you up they are like driving a Jaguar!

Dave was driving just like them and carving them up using his weight, no end. It was a delight to watch. At one point we came up behind a Mercedes whose driver had been a bit slow to react when it was time to go. Dave applied full Alpine air horns and we wet ourselves when he nearly leapt out of his seat.

We met the German guys and sure enough one of them looked like he'd been through a hedge backwards.

"Sorry to hear about your illness, man," I said, not knowing if he spoke English or not.

"Ya. Vas from shit in well, in vasser."

"Do you mean the little bugs in the water? Or do you mean actual shit in the water? Y' know, faeces in the water."

His mate spoke to him in German and had understood what I was asking.

"Ya. Vas the bugs in der vasser. Drinking water in chai shop, was from river!"

His pal took over the story, and it seems that In Afghanistan they have rudimentary hospitals but you have to buy your own drugs. The doctors will not treat you until you have bought them, if you could find them that is. He told us how he'd seen a young girl, victim of a road accident. She was stretchered in and obviously in great pain. She was examined by the doctor, he informed the family which drugs were needed and they had to go and try to buy them. The girl was virtually ignored from then on, and by the time her family returned with the drugs, the girl had died.

I remember thinking how lucky we were back home that we had the NHS.

Dave and I picked up the bikes from the courtyard of the hotel. The sound of these old Harleys starting up brought loads of hotel guests out onto their balconies overlooking the central courtyard. The scent of joss and hash was everywhere.

We rode out into the lunchtime traffic of Tehran. It turned out to be much more fun carving up the traffic on a bike. We rode over to the customs yard and I hung around to help Dave get them loaded and strapped down securely. We had one heart-stopping moment when the forklift driver nearly dropped the pair of them as he was lifting them onto the trailer. He didn't see the rock lying in the way, and one of his front wheels rose up on it and he nearly went over sideways, had it not dug into the floor of the trailer at the front, Jesus H...

Dave and I then jumped into a taxi and headed off to meet Isobel at the main post office.

"Main post office, Aghar," (mister) Dave instructed the driver. But the driver pulled a face and mumbled something about a 'problem'.

"What problem?" I asked.

"No not problem for me. Problem for you," said the driver.

"No. No problem said Dave waving a five hundred rial note under his nose. "There and back, understand?"

"Bali mister, no problem."

And there was no problem. That is until we turned from a side road into a main boulevard. The driver got halfway out and stopped dead. To our left was what can only be described as a rabid mob, complete with Molotov cocktails and other sundry weapons. Burning cars and overturned vehicles blazed away. To our right were the flashing blue lights and specialist vehicles of the riot squad, complete with full body armour, crash helmets and assault rifles. What's more they had just decided to charge the rampaging mob, and we were now right in the way!

Dave grabbed the driver by the shoulder and shook him out of his shock. "Turn round, turn round quickly!" shouted Dave. The driver crunched it into gear and did a passable 'U-ey'.

We disappeared up the side street we'd just come out of, just as the first charging riot squad came past, behind us. "Jesus that was close. What was all that about?" I asked the driver.

"People not like Shah. Want Ayatollah Khomeini return. He kissed a photograph stuck in his dashboard. "Great man," he finished.

"Never mind all that. We still got to get to the PTT agha. You'll have to go round another way," said Dave. The driver started to protest. "Never mind all that," Dave said, again reaching for his wallet.

"My wife and children are at the post office," I said to the driver. "The PTT. You understand?"

"You understand?" said Dave, waving another five hundred note. "But you only get it when we get back to the tourist camping. OK?"

The driver understood alright and we dived off down side streets and alleyways until we got clear of the riot. We journeyed on to the post office where we found the doors locked. This was puzzling as it should have been open. I looked through the window and could see Isobel and the kids, sat in an office.

I caught Isobel's attention and soon the doors were unlocked to let me in. It turned out that the manager had locked the doors and kept everyone inside for their own safety. I thanked him and we set off in the taxi for the tourist camp.

"That's it," exclaimed Dave. "I'm off out of it. It looks like it's all gonna kick off soon."

"Yes I think it's time we left as well," said Isobel.

By the time we got back to camp the manager told me there had been a call for me. He hadn't taken a name but the caller was going to call back at nine o'clock tonight.

"He ask for English Alun," said the manager. "That is you?"

"Yes. I wonder who that is then?"

"It was 'he' so it must be one of the others down in Isfahan. I hope they're alright."

We waited around the office at nine o'clock and sure enough the manager passed the phone to me. The voice on the other end was very faint, but definitely Timus.

"That you Timus? What's up?"

"Well, we're all ready to go on." He said it in such a way as to ask, "Whad'ya think I'm phoning for?" I had after all, been a week or more than I had intended to be.

"That's exactly what Isobel and I were just talking about." I shouted down the phone. "We'll come down on the TBT tomorrow or the day after, OK?"

"That's cool we're all waiting to go." He sounded relieved.

"Yeah! Next bit of the adventure, eh Timus?"

"Fuckin' right man."

"Give 'em our love and we'll see you tomorrow or the next day at the latest."

"OK, Alun. Fuckin' way out there, man." And the line went dead.

"That was Timus in case you hadn't guessed. I think they were really worried that I'd gone off and done something else and left them stranded."

"Well we are a fortnight overdue," Isobel reminded me.

"Has it been two weeks! No wonder they were getting worried. You OK for leaving tomorrow?" I asked.

"Yes, no problem. I'll just stuff our clothes in the bag, and roll up the sleeping bags.

We had a massive cook-up and Dave and all our other friends came round the fire. We smoked well into the night. Dave and I swapped telephone numbers and addresses back home, and promised to meet up when we got back. The TBT pulled out at six thirty the next morning. Dave had got up early with us and drove us to the bus terminal. It was crowded and chaotic but we found our bus. It was still being packed down on the roof rack so there was time to say goodbye properly to Dave. He hugged us both. Isobel got a longer and closer hug than me, *Hmmm*. The kids got a hug as well.

Dave jumped up into his cab, fired up the engine, and, with a loud blast on the air horn, was gone. I looked at Isobel, she was watching him go with a glint in her eye!

The journey down was tolerable. We stopped a few times for meals and toilet breaks. Most of the time I dozed while a well-dressed young man engaged Isobel in conversation. He was practising his English. He asked if he could give the kids some cold Fantas and sweets. He was very polite and I was half listening to some of the history of the area and drifting off to sleep as the bus rocked over the desert. We arrived late in the evening and got a taxi to the camp. Everyone was really pleased to see us. Except Fran. Some of the many friends Isobel had made while I was away driving were there and hugging her and the kids.

The next few days were spent packing and checking the bus over. I was surprised how many friends Isobel and the rest had made. We had a party at the camp site and everybody behaved disgracefully! Thank goodness the kids were zonko in their bunks due to all the swimming and walking followed by huge helpings of their favourite local dinner and fruit. The Bell Helicopters guys came round and drank for the USA. They were loud and wonderfully hilarious as only the Yanks can be. We played a game they'd invented called 'beat the bong'. It was just an excuse to smoke huge amounts of dope through a Hubble Bubble pipe. If you were still standing when the contents of the bowl had been turned completely to ash, you were considered to have beaten the bong. That was all very well but the pipe held over 10 grams of resin, that was a lot to smoke in one go, even for me, whose conspicuous consumption was legendary.

I caught Max, an airframe fitter from New York, with his hand on Isobel's arse. She didn't do much to stop him, despite having his face slapped playfully by Kakey not minutes before. In fact, at regular intervals during the proceedings a squeal from one of the girls was evidence of Max's wandering hands.

A couple of the Bell guys managed to persuade us to let them buy a couple of tabs of acid that we were saving for full moon parties in Goa, India. We kept saying no but they were offering twenty dollars a tab, so we weakened. They were totally off their trolleys for about twenty-four hours and they had to be working the next day.

"Poor buggers haven't seen their wives for months," said Isobel when I remarked that her arse must be black and blue what with all the Yanks and local men pinching her. "Quite honestly, right now I'm too pissed to give a fuck," was her succinct reply.

The local guys got really pissed and were diving into the pool in their underpants. When you consider that they were Muslim, and usually keep their underpants on even in a male shower room! Here they were in their undies in front of women.

Next morning we paid our bill and said our goodbyes. It looked like the whole camp turned out to wave goodbye. We drove at a steady pace and the atmosphere was upbeat. We were all excited at the prospect of Afghanistan and India. We knew that the best hash in the world came from Afghanistan and we couldn't wait to try it. We ended up at the Gol-Leh-Shah motor camp in Tehran again, ready to start for Meshad some four hundred miles distant through a range of mountains that included Mount Damavand where, as legend would have it, an old Iranian despot was strung up inside the peak of the mountain to hang there forever.

As we left the city behind on the Meshad road I was suddenly aware of a taxi trying to get my attention, from behind. "We've got a mad taxi driver behind, I think he's trying to get me to stop. Check it out through the rear window, one of you, will you?"

Charlie said, "It's one of the guys we gave a tab of acid to, for a slab of dope back at the Gol-Leh-Shah camp site. Maybe we left something behind."

"You'd better pull up Al, let's see what he wants," shouted Black Bob.

As I applied the handbrake the guy from the camp and

his very well dressed, in an Armani suit, mate, came on board.

"You have LSD yes?" said the eager man from the camp.

"We have some but we are saving it for when we get to India."

"Please you must sell me some," he said, in a slightly conspiratorial way. "This fellow is cousin to Shah's wife and he is very rich but speaks no English, you understand me? He desperately wants to try this LSD that he has heard of."

We apologised again but explained that the few tabs we had left were more precious to us than money because outside Europe you just can't get good LSD.

The guy from the camp explained this to his Armani-clad pal who looked very disappointed and more than a little irritated at being refused. A thing that he was, clearly, not used to. They reluctantly left the bus with our apologies, got in their taxi that had been waiting and disappeared back toward the city.

We drove on only to be waved down some two miles later by the same taxi as before. This time they wasted no time. "I will give you whatever your price for five tablets of LSD," said the man from the camp, raising his eyebrows and nodding toward Mr Armani as if to say, "Go on, name your price, he will pay it. He is rich and doesn't care about money, he just wants the acid."

Out of the blue and in an effort to get rid of these two, Timus blurted out, "You can have five tabs for one hundred dollars EACH. That should stop this nonsense and get rid of them so's we can get on," said Timus in an aside to me. Neither of us thought for one second that he would agree to this price, it was designed to put him off!

Without a word Mr Armani nodded and gave Campsite

Man a thick wad of dollars and was already heading for the taxi, examining his five tabs as he went. Campsite Man carved off five hundred in twenties and pocketed a still rather thick wad of dollars. He smiled shook hands with Timus and I warmly, and was gone, leaving us all with our jaws on the floor. We'd just made five hundred dollars in the blink of an eye!

Off we went again, this time feeling even higher. We hadn't been going for half an hour when, "Bugger me!" I exclaimed. "I don't believe it!"

"Wassup?" asked Black Bob.

"That bloody taxi's behind us again flashing his lights and waving his arm for me to stop. What the fuck's going on, d'you reckon?" I was getting a bit worried that we'd been set up for a bust or they had changed their minds and wanted their money back. I pulled over. On climbed the camp man again, his eyes wide with excitement.

"My friend is in heaven in the taxi. He has swallowed a tablet. He can see twenty thousand virgins waving him into heaven. He wants another five tablets for the same price!" He waved another wad of dollar bills, same size as before. He parted off the same size commission as before and held out the rest to us.

Timus looked at me. I shrugged. "Speaking for myself and I know for Isobel as well, we'd rather have that fine amount of money."

Timus took a quick vote from the others. "There'll only be one tab left if we do him another five," Timus informed us.

"Do it," said Kakey.

"Yep go for it," said Charlie.

"Yeah," said Glynis.

"I fancied a trip on Goa beach but that's a lot of

money," added Black Bob.

"Do it, man!" I said to Timus.

Two minutes later we were alone again with another five hundred dollars and this time a bonus from Campsite Man of a respectable lump of Afghani hash to boot! We just couldn't believe it! Campsite Man had just made a year's wages and we'd just made more money than all the others had made while teaching English to the Iranian army!

Another light went on inside my head!

We just floated along. All stress from not having any money, was gone. I suggested that as we'd all worked hard and had a bit of luck why shouldn't we treat ourselves to some local clothes and trinkets. This we did in a small town before the border.

It was decided that, in the interests of individuality, we'd all do our shopping separately and then come back to the bus with what we'd bought, to compare. Isobel the kids and I went for full Patani tribal dress complete with belted dagger and what we called 'Shit strainers'. These were trousers of a sort. Conventional waistband but from there down, billowing was the style. A low crotch and falling cloth drawn to a button cuff at the ankles. All this was in local spun cotton. The bodice and wrap-around collar were all Afghan sheep wool. All this was finished off with an embroidered shawl, worn around the shoulders and neck, then flicked over the shoulder to finish. I even took the turban of rough blue-striped cotton. The shopkeeper wound it round my head for me.

"You could be taken for a Patani tribesman like me. You have dark beard and dark sun tan."

"You do me a great honour," I said, and saw that he understood my compliment. "Where did you learn such good English?" I asked as we sipped tea and waited for

Isobel and the kids to try on their new gear.

"I learn from tourist and from western music which I love. My brother in Germany have good job and help me set up business here. I make really good business from tourist so the more I learn English the more I earn. Good eh?" he said with a grin.

Just then Isobel appeared from behind a heavy carpet drape that covered the entrance to the shopkeeper's private quarters. His wife had taken Isobel and the kids back there to try on their outfits. I gaped in absolute surprise to see Isobel with a delicate, tiny, beaded gold strand head band. Her earrings were of jade and gold and of traditional design with exquisite workmanship. She wore a plum-coloured top with embroidery in different natural dyes that glowed. The fact that she wasn't wearing a bra was a little obvious but it just added, in a pure and beautiful way, to the stunning effect. I even heard the shopkeeper take a sharp breath.

She wore billowing trousers that hugged the small of her back, then gave just a wonderful hint of the shape of her beautiful bottom, before falling to cuffed ankles. On her left ankle was a gold bracelet made by tribal craftsmen. The effect was mesmerising!

The lust was dispelled a bit when the kids came tumbling out from behind the drapes. The wife of the shopkeeper had dressed them in identical embroidered outfits, not only that but she'd made up Mellony with traditional tribal henna make-up and ankle bracelets just like Mum. She was ecstatic with her new clothes. She loved dressing up and was definitely showing artistic appreciation. Alun was less amused but was wandering around imitating the local boys with a light leather overshirt, flannel shirt and cuffed cotton trousers with local-style leather sandals. He also wore the hexagonal style hat as many Afghans wear. He looked pretty damn cool.

The bill was enormous compared to the little we had been used to spending but I realised that perhaps we'd been a little mean to the kids, but now I knew that time was over. I had learned things! We bought a few things to decorate the bus. The shopkeeper sent word out that we would like to see some bric-a-brac – it was paraded before us as we drank tea and picked things out to add to the bill, all to be paid to the shopkeeper. He thought he was onto a good thing of course but got the surprise of his life when Isobel started to bargain him right down.

"Is this how it is done in Inglistan, by women? Please sir, you and I." He smacked the back of his hand in the palm of the other, smiling and overplaying it horribly.

"Five hundred rials is a little high don't you think?" said Isobel. "I went for some leather boots down in the shop next to the carpet shop. He had the same clothes as you but a little cheaper. What is your last price?" She fixed him with her gaze then moved in closer so that the gentle jiggling of her unrestrained breasts under that top mesmerised him, and he had nowhere to go.

"Madam you are cruel to me," he said in mock grief. "There is gold and precious stone here."

"Semi-precious stone." Isobel corrected quickly. "C'mon, last price, mister?"

"Madam give me four hundred and seventy and I will still make a little profit, insha'Allah."

Isobel laughed sharply. Immediately the shopkeeper said, "OK madam give me four hundred rials and I will have enough to buy a knife and cut my throat."

"I was going to beat you down a bit but we don't want anybody dying for it," said Isobel with a smile and a final wiggle. Shit! At that point I'd have sold my soul to her, let alone how the shopkeeper felt.

"Thank you madam, now my family can eat and live

good life," he exaggerated.

We paid the bill in the knowledge that out of the four hundred rials, three hundred and ninety five, would be profit. We all gyrated back to the bus to show each other what we had bought. We'd all gone for basically the same thing except Black Bob.

"I have to look a bit western still," he said. "I don't want them to think that I come from round here." A valid thought. If they thought he was English he'd be treated better. If they thought him to be a local, it would be a different story. He'd bought a smart silk embroidered shirt but was still wearing his Levis.

Kakey looked really good. She'd gone with an Indian-style top which was short and tight and ended just beneath her boobs, naked midriff and balloon trousers with the traditional cuffs at the ankles. She also wore an ankle bracelet in bright silver.

Glynis and Fran had gone with the plain female Patani dress but with long flowing silk shawls of exquisite design and quality. Glynis looked more like a nun when she covered her head with the silk scarf. Charlie had Bought an Afghan coat of three quarter length, shit-strainer pantaloons like mine, and a pair of pointed, turned up toe-type sandals.

We thought we all looked the essence of cool and hit the road again. We wanted to cross into Afghanistan at around nine o'clock so that we'd have plenty of time to get to the small city of Herat. It was the first major city and was some three hundred kilometres away.

Before we left we learned that Meshad had a really notorious prison where all the hash smugglers were incarcerated. Upon hearing that there were many British travellers amongst them, we applied to the local police chief to be allowed to visit these people and leave some items for their comfort. We were told in no uncertain terms that as we were not family, we could not visit. If we had any problems with that, we were to contact our embassy in Tehran.

As I stood with my arms folded waiting the chief's decision, one of his minions came over and put my arms to my side. I took from this that they expected me to stand to attention in front of this highly (self) important official. I didn't know it but I'd already blown our chances of visiting anyone by my 'typical western arrogance'. By the time I realised this I decided there was no longer any point in wasting time with this overblown prick, and walked out without being dismissed while he was still speaking in a pompous manner.

As we were driving away, we decided to pull over for some supplies from the rather large general store across the road. A young lad approached us and engaged us in conversation, practising his English. His name was Masood and he was a university student in Tehran. He was visiting his brother who owned a carpet shop in Mashed and asked if we would like to see some beautiful Persian rugs. We were wary of some kind of scam going on ("You come my brother shop. Smoke hash, drink tea, make business. Money no problem."), but as it turned out we learnt a great deal about carpet making, and smoked some fine, fresh Afghani. After all it was the border only twenty clicks up the road.

It was explained to us by the brother that carpets were traditionally made by children. Only their hands were small enough to tie the ten thousand knots per square foot that a good quality carpet requires. They worked in badly lit caves and what we would now refer to as sweat shops. The children often had vision problems and were not educated in any way. Many of them spending their whole lives in the carpet industry. We were told how the Shah of Iran put a stop to young children being used this way and took them out of the caves and gave them an education. It turned out to be a modernisation too far and helped him to be deposed by the religious, right wing mullahs.

We were shown many carpets taken from racks where they were wound up. As we drank tea and smoked dope and lay around in a semicircle, two young boys brought the rolled up carpets and brother flicked and rolled them out before us, with a flourish, one atop the other explaining how they used the marijuana plant for the green dyes and the opium poppy for the deep reds and purples. It really was very interesting. Even the 'sting' when it came was pretty innocuous. It transpired that to export several carpets at a time, he needed tourist passports so that they would be tax exempt as souvenirs. He asked if we would like to earn one hundred dollars and a special price on a lovely Baluchistan prayer rug we'd all liked.

We decided to take a chance and gave him all our passports and an address to send our Baluchistan rug. We parked outside his shop for the night, now wondering if we'd been ripped off but come the next day the brother returned with passports, one hundred dollars cash and a receipt, in Arabic, for posting of one Baluchistan rug to our home address in the UK.

"If I steal from you. You tell everyone on the road and I won't be able to do this again and everybody lose. This way you tell everyone I am good to my word and we all make something."

The next time I heard from home, a large parcel with a carpet inside was waiting for me 'with loads of foreign stamps on it'. We spent a very pleasant evening with the family and they cooked a huge pot of mutton curry and other vegetable dishes, and pots of cold cooked rice. I learned later that evening that they had slaughtered a goat for the meal, a very great honour for us but something I didn't need to know!

After the women of the house departed to eat their

own dinner elsewhere in the house, out came the hash and opium and a half consumed bottle of Red Label. We got well out of order and had to hang around the next day to recover.

The next day which was cold but clear sunshine we said our goodbyes and headed for the Afghan border.

Teybad border was infamous for its hash busts. The Americans were hysterically trying to stop the flood of hash into their country, so typically, they took the 'war on drugs' to the source. Any customs officer detecting hash of any amount was rewarded with a thousand US dollar bonus. There were all sorts of horror stories about huge discoveries. I can remember looking at their little photo display of people they had caught and some of the methods used. Talk about silly ways to smuggle dope, this cabinet had it all; hollowed out bars of soap. False soles of shoes. All these methods were asking to get busted and straight out of Boys' Own adventure stories. It was pathetic to look at and to my mind just a little display that would say to the Americans, "Look what we are doing to stop the dope coming out of Afghanistan. Can we have a few more million dollars in overseas aid please?"

Of course at the time, nobody with any smuggling sense would be bringing large amounts through that small strip of border. The large amounts were going by boat out of Karachi and neighbouring ports as anybody can realise if they read the exploits of Mr Howard Marks in his excellent book, *Mr Nice*. He was doing his wonderful thing about the same time that we were travelling and I recognised many of the places and people that were mentioned in his book.

A story was told to me by a border guard as I looked at the display. One concerned a bus just like ours, only it was a company from London taking paying passengers. On one return journey, the driver had hit a tree when he'd had a front wheel blow-out, and demolished most of the front of the bus. Luckily there were no special bits needed to repair it. In those days the frame was just wood and aluminium panels.

The driver decided to put the bus into one of the many local coach body-building yards that were highly skilled in their trade. After a fortnight, when the repairs were completed the driver went around to collect it. The owner of the yard told him that he wanted to buy the bus as it had a strong chassis and engine. "But I can't sell it to you, I need it to take my passengers back to London."

"Ah, but I can pay you for it now and my agent will collect it from you in London. My brother is there studying at university and will be coming home soon. He can drive it back here for me." To sweeten the deal he agreed to pay two thousand dollars for the bus, half of which he would pay now in cash, up front.

The driver knew that he wouldn't get that much at home and also knew that he could get a newer bus with the money, so he agreed to the deal. What he didn't know, of course is that while the yard had repaired the bus they had also stuffed fifty kilos of hash in the double skinned roof and the brother would have been in London to take ownership of the bus and the safely smuggled, fifty kilos of hash.

The first the driver knew of it was when these wild-eyed customs officers started to tear the roof apart. They did not use dogs in those days but the next best thing. There was a young boy who lived at the border post. He accompanied the officers when they searched a vehicle. A small drill bit would be pushed through a suspected panel. The drill bit was then held under the boy's nose and he would say yes or no according to what he smelt. This is how several big busts at that border were carried out. I learned later that a not very nice fate befell the young lad who was responsible for sending many people to Mashhad jail.

It was no good the driver telling them that the yard workers must have put the hash there. He ended up being sentenced to twenty-five years in Mashhad jail, one of the worst in central Asia. As it happened he only did four years as the Islamic revolution came about in Iran and an amnesty on all foreign prisoners was declared. The truth was that they needed the space for all the murders and torturing that the new regime needed to do to its former enemies.

The other story was more amusing and was told to me by the driver concerned. He'd made a mobile home inside a Mercedes van. He'd run out of money on the way back from India and decided to avail himself of seventy kilos of best Afghani hash and had made a false floor in the van to stash it in. All had gone well until he approached Teybad border. A couple of hundred kilometres from the border a truck had forced him to swerve off the road and caused a large gash in the side of the van when he grazed the rock face. Of course, where did the gash come? Right between the false and real floors. He pulled in to a secluded spot just off the road and inspected the damage. There were plaques of hash sticking out of the tear, so he stuffed them back in and got out his tub of filler, and began to beat out and fill the gash. The trouble was that wherever you stop, even in the middle of the desert, someone will turn up to gawp at you. They seem to come out of the very ground.

Just as he had mixed up the filler a couple of shepherd lads came along and tried to engage him in conversation. He had no choice but to move on after only having repaired part of the gash. The next hundred and fifty kilometres consisted of pulling over and continuing to do the repairs only to be interrupted again by curious locals. These locals would think nothing of reporting strange activity to the border guards.

This happened many times even while he was spraying some aerosol paint onto the repaired bodywork. By the time he'd stopped for the last time he was only thirty miles from the border and the paint was still wet. With what I can only describe as 'shit loads of bottle', he continued on to the border and actually got through without them finding the stash by some miracle.

I don't know about anybody else but the luck, or lack of it, that he had would have said to me, "Turn back! You are going to have big problems." But he kept going, got through Teybad border and stopped in Meshad until he'd sold enough of the dope to some tourists, to make enough to get him moving again. I remember asking him, how the hell did he do it?

"I just put it out of my mind. It's not there and because I convince myself of that, it shows on my face."

There was a lot of sense to that and I learned a lot from him, in fact I was in awe of his courage and conviction. He was in no doubt that if he'd been caught he and his girlfriend would be spending serious years in the worst jail in central Asia. And yet he still went for it! As if that wasn't enough he crossed thirteen other borders, including the Greek and Turkish, both of which were hysterical about dope in those days, Remember the old Eagles track 'The Greeks Don't Want No Freaks'?

He eventually got back to London and sold the lot for a small fortune. The only dope available in those days was mediocre Moroccan. So when he turned up with top quality Afghani, he could sell for top dollar! The one photograph from that pathetic, grotty little display at the border that stays with me, was a picture of a young British truck driver. He was wearing cut-off denim shorts, a T-shirt and flip flop sandals. He had longish hair and his right wrist was handcuffed to a grinning customs officer with several of his colleagues stood beside him. Behind them was the truck, an English-registered Volvo F88. In the foreground were several small-wheeled trolleys piled up with kilos of hash. This had obviously been their biggest bust so far and they were making the most of it. I have often wondered over the years, what happened to that driver. Sometimes I remembered that truck driver in defiance, sometimes in fear.

Chapter 9
Afghanistan

We approached the border at Teybad. After crossing we'd be in our first dope-producing country. We were like kids at Christmas. The border itself was one of complete contrasts. On the Iran side you had a modern building and air conditioning. Once you crossed to the Afghanistan side it was back to Medieval times. There were adobe-walled enclosures with offices and a cranky fan in the ceiling. Side offices for lower minions, had no fan. The customs officer was in tribal dress. He was able to speak and read English. I soon realised that this would be a great status symbol in this country. He obviously had been educated.

He gave us a wrinkly weather-beaten smile that showed his Genghis Kahn ancestry. "Welcome to Afghanistan," he said pleasantly, but from then on he concentrated on writing from right to left in a really neat Arabic scrip. I noted that the stamp he was using for our passports was round, about the size of a digestive biscuit and almost smooth. You could just pick out the moon and star of Islam but around the edge it said, 're c o A ni n' (Republic of Afghanistan). The stamp in my passport for the bus was a piece of art with scrolls and wings in the corner. As we waited for the customs man to finish, I noticed a crate of empty Coke bottles in the corner. They had the trademark, curvy white stripes and the words 'Coca-Cola' but in Arabic, and the bottles were almost opaque with age where they had rubbed in their crates. They had been used many hundreds of times. Something told me we were entering a very poor and primitive country. It was real frontier stuff and very exciting.

As we exited the stifling heat of the border post a sign about fifteen feet high said 'Welcome to Afghanistan'. Those words were printed on the huge advert for Coca-Cola that was the sign. For some reason that sign has stuck in my mind, I guess because if there was one place that Coca-Cola shouldn't be, was that wild and wonderful country.

It was very hot as we prepared for the long drive to Herat. We wouldn't get there in daylight but it shouldn't be too late. I was still worrying about the cooling system. It had almost boiled a couple of times and I had to stop and run the engine up to a thousand revolutions and try to cool the thing down. It was a real headache, and it was getting hotter. The border guard that had stamped our passports suddenly came aboard uninvited.

"You have hashish?"

We misunderstood his question and became really defensive. "No. No. We don't have anything like that," I protested.

"Good. Do not buy from these people, these local people."

"No. No. Of course not."

"They will only rob you, you should buy from me."

"Pardon? Did I hear that right?"

"My brother have farm in Mazar-i-Sharif. Best quality hashish in the world." And he was deadly serious!

Timus was first to regain his composure and get his chin off the floor. My eyes were still wide at the thought of a customs officer offering me the finest hash in the world at an equivalent of two pounds an ounce, when back home this kind of quality would cost you around fifty pounds an ounce IF you could find it!

"How much for an ounce?" asked Timus.

"Huh?" replied the officer.

"Um. Twenty eight... no hang on, thirty grams?"

"Fifty grams, I give you for ten dollars."

"Cool. Yes we'll take it. Can we have a look?"

He produced a large wooden box that was full of a coarse brown powder.

"Hang on. What's this?" I said, dripping with suspicion.

With a cross between a grin and a leer, he said, "Good quality, watch I show you."

He went to our hurricane lamp and lit it with a slightly high flame. He poured a big handful of brown powder and started to squeeze it between his palms, gently heating it over the flame to warm it, pressing it really hard and turning it over and over in his hands. After about ten minutes of this he had a fish shaped piece of black-brown hash. The brown powder was the raw crystal powder of the female marijuana plant. In the heat of the sun this crystalline resin would be secreted by the plant to protect the leaf from too much UV sunlight. When the plant is harvested the granules fall and pile up into the brown (colour depended upon geographical location and strain of plant) powder we'd seen before Customs Man continued to press up the hash for us and we watched and learned.

"I must make heat," he said, as he held the hash over the lamp until it was warm and pliable. He then spent another few minutes finishing off the plaque of hash. It was now black all over and more like what we were used to back home. He finished by carefully laying the slab of hash on the cold metal surface of one of our grill trays. "This must go cold."

We watched, fascinated, while we waited. It was the hardest wait of my life!

Customs Man eventually picked up the piece and sought out a hard surface. When he found one, he dropped the piece from about a foot height. There was a 'clacking' sound as the piece hit the hard surface. Customs Man declared the sound to be correct and all that remained was to press his stamp into it and polish the piece. It looked wonderful by the time he'd finished, complete with government stamp. He then invited us to sample the goods.

What can I say? What words can I use to describe the effect of this piece of the world's finest smoke? All my expectations were met and then some! I was humming along, looking at everything in this new world I was in. The sun fell on me and felt so good. I could see the road that we would be driving soon and I wanted to go now. Finally my head came back to the present and I realised I'd wandered outside the bus and was staring at a group of Waziri tribesmen, looking after their beautifully kept horses. I learned later that these guys loved a game of Buzkashi. A mounted game with about fifty riders in one team and fifty in the other. The idea is to lean down from your mount and grab a headless carcass of a calf. Then you ride with it into your opponent's area until no one else can get it from you. It is complete mayhem of course and demands incredible riding skills. The rules are: there are no rules!

The game originated back in the times of Genghis Khan's hordes but then, instead of a calf's body, they would use a freshly decapitated carcass of an unfortunate prisoner. When in full cry, it is dusty, noisy, and very exciting, with heavy betting on the favourite and famous riders.

I dragged my mind back to the present and returned to the bus, still buzzing very pleasantly. While I was outside a very fragile-looking Timus had paid Customs Man and we were all wasted, giggling like schoolgirls.

"Hello, hello, my friends. Where are you from?" This came from a snappily-dressed youngish man.

It was difficult but I managed to reply, "Hello we are from England."

"Ah! I have friend in England. Where your city?"

"Bristol," I replied, knowing what was coming next.

"I have friend in Bristol. His name Bobby. You know Bobby. He come Afghanistan many times. He always come to me for hashish."

"We have just bought some from the customs officer." He looked disappointed but went straight on.

"My name is Habeeb. I am manager for Miramar Hotel in Herat. Can you give me lift to Herat. I can give you some hash and you can park in the hotel grounds."

I did wonder why a manager of a hotel needed a lift but it sounded like a good deal to me so I asked if everyone was ok with that. They were, so we set off.

The only main highway through Afghanistan was part of the old Asian Highway that stretched from Istanbul in the west right across to Saigon in South Vietnam. Most of it had been built by the Chinese who wanted access to the warm sea port of Karachi. The trouble was it had been built many years ago and it was badly in need of repair. It had been built of slabs of pre-cast concrete about the size of two buses end on end. The sun and the cold had conspired to undermine the gravel bed that the slabs were laid on. This had the effect of making a heavy 'clump' as the weight of the bus went on it, and another as it went off the slab and onto the next one. It had a hypnotic effect, or was that the even better hashish of Habeeb? After about a hundred and fifty miles of blistering white sunshine, I noted that the coolant temperature had climbed very high. I started to go through the routine of trying to keep the revs up in order to spin the fan faster. I noted Habeeb looking over my shoulder.

"Do you have problem my friend?"

"Yes, this is an old English bus and it was not built for this heat. I must make a repair in Herat."

"This is big problem for you my friend, I think."

"Yes it is and I don't think we should go anywhere until we fix it. I think the best thing I can do is take off the cylinder heads and see if there any blockages. Will I be able to do this when we are parked in the Hotel?"

"Why not?" said Habeeb. "I will escort your wife and children and friends if they want, around the very old city of Herat while you make repairs." Everybody agreed to this, bar Fran. I could see they were warming to Habeeb as he told them stories of old Afghanistan. Fran however saw a chance to have a pop at me.

"I thought we'd sorted that out in Greece," she said acidly. "Are you saying we wasted all that money?"

"For a start 'we' didn't fix it Fran. *I* fixed it, if you remember? And we didn't spend a penny on the bits." I turned away as if to indicate I'd finished talking to her.

"Don't you turn your back on me! You're supposed to be the big clever mechanic aren't you? Why haven't you fixed it then?" She spat her words out at me. I looked up in complete surprise. How could she leave herself so open to a verbal onslaught from me? I glanced at the others for some kind of clue as to what was going on. One by one they avoided taking sides. Only Isobel looked at me and barely perceptibly, raised one eyebrow. This meant, "Is it worth lowering yourself to her level?"

I gave a look back that said, "I've had enough of this lazy, crazy cow." Isobel gave a slight shrug and walked down the back away from the impending storm.

"I did my best with what was available. It hasn't completely worked, I know, but I'm not a FUCKING MAGICIAN, and in case you haven't noticed seeing you ain't been off the bus for days, it's fucking hot out there. Anyway if you think you can do better you know where the tools are kept." I should have stopped right there but ole foot-in-mouth did it again by adding as an aside, "That's if you can get your fat, lazy arse under the bus."

"What? What did you say? You fucking asshole."

"Fran shut the fuck up will you? Go and get yerself laid for fuck's sake and give us all a break."

"You bastard. One thing's for sure, asshole, it wouldn't be with you if you were the last man on Earth. I've seen you looking," she finished with a sneer.

"Aluuun!" Isobel's voice came sharp from the rear, but I'd had enough and the old red haze was beginning to drop. I stood up and approached her.

Black Bob stood and put his hand on my shoulder. "C'mon Al. We're in Afghanistan for fuck's sake."

"It's alright man. I just got a few more home truths I wanna speak. I gently removed his hand from my shoulder. At that moment, for the first time, I saw the light of uncontrolled hysteria and hatred in her eyes. "I wouldn't touch you with Timus' dick, let alone mine." That was the last straw as far as she was concerned. She lunged at me but Kakey and Black Bob, stopped her. She took that as them-against-her and flounced off down the back with a muffled shriek.

"Well fucking done," whispered Isobel as she went by. She got off the bus for some fresh air. Again, Isobel with the 'fuck' word!

"Where the fuck did that come from for Christ sake? As if I ain't got enough hassle with the bus I don't need some hysterical bitch on my case." If she heard my comment, she didn't react. Thank goodness the kids were asleep. I was well pissed off that she should act like that in front of them. "I ain't taking this shit from her anymore. What've I done to her anyway? Except drive her to India." I wasn't going to let it drop. "If she ever attacks me like that again..."

"Don't worry arsehole, I'm getting off when we reach New Delhi and I'm going home!" she shouted from the back.

This was music to my ears but I didn't show it. For once I shut up.

The road through Afghanistan carried all the hippies and travellers on their way to India. Most of the hotels, cafés and shops were geared to dope smoking adventurers. The cafés had silk cushions for reclining on while most of the low tables had packets of papers and water pipes here and there. The Afghans themselves didn't use rolling papers but had imported them for use by tourists. That was an indication of how far the Afghans and Pakistanis were prepared to go to make us travellers welcome and thus maximise their profits from those driving through. The shops carried every sort of jewellery and Afghan goat and sheepskin coats that were popular in the west in the 70s Some of the cheaper ones would stink to high heaven as they hadn't been cured properly, The better ones were intricately embroidered with coloured silks. They looked superb but you couldn't ever wash them as the dyes used to colour the silks were not fixed properly and would run at the slightest suggestion of moisture.

Around ten in the evening we pulled off the highway and drove into the town of Herat. It was a typical frontier town with dirt roads lined with trees with white painted trunks. The only lighting was the occasional street lamp, mostly at junctions and crossroads. Habeeb directed us across what looked to be a wide square on the far side of which stood a several story, hotel building, built at a right angle around one of the corners of the square.

Habeeb shouted out to the night watchman who raised the barrier to allow me to drive the bus to the back of the rear gardens behind the hotel. By the time I pulled up I was completely exhausted.

Habeeb asked if we wanted to come to the restaurant in the hotel but I was just too tired. All we wanted to do was crash out for as many hours as possible. I left the others and fell on our bunk into a deep sleep. The heat and worry about the overheating had conspired to sap my energy.

I awoke the next morning to the sound of chickens somewhere nearby. I looked around me in the early sunshine. The bus and whole area were shaded by some kind of creeper and grape vines growing over ancient trellises. There were gardens with what looked like grass but on closer inspection was some kind of succulent grass-like leaves. There was a pathway to what I assumed was the rear entrance to the foyer. It was situated in the right angle bend of the L-shaped four story hotel building. As I got nearer the rear entrance I could see that the build quality was crude with wooden window frames and doors, though ornate, were of low quality wood. The whole construction wouldn't pass inspection back in England but here it stood.

I walked in through the rear entrance to the foyer. There was a reception desk with a young Afghani guy grinning with a mouthful of white teeth like tombstones.

"Good morning sir. Have you slept well?"

"I slept very well thank you. You speak excellent English."

"I am e'student at university in Kabul I study English there and when it is closed during the summer, I am manager here for my father who owns the hotel"

"Oh," I said. "I thought Habeeb was manager."

"Ah, he is manager of top floor," he said, and looked a little shifty. I found out why later. It turned out that Habeeb was the tout for the hotel. He would stay at the border and pick up travellers like us, to take us to the hotel. He was on a small commission for whoever he brought to stay.

"What is your name?" I asked.

"I am Jami-gul but you must call me Jamie," he said proudly. "What is your name, sir? I am receptionist, chef, and cleaner. Do all your passengers come for breakfast later?"

I thought about that and decided for everyone else that, seeing as we hadn't done any shopping yet we might as well have breakfast here. "My name is Alun and I'm very pleased to meet you Jamie." I shook hands with him. "I'm just going to look outside for a while. We arrived in the dark last night and I want to have a look around." I gestured to the front doors which were now streaming with morning sunshine. A bright contrast with the cool and slightly dark foyer.

"OK sir, breakfast will be ready in one hour."

"What is it?"

"We have very good oatmeal (porridge) with local

honey. After, there is fried eggs with green beans and some other vegetables in spicy sauce. I will send out later for some special bread, freshly cooked."

"Sounds wonderful Jamie but do me a favour will you?"

"What is that, sir?"

"Stop calling me 'sir' will you? My name is Alun, OK?" I said with a smile.

"Oh OK Alun." He smiled back and nodded, and looked very pleased that I was, of course, treating him as an equal.

"Right I'm going outside to look around for a while."

"Please Alun do not buy hashish from these street traders. They will steal from you, give bad quality. You can buy good quality from me."

"OK Jamie I'll buy from you later. I'll see you in an hour." I walked to the glass front doors and flung them open.

What I saw, the spectacle of it, has stayed with me over the years. It caused my jaw to drop in sheer surprise. First I noticed the smell of roasting kebabs mixed with the scent of flowers and incense. Amongst the hustle and bustle of taxis and grossly overloaded buses, were horses bedecked with blossoms of some white flower or other. Bullock carts, badly overloaded with some type of crop, were everywhere. Then I recognised some of the smells as being horse piss and dung. As I looked on this scene my eye was drawn to the wide boulevard running away from the square, opposite to where I was standing. At the top of this wide and bustling way was an ancient mosque with a jade mosaic-covered dome and tall minarets each side of it. An absolutely stunning sight. I just stood there with my mouth agape, taking in this wonderful assault on all my senses. If it wasn't for the odd taxi and bus I'd swear I'd been transported back to the Middle Ages.

The morning sun was warm in the dusty atmosphere and as I stood there it suddenly occurred to me like a flash. "Shit man!" I said aloud to myself. "Now we are REALLY travelling!" I felt like such a serious traveller. It was all so different! I must have stood there for an hour or so until I felt the presence of Isobel beside me. "Well! It's certainly different to the centre of Bristol." I said, a little in awe of what I was looking at.

"Shiiit," was all I got out of Isobel. She stood absolutely enchanted and agape at the view that had moved me deeply. Later on we had a wonderful breakfast and were now looking forward to doing some sightseeing and shopping.

During the early morning walk across the courtyard, I had noticed the hotel water tower high up on some stone outcrop. I realised that to get water up to the top floors of the hotel, you would require a reservoir higher than those top floors. Not only that but the pressure at the lower point would be pretty good. I looked around the garden to see if there was a tap. I didn't see one but I did see a young Afghani man about thirty years old. I shook hands with him and asked him if he understood English.

"I speak a little English, everyone here does, or don't make money from the tourists," he grinned.

"My name is Alun. I'm the driver of that bus over there."

"Oh yes I saw you arrive. I live at the top of the hotel. I see everything. My name is Masjood."

Little did I know at the time but I would be hearing about and seeing Masjood on TV in the future. He went on to become a commander in the Mujahideen and fought the Russians tooth and nail when they invaded Afghanistan. He was eventually to die in a bomb explosion. Information was mixed, but he was the victim of two suicide bombers posing as journalists. They hid an explosive device inside the camera and detonated it when they were all together. They were all killed instantly.

We wandered the souks and markets looking at loads of tourist stuff. Whenever you passed, the shopkeepers knew just what to say. "You like some souvenir? Some excellent hashish?" That's the one that usually got my attention.

"You come my shop. Drink tea, make business. Money no problem. Come. Look finest hashish."

"Well! As we're here, there's no harm in looking I suppose." And as Isobel lost herself in the precious stones and Lapis and the finely made clothes and carpets, I sat and smoked a chillum with the shop owner who spoke good English. He told me how his father in Mazari-Sherif owned the shop. It was to sell to tourists, yes, but it was also a cover to meet lots of tourists and sell them varying amounts of hash from the farm up in the Mazari hills. He could see I was interested in how resin was produced and we sat and talked for a long time.

"You know this bus you have would be good for transport hashish. No problem take many kilos to your country."

I explained how it wasn't just my bus and anyway, there was no way I'd do it that way. I'd have to cross thirteen borders, including Afghan-Iran and of course the Turks who are just insane anyway, not to mention the Greeks and Germans, they'd be all over us with sniffer dogs, like a rash. "How you do it then?" he asked straight-faced. "Because if you have way, I can get you best hashish."

"I don't have the money for large amounts of hash, we're on our way to India."

"When you come back through Afghanistan you come

to me. I will give you one hundred kilos, no money." He paused dramatically.

"What do you mean no money?"

With a mixture of a smile and a sneer he said, "You take your country, you sell and come back to me with money."

"You'd trust me with that much?"

"Sure! You are Englishman. Good people the English, good soldier, good fighter. Besides," he said, looking me in the eye, "you rip me off I send my cousin in London to cut your throat." He started to laugh which turned in a guffaw, but there was no doubt in my mind he was serious.

"That's a very generous offer but I'll have to think about it."

"Sure that's no problem. Think. Do it properly and we all make money. You come my shop ask for me, Ferouq, everybody here know me. If I am in the hills they will get word to me."

"Thank you Ferouq. And thank you for the knowledge about the hashish. You have made a friend today."

"That's what it is all about Alun, everybody make money, everybody happy. No need for problem. I left with no doubt in my mind that if a problem came up, it would be dealt with in a ruthless manner. By the time I got back to the hotel everyone was comparing what they'd bought. I slipped out to take up the invitation of Masjood to visit him on the rooftop of the hotel. I climbed up as far as the stairs would take me and then pushed up the hatch to the roof and climbed through.

"Masjood!" I called out. Soon a face appeared out of one of the ducts for the central heating.

"Alun! Come. Through door!"

The 'door' turned out to be an entrance hatch to a large

vacuum chamber of the central heating system, and it looked like one of those water-tight doors you see on submarine films. Inside was a bed with turned wooden legs and striped, wide, deck chair fabric stretching from one end to the other, and across these were the same fabric at ninety degrees. A small paraffin burner and a tea pot were in the corner, which was a bit of a concern as the floor was strewn with fresh hay. Some clothes and a few old text books, in English, and magazines, in German, were scattered around. "Is this where you live all the time Masjood?" I asked, barely able to keep the shock off my face. "When you said you lived at the top of the hotel, I imagined a room on the top floor. Not actually on the roof."

"It's OK here, man. I don't pay no rent and the hotel gives me money and food to look after the grounds and cut the grass. Besides it's only while I am here in Herat. I have home with my parents in Kandahar."

As he filled a chillum with what looked and smelled like finest quality hash, I learnt that he was attending university, a very upper class thing to do, as only the rich could afford higher education. We went outside and sat on the parapet looking down at the hustle and bustle and dust below us. The sun was just touching the dome of the mosque in front of us and a wonderful quality of light made it such a lovely evening.

Masjood lifted the full chillum with both hands to his lips and indicated to me to light it for him. I took out my lighter to oblige and when it was lit, I stopped the lighter.

"No! No! Alun. Never take the flame away until fully lit. Look I show you."

He held the lighter in one hand and put the chillum to his lips and puffed deeply. Each time he stopped a flame would come to the end of the chillum and only when fully bright and burning would the last deep lungful be taken.

Again, and this was most important, I was informed, "The flame must be big after your last breath!"

He then let out the biggest amount of smoke I've ever seen. It was in solid columns from his nose. There was masses of it. He passed me the chillum and I did my best for my country. I took the trouble to puff the chillum into life before taking the big one. I inhaled a huge amount of smoke. It took all the control I had, not to cough and splutter but the flame came to the top of the chillum just as it should. I looked at Masjood who was showing white-teeth-for-days in a big grin. I almost passed out as the THC hit my bloodstream but managed to stay conscious mainly because I was sat down! We both sat looking at the sunset for hours, it seemed, lost in our own thoughts. Eventually I felt able to stand.

"You have an amazing country and wonderful people. I'll see you again Masjood."

"You sure will." He spoke low and didn't take his eyes off the sunset.

Next day with Masjood's help, I managed to attach a hosepipe to a tap in the garden area this was directly under the water tower. When I turned it on a strong jet of water shot from the end in a very encouraging way. I decided to remove the cylinder heads to inspect the waterways for blockages. This would mean draining all the cooling water now in the engine, doing the work and then filling it all up again.

Was this water supply strong enough and was there enough in the tank to fill the cooling system of the bus? All these were nagging doubts but I had no choice. To go on as we were was foolish, especially through the deserts of Afghanistan. We didn't need to boil over out there it would be more than a walk to the nearest garage with a water can!

I set about removing the cylinder heads with an

audience of young Afghani boys, eager to learn about engines. Over the next two days I took off the cylinder heads. I cleaned the threads and laid out each bolt and nut on a piece of white cloth. The crowd of boys now brought me green tea and sweet pastries in return for the knowledge I was giving them.

I showed them how a diesel engine works and how it is cooled and how the power is translated to forward motion. The rear axle and differential action was difficult for them to grasp. It is difficult in English, let alone after translation. In the end I got it across with the help of an Afghani doctor who was staying at the hotel. He spoke near perfect English and translated for me. He was equally interested to learn about engines etc., so it was a two-way street. Eventually I finished cleaning and clearing and time came to put it all back together. I wiped each piece with the white cloth.

"Why you do this?" asked one boy.

"I want each piece to be clean. My idea of 'clean' is when you can use a clean white cloth to wipe the pieces and after, the cloth is still spotless. I didn't know how 'spotless' would translate. He smiled broadly as he understood and then there was a chorus of 'ah's as I explained that it must be very clean. The slightest piece of dirt can do irreparable damage.

The time came to refill the engine cooling water. Would this supply be strong enough, long enough, to fill the system and drive out all the air? Only one way to find out.

"OK mister. Turn it on!" I shouted, after fixing the hose to the lowest drain tap under the engine. The boys were most intrigued to see me sliding under the bus instead of filling it up at the radiator cap. I explained about the possibility of getting air locks in the long pipes and they nodded as if this was most important information, which it was. The hose spluttered and kicked a few times but then a steady stream flowed down the pipe. I came out and stood by the radiator filler cap and waited for the water to come out. I didn't have to wait long as there was a spurt and the water spilled out of the filler cap along with air, rust, scale, and other blockage making, gunk. This was looking good and the boys cheered as they now knew what to expect. When I was sure all the air was driven out I shouted to the boy on the tap to turn it off. He was proud to have been involved with the foreigner and was telling all who'd listen that he was the one who turned the tap on and off.

Eventually, I finished putting the motor back together and hit the starter. The engine turned over on the starter motor and fired up unevenly but as it picked up revs, the motor ran smoother, until I released the throttle and let it idle. It sounded good. I let it run for half an hour without any cooling problems but until the bus was actually working, it would not be possible to tell if the overheating problem had been solved.

All this didn't matter to the local lads who'd been helping me. They danced up and down with huge grins on their faces. I gave them a typical British thumbs up which of course, they took up and gave thumbs up to everyone.

We'd been in Herat for over a week now and it was time to be moving. We had a discussion and decided that it would be good to go into Pakistan instead of going through Kabul. It would mean turning south in the city of Kandahar. We spent a day packing up and getting ready to move out early next morning. That night the hotel put on a special meal for us. We had bought the meat and rest of the ingredients, they had cooked it in a traditional way. We had a wonderful evening with local musicians and dancers and much top quality hash being smoked. Eventually we headed off to sleep but not before names and addresses were exchanged on pieces of paper. The information was written in Arabic and English.

I got up around six the next morning, went to a chai (tea) stall near the front entrance and had a green tea with a pile of sugar lumps. By the time I got back to the bus, everybody was up and having a quick breakfast. The kids were saying goodbye to their little friends that they had made and a few tears were flowing.

"Don't worry. We'll see them on the way back." I said to the kids. I didn't know it at the time but we would be seeing these guys again many times. We drove down the poplar-lined street that connected the town of Herat with the main highway. We pulled onto the main road and settled down to some serious driving. I kept a close eye on the temperature gauge and was pleased that it seemed to be coping with the high ambient temperature which this morning was high eighties. All the windows were open including the windscreen! It could be wound open with a little crank handle just under the dash! A feature sadly missing on modern buses.

The miles rolled on and the light was intense – a bright reflected light that makes you squint. We were all so brown and grizzled by this time, we all looked like desert rats!

As the road surface deteriorated I had to slow it down a bit. Even at these slower speeds and therefore, lower airflow through the radiator, the cooling system seemed to have benefited from the clear out. Probably the first time it had been done in one hundred thousand miles!

The tarmac dwindled down to a single width ribbon. It seemed the local custom when another vehicle approached was to put one wheel off the tarmac and each of you pass, half on, half off, so to speak. I learned that it was a macho thing. You gave way by moving over but only the minimum needed to pass without touching. The only way to play it was to hold your line, exactly half on and half off. Do not slow down, it will be seen as a weakness and you'll end up right off the road and waiting for the other vehicle who doesn't slow down at all. Seeing we were tourists and strangers, gave the truck and bus drivers that extra courage to hold their line and were deeply surprised when the foreigner didn't move off the road. I remember the look of surprise on many a face as it zipped by just inches from mine.

After a few hours of this I was getting mighty pissed off by their reckless driving and was determined not to give way. I would slow and if needed stop exactly in the middle of the tarmac and make the other vehicle drive around me.

We pulled up just outside of Kandahar for the night. We did some shopping for dinner and some fresh barbari bred. We decided that in the evening, we'd drive to the city centre and have a look around. The city was like something out of the Middle Ages with rows of makeshift stalls and homes, selling everything you can think of. Every few steps we would be regaled by street sellers. "Hashish mister? Good Kandahar black mister. Look! Look!" as they plied a one kilo slab of very black and shiny Hash just under your nose. I ended up buying several different lumps, varying from green inside to brown depending which valley it came from. All of it real kick-arse hash of the finest quality and costing under a pound for the bits I'd bought.

We decided that before going back to the bus, we'd have a tea in one of the roadside tea houses. Black Bob was back guarding the bus so we were in no hurry. We stepped through the front door of one of the cafés and were greeted with a full house of turbans flowing robes and crossed bandoleers full of shells over both shoulders. Their rifles and shotguns were at their feet. All eyes shot to us and dark brooding eyes stared at us from black bearded faces. I started to do a U-turn, feeling that we'd come in the wrong door! These were some serious looking tribesmen. Before I could turn, the owner came from behind a huge solid silver samovar percolating and steaming away in the corner. "Yes! Yes! come, come." He grabbed my arm and led us all to a huge pile of cushions and motioned for us all to sit. Everybody else in the place had decided we were just tourists and therefore, no threat. From that point on it was all smiles and nodding to us and Cokes and Fantas were brought for the children. I asked to see one of the rifles that were piled on the floor. I recognised it as an ex-British Army, 7.62mm, S.L.R (self-loading rifle) made by Birmingham Small Arms (B.S.A.). While serving as a boy soldier, I had got to know this rifle so well that I could literally, strip and clean it, blindfolded.

I asked if I could see the rifle. There were a few nervous glances but the owner got up and picked it up and unclipped the magazine, re-cocked it, which cleared the round in the breach. He handed me the rifle minus the magazine. I took it and immediately released the hinge clip. The barrel and breech tilted forward and I pulled out the firing mechanism, dismantled that and placed the bits on the table. The men looked on with their mouths now gaping. I held the rifle up to the light and looked down the barrel. It was spotless and had been cleaned and oiled in the correct manner, however I looked around directly at the owner and tutted in an exaggerated manner and shook my head disapprovingly. The owner looked dismayed and took it from me. "Corrosion!" I shouted. "Rust, rust," I said pointing at the barrel. The owner looked down the barrel, then at me, in dismay for a minute then realised that I had been winding him up and the whole place erupted in much laughter and piss-taking of the owner, who was basking in the limelight and grinning like a twat.

We had a wonderful time with these fierce Kandahar tribesmen and the kids were feted by everyone there. The drinks were in bottles that had been used may times and were almost opaque with scuff marks. The bottles were printed in Farsi Arabic so I guessed they came over the border from Iran. I couldn't imagine an Afghani bottling plant! We had no airs and graces. We ate what they ate and were treated with great respect. When it came time to leave, every man in the place stood up and much nodding and bowing and big toothy, grins on wrinkly, weathered, hard faces.

We were all up early next morning and got underway quickly. We turned south on the road to the Afghan-Pakistan border. It was a long, dusty drive on a very tenuous road surface, still the single width tarmac. I was still getting seriously miffed by the local bus and truck drivers who, seeing we were tourists, were failing to do their share of moving over.

The heat and dust and hours of driving over this out-and-out, desert were getting to me and I was taking their driving as a personal insult. After many hours we decided to stop and cook something to eat. We had a nice meal in the shade of some rocks after which Isobel the kids and I decided to go walkabout and have a look round. I just wanted to get up high and get some space around me. It was late in the afternoon and the light had a particular soft but clear quality about it. We climbed high on the rocks on a pinnacle where we could see the bus below us and the road in which we arrived and in the other direction, the road we had yet to travel, disappeared into the dusty, distant horizon.

I had brought a smoke with me so while the kids explored the rocks around us, I had a quiet puff. Isobel and I sat watching the primordial desert scene now being bathed with a warm gentle wind. We smoked the hash and just sat there for hours. We both would have fallen asleep, so peaceful and beautiful was it there had it not been for the fact that the kids could not be left unsupervised for one second.

I looked down to see Glynis sat on a rock way below us. She was alone and sat in the afternoon sunshine. She didn't see the young shepherd boy approaching from behind her. His flock of goats were trailing behind him. The shepherd was intent on begging a few Afs (Afs = afghanis = currency of Afghanistan) or perhaps a pack of cigarettes. Some of these guys stay out for weeks with just water and a few provisions brought by the owner of the goats and they would roam for hundreds of miles across the semi desert scrub to keep the goats fed. This was one of the reasons we attributed to the fact that whenever we thought we'd found a quiet place to go to the toilet, out of the ground would come some shepherd or other, right in the middle of a desert!

The young shepherd and Glynis were now having a good conversation and the guy gave us a big smile when we arrived at the location. There was no malice in the clear open face of the young lad and we all passed an hour talking to each other as best we could. His brother actually owned the animals and he told us he walked for two weeks just through the mountains and desert floor. His brother would bring him food and water but from there on he was on his own. I found it easy to imagine what life was like for him. Totally uneducated and living from day to day and sleeping wherever he could, to rise the next day and just wander.

By the time Isobel, Glynis and I got back to the bus the others were waking up from a sweaty snooze in the heat of the bus. It was decided that we should get as near to the border crossing as we could that evening, parking for the night and doing the border crossing at a frontier town that delighted in the name of Spin-Boldak about two hundred miles north of the city of Quetta, in North West Pakistan. We drove on for another hour or so until we came to an outcropping of high rock towering from the desert floor. There was a track running off the road and into a cleft in the rocks. There was just enough room to get the bus right off the road in the shade of the rocks. As we were thirty miles from the border we decided to park here for the night and started to unpack the cooking gear. I gathered some large rocks into a circle, lit a fire and placed the steel grid over the top of it, resting on the rocks. It made a fine barbecue and it wasn't long before we had dinner under way.

Chapter 10

Pakistan

I was tired and wanted an early night so we doused the fire stashed all the cooking gear and moved inside the bus. It was completely dark outside by now so we pulled the curtains and started getting the kids ready for bed. We noticed some headlights bouncing along the track towards us. There were several vehicles and I could see quite a few people in the motors. We waited in silence as the cars drew up and footsteps approached the bus. There was a sharp tap on the door. I was nearest so I slid it open. There was a captain of the customs and border police in full uniform carrying a Kalashnikov rifle with a bandoleer over his shoulder. I could see half a dozen officers, similarly armed, behind him.

He came to attention when he saw me and with a big grin, saluted me. "Good evening, sahib and memsahib, I am afraid you cannot stay here."

"What? We have this massive desert area and you come along and tell us we can't park here." Clearly, I was still thinking like a European!

"Oh no! Sahib you must not stay here. It is not safe. There are some very bad men here, bandits. They will kill and steal. You must not stay here you must come with us. I have put my men's life in danger to come out here and rescue you. Please you must come NOW."

Suddenly the seriousness of the situation dawned on me. "I'm very sorry Captain. I understand, now. What do you want us to do?"

"You must reverse back to the road and then follow my Jeep to the border post. It is about 30 miles. We will make provision for you there. When you reach the road my motorcycle and side-car mounted machine gun, will come behind." I was rather concerned to see what looked like a GPMG (General Purpose Machine Gun) mounted in the side-car! "Please sahib, when we get to the road follow me as fast as you can and do not stop for anything, anything sahib. You understand?"

"I understand Captain." Now realising the danger we were in. As I backed out along the track a police officer in Khaki uniform, was watching the rocks above us. He had his back pressing against the front grille of the bus and was walking backwards with a look of fear on his face that I have remembered to this day. He was terrified and white faced.

He carried a 12 bore shotgun and kept it right at the ready. We got onto the now deserted ribbon of tarmac and went hell for leather for the frontier. All the time I could see small arms bristling out of the windows of the captain's Jeep and also, in my mirror the headlight of the armed motorbike rear guard. The bus was driven much faster than I had taken it before and I glanced nervously at the temperature gauge but it was staying reassuringly cool. *Must have fixed it*, I thought in an abstract way.

As each mile went by I was feeling more and more embarrassed at having put these guys in the line of fire and endangering the bus and all of us. I learned later that a tragic story had unfolded not many months before. A young family out from England had made the same mistake we had. Whilst we were painted like some travelling circus, They were in an ex-military, Commer truck, it has to be said, stupidly, still painted in its army camouflage! (so you could argue that Charlie's over-the-top paint job saved our lives!)

When some of the bandits saw what they thought was a Pakistani Army vehicle moving through their tribal area, they opened fire with drastic consequences. The vehicle was raked with automatic gunfire. The young father was shot and killed. His wife took some hits in the legs and was badly scarred. Thankfully, the two little girls in the back were shocked but uninjured. When the bandits approached the vehicle for the arms and money that they thought the soldiers would be carrying, there was pandemonium. They knew that this was a big mistake. It would stop the tourist trade, on which many locals depended. It would mean that the British authorities would be in the area, with all the enquiries and crackdowns that entailed. They we're not going to be popular, big time.

This proved true as, some weeks later, the two bandits who had fired, were found beaten and executed, their broken bodies hanging by one leg, from a lamppost on a large roundabout on the main highway into town. "Well, we couldn't have known. Thank God they came out and got us," said Isobel, who was sat in her usual place on the left of me.

"Yeah. You can imagine what they're saying to each other. 'Bloody stupid tourists. I could be safe and warm in my bed but I have to risk my life for some stupid tourists'."

"Well it's not as if we haven't been careful all the way across." She was right. If ever there were warnings we would make sure we parked near the police station overnight.

"Suppose we put this down to experience and be more aware. Still embarrassing though. Do you think they are going to arrest us?"

"What for?"

"I dunno. Endangering a police officer's life? I'd be seriously pissed off if it was me."

"I suppose we'll find out. It looks like we're coming to somewhere with all the lights ahead," said Isobel.

We swung into a fenced off compound and the captain came towards us. "'Ere we go," I said, expecting a telling off. The captain came right onto the bus this time and saluted us all and made sweet little noises at the kids, who were now way past their bedtime.

"Please, you were not safe there we must bring you here for safety. We have very big fire in restaurant, many cushion and we will give you blankets. You can make bed by the fire and be very warm for sleeping. It gets very cold here at night, sahib."

"Captain I'm so sorry to have put you and your men in danger, I'm sorry we just didn't know..."

"Oh no sahib. Do not be sad. You could not know. You are very velcome to Pakistan. Ve not vant you die here but have good visit. Vhen you are settled you must come have supper in the restaurant and then sleep around the fire."

"But what about the bus, Captain? Will it be safe here?"

"You are in the police compound sahib," he said proudly. "You vill not be bothered by thieves. Anybody here know that if he steal from me or my friends, I cut off his hand."

I looked at him and waited for the toothy grin but it never came. He was deadly serious and as I looked into his eyes I had no doubt in my mind he was serious. "As you are my guest, you will be treated with great respect," he said rather formally, but broke into a big grin. "I will see you in the restaurant shortly." He saluted us again to a chorus of 'thank you's from all of us.

"I think we are going to remember this night for a long time. Did you see that guy's face, the policeman at the front of the bus when I was backing out onto the road?"

"Yeah!" said Timus. He was frightened and the two on each side were pale and shaking.

"Yes the bloke at the front was pale as a ghost and sweating. Y'know that was probably the most danger we have been in since we started?" There were general murmurs of agreement and embarrassed looks.

"So c'mon then who's up for some supper and if we can sneak away somewhere we can have a smoke? Let's go inside and see what it's like!"

Again general grunts of agreement and we all got ready to meet the locals and probably have the piss taken out of us for being stupid tourists and making bother for everybody.

I couldn't have been more wrong. We were greeted with, "Yes, yes come come sit," by a very enthusiastic patron. He led us over to the fire and verbally harangued some men who were hogging it. They saw us and quickly shuffled aside.

"No, no," I said, and started to protest that they should not go into the cold for us.

"He is Muslim sahib. If he does not make you comfortable he will not go into paradise. It say in Koran must always be good to traveller and stranger and feed and shelter them. It is same in Bible eh? Commandment yes? beside these two curs are too wicked for other reasons." He grinned and lightly kicked and verbally harangued the two that had moved. This brought laughter all round as the patron translated what I had said, and his own reply. I was warming to their kindness and readiness to have a joke and laugh.

I still got the impression that if you crossed them they'd skin you alive. The patron appeared with large steaming bowls of spicy smelling bean and vegetable stew with chicken and potatoes. We were closely watched as we tentatively started eating. The dinner had a considerable after burn and I think the locals were waiting for a reaction as they were watching me closely. I lifted my plate to them and tapped it with my spoon to indicate how I was enjoying it with a thumbs up. They all grinned and looked impressed and were giving thumbs up all round.

After the dinner I noticed the captain had come in. He saw us and came over, saluted, and asked if we had enjoyed our dinner. I assured him that we had and that it was the act of an officer and a gentleman. He puffed up a little to my flattery, knowing that the patron was translating for the benefit of all in the restaurant.

"Please join us Captain," I said.

"I have time for a chai and wada," he said and quietly gave an order for such, which was immediately obeyed. A 'wada', it turned out, was a variation on our 'bubble & squeak' only ten times more spicy.

"How is your trip?" asked the captain.

"We have had our ups and downs but it's been the voyage of a lifetime so far," I replied. "I find your roads a little strange though, Captain."

"Ah yes. The roads here are basic, to say the least. We

send out the grader to keep the dirt roads flat and we cannot afford to tarmac the whole width and the sun here is so hot sometimes that the tarmac melts and breaks up."

"Where are you going?"

"We hope to get as far as India and Nepal but it's still a long way to go," I said.

"Many travellers to India don't come this way. They go straight across the top of Pakistan through Peshawar, Islamabad, Rawlpindi and Lahore and they miss most of Pakistan. We have many things of interest for you here."

"Well!" said Isobel, standing up. "Thank you for rescuing us and I'm sorry we put you and your men at risk. I'm taking the kids to bed now so I must say goodnight."

The captain stood and saluted as Isobel walked out to the bus.

"In England when dinner is finished the ladies withdraw, leaving the men to their pleasures, is that not correct?"

"Yes captain that is how it used to be. Not anymore. Only in the richest households, then only on very formal occasions. Like the British Raj, it was over many years ago." The captain smiled at the mention of the Raj, the British administration of India that ended in 1947 with the birth of Pakistan and millions slaughtered in the inter-ethnic wars that followed.

"OK I think you would like something to smoke, yes?" said the captain.

We all darted furtive glances at each other and I ventured a tentative, "Yeeees," thinking I could always say I thought he meant cigarettes! He pulled out what looked like a brown paper sweet bag, stained with something. We didn't have to wait for long to see what the stain was.

The captain handed Timus the bag and said, "Help

yourselves." Timus pulled a fist full of green chips of hash. "That is finest green hash from Chitral valley and the brown hash from Kulu valley. Smoke, smoke!" encouraged the captain.

Timus looked at me with a mixture of delight and paranoia. As if to say, "Look at this, but he's a copper."

"Ah! Ha, captain um, ah... we aren't used to smoking hashish with a police officer, to say the least. In England it is against the law."

"It is here as well but we don't make a problem unless smuggling is involved. We have had hashish in our history for many thousands of years so it is just quietly left alone, besides, most of it is farmed up along the Afghan border and this is an area where even the military or police don't go, and is under complete control of the tribes. It has been that way for thousands of years. Tourists are not allowed to go there."

"Sounds like a wild place," said Timus.

"Oh yes it is very bad place. They make and sell guns and rifles and will shoot first. You can take any kind of gun and they will copy for you, any kind at all. They have control over the hashish and the poppy and they export tons of both. They have their own laws and tribal elders and take no notice of the government in Islamabad. All of the Kaiber pass an surrounding area is run by them. If you want anything to go through the pass, you have to pay tolls to them."

"It sounds like a real frontier place. My old man was out here, stationed in Rawlpindi, before the war."

"Ah a good time for all people. The British were here in force. The tribesmen would steal everything form soldiers. The British had a large garrison under canvas on the Peshawar road just outside Rawalpindi."

"Yes that is where my father was stationed, Rawalpindi.

He used to tell me stories of how the locals would rip off everything from the tent during the night." They would strip off and cover themselves in 'tiger grease', a local lubricant similar to our Vaseline. This would be done so that if the hapless sleeping squaddie should wake up and make a grab for the intruder, he would literally slip out of their grasp and disappear into the night. If the squaddie didn't wake up, he would wake in the morning to an empty tent. Even the blankets and sheets would be stolen from under him. The thief would use the technique of blowing gently in your face while you slept. This had the effect of making you turn away from the breath, in your sleep. After a couple of applications of this the blankets would be pulled from under him!

The thieves never used arms or knives of any kind and on the rare occasions that the thief would be caught, a good slapping with a British Army web-belt was the usual fate for him. My father said that it was considered a 'sport' by both sides.

We smoked and chatted well into the night and I learned a lot about Pakistan. The captain was at pains to point out the wonderful time to be had in Southern Pakistan and recommended several places to see. I awoke next morning to a clear sunny and warm morning. We had crashed out around the fire and the young 'chai wallahs' were getting large numbers of chai glasses together for the morning rush and the beautiful silver samovar was steaming away, and boiling drips of water were dripping from the ornate silver tap.

We got everything together and as the others finish packing up Isobel and I sought out the Captain of Customs. We were ushered into his office and he stopped what he was doing and showed us to some chairs. "So sahib, memsahib you are ready to continue your journey. Please when you see other travellers and tourist, you will tell them that Southern Pakistan is good place, yes? These people are good hard working people and a little tourism would be good for them."

"Captain you have my word as an Englishman that I will tell this story to everyone I meet and I sure will mention your bravery and that of your men, have no fear about that." It was a little over the top but I spoke in such terms as I wanted there to be no mistake that we'd learned our lesson.

"You saved our lives last night Captain, and everybody on that bus is grateful to you, and your brave men," said Isobel. The captain translated for his men and they broke into big grins and swelled their chests out, and rightly so.

"Good sahib, good madam," was all the English they could come up with to show their appreciation, as they pumped our hands. "Before you go please, I have something for you." The captain put his hand in the brown paper bag we'd seen last night and brought out a handful of green and black hashish which he put in my hand. "Enjoy this sahib, and please tell other tourists."

"No problem captain." I turned to the others. "Shukrea," I said, and shook their hands.

From the captain down, they all came out from the customs post and from the restaurant to wave us goodbye. What a wonderful introduction to Pakistan. Sure, they wanted to impress us so that we would give them good 'press' but what the hell? They had made us feel welcome and protected us and shown great kindness and generosity. So they made a few rupees here and there with slightly over-inflated prices but that was alright by me, let's all make some money! Later in the journey, that attitude got me real respect because I was straight to my word and the people around me prospered also. This was not always the case. Some travellers took advantage of the trust and generosity shown by poor, local people. Mind you, how these guys expected to make any money when they wouldn't take a 'paisa' from us for the supper and breakfast, saying it was customs business and they would pay the bill. They would take no money from me, so I asked if I could just tip the working boys and waiters.

I went onto the bus and dug out some t-shirts I didn't need and gave them to the young lads and to the older ones I gave ten rupees each. They all but kissed my hand as I'd just tipped them a with a week's wages. The drive on into Quetta was very hot and dry. The desert and mountain road was just a single carriageway, a single strip of tarmac.

As we came into the city, I was struck by the similarities with the part of London that I was born and brought up in. Woolwich! There were large advertising hoardings, proclaiming 'Smoke Capstan Full Strength' and 'Brook Bond PG tips' etc. There were red double decker buses everywhere. It really did feel like I had just stepped back into 1950s London.

We found a quiet street to park up in and started to get the bus cleared up from all the dust and chaos of long distance, desert and mountain driving.

"Hello my friends."

We looked around to see a rather comical looking man of about forty. He looked comical to us, as he had long fluffy sideburns like a 1970s Elvis Presley. He was dressed in a full worsted suit in the boiling heat, with an immaculately laundered handkerchief protruding just a little too far out of his top pocket. His hair was shiny and smarmed down both sides of his head. He had a certain quality, poise and easy charm about him. "Welcome to Pakistan," he said in perfect English. "Welcome, what can I help you with, my friends? Ahh! What beautiful little children!" He seemed genuinely delighted to see them.

We were a little reserved but said hello and thanked him for his welcome. "These are my, and Isobel's, children. This is Alun Junior, my son, and my little daughter Mellony."

"They are fine children." He beamed. "Hello babies," he said as he lightly touched their hair.

"Please come aboard and meet everyone." He seemed so polite, standing on the bottom step until invited. That showed manners, to me. Not like some of the pushy tricksters and con men all out for something. This guy seemed to just want our friendship, but still, I was wary of a con. "My name is Antony." He smiled at our surprise. "Actually my real name is very long and starts with Mohamed, but most of my friends call me Antony."

"Hello Antony. My name is Alun Senior. You have met my wife Isobel."

"Ah yes! Spanish for 'beautiful one'. How apt," he said easily. He smiled charmingly and shook hands as an equal would.

Isobel smiled her thanks to his compliment and continued the introductions. "This is Fran, Cathy, Tim, Bob." He displayed not a flicker of hesitation at Black Bob's outstretched hand. I was beginning to like this guy. "Charlie and his lady, Glynis."

Antony sat and drank tea with us and chatted for a long time. It turns out that he was educated at Millfield and Oxford. He knew England well, as he had taken time to travel round the British Isles. I thought he must be quite well-off to have had such a privileged upbringing. "Yes my family owns some land up by the Afghan border. The land is shaped like the moon and star of Pakistan." He pulled one of our maps over the table and indicated an area about the size of Ireland!

"Your family owns all this land, Antony?" I asked in surprise.

"Yes it is our tribal area. I would love to show it to you,

if you have time."

"Well that's very kind of you. I hope we will be able to take up your invitation. As yet, we haven't decided what to do. We thought we'd have a look round Quetta and buy a few trinkets for the kids, and maybe something for us older children," I said, grinning and raising my eyebrows.

"Ah! I understand. You would like some good Pakistan black hashish? That is what most of my tourist friends usually ask for. My friends, I will return after an hour and take the men to a special place where I'm afraid, women cannot go. After this we will return for the ladies and children and you will please, allow me to provide you with supper, Quetta style, Oh yes!" he said with a big smile.

We were excited to see what was in store and many theories were put forward as to where we were going. We had the predictable, sniffy response from the women, especially Kakey, but we were able to retaliate that it is not our tradition but theirs, and we ought to be able to respect that. Ha ha! Antony arrived back in a large taxi able to take us all, and he spoke some curt words to the driver, who whisked us into a central area of the city. There were trucks, buses, cars, bicycles, ox carts, auto-rickshaws and barrow pushers, everywhere, but our driver managed to miss everything by the thickness of a cigarette paper.

Eventually we arrived at a regular looking tea shop perched on the side of a sloping side road. It looked busy with men coming and going. The inside was filled with steam and noise. The young boys were running to and fro with big, engraved silver trays full of small glasses of tea. "This is most famous tea house in Quetta," smiled Antony. "Very special." He grinned again.

Then suddenly I caught the reason for his grin. The strong, pungent smell of hashish was in the air. "Is this a smoking café?" I asked.

"Yes my friend. This is the Habbeybulla hash shop.

Known all over Quetta and most of the hippy world," he laughed. "But you are not hippies. Your bus is clean and does not smell bad like some I have visited. Come this way." Antony always wore a camel hair coat in the winter with one of those furry, embroidered side caps that Pakistani gentlemen like to wear. I never did learn the name of these caps, but along with the other fine clothes, they had a flavour that was 'Eastern' and distinguished. He liked to wear his coat around the shoulders, casually, and would discard it to the hands of willing servants, with a flourish.

He walked toward the counter on which stood a silver samovar with exquisite silver kettle and teapot for the owners use only, and a large pile of fresh pastries and Indian-style sweets. The man and boys serving the tea stood aside respectfully as Antony approached and I noticed the large manager lift Anthony's hand and kiss it, while mumbling a deeply respectful greeting.

Antony gently and kindly, with an air of smiling, said, "Please don't fuss over me," removed his hand, and motioned that they were equals, which was a boost to the café manager because, although relatively affluent, he definitely was not on the same social level.

The reason for this, I learned later, was that Antony co-owned the tea house and had saved it from bankruptcy, He had put the owners and workers children through private school. This was nothing compared to some of the other work he did in the community. I suddenly realised that Antony was an important and powerful man. In his quiet way, he supported many families and indeed, whole tribes who were not as fortunate as him. This highly educated and deeply committed man of his people, was a true local hero and a gentleman. Not the gentlemen one saw in 'the city', with their sickening greed and hypocrisy, but a practitioner of the true art of being a gentleman, with all the obligations and responsibilities to the servants and workers, that that entailed.

He didn't lord it around in some solid gold Rolls Royce, though, believe me, he could have bought a solid gold Rolls for each day of the week and not even notice the difference between them! Nor the insignificant drop in his bank balance!

Meeting Antony was one of the defining moments of our trip, so far. All the cynicism, all the deceit, that is the daily struggle for life, whether it be here in the dust, and Betel nut-spattered grime of Quetta, or the financial district of London or New York, all that cynicism was wiped away. Here is one man in, what seemed to us soft westerners, a world of hustlers, con-men and tricksters, who was genuine and wanted nothing from us bar that we enjoy his hospitality. I realised that cynicism had crept up on me, big time! Possibly from all the hustlers along the road who after all, were just trying to survive in a world without social security. Just their sense of duty to one another and loyalty to their kind.

For one moment I thought we were going to all stand behind the counter, but at the last moment I could see a small arch in the wall behind the steaming samovar, which was about five feet tall. We ducked through to a large, very tall, white room with a brazier of charcoal smouldering in the middle of the floor. There were some high-up windows that filled the whitewashed room with light. Brick stairs built into one wall, led to the roof terrace.

"We like to come here and smoke hashish. It is quiet and we do not get bothered by anyone. We smoke hash, drink tea and afterwards we like to eat these sweets. Sweets are very good for after hashish, oh yes! The sugar restores your balance after smoking. So you can go home sober as judge, Oh yes indeed."

We laughed at his use of vernacular English.

"Come! We smoke," he said, as he indicated to one of

the young boys who stuck beside him as if glued.

The boy went over to the man who ran the smoking side of things. He sat on a pile of cushions and had a cash drawer to his side. The other side, and I was still gaping at what I saw, was a huge pile of chips of hashish, ready for smoking.

There were a dozen or so men in the 'den'. They all stood, quickly and immediately, on sight of Antony. He motioned them to sit, and we all relaxed. As I looked around at the other men, each in turn nodded respectfully, back at me.

"Please tell these men that I am sorry for all these Englishmen tumbling in here disturbing their calm but we are very happy to be here."

There was a chorus of, "Oh no, sahib, velcome, velcome." They beamed.

I sensed Antony was pleased at their welcome. Like a proud father.

"Many of these men are from farms or roadworks, gangs, but over there is the Mayor of Quetta and his secretary.

I looked over to see a large-gutted man in a tailored shirt and trousers. His tie was loosened and his jacket over his arm. He noticed us looking at him and stopped talking to his secretary and gave a formal nod with hand on heart, in our direction. It was a respectful nod but not too much, after all, he was the mayor!

Antony nodded in return but without the hand. It seemed so funny to me to see their suited gentlemen, of obvious social importance, with their assistants talking over papers and dictation, whilst toking on a chillum!

"If we throw some rupees into the centre of the floor, the boy will see to picking it up. He will then buy some chips of hashish from the man. Everyone in the room will be able to smoke from your generosity and it is a good thing to do. The boy will make some rupees and all will be happy, you understand?"

"Yes of course. How much do you think would be right?" I was ready for a bit of a sting.

"Twenty rupees or something like this would be good, oh yes, indeed."

I counted out thirty and looked at the others, they readily agreed. "Just throw them there." When I did so, the boy picked it up and shuffled over to man in corner. He just grabbed a huge handful of hash and gave it to the boy. He placed some of it on a silver tray along with some tobacco and a chillum. The chillum, shaped like a hollowed out carrot, about ten centimetres long and made of fired clay, was filled by the skilful hands of the boy. A small, dampened, square of cloth was offered as a 'sofie', a cloth used as a filter and stuffed into the palm of the hand that holds the bottom of the chillum to the mouth. The idea being to draw the smoke through the wet sofie.

Antony raised the chillum to his lips and indicated to the boy to place the red-hot charcoal on the mixture at the top wide open, end. He took several small, puff-like tokes, then when he thought the time was right, he took the deepest breath I'd seen anyone take for a long time. As he finished, a mass of smoke was in the air and a little flame erupted from the end of the chillum. On seeing this flame, all the other men uttered a word of congratulation in unison, while clouds of smoke exited from Antony's mouth.

"You see, Alun. It's is not alight unless you have fire at the end. This way is respectful to our host and to the hashish. It is like lighting a fine cigar. It has to be lit thoroughly and properly. He glanced around to a sea of grinning, nodding, white teeth in black beards.

"Ok, my turn." I raised the chillum to my lips and

toked for my country. A nice little flame was going as I handed it to Bob. I then had to sit down fairly rapidly as the green, Chitral hash entered my bloodstream. And nothing was the same again. "That's some fine hash Antony, sheeeyit."

"Thank you my friend," he beamed. This is From the Chitral Valley, a very beautiful place, Oh yes."

It was a fascinating ritual. One either sat down on the bench or squatted on the floor. The lad would bring you a couple of red coals when you felt ready, the chillum would be lit and the toke, taken. Often the lungs would rebel at such treatment and each man had his own sound when coughing. The coughs would then trail off into laughing.

We all got wrecked, in the extreme! Chillum after chillum went by. Loads of laughing and pantomime and sweet, green chai. "These people are very impressed that you have not fallen over. Many tourist men fall over here!" Said Antony, with a grin.

"I don't think we'd do that, d'you Bob?" I looked over and instantly saw what a gamble I'd taken, asking him for an opinion at this stage! However I was pleased to see effort being made. He sniggered convincingly. Turning to Timus, he continued, "Well, I can't speak for these two but, knowing them as I do, I think we can consume kilos of the best you have and we'll all walk out of here."

"We are English, after all," added a bleary-eyed, but still standing, Timus.

"Bravo," I nodded to Timus. "As for me, Antony I, of course, can smoke anyone under the table," I said with a straight and serious expression, brow wrinkled in mock concentration.

Antony translated for his people and at one point, as he was speaking a great cheer went up, with cries of "Elephant, elephant!"

I looked around at Antony. "They're bringing an elephant here?" I asked.

"No. It is the name of the water pipe which you now must smoke, as you have sent out the challenge, Alun."

I looked around and all eyes were on me. "Elephant! Bring it out here," I cried in false bravado. They all said things like "Good sahib!" and "Yes! Yes! Sahib."

When I saw it, I steeled my face to stop any shock showing! It was bloody enormous! The base was about a foot and a half high. It was a pot-bellied pot, three quarters filled with water, glazed and with a huge aperture at the top. Into this was stuffed two bamboo tubes, tied together at the bottom, with a bandage of cloth wound as to form a big stopper for the top of the pot. One was the tube that you smoke it through, which reached all the way up to your mouth and the other short one, carried the bowl for the hashish. That bowl was the size of a standard tea-cup! The pipes were positioned in such a way that the smoker was pulling the smoke through the cooling water inside the pot. Of course, you didn't have to use just water. It could be whiskey, brandy or, my favourite, coconut milk. After pulling pure grass through it, no tobacco, one could drink the milk!

"That must hold at least half an ounce," Timus guessed through blood-shot eyes. "You sure of this?"

"Oh ye of little faith." I grinned.

Apparently the method was to bind the two tubes, so that the binding wedged into the large aperture at the top. You then soaked the binding in water thus aiding the seal formed by the rag in the top of the pot. The correct pose was then to stand up on one foot and use your other foot to jam down the tubes and rag. The boy would load up with chips of hashish, topped off with a couple of red-hot charcoal pieces to light it.

This is it, I thought. *This has to be lit correctly, and smoked properly, and I have to walk out unaided, or I'm going to look a complete twat!* I took the big tube in my mouth and began a slow but repeated series of short puffs, keeping my eye on the coals and noting with satisfaction, that they were glowing bright red with my puffs. When I felt that I'd built up just enough momentum, I emptied my lungs as far as I could, even crouching down to expel every last bit. I then went for it! I rose to my full height while inhaling for all I was worth!

When my lungs just wouldn't expand and more, I ripped the pipe, sideways out of my mouth in a dramatic fashion. It worked! There was a 'poof' sound and the hash in the bowl burst into flames. There were sparks and spits everywhere. "Yes!"

The watchers were unrestrained in their slack-jawed, open-eyed, wonder. They shouted the same word as before, in total unison and even applauded. It wasn't good to allow the hash to be in flame so I put it out by damping it with my hand. One must never allow hashish to burn. It must smoulder. I took my accolades, even though I felt weak at the knees and my sight was coming and going! With gargantuan effort, I pulled myself up to full height, the effort of which nearly made me pass out! I walked steadily to my seat, surveyed my audience and sat down with straight back. The place erupted with delight!

"No Westerner has ever smoked that pipe and walked away from it unaided," grinned Antony. "Indeed, no! You will be famous, Alun."

I decided now was the time for bravado. I stood unexpectedly but steadily. I grasped the still smouldering pipe and casually passed the pipe stem to Black Bob, who had been anticipating his turn, and winked at me. As he prepared, I turned to Antony. "Please ask your friends when are we going to get down to some serious smoking?" I even managed to keep a dead-pan delivery!

Antony translated this to jeers and cat-calls and much laughter. In the end, I cracked as well, and the full, 'stoned-out-hippy-grin' that goes from ear to ear, was on display.

Bob, meanwhile, was making a good fist of smoking the pipe and Timus was filling in the gaps. Many of the local guys joined in with a toke. Charlie had stayed behind as he was suffering from the 'Tehran Trotts'. And didn't everybody know about it!

Antony sent one of the boys to fetch sweets and a tray of chai. We managed to climb the stairs to the roof.

"Salam wh'aley coom," said the guy who sat in the chair. He didn't rise when he saw Anthony, because even though he was of lower class, they had been friends since they were five years old.

"Excuse me while I talk to Habby," said Antony, and they continued in Urdu. From this, I gathered his name was the same as the café, and he was the other owner.

Not only had we beaten the 'elephant' but we had made it up to the roof for sunset. It was a beautiful sunset and we all sat around smoking and talking. Habby asked if I liked Kashmir hashish. I replied that I'd only seen a few pieces before. He pulled out a big chunk of Black Kashmir and applied some heat with a match. When the hash started bubbling with oil, he gave it to me to smell. It was spicy and black all the way through.

We smoked some of it as the sun went down. Habby told us that we could have as much hashish as we wanted. He would make us a deal. We could have as much as we liked, on credit!

"I can tell you are serious people, you bring bus from England. I give to you; you take to your country and sell. You come here, pay me, and we do it all again."

"That's very trusting of you Habby. What's to stop me ripping you off?"

"You are not ordinary tourists. Also I have many family in England and, if I ask, they will come and kill you," he said with a slight smile. I didn't doubt it for a second.

"Thanks for the offer, Habby but we are going the other way. We are on our way to Goa in India."

"No problem! You take to Goa, sell to other tourists, make good profit. We don't give Kashmir for this. We use best Afghani," he leered.

"I think we'll probably do a deal with you Habby, but right now we'd better get back to the Memsahib, they'll be wondering what has become of us."

We went back down to the saloon and as a parting shot, I thanked our new friends for their hospitality and added, "And look here, we are walking out under our own steam!"

There was babble of Urdu, then in clear English, "Under our own steam!" Then on in Urdu.

"We will see you tomorrow Habby, and we can work together."

This pleased Habby very much. It also got me thinking. Very, very deeply!

We bade good evening to Antony and caught a taxi back to the bus. We had a funny conversation with the driver who wanted to become a taxi driver in London. "My brother in Full-ham," he over-pronounced, "he have two taxi."

We pulled up beside the bus. There was a small gathering, watching every move. They didn't see too many English buses and hippies in the Southern part of Pakistan. Most travellers just dashed across the top of the country i.e. Peshawar, Islamabad, Rawalpindi, Lahore and cross at Attari Road crossing just outside Amritsar, India.

The driver of the taxi would not let us get out of the

cab without filling my cupped hands with some very nice looking and smelling, brown hashish. "You are all welcome in my country," he beamed. We were delighted by his generosity. That's an understatement. Here we were in a dope-producing country and our fantasies were coming true. People were literally, forcing prime quality dope into our hands! We were in heaven.

"Can you imagine this happening in London?" asked Timus. "A black cab, dropping us on the Embankment and not letting us get out of the cab before giving us a handful of hash!" We giggled like schoolgirls, the driver as well.

"Mister. You need cab again, I am here, no problem. Mohamed Babu. You speak, I come."

"Thank you Mohamed 'B', we will see you tomorrow."

He drove off very happy, repeating, "Mohamed 'B'." To him, that was as good as a contract. We cooked and had a good time recounting what we had been doing.

Charlie was no better. "Antony said the best cure was to go to the government opium shop! Take a small piece the size of a pea of eating opium, it will bind-up your guts and stop the cramps."

I smiled as if to say, "Ain't that some shit, man a government opium shop," but Charlie was in a bad way, and I actually felt sorry for him!

We decide to visit it tomorrow and just buy fifty pence worth of eating opium and fifty pence worth of smoking opium. The shop was only four doors down from the Habbybulla.

We spent the next day with Antony in his mountain village. He arrived early. With breakfast of spicy hot soup and fresh chapatti with several side dishes of chutney, coconut sauces and chilli pepper puree, followed by yoghurt and local honey. Antony told us that the bees lived in hives that were situated near the fields of marijuana and that the bees often sought pollen there.

"I'd better not give the kids any then."

"Don't worry Alun. We have ordinary honey as well so the little ones will still have the sweetness, oh yes." He smiled at the kids who were at the time, hanging off his arms and being spoilt rotten by him.

His family house was massive and used to be a summer palace for one of the Maharajas. I drove into the courtyard and we all got off to go in the house. I started to lock up the bus. "Do not worry; these people will not come near the bus. They know you are my guest and you could leave five pound notes all over the floor and every one of them will be there when you come back."

"I'm so sorry Antony I didn't mean to insult anyone. It's just that we have had so much of our stuff ripped-off on our journey."

"Oh, don't apologise Alun. If you weren't with me, they would rob you blind, very bad fellows, oh yes indeed!"

We both burst out laughing. Antony took me on a special tour of this huge palace that was now his home."

You know Alun, when the British were here they used this place as a hotel and banqueting house. The kitchens are down there." He pointed to what looked like a marble hall about half a mile long!

"I should think the food was cold by the time it got to the table!"

"Ah but there was a one eighth scale, model railway that ran from the kitchens to the banqueting hall, each carriage had an oil burner underneath to keep the food hot."

"You are kidding me. A model railway to carry the

food?"

"But you know the most remarkable thing? It was made of solid Silver!"

"You are kidding me!"

"No, Alun I am serious. Come, here are some photos."

I looked at some very old photos. They were black and white and very formal. Victorian ladies, in their lace and black jackets. Elaborate hats with huge black ostrich feathers. The cars that they were all sat around in were quite remarkable as well. Rolls Royces with Park Ward of Mayfair, hand built, custom bodies of luxurious quality with matching leather interiors and cut glass, Waterford crystal, for the built-in decanters.

Other cars, such as a rare Hispano Susa, a Cadillac saloon that looked about a mile long, and loads of Jaguar MK9s. Not forgetting the Mercedes and a Model T Ford flat-bed truck for the bodyguards and servants, who sat facing each other in the open back of the T Ford. And a picture of my dream car, the Ford GT40!

"This is my favourite car, Antony. I have studied them since they were first made. If I had the money to buy any car this is the one I'd buy."

Then I spotted it! A genuine D-Type Jaguar in full Le Mans livery and a smiling driver who was obviously the owner of this palace at the time of the photos "A D-Type! An original too!" I gasped.

"Yes. This fellow, the two hundred and thirty second Maharaja of Baheraat. He won Le Mans three years running, until the Ferraris started to compete. We still have these cars!"

"Do you know what this D-Type is worth?" I asked incredulously. It was a rhetorical question as I knew already. One had gone in a Sotherby's auction, recently. "It went for three and a half million pounds to a collector in

New York!"

"Oh yes Sotherby's people in New York, tracked it down from Jaguar's records and keep pestering me to put it into auction."

My stunned mind just recognised what he had said earlier. "You still have these cars? I gasped. I'd love to see them please."

"I will get the servants to open the garage," said Antony. A building the size of the average four bedroom property with its under-floor heating and air conditioning.

The house and grounds and also all the other buildings were not powered from the electricity from the city, but from a Rolls Royce, turbocharged, V12, twenty-two litre, 250KW, generator, installed in a forty foot shipping container. What was known as 'Hush-Power'.

Under medium loading these were so sound-proofed, that the only way to tell if they were running was to put your hand on the container and feel the vibration!

"I bought this from the management company of the Pink Floyd," said Antony. "It was for extra power at venues that didn't have enough."

"Must have cost you a fortune to get it out here," I said.

"I had it reconditioned at Rolls Royce and they shipped it straight out here to Karachi and then by truck, to here. Because of high import tax, it was cheaper to buy a second hand set and have it reconditioned than to bring in a new one from a Far East supplier!

We had a wonderful meal of spicy mutton and potatoes, with every vegetable you can imagine. Followed by, mangos, kiwi fruit and coconut. The kids were playing with some old Tri-ang train sets so we wandered out onto the huge veranda and finished our brandies. After a while a servant came along and bent to talk to Antony.

"This fellow tells me the garage is ready, would you like to see the cars as well, Isobel?" The children will be safe with my servants.

"I wouldn't miss this for the world," smiled Isobel. She had become a bit of a petrol head since hanging around with me and could discuss the merits of a hemispherical head and fuel injection.

We drove to the garage, now lit and shining brightly through ivy-covered windows. When we entered through the doors I had to blink a couple of times. There was the D-Type, looking as if it'd just been built. Alongside it was the Rolls Royce. Beside that was an original A.C. Cobra, a 427 cubic inch V8 engine and all original!

"Do you know what this would be worth in England? Of course you do why am I asking you such a silly question?" I babbled. I was in shock. Never had I seen such a collection of cars under one roof. A gull wing Mercedes, a Vanwall from the fifties, Formula One. A Cooper Climax from the same racing stable. It was too much to take in! Why was Antony grinning so much? We wound our way past some cars under dust sheets and standing on blocks to relieve their suspensions of the static weight of the car. I came to one shape under the dust sheet. It was so familiar. Why was Antony grinning so much? I looked at the wall there were a few pictures of the greats of Le Mans Twenty-Four Hours, Jacky Ickx and Jacky Oliver. Pictures of them in a familiar car doorway, looking dirty, tired, but jubilant.

"Nooooo!" My jaw dropped as I looked at Antony who was still grinning from ear to ear.

"Yes my friend, it is their car," and he whipped off the cover to reveal a Ford GT40 in original John Wyer automotive livery. This was the car I idolised ever since it came into existence at Ford Advanced Vehicles Operations (the same unit that gave us the legendry

'Escort Mexico' and the Twin Overhead Cam, Escort 'Twink' GT. Both won more trophies and race records than I have time to detail), which I seem to remember was in Slough at the time.

The Ford GT40 came into existence because of a feud between Henry Ford the second, and Enzo Ferrari. The story is well documented elsewhere but in the end Ford poured hundreds of millions of pounds into developing a Le Mans car for one sole purpose: Beat the Ferraris at all costs! Ferrari had been winning the twenty-four hour endurance race for twelve years running.

Built and designed in England, not only did they beat the Ferraris but to use the parlance of the weekend GT racers, "They widdled all over 'm!" They came in many laps ahead of the nearest Ferrari and went on to win the race, four years running. It was only rule changes to the race that made them outside those rules and very expensive to bring them inside spec. By that time, Ford had proved their point, and moved on.

For car enthusiasts, I was in the presence of God's chariot! I looked at the driver's seat, way down low. The name GT40 came from the fact that they were just forty and a half, inches tall!

The old canvas seats were oil-stained, at least I hoped it was oil! At over two hundred miles an hour down the Mulsann straights, braking technology being what it was then, it could have been anything! The chassis numbers were all there. The provenance was impeccable. I touched the old leather gloves that could have been worn by the legendary winners. I sat in their car! I looked down on lesser mortals from Olympia. Isobel told me later that she had tried to talk to me but just got grunts of non-committal monosyllables, in return. She gave up, so she and Antony carried on looking at other cars, and left me to my first automotive love, the Ford GT40.

I won't go on… much! But you can imagine what was going on in my fantasies. Anyone who appreciates cars and engines will know how I felt at that moment. There was no ignition key of course, just a big red push switch. All the dials were at odd angles. *What?* Then I remembered: The gauges are positioned so that when everything is normal, all pointers will be directly vertical. This saves you having to read each gauge when checking if all is well on a 24-hour race. The slightest variation of those needles is vital to spot as early as possible, so a pit stop and back-up can be implemented.

At over two hundred miles an hour, a quick flick across the dials is all you can afford. By then, at those speeds, you've travelled miles in that flick of an eye! I found my hand hovering over that red push button. I wasn't going to push it. I already knew that it had been drained of fuel and the engine oil drained for storage. But I couldn't resist asking Antony if I could lift the rear end and see the engine and transmission. This he readily agreed to and I went straight to the retaining clips and catches that allows the whole back end to tip up, so that the mechanics have easy access to everything.

I think he was impressed as only a sad anorak, like me, and the people who built and maintained it, would know where the clips were. I lifted the back end to see a well-used but superbly engineered, full-race, engine, trans-axle, and suspension. The convoluted, extractor exhaust, looked like the snake-pit at a zoo! There was stainless steel brided pipe work, and anodised blue and red aluminium couplings. All incredibly expensive but real engineering beauty. A costing department i.e. the soulless 'bean counters', had not been allowed within ten miles of this beauty. Engineering to a specification, not a budget! Pure! This was the nearest thing to time travel I'd ever experience. I closed the covers and took a deep breath. I couldn't sully that moment by discussing monetary worth but with that provenance, we must have been talking about two to three million pounds. That's if you could find one.

They only made around one hundred and ten. In the years that followed they were even re-building written-off, wrecks, just because of the authentic chassis numbers! I dragged my head back to the present. We finished our wonderful dinner with tales from Antony about the British Raj and its excesses. Those horrible pictures of some white, elite, member of the Raj, in full Putties and Pith helmet, with his foot on the lifeless tiger's head. And swaggering with rifle in the other. He probably shot from the safety of the back of an elephant.

Row on row of dead lions, tigers, water bucks, and water buffalos. Hundreds of carcasses. In front of the carcasses were tusks and antlers, by the dozen. Rhino horns, all laid out in rows. My face must have gone black. I just couldn't understand such wanton destruction just for pleasure. "It was another time, Alun. These fellows knew no better."

"I'm sorry Antony, but it still exists. There is a sickness in the mind of man that likes to torture living things for no other reason than his own pleasure at inflicting that torture. It's what led to the slaughter of six million Jews in the war."

"Don't you dare bring this wonderful evening, down like that," scolded Isobel with mock gravity. She turned and kissed Antony on the cheek and squeezed his hand. Thank you for a wonderful evening, Antony. The kids have loved it here and have learned some things from your servants. Thank them all from us."

All the girls kissed Antony goodnight and it seemed the whole mountain village came out to wave goodbye.

It was wonderful getting to know Quetta. And, as I've mentioned before, it strongly reminded me of East End London of my childhood. In fact, the only difference would have been the evidence of 'Betel nut' chewing. This was a foul habit. Betel nut is a mild narcotic, like nicotine. One chews the nut like a cow and her cud. This produces a mild euphoria and copious amounts of saliva which is deep, red in colour. The idea is to hold the fluid in the mouth until you can hold it no more. It then gets spat out on the pavement or floor and like disgusting chewing gum, it was everywhere in huge gobs on the floor. I said it was disgusting!

Many women begging on the streets would be holding children for the sympathy vote, while their lips were stained red and with glazed eyes.

"Bloody Mary's chewing Betel nuts,

She is always chewing Betel nuts,

Bloody Mary's chewing Betel nuts,

Now ain't that too damn bad!"

The words from the nineteen fifties Rogers and Hammerstein's musical *South Pacific* kept coming back. We decided that we had better move on, so the next day we said our goodbyes and invited Antony for dinner aboard the bus. Before that we had gone to the government opium shop. It was actually only a shop front with a wire grill through which purchases could be made. We asked for a couple of rupees worth of cooking and eating grade. We reasoned that we'd be crossing into India soon so we didn't need much, just enough to last us to the border.

The shopkeeper came back with handfuls of each, for just a few rupees. The equivalent of fifty pence worth of each! What were we going to do with all that opium? It only took a small ball of it to bind Charlie up. The rest we tried eating to settle our stomachs and then what was left, we threw away. We had a great time with Antony and he left us that night only after promising we would return to visit him one day.

We headed out to Sukkur and Multan. Just outside Multan there was the sound of twin Alpine air horns behind me. I looked in the mirror to see the Simontour truck behind me. He was driving like a maniac as he came past grinning and waving, his trailer cover flapping in the wind, where he hadn't bothered to do it up. He was a rarity on these roads. The Pakistani transport system still relied on four-wheeled Bedford J-Types. To see a British registered, Scania 110, here, was very rare indeed.

We drove on to Lahore. We arrived late at night and I just pulled up where we stopped. We hadn't any hash that wasn't well packed, so we walked over to a stable nearby and sat around the brazier with some of the horse-drawn taxi drivers. They invited us to chai and before long, some very good chitrali was brought out. I just had a few tokes and left them all to it.

I was awoken early in the morning by traffic and air horns going off. It seemed we had parked on a roundabout and nobody had moved us on, they were just driving around us. I stuck my head out of the door and was greeted by dusty chaos of all kinds of traffic. Trucks to ox carts to taxis. We moved over off the roundabout onto a side road and made some breakfast. It was decided that we should cross into India tomorrow via the only crossing left open since the Pakistan came into existence. The various wars and slaughter that came about when the British left India, was now reflected in the fact that despite several thousand miles of shared border, the Attari Road crossing, was the only way in. Every day at Attari Road, they would have a ceremony at around 4 o'clock in the afternoon where in full ceremonial uniform and practised drill, they would each slam the gates shut across the road and all but thumb their noses at each other. They would then stand glaring at each other from behind their gates. Between the gates was a hundred yards of no man's land and customs offices at both ends of the compound.

We arrived too late to cross that day, which pissed me off for no reason I could think of.

As I walked back to the bus with the papers and passports, a Cockney voice behind me said, "Alright sun?" I turned but there was nobody there except a cakes and pastries salesman with his tray of cakes. I went to walk on. "Bleedin' 'ot init moosh?" There it was again no mistaking it. It was a South East London accent. I turned again but there was nobody there. This time I turned as if to walk on but I turned again unexpectedly to catch the cake seller mimicking like a parrot, a Cockney accent.

"That's you isn't it?" I said to the seller.

He grinned and came out with "Alright mate," and I swear he had it off to a 'T'.

"Where did you learn those accents?" I asked.

"Only from traveller, sahib. Like you."

"How many voices can you do?"

"I can do Birmingham and Scotland and many others. Yowm aoright ar kid?" he said, in a perfect, Birmingham accent. "Come ached. Eh! Calm down ar kid. Arr eh. I was made oop, ar kid." That was Liverpool and every bit of it sounded authentic.

"Wow that's pretty good. You had me fooled."

"Can you buy cake sahib?" he asked, now very earnest. "I sell to pay for food for my family; we are very poor people sahib."

"Go on then give me fourteen of them, please."

"Fourteen? Oh yes sahib, no problem." He wrapped two big bags in old newspaper and all but grovelled at the large order I'd given him. "I will go to my home and bring the rest to your beautiful bus, sahib. My home is nearby."

"OK. You bring them as soon as you can. We will start cooking our dinner now and everything should work out fine. When you come to the door you must bang hard because we have music and much talking inside." I gave him a one hundred rupee note. His eyes widened. It was about what he made in a month.

"Oh sahib I do not have change for this."

"OK bring me change when you bring the cakes."

"Very good sahib, I will come soon."

I could see he was a poor man. His plastic shoes were nearly worn through and his clothing was worn.

When I got back to the bus, Isobel and Kakey had cooked me a wonderful meal and I ate it without interruption. After a while there was a knock on the door and there stood our cake seller with a huge tray of warm cakes, many more than I'd ordered. The kids were excited at the prospect of all those sticky buns. Behind our cake seller, just in the darkness, we could see the sellers' wife. She was dressed in a sari and carrying a tiny baby with her.

"Come in, come in, please sit down," we said to the lady. She didn't understand.

"Please your wife must be tired. Please ask her to sit down while we finish our business," said Isobel

The wife came aboard very shyly. We all peeped at the little baby which could have only been a few days old. There was much grinning and smiling from the proud dad. Mum looked a little shocked at our appearance and lifestyle but beamed at us when we looked at the baby. We introduced our kids to her and they both wanted to see the child close up. I noticed Mum had dark henna around her eyes with huge gold earrings and many gold necklaces. Her nose was pierced and a rather large gold ornament was fixed there. She also wore many coloured glass rings on her wrist. They were very popular and many were piled up the arm. Her sandals were intricately carved leather and the whole effect was in contrast to the poor clothes that he was wearing. I guessed that he always wore old clothing to help sales of his wares to the foreign traveller.

Many people here liked to buy gold instead of putting their money in a bank. Who can blame them? Corruption is rife in the banking industry. Even in Europe and the USA. So they preferred to turn profit into gold, and it is then worn by the wife. A kind of human strong-box! We made coffee for them both, and we chatted as much as possible, for quite some time.

"Sahib we must go now, the baby is hungry and must be fed. Here is your change."

"Please keep it and buy something extra for your beautiful baby," I said, to choruses of agreement from the others.

He was beside himself with gratitude. "If you come back this way I will see you again, sahib. Good night madam and thank you very much." He waved to us all. We all touched the baby gently, on the way out and explained this was our way of saying good luck.

They disappeared, smiling, into the darkness. I often wondered over the years, what happened to that baby and what he grew into. Guess I'll never know.

We arose early to catch the border post as soon as they opened. Isobel tried to change some money, but the money change wallah, thinking we were just dumb tourists, tried to give us a very low rate of exchange. Isobel was so pissed off at this, she complained to the captain of customs. He promptly kicked the money changer up the backside and told him, in English, that if he didn't give the memsahib the proper rate he would be be banished from the border crossing! Imagine a British customs officer getting involved in money changing. Some chance! There was much stamping of passports and stamping and writing in the Carnet de Passage. The Seik border guard, immaculate in his white shirt and a tropical suit, came out to inspect our bus. He found our stash of Playboy magazines which he had to take away.

"I am sorry sahib. I must take these to determine whether they are pornographic and may have to be confiscated."

He disappeared quickly and we never saw him again. Our papers were cleared and we left them to their determinations!

A few hours later we arrived in Amritsar, just on the Indian side.

Chapter 11

India

WE HAD MADE IT TO INDIA!

We were over the moon and decided to have a celebration that night. We had been told by other travellers that the best place to stay was at the Y.M.C.A. at the edge of town, on the Delhi Road. There was plenty of room to park the bus and showers and a restaurant. No Indians were allowed in there and it was free from hassle.

We decided it would be a good idea to buy a kilo of good Kashmiri hash to top up the stash, and take it to Goa to sell to the tourists. Isobel and I took a rickshaw into town. We asked the driver to take us where we could buy some hashish. He took us down some back streets to a decidedly dodgy looking area. We sat in his rickshaw and waited. A man in western-style clothing came up to the rickshaw.

"Oh sahib, madam, You should not be here. This is not good place, there are bad people here. They will rob you, please do not stay."

He spoke excellent English so we explained we were waiting for our driver and then going back to the hostel.

"That is best sahib, goodnight. Goodnight madam."

"Goodnight," smiled Isobel, "and thank you."

Our driver reappeared with a tall man wearing the turban and dress of a Sikh.

"This is Mr Singh, sahib. He has the kilo for you but he will bring it later to the hostel. I was waiting for the 'Give me the money now. I will bring it later' routine but it didn't come. We just paid for the piece he gave us and agreed to meet him in about two hours. I made a smoke on the way home and got pretty shit-faced. It was good stuff.

I told the others what we had arranged and we all had a smoke and it was agreed that a kilo of this should be purchased for smoking and selling in Goa.

The Kashmir made a nice change from the Afghani we'd been smoking. After a while there was a knock on our door and one of the servants of the hostel told us that a Sikh fellow wanted to see me.

"OK tell him to come over."

"I cannot do that sahib. These fellows are not allowed to come in here. Only tourist here sahib."

"Oh, OK I understand. I'll go to him. Thank you."

"Be careful sahib these are not good fellows."

I could see Mr Singh waiting at the gates. He had a brown paper carrier bag and looked for all intents and purposes, like he had just come from the takeaway.

"Good evening Mr Singh, you have something for me?" His head nodded from side to side as they do in India to indicate that they understand or 'all is good'.

He handed me the bag and I saw inside wrapped in the *Times of India* newspaper, was a couple of fine-looking slabs of black Kasmiri hash. It had a white powder in places. I was immediately suspicious.

"What is all this white stuff?"

"Oh sahib it is just the water that they use to press the hashish when it is fresh from the plant. It makes it easier to stick together, otherwise you must use heat and that is not good sahib."

"Mr Singh, would you please wait while I try one smoke of this?"

"Take one piece, sahib. Make smoke, no problem." Head going vigorously, from side, to side.

"Now Mr Singh, this is top quality, like I asked for? First quality?" I asked, as I broke a lump off. It certainly smelt pungent and spicy.

In answer to my question, he came out with a saying that lasted the whole trip. Even to this day, we still use the words he spoke. "Oh! Don't vurry sahib! Soon you vill be floating!" He said it with eyes wide and head going from side to side. I laughed very hard at this phrase. It encompassed everything.

"Don't vurry sahib, soon you will be floating," I told the others as I prepared a chillum full of Mr Singh's hash. We fell about laughing. We passed it round and it turned out to be very good hash indeed.

"OK. I think we are agreed then. It's worth the money."

"Wish we had a load of it in England," said Black Bob.

"Not many," said Timus. "I could sell twenty kilos right now."

"Funny you should say that, I've been thinking the same thing," I said. Oh yes! I'd been thinking, alright! "Anyway, I'd better give him the money and get the hash before he wanders off."

We counted out the notes. The equivalent of forty pounds, sterling! When I got to the gate I couldn't see him but he was sat in the chai stall, opposite the large gates. I walked over and shook hands. "What's up? I could sense his unease."

"I am just a low class fellow. Here we are called 'untouchables'." I looked around at the many faces and all classes, drinking chai, they seemed to be watching my reactions closely.

"Oh I see! Well, Ahem! Where I come from, we don't have that crap anymore. A man is a man, whether he runs a bank or cleans a toilet. If he is a straight man, he will be respected."

I heard mumbled words of Punjabi amongst the chai drinkers. Most of it was incomprehensible to me but all of a sudden amongst those words, in English, "Ve don't have that crap anymore," then back to Punjabi, to finish the sentence. Many times that happened. Right in the middle of a sentence in Punjabi you would suddenly hear some English words where there was no equivalent. Sometimes they would use English like this and it sounded funny to us. I sat down quietly and gave Mr Singh the envelope containing one thousand two hundred rupees.

"Oh thank you sahib." His smile became much broader. He put the envelope in his pocket. One of the chai drinkers spoke to him in Punjabi. "No! Sahib is English. They are honest people. He is not some Tajik or Waziri, rouge fellow. I do not need to count," he said with a little mock annoyance and in English of course, for my benefit. I was still impressed though.

"We will be here for a few days… I'm sorry I didn't get your name. My name is Alun."

"Ah Mr Alun, sahib."

"No, my friend, Just Alun. Only Alun. No sahib. No Mr. Just Alun."

He wrinkled his brow a little with the characteristic side to side, head shake.

"Mr. Or sahib. It makes me feel as if we are still in the British Raj days. I am just Alun. My friends call me Alun or Al."

"My name is Pekoo Singh-Sarl. I am Punjabi Sikh." He said proudly. Now I knew he understood what I meant. I was very impressed with the Sikh peoples and the Punjab in general. It was green and lush, and had plenty of dairy products too. Much of the Punjab resembled the West Country of England, in summer.

I learned a little of the history of the Sikhs. The religion came into being, to try to join together the Hindu and Muslim peoples. The leader and founder, the guru Nanak, apparently went for a swim in the river, one hot afternoon and nearly drowned. In the moment between life, and death where you can turn either way, he was taken before the supreme power. This entity told him he must found the new religion to bring the people together.

He found himself back on the bank and alive. He spent the rest of his life doing good works and trying to obey the will of God. He was also instructed not to cut his nails, hair, or beard, anything that grows on his body. He must keep his hair in a 'top knot' so that God may grab it easily at the appropriate time, and pull the good person up to heaven.

Many of the Sikh men of business would wear western-style suits and have their head covered with a tightly tied turban. From the turban would be a discreet band under the chin, where it meets the neck. In this, they would roll their beards and everything would look tidy. I will always get the image of a man in a smart suit with an impossibly, white shirt and dashing tie. All topped off with a pastel-coloured turban. They were the business people of India, it seemed to me.

They all have the name 'Singh'. Even to this day Isobel and I will refer to a Sikh as Mr Singh Amritsar, the place we were currently parked, was the most important city to the Sikh peoples. It is the equivalent of Mecca, to the Muslim. It's interesting to compare at this point, the welcome received when we did visit the Golden Temple. It was proud but welcoming. Compared to the glares and hostility and hatred, we received when we inadvertently, drove the bus around the Mosque in Mashhad, Iran. Islam's second most holy city!

We were Western infidels and were much too close to the shrine! Nice eh? The best story for me about the Guru Nanak was when he awoke, under a shady tree, one morning on his travels. He awoke to find himself surrounded by angry villagers.

"How dare you sleep with your feet toward God," they demanded of him. Apparently one had to sleep with one's head, NOT the feet, pointing toward the temple in the village, or something like that.

He rose and asked, "My friends. Show me where God is not. I will gladly point my feet there."

They took him as their spiritual leader. The rest is history, as they say. I was so impressed with the Sikh people. Their friendliness and loyalty to friends and family, that I still wear one of the 'five signs' of Sikhism. The uniquely shaped Kara, a steel wristband, worn on my right wrist. When I come across a Sikh person in England, they sometimes just tap the Kara with their finger nail, discreetly.

I always say "I'm 'Sudagee'." (I am a Sikh). It always gets a big smile.

In the next couple of days, we visited the Golden Temple. It was a stunning vista. The whole area, about the size of two football fields, side by side, was enclosed by cloistered and pillared walkways, with water filling most of the inside area.

There was a pathway out to the temple itself which was in the middle of this huge pond. There were flowers and plants and creeper vines everywhere, and the place was immaculately tended. I recognised lotus, and huge water lilies, and smelt jasmine in the air. The temple in the water was made mostly of gold! Hence, the name.

To show respect, we all covered our heads, and took off our shoes. We washed our feet at the water troughs, which flowed continually. We were shown around by Peekoo Singh, who delighted in the status afforded him, by having English friends. It was he who suggested that I become an honorary Sikh. He took me to the man who made the Kara, from stainless steel. It took a whole day to get it on and I won't go into detail, but it was a very tight fit!

Isobel and I found the sight of young boys of around twelve years old, with hair down to their waists, or done up in an untidy top knot, riding their bicycles, to be charming.

The only time that Isobel didn't like, was when coming back to the Y.M.C.A in a taxi, we passed a large roundabout. In the middle of the roundabout was a sadhu, a holy man. He had long dreadlocks and religious signs were tattooed all over his chest. He was dressed only in a loincloth. He sat in a pile of ashes which he threw over himself, now and again. He was white with ash.

People would bring him bowls of rice and fruit. He would sit still for weeks at a time. The taxi driver told us that he was a Brahman. That is, a member of the top class of Indian society. He also is a holder of the Victoria Cross, for his bravery during the Second World War.

"You're winding me up," I said with incredulity. "That old semi-naked guy?"

"Vinding up, sahib? Vat is this?"

"Sorry. I mean you are telling us a story, you know. A fable."

"Oh no, sahib. It is true. He was a major in the Indian Army. He charged down an enemy machine gun post and killed the enemy soldiers. Very brave man, sahib."

"But why does he live like this?" It was all like something out of *Black Narcissus*, one of my favourite films.

"They say the war affected him and now all he does is spread the message of peace. The people look after him and bring him food."

"He frightens me," said Isobel, "but there is also something impressive about him."

The driver then said something profound, and as it turns out, very true. "But you will remember him and the message he brings, for the rest of your life."

The Punjab made a big impression on us all. Trouble was it made another kind of impression on us, as well!

Next door to the Y.M.C.A. hostel was a patch of open ground, with a pond. This was the breeding ground for mosquitoes! At night you could see them in droves coming over the wall and caught in the perimeter spotlights. We were being eaten alive! The only way I could keep them off me was to use the same method as we used in Greece: two cigarettes crumbled into a saucer of water. Soak for two days then dab the water all over the exposed skin. You may stink of tobacco but you will not get bitten! The reason for this is obvious when you think about it. Most insecticides were based on nicotine, one of the most deadly poisons, in its concentrated form, known to man.

This night was really bad. I'd pulled out all the stops. Tobacco water, sleeping under a fan, burning one of those curly smoke-making burners, but nothing was stopping these blighters. At two in the morning I'd had enough. I roused the manager, paid our bill and got everyone, reluctantly, on the bus. I drove off toward Delhi. Just getting away from that stagnant water, got rid of them. There had been several attempts to eradicate the mozzies. They sprayed DDT on the breeding grounds of the mud, by the pond and such places. But the DDT had got into the water supply and contaminated the wells. The mozzies had died out for a while, but the effects of the DDT took years to go. We travelled on over roads that looked like a patchwork eiderdown. The suspension was getting a hammering.

We came across many accidents and hazards. For instance, if a truck broke down with say, back axle problems, that truck would stay right where it was. The axle would be removed and taken to be repaired. It did not matter if it was in the middle of the road on a blind bend. It stopped where it stopped. You may have been lucky and seen a single wick, paraffin burner to warn of the hazard but mostly all that you got was a line of stones from the side of the road which were supposed to guide you out round the obstruction. The stones were, of course, totally invisible at night.

Many times we would come across a truck on its side or a broken down, overloaded ox cart with no lights. There could be anything round that bend, anything at all. It demanded total concentration. We passed through towns like Ambala and counted down the kilometre signs until we were just outside India's capital, Delhi.

I wanted full daylight to drive through that madness. Most of the others didn't want to stay too long in the city and I agreed. By the time we got into the city, it was getting on for midday and getting really hot. It was bearable while we were moving but when we stopped it was vital to have some shade. Temperatures inside the bus were decidedly uncomfortable when we stopped.

We had all become accustomed to long distance travelling. I'd look at the others sometimes and think to myself how sophisticated they had become, when it came to living in close proximity like this under the pressures we were under. Thank goodness the work I'd done on the engine in Herat, Afghanistan had virtually cured the overheating problem. I didn't need another problem in this heat.

The other reason we'd had to come into Delhi was that Fran still wanted to go home. We hadn't rowed, in fact there was a tolerant silence between us, but she was determined to go. We had all learnt a bit about being on the road and living in a group. Charlie still tried to dominate everyone by telling them how this or that should be done. I'd learned to just let him get on with it, and then do exactly what I wanted to do.

To get to the embassy, I had to drive the bus into the diplomatic area of Delhi. The British Embassy was set in lavish park land with water sprinklers everywhere and sculptures lining the route. We parked right outside the British Embassy gates and a policeman stepped forward to move us on.

Before he could say anything, I whipped out my passport and said, "This is my embassy and I want to park here as I have business to attend to and I need to park my bus in the shade so that the Memsahib and children can stay cool."

"Well actually sahib, I vas just going to suggest you bring all your guests into the air-conditioned foyer."

"Oh I see," I said, much taken aback. "Thank you very much. That's very kind. Your English is excellent."

"Thank you sahib I was brought up in a British school and learnt English as a child. It is almost my native tongue and is a requirement of my job here at the embassy. I am in Special Diplomatic Protection Corps."

"Even your accent is perfect." He smiled in a modest way and the head went from side to side.

The others got Fran sorted with a repatriation ticket. You can go to any British Embassy in any country and demand to be repatriated if you have run out of money. They take your passport away when you reach the UK but you can get it back again by paying off the ticket expenses to the Passport Office. British Airways always kept a couple of seats free, for emergencies such as this on every flight, paid for by the embassy, even if unused.

She was to fly in three days' time. Timus suggested she take some of the Kashmir with her to sell and send us the money. To my utter amazement, she agreed. So I spent a few hours carefully opening a packet of 'Dhoop' which is the perfumed substance, one finds on joss sticks. It was wrapped in a heavy waxy paper and ideal for the job. It resembled a giant squeeze of toothpaste, about 10cm in diameter. I cut down the length with a sharp blade, I then scooped out the middle and refilled it with Kashmir hash, about a quarter kilo. I put the two halves back together and when I'd finished you couldn't tell that it had been worked on. I took special care not to leave any prints on it. Hardly big time smuggling, but best to be safe. I learned later, that the guy that I had told her to post it to, had received it and started to sell it to friends. They were bringing it back for refund with the same tale of 'funny tasting' and 'smells flowery'.

"I knew you wouldn't bother to send me crap back, so I just couldn't figure it out. Then I happened to notice that where I'd cut the stuff in half, there seemed to be a different coloured core. So, OK I thought, best try that."

"And?" I asked.

"Well the next thing I knew, I'd been sat on the stairs staring at the wall, for about an hour, absolutely ripped to the tits!"

Either way, he never paid me any money. Giving me some feeble excuse, about nobody wanting to buy it. All he had to do was give one of them a smoke of the real stuff, and they'd have been all over him like a rash. I guess he ended up smoking it all himself. Shame really because he was a close friend. Bit disappointing.

So there we were. Minus one more! I personally wouldn't miss her but it was a shame. She wasted such an adventure because she just couldn't deal with it. We got out of Delhi as soon as possible, but not before checking the Post Restante for letters from home. There were some from Isobel's family and some from my brother, mum and dad.

They were enjoying a heat wave at home, missing the grandkids but hoping we were having a wonderful time. We had been asked by some 'Orange People' to take them through to Goa. They were devotees of Bhagwan Shree Rajneesh, They wore orange robes and had a Mandala round their necks. This was a necklace made from small wooden beads with a picture of Bhagwan hanging like a fob. Bhagwan had his Ashram at Poona, beloved city of the British Raj. You could tell this because it strongly resembled Cheltenham or one of the Gloucester cities, with some stunning, Baronial, architecture. Spike Milligan, the much loved zany comedian, was born and brought up there.

Bhagwan Rajneesh was a guru who brought the westerners, seeking spiritual enlightenment. Typically, Americans with more money than sense. They would 'donate' millions of dollars to his ashram. He had a yellow Rolls Royce that never went on the roads. It conveyed him to the lecture hall, from his private bungalow in the grounds of the Ashram, about half a mile in total.

He would lecture to a silent, adoring audience, all of whom had to be 'sniffed' when entering the hall as, "Bhagwan doesn't like artificial smells." So if you were wearing antiperspirant or aftershave, you were ejected by Bagwan's heavies. The place hit the headlines in the western newspapers because of the free, tantric love and sex that was going on there, as part of the indoctrination process.

I must admit some very fine-looking girls tried to get me to join the movement. I took what they offered and went to all the parties, and there were some wild parties, let me tell you! But all along, I'd seen Bhagwan for what he was: a con-man, pure and simple. Just like Maha rishi Mahesh Yogi who conned the Beatles, to Maharajii Jay, leader of the 'Divine Light,' cult. And of course, there was the Scientology cult, as well. Every one of them, charlatans. This turned out to be the case. Maharajii was questioned about illegal arms smuggling. What did a guru of peace want with three Phantom fighter jets?

Bhagwan was prosecuted when he, allegedly, tried to smuggle diamonds into the USA when India had had enough of him and he left to set up in the states. As for the Scientologists, well they are just plain evil. These organisations pander to the weak-minded. If they are rich, too, so much the better. It goes without saying of course that native Indian people were not allowed into the Ashram. To me, that said it all, these people, mostly Americans from, where else but the 'capital of weird', California.

They were boring people when they started upon their preaching of how wonderful Bhagwan was, blah-de-blah. In the end I had to ask the ones on the bus to stop their high pressure sales, because we just weren't interested. I had to back it up with, "If you don't stop it we'll ask you to leave the bus." That worked! And believe it or not, they turned back into nice people again.

We were doing some serious mileage every day heading for Bombay, as Mumbai was known then. We'd smoked most of the hash we'd allowed ourselves from the Kashmir we'd bought to sell.

I didn't mind the gargantuan driving sessions. And they were long hours of driving, day in day out. It never ceased to amaze me that I could drive all day, look to my left and right and just see land and jungle stretching out to the horizon on each side. I'd drive all through the night, and at first light, I could still look to my left and right and see the flat landscape disappearing to my left and right. This went on for days before the scenery started to change as we entered the Western Ghats - a mountain range, on the western coast of India.

As we came round a fairly elevated mountain pass, there was a sadhu sat on a rock.

"Hey let's stop and turn this sadhu, on, man!"

"Huh?" I grunted. Brought out of my concentration, I'd been driving for hours and I'd welcome a break.

I braked to a halt. Everyone piled off the bus and was greeted with a wonderful smile from the sadhu. He was gentle and welcoming especially to the children who warmed to him immediately. When we left England it was for several reasons on my part. I have always wanted adventure, travel and excitement beyond what a mortgage and 14 days paid holiday could bring. The one reason for going to India that did not appear on my list, was to gain 'spiritual enlightenment'. Nor did I believe that the 'Mystical East' had the answer to everything. As far as I was concerned India was a vast country with history and a desperation, like everywhere else, to survive. If you have to start legends and religions and handed-down, stories along the way, well, that was part of the whole picture. But for me India was no more spiritual than the Mile End Road, London, England.

India was exciting, beautiful, and so different. There were lessons about raw life, to be learned, for those who listened. But spiritual? Nah! But this guy was different! He wanted nothing bar our company on a sunny evening in the Western Ghats of India. It was all known, and expected, that we would come and sit with him a while.

We sat quietly draped in the shade of a small tree. The kids were dozing around Isobel's lap. We weren't talking a lot. We saw the vast valley and mountains in the distance. We seemed to be on a high plain, above it all. The sadhu wore a plain shoulder bag of woven wool. From it he brought out his small polished copper bowls, from which he ate what the local villagers brought him, as he travelled through their area.

He laid them beside a staff that he carried. It was just short of two meters long and decorated with symbols in what appeared to me to be Sanskrit, and picked up his chillum and started to fill it with 'sacred weed' from, we learned, Kerala, which is in the south of India and famed, among other things, for the quality of its 'erb.

When he had finished his preparations, he sang, in a full baritone voice, his mantra. His song praised the gods Shiva and Shankar for providing. We all sat transfixed as the low-lying clouds made it appear as if we were on a floating cloud looking down on the world.

He lit his chillum with a Bic disposable lighter! We all laughed at the practicality of that. He looked at the lighter, understood, and smiled as he shook it. We all had a puff on the sadhu's chillum. When it came to me, I had a chance to study it closely, after I'd had a deep lungful of pungent and spicy-tasting weed, of course.

I raised it to my eye level and saw the intricacy of the carvings of this piece of art. For a start, it had a cobra's hooded head protruding from one side and coiled down the length of the stem. After what seemed like an hour of travel round the chillum, I was aware of someone talking to me.

"It's beautiful isn't it," said Isobel, who had an eye for beautiful objects.

"Absolutely stunning! And it's made by a guy called 'Hampi Baba'."

"How do you know?"

I didn't have a clue how I knew this. "If you travel to Hampi, and seek out Hampi Baba. He will fire and carve a clay chillum from what he feels about you. You must do something in return for him. That is the price."

"Like what?"

"I don't know but it sounds intriguing. I must have heard someone talking on the bus. What would you do for a piece as beautiful as this?" An hour or so had passed since we first pulled up. One of our 'Orange People' made some tea. We offered some plain chai to the sadhu and thought he would like it that way but when he saw the condensed milk and sugar he steamed in and made 'builder's tea'. He grinned at us and held the tea under his nose. We all laughed.

"Sadhu, Baba. We would be honoured if you would like to taste some of our hashish from Afghanistan," said 'Prabu'. His name was Ted Marston from Healdsburg, California, but they just had to be given names by Bhagwan. Inspired to name them, as he was, from a physical presence before his fakeness, or he could do it form a photograph, for just forty dollars. Please-make-cheques payable… etc. Prabu was actually quite a nice bloke for all his fanaticism. He really believed in the cause, and tried to live it.

The sadhu smiled and thanked him by putting his hands together as if praying. We had no idea if he understood English but I prefer to believe he did. He certainly enjoyed smoking the Afghani hash. We all decided to get a few more miles in before darkness and everyone said their goodbyes. The sadhu smiled and nodded a lot. I don't know why but I waited back a little. "Sadhu Baba, I don't know if you can understand me, but you have shown me things today. I don't understand if it was the fine ganja, or just being tired from our journey, but I understand a few things better than I could ever have hoped. Just by stopping here with you." For some strange reason, I felt very emotional. Stupid I know, and probably the result of loads of smoking and long, long bouts of driving, requiring enormous amounts of concentration. But I don't think it was just that.

I got up to go and to my surprise, he turned to me and fixed me unwaveringly, in the eye. His eyebrow raised and he inclined his head toward the superb evening sun as if to say, 'It's out there, everything is out there. Enjoy it'.

Then he turned back toward the sunset. I was already gone. I looked back to see him sat in the lotus position, just staring into the sunset.

We ploughed on into the night. I just wanted to get to Goa and see all the friends we had made on the way down, catch up with their news etc. I also recognised that I was exhausted. The kind of exhaustion that builds up over time. I needed to rest and get some time with just Isobel, the kids, and I. I was looking forward to swimming on the legendary beaches. I also heard that nobody wears anything on the beach, in Goa. That I was looking forward to as well!

We drove late into the night. Strangely most people stayed up with me, and of course Isobel, navigating. We followed some trucks toward a mountain pass. It was steep with hairpin bends and nothing between you and a hundred foot drop, on the other. As we slowed to a stop on a very steep and twisty part of the road. I watched, slightly horrified, as all the drivers' mates got out of their cabs, ran back with a massive boulder and rammed it under the rear wheels of their truck. It occurred to me that only one rock needed to be out of place and they would all come rolling back on to me. The domino effect, but with trucks. I felt a swell of panic as I remembered that here in India, if it moved you could take it on the road. No road tax. No insurance. No restriction at all. Just as in England after WW2, all you needed was a truck. It didn't matter what state it was in. In India there was no M.O.T. inspection. No highly trained inspectors crawling over it, once a year.

Eventually the long line of trucks began to move but it was only a few metres, and out came the driver's mate with his boulder! A few more metres. Should he and boulder get into the cab? No! Stopped again! Running like a sweating Buddha, carrying his boulder across the belly, with him. It wasn't like the mountain passes in Europe. There they had Armco barriers where the road edged along a long drop. Here, it was just a beaten earth surface that was likely to give way if it had been raining or too many heavy trucks had used it. You could be certain of nothing crossing the Western Ghats.

Not only that but it was pitch black. Perhaps that was a small mercy, as sometimes I'd look over the precipice that my front wheels were oh-so-close to, and all I could see was rock face disappearing into the darkness below me. Just do as I'd done many times before. I said to myself, "If these guys can do it, so can I. Grit your teeth and follow the bloke in front!"

In the end it got too silly. We were getting nowhere fast. We came to a pull-in amongst the trees and decided to stop for the night and let some of these trucks dissipate. By the time I'd parked up and seen to the bus, Charlie, much to my annoyance, had sparked up a spliff. By the time he and Black Bob had sucked the guts out of it, there was very little left for me. We had stashed all our other hash in a difficult to get to, hiding place. We now had just enough for one spliff.

"I've been looking forward to a smoke after a day's driving, thanks a bunch!"

"Oh stop moaning there's enough for another," said Charlie testily.

"Oh pardon the fuck outta me, for moaning that I don't get to smoke a joint, after a day's hard driving." I was winding up to full 'fuck-you-you-inconsiderate-bastard', mode, and I could feel the anger, not so much rising, but the red mist just dropped and I was going to grab him by the throat.

Isobel stepped quickly in between us. "Alun! The kids want to say goodnight to you. Besides we'll be in Goa day after tomorrow and there'll be plenty there."

I stood there snorting. That had been a close thing.

"OK give the rest of the hash to Glynis so that we can have, at least one smoke tomorrow."

I didn't wait around for an answer. I wanted to be with my kids rather than tear him a new one. I slept for a few hours until daylight. Most of the trucks were travelling freely, so after some breakfast, I ran up the engine. When it was warm we moved off with most people still asleep. "I'd really love a smoke right now," I said to Isobel, who of course, was sat across from me, navigating.

"Here you are." Isobel handed me the bag with our last bit of hash in it. I heard some movement in the rear so I assumed everyone was now up. I caught sight of Charlie, so I though it a good time to roll up and we could all have a last toke.

"I thought you gave that to Glynis!" he said loudly.

"She gave it to me because she didn't want you getting heavy over it. Alun's doing all the work right now, so I thought he should get a good smoke of it! There's some for all of you."

"You fucking cow," he spat.

Looking back, I'm not sure whether he was talking to Isobel or Glynis. It didn't matter, right then. I slammed the brakes on and yanked the handbrake on, before the bus had stopped fully. I grabbed Charlie by the head, opened the sliding door, and threw him down the steps to the ground. "Don't you ever talk like that to her again," I snarled as I slammed my fist into his face. We tumbled over and over. All the frustration and listening to his whingeing voice for the last thousand miles of very difficult driving boiled over, and I was going to give him a pounding. "You might talk to Glynis like that. But you (whack) talk to Isobel (whack) like that and (whack) I'll punch your fucking lights out (whack)." I was vaguely aware of some local people trying to break us up.

"No, no sahib. This is not good."

I felt his hand round my arm. He was smaller than me but spoke with such authority that I stopped beating on Charlie. And stood there completely spent.

"I am so sorry." I felt totally ashamed. "This has been building since we left England. I'm so sorry, Baba."

"Sahib you must be calm," he said with a little sideways shake of his head.

"Yes you are right. Thank you and, again, I'm sorry." I stuck out my hand and shook his. He leaned closer to me.

"Now you must do this with him." He nodded towards Charlie.

"Goodbye and thank you."

By this time Charlie had got up, brushed off the dust and was back on board complaining, loudly, of how I'd beaten the crap out of him for nothing.

"Charlie shut the fuck up and don't you ever, EVER speak to Isobel like that again. DO YOU FUCKING UNDERSTAND?" I shouted about two inches from his face.

"Fuck off you arsehole," he spat.

I had my fist in a ball, ready to smack him again!

"Alun! Will you fucking well stop it!"

Whoops! Isobel with the 'fuck' word again. She was pissed off big time.

"What do you think the children felt like, to see you and Charlie rolling around, fighting in the dust?"

I hadn't thought of that and it brought me down. Quickly, I sat down and smiled at them.

"Don't worry, we were only having a silly row over nothing."

"But you were hitting him, Daddy," said Mellony, close to tears.

I felt absolutely rotten, desolate. I just held her tight and said I'd been silly but it was all over now. I just wanted to go to Charlie and say sorry. I didn't mean it to go that far. I felt really bad. Just like when my older brother and I would fight. I could say nothing, male egos being what they are. Charlie had selflessly jumped into a lake when he thought young Alun was in trouble, and I owed him big time. How did we get to this? There have been a few occasions since then I have had to use my fists in self-defence, or some bar-room fight but I can tell you that, to this day, I deeply regret letting it go that far.

I sat in the driver's seat and pulled myself together. Eventually I drove on. A couple of the Orange People tried a little calming psychology on me and actually, it did help, but I wasn't having any of that Rajneesh 'peace and love' crap that they were about to use on me.

"Look guys it was just something that has been building since we left England. You know how I feel about Rajneesh, so thanks, but no thanks."

"Will this take your mind off it?" asked Jean, another 'orange person', from Venice Beach, California. His fakeness had given her the name 'Sky'!

She stood and opened her orange robe to reveal a rather beautiful and totally naked, body! I spluttered into my steering wheel. Nobody except Prabu, Sky, Isobel, and I were at the front of the bus. We all laughed but the shock of such an event brought me back to the moment. I stared openly. "Right, that's got your attention, now breathe deeply, and relax."

"Breathe deeply? You've got me panting, I don't know about 'breathe deeply'."

"Over to you, Isobel," said Sky, closing her robe. We all laughed and the atmosphere got a bit lighter. But the sight of that beautiful body remained with me, little did I know I was to see it again, very soon. We decided we couldn't pass Agra without going to see the Taj Mahal. One of the wonders of the world. It was built by Shah Jahan as a shrine to his wife, in fact, a shrine to love. In those days it was still possible to drive right into the outer courtyard. This I did and pulled up. It was just getting dark. We started making dinner and while it was cooking, Isobel, the kids and I, wandered toward the huge entrance to the Taj water fountains and gardens. Sometimes without any conniving or conspiracies of coincidence, things just come together in perfect timing that can only happen by the purest of chance and a little sprinkling of stardust.

Visiting the Taj Mahal that evening was one such occasion. As we rounded the huge archway with its twenty-foot high wooden doors covered in forged steel hinges and cast iron latches and giant handles, we just stopped dead, right in the middle of the arch. Never before or since have I been so stunned by such a sight.

I had the kids in front of me, at my knees. Isobel had wrapped her right arm around my left and was close to me. We were just stunned to silence and the rest of the world disappeared as we took in this wonderful sight. We didn't plan it but we had arrived on the full moon, on a completely clear night. Again by no plan, we had picked the perfect time of day, to view by full moon. The Taj is all white marble and the angle of the rising full moon through the dusty atmosphere had turned the marble pink. The moon hung over the building, it couldn't have been more perfect. Goodness knows how long we stood there but with the rising of the moon, the building had gone from pink, through steely blue to pure white moonlight. I just don't have the vocabulary to describe the wonder of it! The immaculately kept water gardens and park lands, stretched out toward the building and oil lamps burned here and there. The scent of Jasmine was everywhere. It was magical.

I was first to speak, and broke the spell. "I... I... Ah... Ah... I... Phwar," I said articulately, expelling my breath.

"I've never seen anything like it," Isobel replied, almost whispering.

We thought it'd be a good idea to visit the actual building in the daylight so we wandered back to the bus, had dinner, and slept right there.

The next morning was hot so we did the tourist bit early on. There were a few Indian and foreign tourists around but still very tranquil. There were signs here and there asking visitors for complete silence as the slightest sound will echo around the marble and will actually build up sound like an open microphone will sometimes scream with feedback! Screaming or giggling children were definite discouraged, inside.

We stayed longer than we had planned because Agra in

those days didn't have an international airport, nor the Oberoi Sheraton, five star hotel. It was still very quiet for a place containing one of the wonders of the world. We frequented a little restaurant, whose owner introduced us to the delights of 'bhang lassi'. Bhang lassi was a yoghurt like drink, infused for twenty-four hours with marijuana. The milk base acts as a solvent to THC and maximises its absorption into the bloodstream. It resembled a glass of milk but with a green herbal suspension.

I don't think I ever finished one. Eating or drinking THC has a very different effect than when you smoke it in the form of herb or resin. It's physically and mental debilitating and you have to be prepared for a few hours of three times atmospheric pressure, pushing you, prostrate, into the carpet while waves of relaxing pleasure wash over you. There is a danger that you may crack jokes and laugh a lot, drink coffee and get intricately involved in the music playing. Not to mention the aphrodisiac effect! Who needs Viagra when you've a good smoke, right?

While there, Isobel managed to use her bargaining skills to obtain a handmade statuette of the elephant god, Ganesh. It was hand carved from pale green and yellow marble. We managed to carry that statuette all the way back home without a scratch and as I write this, it has pride of place on the mantelpiece. I ended up visiting quite a few places while in Agra, including the ganja store from where our host would buy his ingredients for our evening bhang lassis. It was just a huge store room full of sacks of grass from Kerala, Manali, and Kashmir. The other place I visited was the Red Fort. I just wandered off one afternoon when everyone was having a siesta in the shade of the afternoon heat.

A wide parapet ran high between two towers of the fort overlooking the river. The Taj Mahal was predominant on the south bank, while the foundation for the 'Black Mahal' a huge foundation plinth for a similar, black marble, mausoleum on the north bank. It never got built but the marble foundation was still there, glimmering blackly in the sunlight. On the parapet of the Red Fort, were two huge marble slabs like low plinths, on pillars. One was white, the slightly smaller one opposite, was black.

Here, on the white one, would sit the Maharajah and his wives and children being fanned and shaded by servants elaborately dressed and holding huge peacock feather fans. Opposite would be his Grand Vizier and accountants etc. All resplendent in rich livery and jewels. The Maharajah would keep himself as fat as he possibly could, because every year his subjects and serfs would be expected to balance his weight in gold. That was their tribute, or tax, to him. His vaults in the castle were huge and full of gold and jewels. It was said that when he went visiting, a fully liveried elephant column, with hundreds of elephants, drivers and flag bearing attendants, would stretch for up to twenty miles. Complete with blaring trumpets and a cacophony of music and sound. All this while his people starved and lived in poverty. He would sit in a giant spice balance, and province by province, dignitaries would parade past with their tribute, in gold, with their appeals for this or that, for him to consider.

No wonder the Maharajahs had their assets seized and were pensioned off when independence came to India.

I sat for a while, on the white plinth and gazed down river to the Taj, shimmering in the afternoon heat. It was easy to picture the scene here against the back-drop of the Taj. I eventually left the Red Fort, and wandered down where the walls met the river. I was delighted to come across a little wild marijuana patch growing in the shade of the fort walls. There were some flowering female plants that were spreading their sweet perfume and just as I'd always dreamed of doing, I picked some and let it dry in the windscreen of the bus.

Time was getting on so we couldn't spend as long as

we would have liked. But we vow to return and as it turned out, we returned many times but it never was as special as that first time. For the next few days we were into some heavy driving. Through places like Pen, Pune (Poona), Satara, all along the road known as NH17 and NH4. It was several hundred miles long and threaded through the mountains before dropping down into Goa. Charlie and I avoided each other as much as possible. He looked a bit bruised and battered and I was covered in scratches and bruises but I could still hear his mouth going full bore. Driving took up most of my time and when we stopped the orange people went into high gear and did all the cooking and tea making.

Days went by with the scenery getting more and more tropical. We stopped just before crossing into Goa, in a town called Belgaum. Goa was an ex-Portuguese colony and it showed. Most of the people were called D'Souza or D'Silva and they were Roman Catholics. They considered themselves separate and different from Indians. After the all-covering Indian saris, it was a pleasant shock to see young Goanese women in miniskirts!

***

We started off early and only had a hundred or so miles to go. The end of the main journey was in sight. I could almost smell the fresh sea breeze, a pleasant prospect after the heat and dust of the interior, the long hot roads filled with bustling people, cars, buses and ox carts.

Now we drove past a town called Mapusa, almost there, according to the map. There were coconut palm trees now and vines, very different from the Western Ghats. Waterfalls from the rocks, creepers and vines and very green all round. Being nearer the equator, the seasons didn't change much. Here we were in late November and it's hot! We passed what looked like paddy fields as we approached the coast. I drove round a corner and looked at the road ahead. At the far end of it, I could see the glistening sea.

"Sea!" I shouted. After all these miles, I was looking forward to a swim. A cheer went up in the bus. The kids were dancing around in anticipation. "From here it looks like the road just ends," I said. It looked like that and when we drove up, that's just what it was! The road ended right in front of us at the top of some, not very high, cliffs. I could see other cars and buses parked in amongst the palm trees at the top of the cliffs.

I pulled on the handbrake. I heard a groan from Sky. "Oh my god would you look at that!"

We did look at that, and for an instant we were held in sheer wonder. Here was your palm-fringed, golden sand beach of tropical dreams! The sea air was fresh and crisp. The sea sparkled with its own special intense light. It lapped gently at flawless, and mostly deserted, golden sand. It was like paradise and we had made it!

Sky and Prabu, and the other orange ones, were already heading down to the deserted beach, shedding orange robes as they went. I let the engine run down as Isobel got the kids ready for the beach. Eventually I stopped the engine and in the quiet it really felt like we had come to the end of our journey. I had parked the bus between some palms, overlooking the sea, and I sat there for a moment drinking in all this tropical beauty.

I noticed Sten's bus parked further down the track but there seemed to be no sign of any of them. Eventually we all ended up in a group on the beach. It was deserted, so all of us, including the kids were naked and loving the water and beautiful golden sand. It was such a wonderful change from being behind a wheel for twelve hours a day.

We had found a small cove just round the rocks and most of us were lying in the shade of the rocks or out in the sun messing about on the beach. Time went on and the sun got a bit lower. Just then Alun Jnr., came around the rocks with Sten behind him. He was really pleased to see us and we greeted each other like the comrades of the road that we were.

"You guys made it then," he said with a grin. He was also naked with a great all-over tan. Most of Sten's passengers were there also and soon they had all come over to join us.

"What a drive man! Those mountains and the trucks were a bitch. Jesus! Sten. Doesn't anyone wear any clothes here?" I asked, looking at his passengers. The group on the beach had swollen in numbers and resembled a nudist beach.

"Nah! Nobody bothers on the beach. The only time we put anything on, is when we go off the beach, but even then it's just a 'lungi' or a pair of shorts and sandals. The girls may put on a top but that's about it."

I must admit, it was wonderful to just wander around in the sunshine without the hindrance of clothes. And there was something special, something primordial, about swimming in the sea, naked. Nothing man-made, just you and the sea. It was stunning. The beauty of the place, the sea, and the complete freedom to do more or less anything you wanted, was beginning to have its effect on me.

"Time for the sunset chillum," announced Ron, one of the guys from Sten's bus.

"Sunset chillum?" I said, intrigued.

"Everyone on the beach or rocks stops what they are doing when the sun touches the horizon. The idea is to watch the sun go down. It's a bit of a special time of day."

Most of the people I could see were rolling a smoke or filling a chillum in readiness for their daily ritual of the sunset smoke. I did the same and we all sat around on the rocks and beach while this natural display went on before us. The sun eventually dripped down into the sea and it seemed to break the spell. We grabbed our stuff and started back towards the bus.

"You guys got any provisions? Y'know vegetables, rice, stuff like that?"

"Yes we've got some, but we haven't done any shopping yet," said Isobel.

"Well why don't you bring it all round to our bus and we'll have a big cook-up?"

"That'd be great. We can catch up and have a good session," I said.

"Yes that's this place, all over I reckon. Total hedonism," said Sten. "By the way, one of my passengers has brought a load of coke with him. We did most of ours not long after we left Amsterdam. It was supposed to last us to here," he said with a grin, "but he stashed some for later."

I looked at Isobel she just shrugged slightly. Neither of us had got into cocaine. There just wasn't that much around in the UK but I had tried it before a couple of times. I enjoyed it but still preferred a smoke.

"OK. We'll see you in a while, Sten."

When we got back to the bus, three Italians were sitting around, dressed like Buddhist monks. They had bamboo 'bongs' hung around their neck and shoulders. These bongs were made from a section of large bamboo stalk, about three inches in diameter. They were cut from just below one knuckle to just under the next one. This made them about eighteen inches long with a natural base formed by the bottom knuckle. The small diameter pipe, made from smaller bamboo, was fitted through the wall, about a third of the way up. It was fitted at an upward angle so that the bottom end of the small pipe was under water inside the bong. The top end of the small pipe was where the grass was smoked. The idea being that a large pinch of weed would be stuffed into the top end of the small pipe. You then put the open end of the bong to your mouth and inhale while holding a flame to the weed. You then breathed the smoke through the water until all the weed was burnt into a grey ash, which was then pulled into the water, leaving the pipe clear for the next charge.

The bong had been developed in Thailand hundreds of years ago in order to maximise the weed after a particularly bad harvest of marijuana left very little to be smoked. Up until this time I would have sworn that no matter what implement you use to smoke marijuana or hashish, nothing would improve the effect. The strength of the smoke was down to the quality of the plant and strength of the THC content. Since smoking a real bong I have had to modify that view. The only scientific theory I have for that fact, is that the column of air being pulled through the bong is concentrated at the point of burning, therefore igniting the weed at extremely high temperature (it's a bit shaky as a theory as THC comes out of the weed at a temperature much lower than needed to ignite the vegetable matter. By the time the weed burns, the THC is long gone). That and the fact that every single microgram is burnt and all of the smoke is inhaled. If you roll a joint with tobacco then up to thirty per cent of the weed or hash, goes up into the atmosphere as it smoulders in your fingers between tokes!

The three Italians were accompanied by another guy not dressed as a Buddhist monk.

"'Ello, my name Ronaldo. I am guide for these men."

"Hello Ronaldo," I said. "We have just arrived and don't know what the scene is here yet. What are you guys up to?"

"'Dis boys they take'a de vow of no e'speak." As

Ronaldo told us their story they smiled a lot and nodded in what they thought was a very spiritual and mysterious way.

It seems they took it upon themselves to take a vow of silence and come to Goa in order to turn as many people onto smoking bongs as possible. In return for this, they would ask for alms and were surviving on what people gave them. This ranged from fish and fruit to money from other travellers. I formed the opinion that they were a little bit pseudo. They were not Buddhists but while they wandered around with a massive bag of weed, introducing newcomers to the delights of a bong and top quality Kerala weed, what was the problem? I don't know what the Buddhist robes and vow of silence were about, but it was good for effect.

I smoked two pipes of their weed and got totally shit-faced. It was difficult to talk and we just giggled and laughed. After a while the Italians and their 'minder' decided that it was time to move on. They would take nothing from us and formed a line and danced off, Hare Krishna style, and to the sound of finger cymbals, they moved off between the palm trees. Now out of sight, the cymbals still sounded in the distance.

I sat and watched as they went and laughed to myself at the delightful little episode that had just happened. And I'd learned how to make, and smoke, a bong. The Italians, I learned later, had a bit of a reputation on the road. They were the ones who were usually into heroin and all sorts of other scams. They would have no money or passport. The passport having been sold as soon as they ran out of money and couldn't buy any smack! They would hassle other travellers for money or cigarettes etc. They would steal from other travellers and were just unpleasant. They really gave other travellers a bad name.

Sometimes the local police would have to act and round up a few of them without passports or money, and deport them. On one occasion the police had been round checking everyone passports and they had ended up with a bus full of Italian deportees. They handcuffed them all together, chain gang style, and put them on the bus along with four armed guards and headed off for Delhi. At a chai stop the guards had all gone for chai and left the Italians unguarded but chained to the bus. They managed to free themselves from the chains to the bus and decided to escape, en masse, into the local jungle, all still chained together!

Imagine the guards and driver returning to the bus to find it deserted. The incident made the local papers and we laughed hard and long at the story. Typical Italians!

We had a wonderful evening and a great meal. We cooked around an open fire and had a good meal all finished off with local fruit. We caught up and swapped stories with friends on Sten's bus. Halfway through the evening a Swedish-registered VW microbus arrived. They were two guys from Sweden who had driven to Goa for Christmas. We invited them to join us and before long they had positioned their VW so that everybody could hear the new Floyd album that they had brought with them. It was called 'Wish You Were Here'. *How appropriate*, I thought. Here we were in paradise saying 'wish you were here'. Whenever I hear that album I'm transported back to that time. I can smell the camp fires, the sea, and the whiff of fish and coconuts. It seemed to be the background music to Goa. You could hear it all over the beach or cliff tops. Somebody would always be playing it.

The next couple of weeks were spent in getting to know who was here and what was happening. Once a month, at the full moon, there would be a big beach party. Everybody from the other beaches would come to Anjuna Beach for the full moon party. It lasted all night and all kinds of drugs were available. There was also a pretty good sound system and the place would be surrounded by locals selling all kinds of stuff, and chai was being brewed in most places. Clothing was optional. The beach was stunning in the full moon and many couples were wandering off to have a romantic break from the dancing and social round.

Anjuna beach was about two miles long, with the rocks that we were parked on top of at the north end and a small headland at the other. Between the two was just palm-fringed, beautiful golden sand and sparkling sea. There was a small group of fishing boats hauled up the beach and one or two groups of travellers, but mostly the beach was deserted.

I wandered down the beach one day on my own. I'd just wanted to explore while everyone else was doing the shopping in Mapusa, the nearest market town. The first thing I saw as I climbed down to the beach was a temporary shelter that had been made from woven palm leaves, and raised up several feet by four bamboo legs. The front was open to the sea view. I could see a couple of sleeping bags, a little cooker, and a few pictures on the walls. But the thing that really caught my attention was a huge banner on the roof, fluttering in the on-shore breeze. It read, 'ROCK & ROLL, SAVED MY SOUL!'

I learned that the shelter was owned by a Swiss couple who had done more or less the same journey as us, but in a Mercedes car. Halfway along the beach was a chai stall called The Rose Garden. It was back between the trees but right on the edge of the beach. It too was made of woven palm leaf panels and had some tables and chairs. You could buy all sorts of stuff there as well, like cigarettes, potatoes, biscuits and other munchies, also soap and spices etc., etc.

It was possible to just laze there for most of the day and wander down to the water now and then when it got too hot. I'd been there for a few hours getting to know the owners and having a smoke with some other German and French travellers. It had gotten really stuffy so I left the others and wandered down to the water's edge. I stripped off the shorts and sandals and waded out into the crystal clear and cool, sea. I was having a great time swimming and splashing around. All of a sudden I looked up to see a massive turtle paddling alongside me. It seemed curious about me and not frightened in any way. I was in his element!

I was part fascinated part scared. I'd never seen a real big turtle before. Would it attack me? I trod water trying to be as non-threatening as possible. It paddled around a couple of times and then parked alongside me and took a good look at me. I noticed that its shell was covered in places with small barnacles.

As I swam back to shore I noticed a group of people on the water's edge they had been watching the fascinating sight I had just been part of. As I got closer I noticed that it was the five girls I had noticed before. They had rented a Portuguese-style local house near where we were parked. There was an English girl, two French girls, one Swiss, and one Italian. They were standing near where I'd discarded my shorts and sandals! *Oh shit*, I can remember thinking. *I'm going to just have to brazen it out.* I was sure that when they realised that I was naked, they'd turn around while I got dressed.

No such luck, so I just thought, *Fuck it*, and walked out of the sea. Far from turning round one of their number even came toward me! "You're from that English bus parked by our house aren't you?"

"Yes hi. My name's Alun, I'm sorry I didn't expect to see anyone and I really wanted a swim."

"Oh don't worry, we've come for the same reason, it's just so hot. My name's Cindy, I'm from Cardiff."

"You don't sound Welsh."

"No I was born in Stratford, East London."

"Oh, I was born and brought up in South East London, in Greenwich. What are you doing with these other girls?"

"We're all students at Cardiff University and we decided to take a year off and come travelling. We flew into Delhi and took the train down to Panjim and got a taxi from there."

As we chatted, I did my best not to notice that the other girls were stripping off and putting clothes and towels down to sunbathe on. Cindy was still chatting away, she turned and noticed that she was the only one with clothes on. She started to undress.

"Was that a turtle I saw you swimming with?" She shook off the lacy white cotton dress she was wearing while we chatted without any hesitation or embarrassment, and was naked underneath. Jesus! Was I really sitting in paradise with beautiful naked girls around me?

I chatted for a while. All of them spoke English and were impressed that we had driven out from England. I was getting relaxed but knew it was time to go back to the chai shop and find some ice to stick down my crotch!

"I'd better get back to the chai shop, I'm dying for a coffee." I picked up my shorts and climbed into them. "Why don't you girls come over to our bus tonight? We'll be cooking up a meal with the other bus and we'll build a big fire."

"Yes we saw and heard you all zee ozer night," smiled one of the French girls.

"Oh sorry we all got a bit wasted that night yu' know, a celebration after making it here," I mumbled

"No problem. I was loving zee music."

"Anyway come over and say hello, even if you don't have dinner with us."

"That's really nice of you. We've already made our dinner but I'd like to come over later and meet everyone," said Cindy.

"We've got some real nice Kashmir hash and one of the guys on the other bus has some 'hooter' if that's your thing."

"Hooter?"

"Yeah. You know, coke." I mimed snorting a line.

"Really?" said three of them in unison, perked up at the sound of drugs, especially coke. "Can you help us out? We've been dying for a smoke but have been too paranoid to score. We heard of so many rip-offs going on, we were too scared."

"Yeah we can sort something out this evening, see you later girls." I waved to the others and winked at Cindy. She coloured up a little. I walked back to the Rose Garden and ordered a chai. As I sat there I had to ask myself if I was dreaming! Here in front of me was a paradise complete with naked young ladies, now cavorting nearby with a Frisbee they'd brought. It was mesmerising. Even now I still remember that picture.

I was now alone on the chai shop veranda. The owner was in the back, cleaning up. It was then I remembered I'd brought a chunk of Kashmir with me.

"Hey Cindy!" I called out. She waved and that beautiful body walked over toward me.

"I just remembered. I have this chunk in my fag packet. Do you have skins or a pipe?"

"Oh wow! Yes we have a small pipe we bought in Delhi."

I broke off enough for a couple of smokes worth and gave it to her. She took it and put her hand on my shoulder and came in close to give me a kiss on the cheek.

I felt her breast bush my arm. *Oh my god!* I broke away quickly.

"Yeah, ahem... No problem. I'll see you tonight then." I watched mesmerised, as she walked back over to the others. *Jesus she has a beautiful body*, I thought to myself as I sat down again. This was beginning to border on painful. I was going to have to get this under control! Well, I was a young, heterosexual male, in the hot sun, after all.

Over the next weeks we met all sorts of people. There was Valentino, a very gregarious and handsome Italian who used to dress like Lawrence of Arabia and dance, everywhere he went. He always had loads of children dancing along behind him. Mellony though he was wonderful and would dance along as well. Many a full moon would be preceded by Valentino doing a solo dance routine up on the low headland, under the full moon, singing his head off.

There was also a thriving scene amongst those who lived in Goa, as opposed to those just visiting. Many little 'firms' were preparing and building stuff for exporting hashish in. Many of these people had rented houses from the Goans, and stayed there permanently. The weeks went by quickly in a round of sun, sea, sex and drugs, and rock and roll. As far as I was concerned, it was paradise. And then there were the full moon parties as well, when it got really wild!

Among the characters we met was an American named Dale. He was tall, at about six feet five inches. He reminded me of the guy off the 'Panama Red' T-shirt. A Willie Nelson look-alike, with a long moustache, and long hair underneath a cowboy hat. He spoke with a Texas drawl. He lived a mile or so back up the Mapusa Road, next door to Nelson's Bar, a well-known bar for 'coconut feni', a vicious, clear spirit brewed from the coconut palm that would strip the skin off your mouth, as it burnt its way down to your stomach!

Dale was technically, 'on the run' from the American authorities for running weed up from Mexico. They had been doing this for twenty years. He and his partner would bring it up by the truck load. They would book into a plush hotel and set about telephoning their chosen customers, to tell them where they were, and to come with loads of money ready.

They would book two adjacent rooms with a connecting door. The buyers would come in one door, pay their money over to be counted, then pass through the connecting door to the next room where their purchase was already weighed up and stuffed into a suitcase or two. They would then exit with their purchase, all in the space of ten minutes or so. After a half day at the first hotel they'd move to another hotel or motel, and start all over again.

This was a regular thing for Dale and he made lots of money until someone got a bit stupid, got busted, and was looking at some serious time behind bars. The only bargaining chip he had was Dale's name, so the lowlife grassed him up to the Feds. They put surveillance on him and caught him red-handed with a truck load of Mexico's finest. He went through a lengthy trial process. In the end he was looking at twenty-five years in jail.

For some unknown reason, in those days in the USA, if you were looking at a long stretch, your lawyer could apply for bail before sentencing, so that the defendant could settle his business affairs before being incarcerated. He had enough money to meet the five hundred thousand dollar bail. They even gave him his passport back.

Needless to say he skipped bail and ended up in Goa. He rented one of the biggest houses around and was busy building his entourage around him. He was trying to put a team together for some serious smuggling of hashish and marijuana into the USA and Europe, especially the UK. He definitely wanted me on the firm and I spent many hours in his house talking over plans for what he wanted to do.

He had plenty of money and the house was a centre for lots of different people and always a handful of women of all nationalities around as well.

Dale would hold court in the evenings and his ego demanded that he dominate the whole scene. But he was very generous and we had some wild times at the house. It was a 'clothes optional' scene, inside the house. I must admit being in awe of Dale. He did have a way with him. Larger than life and a 'can do anything' attitude. Plus all the exciting stories about smuggling. His attitude was to just go for it, and do it big time. He was very loud, with some questionable habits, but we had a good rapport and we got on really well together.

I got to know many characters, for instance, there was a guy that looked like a slightly wilder version of Kevin Kline, the film star with a black goatee beard. His name was Jumping Jack Flash! I didn't believe him, so he showed me his passport and there inside, was printed his name, Jumping Jack Flash. He had badly scarred legs. A gift from his time in the Vietnam War. He and his patrol had crossed a clearing in the jungle to be shot up by 'Charlie'. He'd been invalided out and was given, as a perk, the right to turn up at any American Air Force base, anywhere in the world and demand to be put on any Air Force flight of his choice. He could travel to almost anywhere in the world, free of charge. This was a lifetime concession. Another face, was a guy whom everyone called BMT. He had quit his job as a New York underground train driver, to come and live in Goa. There was an Australian, a Kiwi and a Canadian guy. I used to wind them up every now and then, when we were all together, by referring to them all as 'dammed colonials' which always got a laugh. As time went on, we found we were spending money but had nothing coming in. I mentioned this to Dale and the fact that I was going to have to do something about it or we were going to have to think about getting home. I told him I was fast getting fed up with being tied to the others on the bus as I was sure with what I'd learned, I could make more money on our own without the others. He convinced me it'd be a good time to strike out on our own.

Isobel had made friends with a French girl called Regine, who had been recruited by a guy in Bombay, to fly to Laos, buy some smack, and come back to Bombay. He said he wanted women to do it because they have one more body cavity than us lads.

I convinced her that it was a really stupid idea, and that she should give him the expenses money back and forget all about it. "Why mess around with smack? It's a killer and really bad karma." The evidence was everywhere in Goa. There were smack freaks everywhere. Many times you would hear of a heroin addict coming to Goa for cheap heroin.

The trouble was, they had never come across smack as pure as it was in Goa. It was in from Thailand and uncut (undiluted), not like the stuff they were used to on the streets of London, Paris or Rome. By the time it got to addicts in those cities, it would have been cut some sixty per cent. In Goa, they would mix up their usual amount, but because it was so pure, they would overdose and die!

Regine rented one side of a large Portuguese house and Isobel and I ended up sharing with her. I had the pleasure of sharing a room with two beautiful women.

Dale came by one day to say that he needed to go to Bombay and asked if he could hire the bus because lots of his hangers-on wanted to come as well. I said he'd have to talk to the others and we all went over to see them, or what was left of them. Black Bob had moved in with his friend from Sten's bus and they were living in a house further down the beach. Kakey was shagging some American guy and Timus was hanging out with the Orange People.

We got them all together and it was agreed that Dale could hire me and the bus for a couple of weeks. Isobel and the kids were to stay behind in Goa with a girl called Annie, whom we'd bumped into at the flea market one day. Annie had been one of our friends back in Bristol. She often used to come round and share a smoke with us. We'd look over the rain-soaked roofs of Bristol and fantasise about being on a tropical beach. Little did we know that some six months later we'd meet in Goa. One day she'd just decided to walk away from her University course and come to India. "All your bloody fault, Alun. Nobody thought you'd actually do it. It real really did excite me. I just couldn't stop thinking about it."

Annie needed somewhere to stay, so she moved in with us. The kids had their own room. We had the main room and small kitchen. It was owned by a Goanese couple who were taking advantage of the increasing numbers of foreign tourists coming to Goa for Christmas. They were Roman Catholic and desperately poor, but their situation was improving, thanks to the money coming in from renting. They had a young boy named Joseph who was delighted to have two English children to play with and they'd spend hours in the tropical garden. They'd get up early and go down to the beach with Joseph's dad, to help the fishermen drag the boats in. The fishermen would not allow them into the water, at that time of the morning, and they were under strict orders, from me, not to go in the water until myself or Isobel were there. The fishermen would pile them up with fish and villagers would give them fruit. We'd all have the fruit for breakfast on the porch of the Portuguese-style house.

After breakfast we'd all wander down to the mostly deserted beach. We'd lie around sunbathing. Now and again, people would come by and maybe, stop for a smoke and a tray full of chai from the Rose Garden, just at the edge of the beach. It really was a beautiful life. We'd got to

BEYOND THE 'BUT' *A Long Road to India*

know a Dutch guy called Hank. He was one of Dale's entourage and a nice bloke. He would spend a lot of time with us on the beach, and we'd all go body surfing when the waves got up in the afternoon. Hank was getting a bit sweet on Annie, which only met with limited success as Annie was in love with Isobel. I, of course found this delightful. It was a wonderful time.

***

The run up to Christmas 1975 was one of sun, sea and partying. Thousands of tourists had come to Goa for Christmas and the whole place was buzzing. Quite a contrast to when we'd first arrived The day came for me to drive Dale and his mob up to Bombay. I arrived at his house, with the bus, Isobel, kids, Annie and Regine, at about midday. Isobel and the kids were going to walk back to our house after seeing some friends nearby. Isobel would spend as little time as possible in Dale's company. She couldn't stand him, or his loud, belligerent, ways. As I waited for them to appear, I altered the destination plate, in the front, from 'Afternoon Circular', to 'The Races'.

Dale emerged first from the house, looked at the plate and said in a Houston Drawl, "Dig it man! We're going to the fuckin' races!"

He looked so comical, stood there in his Willie Nelson mode, you couldn't help but laugh.

I had a chai at Nelson's Bar across the track while I waited for them to move their stuff on board. I noticed we'd be taking both of Dale's women, and Hank the Dutch guy Isobel and I had got friendly with, and a guy that gloried in the name of 'Hollywood Pete'. There was another French girl who I'd never seen before.

"Hey Al. I got a bag full of Afghani slabs here. You OK with that?" asked Dale with no subtlety whatsoever.

"I know nothing, and don't want to. BUT I don't want any smack on board, OK?"

"Shit man! I won't have the crap near me. I ain't got no time for smack freaks, man. Now C'mon you people let's hustle. Let's do it. To it." This was a phrase he used quite a lot.

I said goodbye to Isobel and the kids and gave them a big hug.

"Be good and if you can't be good, be careful," I said to Isobel, Annie, and Regine with a wink. "Look after each other."

"You just be careful yourself, and don't come back with any nasty infections," laughed Isobel. Not that I was going to risk getting something nasty but she knew I still liked to party.

I drove for the remainder of the afternoon and we crossed the state line about eight in the evening. It was dark and there were two Sikh officers on duty with a few trucks clearing their papers. I pulled up because I knew that they like to just inspect passports but without any other hindrance.

As I got up to take the passports, Dale pressed two five hundred rupee notes into my hand. "Whatever these clowns want, just make 'm disappear, man. We don't want them coming aboard, man, dig? Treat them like they are beneath contempt. Tell them they gotta take their shoes off if they wanna come aboard. Use some of that British superiority shit, man."

"Yeah no problem. They should be OK."

They were more interested in seeing no untaxed gold and other contraband was being smuggled out of Goa. Also, there was a thriving gold-smuggling economy, with many locals deeply involved, just like it used to be in Cornwall, most of the villagers were involved in smuggling

French brandy and guns. Here it would be gold from Saudi Arabia or guns from Singapore, all coming ashore with the fish, here in Goa.

One guard stopped me on the way to the office. "Don't bother to go in there sahib." He held his hand out for the passports. He looked at the top one which was mine. He gave them all back to me

"Thank you sahib, please drive carefully, some of these fellows can be very crazy at night."

He gave me a salute and that was that. I got back on the bus.

"Everything OK man?" asked Dale.

"Yeah. No problem. Here." I went to give him the thousand rupees back.

"No hang on to it. You'll need gas soon won't you?"

"No, but I will be needing diesel. We cook with gas in the UK."

"Oh I'm so terribly sorry, old chap. Diesel it is then, old man." He did a very tidy mimic of an English accent. "Goddamn, bloody Brits." He grinned.

"Dammed colonials," I muttered, just loud enough for him to hear as I swung back into the driver's seat.

I had been driving for about five hours by now. The general agreement was to get to Bombay as soon as possible so that the partying could begin, city style. All of a sudden an arm appeared with a hand holding a small silver spoon with a pile of coke on it.

"You vill sniff, now, yah?" It was Hank offering the cocaine. *Yeah, why not!* I was feeling a bit tired.

"Bring it in a little closer please, Hank." He got it just under one nostril and I sniffed hard. The powder disappeared like dust up a hoover. He refilled the spoon and did the other side. The coke hit me and I was rejuvenated. I drove on and on into the night. While they all partied in the bus, I drove on and on. I drove through jungle, I drove through mountains, I drove through river beds, I drove across plains. Like a portable tunnel of light, I drove on and on, through the darkness. Shiva sat beside me and Ganesh the elephant god pointed my way. Blue-skinned deities swirled about me with almond shaped, half-closed eyes that were emphasised with black mascara. I was totally in a world of my own! The need to stay alert did away with the sensual side of the coke. This time I was using it purely for the stamina benefit but when we stopped for a toilet break or whatever, I drifted off into a dreamlike state and let the coke take me where it would. I remember a chai stop where the sound of the bus engine seemed like it had been put through a phasing effect. It also made me incredibly horny.

Time to put the frustration to constructive energy. We drove on. I was getting a little tired again. I looked for a clearing or something that would get us off the road. I just needed to stop for a couple of hours sleep. That's all I needed. Just to sleep for a couple of hours and then we could go on again. Just as I was thinking this, I felt a couple of arms round my chest from behind. The nails on the hand and the way they touched my chest let me know they were female. I tried to turn but there was a quick ducking movement and her hands went way lower than my chest!

"I can do anyzing to you and you must drive." That heavy French accent could only be one person. Her name was Phillipe, a girl of about 25, and very attractive.

"Ahhh ha ha." I shuffled as far as I could. The tops of her fingers were now just under the draw-chord of my white cotton trousers. "Jesus Phillipe, are you trying to drive us off the road?" She was now so close behind me I felt her breath on my ear and smelled her perfume, it was dizzying and God! Now I felt so horny. It's not a drug to take on your own!

"Seriously, you're taking your life in your hands doing that. Especially as I've just had some hooter. It makes you very horny y'know," I babbled.

"'Ow you say 'ooter, 'orny?" she asked, puzzled.

"Uh, hooter means cocaine. Horny means, y'know, makes me wish I was with my wife, right now."

She removed her hands and sat on the dashboard with her back to the windscreen.

"My faz'er was truck driver." She said it in such a way that I wasn't sure why she had told me that.

Just as I was thinking about that, I saw a clearing under the trees and made a dive for it.

I let the engine run down before stopping it. By the time I walked toward my bed, they were still partying. A mirror, with some large lines of coke, was just being passed around.

"Hey Al. What's happenin' man?" Shouted Dale over the noise. He was draped in a topless Lilliana, an Argentinian girl, on one side, and Rita the Kiwi, also topless, on the other.

"I gotta have just a couple of hours sleep, I'll be ok to carry on, then."

"You not vant anudder line?" asked Hank.

"No thanks, Hank. To go on now would be dangerous. All I really need is to sleep, even if only for two hours, then we can crack on."

"Hey that's OK man!" shouted Dale. "When you gotta sleep, you gotta sleep. I ain't got no intention of sleepin' though." He cackled. He leaned over and stroked Lilliana's breasts.

She giggled and slapped his hand away but I thought to myself that the bus would be rocking soon.

I stepped through to my double bunk and closed the curtain behind me. I shrugged off my shorts and sandals and pulled off my cotton waistcoat. I climbed up to the bunk and just flopped down. It was much too hot for bedclothes. The fatigue overtook the coke.

As I drifted off, The noise and movement of the bus faded into the background. Suddenly the curtain opened for a second. I thought I'd dreamt it but what happened next had me wide awake and my heart thumping. It was Phillipe! I could just make her out in the darkness. She was totally naked! I gasped. She put her hand gently on my mouth as she climbed in beside me. I should have sent her away, but I'm only human and what with the heat, the coke and the desire, thumping through my veins. I just couldn't.

I woke after four hours but when I looked at the rest of them, I decided to go back for another couple of hours. They were blotto with the evidence of empty alcohol bottles and smeared mirrors. By the time I'd had a couple more hours, it was getting hot in the bus. I grabbed the gas and kettle and went outside to make some coffee. I heard the door open after a while and Phillipe came and sat beside me.

"I'm real sorry Phillipe. I..."

"Why sorry? Did you not enjoy eet?"

"Are you kiddin' me?" I said. "Of course I did, it was wonderful but I already have a wife and two kids."

"I know zat. What 'appen last night was last night. M'ybee it 'appen again, m'ybee not. I expect nozing." She kissed me lightly on the cheek.

"You are a lovely lady," I said. She smiled and went back to the bus.

When I got back, hardly anyone had moved. Lilliana was laying mostly naked, next to Dale who was snoring heavily, with an empty bottle of Jack Daniels still in his hand. I got into the driver's seat and fired up the engine. *Jesus they sure like to party*, I thought to myself. I moved off and pulled out onto the patchwork quilt roads again.

Driving in India was a series of reasonable tarmac, alternating with really bad pot-holed stretches that went on for miles. It was a series of accelerating and then heavy braking before the bad bits. Add to this the grossly overloaded ox carts, bicycles and pedestrians. This went on for hours and was very tiring. Not only that but Dale's continuous dialogue on what he thought of life, went on and on. Typical Yank. You could hear him over the noise of the engine. He just had to be the centre of attention. Trouble was, what he was saying, was what he had learned from experience. I would have been a fool not to take aboard the knowledge he was imparting. In a way, he was just like Bhagwan Shri Rajneesh. He was a cult leader, led by the force of his personality. Of course like Rajneesh, a lot of what he did and said was for effect and mostly, bullshit. I took the time to educate him on the delights of Cockney rhyming slang. I would end up teaching around five 'colonials', about things like 'frog and toad' (road), 'dustbin lids' (kids), and one they would have extra trouble with, 'thrup'ney bits' (tits), 'septic tanks' (Yanks), etc., etc. To do it properly, you just used the first word i.e. 'I'm just going down the frog' (I'm just going down the road).

A couple of days later, Dale breezed into the room where myself, and some of the other Yanks and Canadians, were having a mid-morning chillum. "Hey Al, I'm gettin' this Cockney thing together, man." He grinned, full of his own self-importance. "You call us 'septics' 'cos it's 'septic TANKS'. Rhymes with YANKS, right?"

I mustered all the stiff-upper-lip attitude I could, and announced in a subdued voice, "No, old man. It's because you're full of shit!" The place erupted with sputtering, guffawing, laughter we were all wetting ourselves, give him his due, Dale too.

An overloaded ox cart dragged my thoughts back to the road. We were now passing the first signs of Bombay city. Some high-rise slum blocks, surrounded by pools of stagnant water, here and there. These were breeding grounds for mosquitoes of course, and the whole are a stank of rotting vegetation and open sewers. Believe me, you haven't seen hopeless human poverty till you've seen the slums of Bombay.

We were all awake for the drive into the centre of town. We headed for the 'Gateway to India', a magnificent archway, similar in size and appearance to the Marble Arch in London. On the way in, we got a good cross section of the architecture of the city. The British had built some magnificent buildings along the style of the V & A Museum or the Houses of Parliament. Bombay had incredibly stunning architecture and tumble down shacks by the millions. People built polythene shelters right along the train tracks. Trains would rattle through, inches from some of the structures, and as soon as they had passed, life spread out across the tracks again.

Then there was the street life of all kinds. You could get ANYTHING in Bombay. Sex, including the most distressing sight of child prostitutes in cages. Yes! Cages. They may have had silk pillows and feather beds and soft fittings but cages they were. Made from steel bars! You could have a shave from the 'shave wallahs', or have your sandals re-soled. The new soles would be made from old car tyre treads and therefore last for years. The leather would rot before the tyre sole wore out! You could have pots mended, bicycles and punctures, mended and even non-refillable, cigarette lighters, refilled with gas! There was even a guy with a bedstead-like contraption for re-fluffing the stuffing in mattresses. It was all right there on the street.

We pulled up on the seafront in an area just down from

the Gateway on a road that gloried in the name of PJ Ramchandi Marg, an area known as Colaba. It was a long sweeping causeway. The sea on one side and some fairly up-market houses and hotels with palms, stirring in the heat, on the other.

"Hey I'm gonna check out these hotels, man," said Dale.

"Don't bother for me. I'll sleep on the bus. I'd like to be able to use the bathroom of course, but I never leave the bus on its own."

"OK man. Your choice." I didn't add that I would need a place of refuge when that 'I know best', loudness got a bit too much.

We ended up doing a deal with the Shelleys Hotel for me to park the bus in the hotel grounds, in front of the hotel, overlooking the seafront and all the Bombay life, going to and fro. Dale and his entourage moved into the hotel room and I tidied up the bus. There was a tap on the door it was Hank and Hollywood Pete.

"Out for a rest on the eardrums?" I grinned.

"Ya. Man he don't stop, ya?"

"He is a bit much sometimes, but a lot of it comes from experience and is good advice, it's just the intense way he puts it over. I like the guy actually, it's just that he is the typical Brit's idea of a loud, Yank. No offence, Pete."

"Hey! none taken man," said Peter with a smile. "We see you Brits as being prissy, queers anyway."

"Fuck you, and the horse you rode in on." I grinned at Pete and we all laughed.

"Dale is supposed to be seeing an Afghan guy here, tomorrow. Some rich guy called Habbib from Kabul. I reckon he's picking up a couple of hundred kilos of hash,"

"Hmmm didn't know that. Carrying large amounts of

dope around is well iffy, even here."

In those days, hash in India, was looked upon as something old and traditional. As long as you weren't blatant about it, you were left alone. Trafficking was a different matter! That meant that big money was involved and palms had to be greased for that. Play the game and you were alright, but not to pay the bribes was asking for trouble. Anybody who has read Howard Marks' excellent book *Mr Nice* will know how things were in those days.

"I'll have to renegotiate my fees for that."

"Ya. Ve all go to some place called Sucolaji Street. In de Crawfoot Bazaar, market area. Is vell known for its prostitutes und opium dens. Bring only a couple of rupees and leave your passport here."

"Why's that?"

"If you drift off, you vill have nothing to lose from your pockets."

"Sounds like fun. When do we go there?"

"Better come to the room and we can decide when we're going and how we're going there," said Pete.

"We'll take the bus, I don't want to leave it alone at any time."

We left the women behind and headed for the opium den. The hotel, knowing where we were headed, sent two of their men with us to look after us, and the bus.

The place was called 'Rashids' and was a very old building. To get to the opium den, we had to walk through low, dark, wooden beamed rooms to a salon out the back. It was dim lighting and there were cane mats, rolled out each side of the room towards, the middle. In between each mat was a little burner filled with paraffin, and a little wick, sticking out the top.

We all filed in. Nobody took a blind bit of notice. The

place stunk of opium and sweat plus the odd open sewer, somewhere. The proprietor came and led us to a mat each. A youth came and sat between the mats. His job was to fetch the opium and cook and prepare it for smoking.

I sat down on a mat and noticed a small, wooden, two-legged stool, about six inches high. I couldn't work out what they were used for. "You'll need to buy about two cups. I've never been able to do more than two," said Dale. I didn't know that I wanted to do any at all, in this place. It just didn't feel right.

The lad who did our cooking came and sat down cross-legged between me and the Kiwi girl Rita.

He had with him a couple of egg-cup shaped containers of opium. It was different from the opium we'd bought in Quetta. This was highly refined and resembled a thick jet-black syrup, only much thicker. I watched, fascinated, as the lad prepared our smoke. He had a small metal rod, about six inches long. This he dipped in the liquid and removed a large drop. He cooked this over the wick. The opium pipe was about eighteen inches long end to end. On the far end was a glazed ceramic, elongated egg-shaped, chamber. There was a pinhole round about the middle of the chamber.

The lad finished preparing the opium by mashing it against the smooth ceramic egg and using just the right amount of heat. When he decided that it was just right, he formed a 'doughnut' around the bottom of the thin metal rod. The rod just fitted the hole in the ceramic egg, he inserted the rod as far down as the doughnut and waited a while for the opium to solidify. When he thought the time was right, he gave a sharp downward movement of the rod. This had the effect of sticking the doughnut evenly round the hole, at the same time, releasing the rod from the now solid, opium.

I watched absolutely fascinated and realised this ritual

had been going on for thousands of years. It was now I realised what the wooden constructions were for. You were supposed to lay on your side facing the flame, your head supported by the wooden stool. You held the pipe to the flame and off you go. You then drew the flame through the hole, bubbling the opium, and turning it to smoke, as it went through.

I filled my lungs with the smoke and passed it to Rita. She was laying opposite me.

By the time the pipe came back to me, I was already floating down the slippery slope. Waves of dreamy pleasure were washing over me. I took another hit. As I lay there in complete ecstasy, I felt some hands on my legs. I opened my eyes to see a man dressed only in a loin cloth. I began to push him away but the cooking man stopped me.

"Sahib. He is Nepalese man. He is expert masseur. For only a couple rupees he vill massage you properly. He lives here, he smoke vhat is left over."

"Oh. OK, go ahead then. What's a few rupees?" I passed him one of the ten rupee notes.

The Nepalese guy brought his coconut and aloe vera oils and asked me to turn over.

He started at my shoulders. His hands were like velvet pinchers. His fingers seemed to get between every muscle. He worked his way down my back, buttocks, thighs, calves and feet. It was wonderful. I just let the waves rush over me and I sank into a semi-dream-like state.

I struggled into consciousness a couple of hours later. There were a few more people in the den including some scabby looking Westerners, conspiring with the owner who was passing out what looked like little packages of smack.

Sure enough, a moment later one of them starts to cook up a fix and prepare his needle and tourniquet. He turned and looked at me with black, wasted, eyes. The emptiness of his face and the single mindedness of his actions jolted me. With dawning revulsion I looked around at the people I'd come with. Without exception they were all 'gauched off' in the same dream world I'd just been in.

I had to get out. I stood on wobbly legs and walked through the labyrinth of wooden beamed passages. My head was swimming and claustrophobia came upon me quickly. I started running and just made it into the street, whereupon I deposited the contents of my stomach, into the gutter. I'd noticed that about the opiates. At some time you are going to throw-up. It isn't the muscle cramping, retching, kind of vomit, but an effortless up-chuck.

A couple of local guys looked at me with disgust. I stumbled on down the road. I passed gaudy brothels with women, men, young boys and girls, transvestites homosexuals. What did you want? It was all there and well on the way to being deeply bizarre. I felt disturbed and just wanted to be away from the place. And if one more pimp whispered, "Heroin cocaine, boys, girls," in my ear, I was going to smack the bastard. I arrived back on the bus and stumbled aboard. It was good to be amongst familiar things.

The guys from the hotel were still there. One was sleeping, the other wandering around, nervously. "You fellahs want some chai? Take this and get us all some chai and samosas or something, whatever you like."

He took the money and disappeared, to return loaded with tea tray and a load of sticky buns and local style sweets. He went to give me the change but I waved it away.

"Both of you have a chai later, OK?"

"Thank you sahib." I gave them a couple of rupees each, which was about what they were paid per day, by the hotel.

We sat and drank the chai and talked for a while. The

two hotel guys were from a village to the south of Bombay. They had come to the city to work. "Not big wages here then?" I asked.

"The only other work sahib, was to work building apartment blocks, at a rupee per day."

This was a fact. I had watched a building site just behind the Taj Mahal Hotel, a five star intercontinental hotel just behind the Gateway. The construction was five storeys. The scaffolding was made from large-diameter bamboo poles tied together at the points where, we in the west would use scaffold clips.

Lines of women in Saris, with shallow baskets carried on their heads, would file up the ladders. In the baskets would be cement or sand and even bricks. These women would work for ten hours a day, and then sleep on the site on just a rush mat and maybe, one blanket. Whole lines of workers, just sleeping on site. At night when all of them were sleeping, the rats would run around amongst them. And they were big rats!

What a contrast, I thought. There, in the shade of a five star, luxury hotel, was intense poverty. We finished our chai and I asked one of them to check and see if Dale and the others were conscious yet. They weren't, so one of them stayed behind to bring the others back to the hotel. I was going to leave the area, now. I didn't feel that safe here and the hotel guy just wanted us to go. I was able to drive, though still a bit dreamy! Anyway, it was only a couple of streets over, I would've been able to walk it, sober. We made it back and I parked it in the drive and collapsed on the bunk. By the time I surfaced again it had just got light. I was amused to see the joggers and dog walkers along the seafront. Most of the dogs ate better than the street beggars that were everywhere. I happened to see a large, well fed, cat in the gateway of the house next door to the hotel. It was a large, ornate building, owned by an English woman who stayed behind after independence in 1947.

The cat sat in the gateway and watched the early morning life go by. All of a sudden, a large rat appeared around a gatepost and walked right in front of the cat and strolled off into the hedge. The cat stiffened slightly, but discretion being the better part of valour, didn't move! He just turned his head to watch the rat pass, ready to spring away if the rat attacked! It was that big!

By this time, Dale and the others were arriving back in taxis. "Sorry mate but I just had to get the bus out of that area, it didn't feel safe."

"No problem, man. I'm having some breakfast sent up to the room, yu' commin'?"

"Yeah, be there in a while."

The hotel sent out young lads to fetch breakfast for us, and sumptuous it was.

While we ate, Dale talked about how he saw the future of his little firm. He was to sit at the centre of the web and his couriers would go out into the world. Simple as that! He had the money, contacts and the 'front'. He could talk his way out of any situation. He could get anyone to agree with him! Except Isobel. I suggested a few moves and constructions we could use and I must have sounded convincing as he seemed to be enthusiastic about my ideas. As we talked on, it became obvious to me why he needed someone like me. He had no practical skills whatsoever! He was an organiser. 'Do your best work but if that fails, blind them with bullshit and throw money at it', was his thing, and I have to confess, he was a master at it! "I still need a man for the UK. Or are yu' gonna build Jaguars in Coventry for the rest of yu' life, man? Remember, dude, you are exactly where you WANT to be."

"What's the deal on that, then?" I asked.

"Hey man, here's the thing. I'm gonna be sittin' on two hundred and fifty kilos of Afghani, fifteen litres of

Kashmir oil of top quality, and fifty kilos of Thai weed. All we gotta do is work it, man. Yu' take watcha need, you do yu' thing, y'come back here and we do it all over again, but this time YOU are calling the shots. YOU get your man for the UK and so it goes on. We all make money like you've never seen, man. I can get as much hash as I need, straight from the farm in Afghanistan, man."

"But what about flight tickets? Round trips to London ain't that cheap, especially when you are not trying to do it budget-style," I said.

"Hey man! Didn't I just say yu' take what yu' need? If it cost, such and such, to go on the days you need, you pay that cost and you smile. We ain't fucking around, here man."

I took that to mean anything can be done as we have the money. I'd not been in this position before. I'd always been constrained by not having much money but now that it was not an issue, my head swam with ideas and excitement. I was mesmerised by the possibilities and was seduced. The more I thought about it, the more I was convinced it was the way to money and adventure.

I now put these dodgy decisions down to the fact that I had, at the time, more balls than brains and the road I was now on was a very narrow ledge above a precipice. Place one foot off the track and you fell a very long way! But, to hell with it. I could do anything!

Looking back now with twenty-twenty vision, I must confess to doing some really stupid things but as is often the case, these stupid decisions often lead to great adventure, of one kind or another. I had seen other little firms in Goa who'd be broke one week, one of their number would fly out and hey presto, a week or two later, return with money coming out their arses. It just seemed so easy. Customs weren't so on the ball in those days. However, they soon caught up when Semtex and heroin came into the picture.

For the next couple of weeks we just hung out waiting for the contraband to arrive. It came one morning in a taxi. There were four, very large, wheeled suitcases which I buried under loads of junk in the boot. An English girl and her Indian girlfriend started to hang around the bus. Dale was taken with the Indian girl. Not surprising as she was a beauty and came from a very high caste, rich family. She was slumming around with western hippies just for the hell of it. One day I came back to the bus to find it tastefully decorated inside with some really nice drapes, Batik, and materials including a woven Baluchistan tassel, hanging from the gear lever.

They had taken to sleeping on the bus as well which was a bit strange. I really didn't fancy the English girl. She had 'track marks' all along her arms and was a bit scabby. I noticed the marks one morning when she woke and walked around naked. Believe me it was not a nice sight. She obviously spent more money on smack than on food.

"I've seen the needle and the damage done,

A little part of it in everyone."

Neil Young's words kept returning.

They moved into the rooms with the others for a few days but Dale's play for the Indian girl had been rejected. This pissed him off, big time, and he threw both of them out. He had been rejected in front of everybody so retribution was swift and verbal. They ended up having to knock on the bus door and ask to sleep the night. I couldn't turn them away in the middle of the night in Bombay.

The English girl, Penny, also from a very rich family and ex-Rhodene pupil, may have been a wreck but the Indian girl, Reena, was a different story. She was the typical Indian beauty with dark eyes and sensual movement and the poise of a Brahman, high caste, Indian. Her parents really were fabulously wealthy. She wore, mostly western clothes. Levis and a silk top. But the first time she turned up in a sari was breathtaking. To see her walking around first thing in the morning, in just bra and pants was exquisite torture!

"There's some blankets over there, just sort yourselves out." I just wanted to get back to sleep.

"By the way, girls I don't want to see any smack on this bus, OK?"

I went back to sleep. Day broke across the bay. The sun came up, as it went down. Blazing hot. I lay in my bunk thinking how hot it was getting. Then I noticed the smell of coffee brewing. It got me up and dressed. The girls had got some breakfast together and it was tasty.

We sat at a makeshift table in the shade of one of the trees and watched Bombay come to life. Penny told me a bit of her story. She was a smack freak and had been for a couple of years. She had flown to Goa for Christmas and just hung around. There was plenty of Thai heroin around, so why go home? She'd met Reena at Rhodene and they had become friends, because their families were more or less the same. Pots of money and no time for a rebellious daughter. Just give her a hefty allowance and a ticket to somewhere. Now that Penny was a heroin addict, Reena saw it as her job to clean her up. Trouble was that they would both end up partying and going to all the wrong places.

Dale came down from the room, looking like thunder. "What the fuck are you doin' still here? I thought I told you to get the fuck outta here. Now pick up your shit, and get the fuck outta here, now!"

"We are staying on the bus. It's Alun's bus, nothing to do with you. Why are you being so nasty?" Reena really couldn't see what had happened. She didn't hesitate to use her femininity when it suited her but held out when some guy got interested. She definitely played a dangerous game. She had done it all her life and now she was using that power in a bad way.

"It may be my bus but Dale is paying the bills so I gotta give him what he wants. It'd be better if you got a hotel room."

Without another word they went and got their gear off the bus. Dale sat down with me.

"Fucking freeloading skag freaks. Just fucking take, take."

"Didn't get your leg over, then Dale?"

"What's leg-over?"

"A shag. Y'know, didn't get your end away."

"Oh yeah. End away? Jeez, you limeys! She just wouldn't come across, man. She thought she'd control all us men like she has done, every man she ever met, since she grew tits."

"I know. Shame really. Nice body but snotty attitude, what we in the civilised world, call a prick teaser."

"Fuckin' 'A', man."

I took the opportunity to quiz Dale on his next move.

"I've got everything we need, but it's the dope, man. It's all in plaques and all different weights. We need to make it into kilo slabs. I don't want to take it home an' do it. Too many people, man."

"Why don't we take it to a beach just down from the city. There must be somewhere. We can put the dope on the roof, from inside. It'll warm up the slabs nicely and do all the work inside too."

"Good shit, man. That's what we'll do. I'll get the others together an' we'll ship out today."

"Yeah that'd be good, I'm missing my family."

We had been having a great time hanging around all the haunts of the hippies and travellers. Getting wasted most nights, until the morning I woke up with Rita lying next to me, semi-naked. I couldn't remember whether we'd done anything. It was all a blank.

My moving around, woke Rita. She sat up and her beautiful body was barely covered. I suddenly wished I could remember... badly!

"Uh Rita. I, um, ah. Did we, ahh...?"

"Relax, Alun. You were asleep and snoring. Besides you must have cracked it by now, it's Dale I want. Nah, man I had a row with him last night and I just wanted to get away from them all."

"That's why I've been sleeping on the bus." *Shit!* I wished I'd been awake.

"You are an attractive man, but, as I said, it's Dale I'm here for."

I'd just been rejected in a Kiwi accent! "You must be well pissed off, with Lilliana and Reena, hanging around."

"I can handle Lilliana, she was here before I came, it was the way he went after that Indian slut."

"Ah well I can tell you he got a knock-back there. I really think you should take another lover. It'd concentrate his mind. I'd like to apply for the, ahh, position."

We laughed and she came a little closer.

"I'll put you second on the list," she teased.

"Story of my life." I grinned. I thought it a good idea to step away from her, just then. My body was beginning to react to her invasion of my personal space. I was really missing Isobel!

Dale didn't have enough cash to pay the full bill, and

BEYOND THE 'BUT' *A Long Road to India*

get us back to Goa so, using all his blag powers he pointed out to the management that it was 'off-season' and they were lucky to have anybody in that room. If they wanted to call the police then they could but that way they wouldn't get anything. He gave them a few hundred rupees which paid most of it, and told them he'd be back soon, with the rest. They seemed happy with this, as in fact, they were lucky to h ave anybody in the room.

We drove down the coast road. It was off the tourist track and was little more than a very patched up tarmac, double carriageway. The scenery made up for the heavy going of the rough road. We parked up eventually, down a dirt track, toward the sea. There were a few houses in the distance but we were well away from anybody. I unpacked the boot and dragged the hash in the cases, inside the bus. It stank to high heaven. I set about making up a mould with the bits we'd bought before leaving Bombay.

Most of the heavy work was being done by Hollywood Pete, and Hank. We set up a little production line. First the hash had to be made pliable so we decided to lay it all out on the roof of the bus. When it got warm enough, it was brought down and, using the bus's hydraulic jack, pressed into one kilo slabs. It was intensive work and by the time the sun went down, we hadn't done half of it. The night was balmy and the sea was fairly still. I went down by the water's edge to have a smoke on my own. The bus had been getting noisy again as everyone relaxed after a heavy day. By the time I got back the mirror was out and lines of coke were disappearing up people's noses at a sub-sonic rate.

I didn't complain as it got everyone up and doing stuff. The interior of the bus was being cleaned and dinner was on its way. Best way to use a coke rush, was to be occupied, do stuff, instead of the 'coke rap', which consisted of sitting round talking complete bollocks. There was a tap on the door. I opened it to see two local girls dressed up to the nines.

"Hello what can I do for you?" They just smiled and wiggled around a bit.

"Uh, do you speak any English?" I asked. One of the girls smiled.

"No English mister," one of them said. They looked very young.

"I reckon we've got a couple of working girls here."

"Hey no shit man. I've alvays vant'd to fuck, Indian girl, ya!" said Hank, a little too eagerly. Peter was right beside him as well.

"We could probably get them for a few rupees, man," said Pete.

"Little bit young, Pete," I said.

"Yeah, but look at 'um."

He did have a point. They were very attractive in a native way with their saris and ankle bracelets.

"Let's not get too picky here. You fuck those two, the whole village eats tonight," said Dale.

Without much more a-do, Hank and Pete head for the back of the bus with the girls in tow.

"Don't use my bunk!" I shouted after them. Eventually Dale went back and got a blowjob. He just couldn't resist. This pleased his girls, no end. it looked like either, Pete, Hank, or myself, would be getting some pay-back action. Unfortunately Phillipe had met a German guy in Bombay and had decided to stay with him and fly back down to Goa. I just wanted to get back there, as well. I was missing Isobel and the kids. Not only that but I had heard from other friends that Isobel and one of the guys off of Sten's bus, by the name of Eric, were getting very close. I need ed to get home.

I know we were all a bit free with who we slept with in those days, we both had a good time, but I didn't want it developing into anything long term. However things were getting interesting. The interplay between the others was tangible. And as I hadn't been disgusting enough to take advantage of the young Indian girls, I was the target for revenge sex. After a really intensive and sweaty day, I just wanted to get cleaned up and cool down. I took some Hash and my wash kit and headed for the beach. It was absolute paradise. I shed my clothes and started for the sea. There was something primordial and a wonderful feeling, to swim completely naked.

A good swim around would loosen all the coconut oil I'd been smothered in. The sea and intense sun dried your skin and frazzled your hair. The only way to keep skin and hair together was to just smother yourself, hair and all, with oil, every morning. It kept the mozzies at bay and gave you a wonderful tan.

I lost track of time while I swam and body-surfed. The sea was wonderful and some large fish swam alongside me. They would surf almost to the shore and dive away at the last minute, leaving me feeling like something out of its element. When I swam out for the next wave, there they were again, swimming beside me.

A larger than normal wave, took me inshore at a rate of knots. At the last moment it dumped me on the sand. I lay there at the edge of the waves, exhausted in the glaring sunshine. The waves washing over me at just the right intervals so as not to burn. I decided that it was time to get the soap out. I stood and turned to head for the shade where I'd dropped my wash bag and towel. I checked my step when I saw Lilliana getting undressed. "Oh you 'ave fini? I come to swim also."

"No," I spluttered. "I've just come to get my soap." I indicated my wash-bag.

"Ah you 'ave ze bath in ze sea? Come, I wash be'ind for you."

"What! You wash my behind?" I patted by backside and she snorted with laughter. "In English we call this the behind." I patted my bum again.

"No, no," she giggled and patted herself on the back. I pretended not to understand and she actually came up to me and reached round to indicate my back.

A shock of contact and a deeply drawn breath from me, served to lift all pretence for an instant and we looked at each other and, God! I wanted her right then, right there. I hadn't had too much contact with her since we left Goa. She just seemed to hang around Dale all the time. She didn't smile too often and to see her smiling now was a tonic. It opened up her radiant Latin beauty and transformed her. The fact that she had a beautiful, full body and skin like coffee, was just icing on the cake as far as I was concerned.

I broke the spell by grabbing my wash-bag. She was after all, one of Dale's girls. I didn't want to spoil the working relationship between Dale and I. We definitely were good for each other. I had the practical skills that he needed, as the coming months would tell. I could tell he was impressed enough with my abilities. Most of the people around him were partying and having a good time while freeloading.

Dale figured that this was OK as it made him the 'place to be' and lots of the 'pretty people' hung around for the drugs and the sex and the music. There weren't many places with electricity and a stereo with speakers the size of a wardrobe! I was always included in the little group that would be mostly, separate from the circus, going on in the rest of the large Portuguese-style, house. *Best not to muddy the waters*, I thought to myself as I watched her walk down, in front of me, to the water's edge. She had such a beautiful figure from behind!

With gargantuan effort I drew my mind back to washing. Lilliana had gone right in for a swim and was now floating on her back, observing the effect she was having on me. I sat down at the water's edge and began to soap up. It was wonderfully refreshing and the sand stuck to the soap and acted as an exfoliant. I was tingling clean all over and waded out a little and then dived in. It was wonderful and cooling.

When I surfaced, I was alongside Lilliana and she grabbed my arm to help her tread water. A wave threw us together and we made full body contact! *Jesus*, I thought as I swam away from her. *C'mon, I'm only human!*

"Why do you go?"

"Lilliana, you are very beautiful and I desire you. You understand? I really desire you. But you are Dale's woman. You understand? You and Dale. Not possible, you and me."

I tried to put it in terms she'd understand. Her English was not that good and I wanted her, desperately, to understand clearly, that the only thing stopping me was that she was Dale's woman.

"Oh Dale, poo, poo." She pulled a sour face. "Not possible?" We were treading water by now and she was hanging onto me again. Again a wave threw us together but this time neither of us drew away and we kissed and our bodies came together.

"I think we'd better go back to shore now," I said in a very excited state.

I can remember thinking how glad I was that the water was cooling my ardour and my thumping blood pressure was dropping. We lay side by side in the sand. When the sun had dried us off, we sat in the shade of the palm tree. I made a smoke and we got giggly stoned, as the shadows got longer and the sun got deep gold and red as it dipped towards the horizon. Lilliana lay with her back on my waist, propped up to watch the sunset.

I have to admit that in the battle of whether to watch her or the beautiful sunset. The sunset lost! She turned and caught me watching her. I looked her up and down, purposely. She saw the effect she was having on me and smiled.

"Lilliana. I know what you are doing here, and I love it. You want to use me to show Dale you do not care. I just wish it was different, you understand? No Dale!"

She frowned.

"We'd better get back to the bus before it gets dark." I tugged on my shorts and sandals, Lilliana just wrapped a lungi around her waist. She looked charming in bare feet with an ankle bracelet. We walked, arm-in-arm, slowly back to the bus.

"I love'a today Alun. Swim'a, talking, smoking. Quiet. Tanquillo, understand?"

"Ce, mi amiga, io comprende. I have had a good time. You are very beautiful but normally you would not look at me. So I ask myself, why? Do you know which answer I got?"

"No. What?" she asked wide-eyed.

"I got the answer that I don't give a fuck what the reason is. Right now I'd do anything to make love to you." Again not words I'd normally use but, needs must. We were just outside the door of the bus now. The curtains were drawn and the interior lights on. The sounds of partying were unmistakeable. I grabbed Lilliana close to me.

"I don't care what the reason is, I just want you, badly."

She answered by kissing me.

The door started to slide open. We broke away in time

as the hash smoke wafted out the open door.

"Hey Al. Y'gotta come an' see this, man!" Dale said with a leer, as he looked at Lilliana and me.

We all went up the steps to be greeted with quite a sight. Two of the young girls were dancing around naked. They had brought some of their friends and Dale, Pete, and Hank, also naked, were having a whale of a time. Every time the girls did something, the guys gave them more money. I took one look and decided that I would sleep off the bus tonight. "Hey you lot. I'll be sleeping on the beach tonight."

"Come and get your dick sucked, man. She'll do anything you tell her."

"No thanks. But if you don't mind, I'll have one of those lines. I know it's a bit extravagant, but it's nice to drop off to sleep with." I caught sight of Lilliana and Rita. They both had faces like thunder.

I snorted the line and grabbed my sleeping bag and went for the door. I sorted my space under the palm that we'd used earlier and decided to have a smoke. Coke and hash go together quite well and I was just lying there listening to the waves and the balmy breeze as it shifted the palm leaves. All the swimming and other work started to drive me into a wonderful euphoric state of relaxation. Waves of pleasure were driving me to dreamland, and I don't mean sleep, though that usually followed when the effect of the coke wore off.

I heard the bus door slide open. I could see Dale, Lilliana and Rita had come out for a free and frank exchange of views! I couldn't hear the girls clearly but I heard Dale's answers. There was plenty of angry arm-waving and gesticulation. Dale disappeared inside the bus sliding the door shut with way more force than needed. "Bastardos!" Lilliana spat out like a shotgun.

I closed my eyes again. I didn't really want to be disturbed by it. It sounded like they were partying well on the bus and sound and light were emanating from it on an otherwise deserted beach. Suddenly I sat up. Lilliana had sat down under the palm, next to me, Rita was the other side.

"Hi girls, fed up with partying?" I asked with a grin. Both of them seemed a little more relaxed now. "I think a smoke would go down well right now." I started to skin up. One of the advantages of being in Bombay was that you could get RizLa+, papers.

"I guess they've still got the girls in there?"

"Fucking bastard," said Rita.

"But you must know what he's like. I mean for a start he has you two on the go. Do you really expect him to not mess around with other women?" Rita got up and walked off down the beach.

"You could always stay with me tonight Lilliana. It's quiet here and..." Before I got the last words out, she was all over me, like a cat in heat, with all the passion and surrender of a Latino.

I woke at first light. Lilliana was still close up to me. Rita was the other side, quite close as well. It seems I'm always asleep when she gets into bed with me!

I was going to light the gas but as there was enough driftwood left from last night, I decided to save the gas and re-light the fire. There was already the smell of burning wood from the houses, nearby. We made some coffee, black of course. There was no way of keeping any kind of milk. Powdered milk was OK, but even UHT lasted only a couple of hours in 110 degree heat and 95 per cent humidity!

By the time we'd finished the coffee, the sun was up and burning off the morning haze.

"I'm gonna get me a bath." I grabbed the soap. As I

did so, both Rita and Lilliana giggled and darted down toward the waves. I ran after them and we all went cascading into the sea. I had a great scrub down, but unfortunately, had to wash my own 'behind' this time. Rita waited until Lilliana was out of earshot. "So you guys spent the night together?" grinned Rita. I realised that'd be just what Rita would want as it might clear Lilliana out of the picture.

Alas, it was not to be. I just grinned at her.

We returned to the palm and put some clothes on. Just as we arrived at the bus, Hank came out coughing and gasping. There was no sign of the Indian girls.

"Good time then Hank?"

He grinned sheepishly. "Yah if Dale 'vas right, dey eat for a week, ya!"

"Hank you are disgusting," said Rita.

"Yah. But I just can't help myself."

We all got down to work laying out the slabs on the roof to soften them up. Dale showed up halfway through and joined in the work. There was no word of the activities of yesterday. Eventually we finished pressing up the hash into one kilo slabs and it was packed away and stashed in the boot. I slumped down into the driver's seat, it was mid-afternoon, and very hot. Dale came and sat in the seat opposite.

"Time for a swim," I announced. "I need to wash off the sweat and cool down."

"Bit more skinny dipping, man? I saw y'all havin' a good time yesterday."

"Don't have a problem with that do you?"

"Shit. No man. I've been telling her to get herself fucked for months now." He put it so charmingly.

"So what has happened on the road, stays on the road?

Fair?"

"Man, I love having her around, but they both understand that I ain't gonna be tied down to one woman. An' what they wanna do is their business, cool?"

"Way cool. I didn't want to piss you off but you were busy and she was there, and she is fuckin' gorgeous..."

"Shit no man! You fuckin' Brits crack me up, man. You even apologise for stealing a guy's wife, man."

We laughed and there was no conflict at all. Not so between Rita and Dale. She was still unimpressed with it all.

"I think we can get rolling again. We've finished doin' the hash so why not? We don't have to touch the grass or the oil," I said.

"Yeah. You gonna be able to do anything into England?"

"Yes I've been thinking about it." I decided that as nobody was around, I should lay it out to him. I took my shot. "I'll have to do something soon as I'm getting low on money. Anyway here's my plan: We go back home and set up a production area. We get my next-door neighbour, Jackorice, who's a carpenter, to make up some half-sized tea chests. We make the frame of the chests from two inch square wood which we drill out and stuff with grass."

I had his attention.

"We buy some trinket or piece of local art, say, a jug or porcelain plate, y'know. We get a little team of trusted people to bind the weed onto some pre-cut sticks and call it Thai sticks. Back in England, Thai sticks go for silly money, right? So we are maximising our profit. It's fucking kick ass weed anyway, so nobody gets ripped off right? The hash can go out like this as well, but better for the hash to be sold to the hippies on the beach in Goa. The rest can go out in book covers, or any other way we can think of. We've got the main post office in Panjim and there's air freighting facilities there. If we get a bent customs man there, the sky's the limit. These guys are the most corrupt officials in the world. You can't blame them, they are working for a few rupees a day."

Dale was now listening intently.

"That leaves us with five litres of hash oil."

"Best quality, uncut, Kashmir Black oil," said Dale pointedly.

"Exactly! Brits love the stuff! We get it back to Blighty and cut it a bit with surgical alcohol and we make double the money. It'll still be stronger than anything on the street in Blighty and I've got a mate who'll take all we can send."

"Well! You sure have been thinking about this, man. But how are you gonna get the oil in?"

"I'll swallow it!"

"Say what?" That took him by surprise!

"Yeah. Think about it. That other little firm down at the end of Anjuna do it all the time. When they get a bit brassic, one of them swallows a load of oil wrapped in condoms, and hey presto, flies back the next week! They were telling me how to do it. You just make sure that it's un-cut and you will be able to make three litres of good quality oil, better than what's there now. Now I figure a regular Christmas dinner must be around a kilo of food, specially when you add the trifle," I grinned.

"What the fuck's 'brassic', man?"

"Brassic lint means skint, which means without money. Didn't you listen to my rhyming slang lectures? Try and keep up. Bloody colonials," I said under my breath.

"Fuckin' limeys. Get on with it, man," he laughed.

"That's about it really. That's a lot of work and I'll need some expenses for the family while I'm away, plus a return ticket, of course. I reckon to go just about January, just after Christmas. We can raise the ticket money by sending out the crates and books. That'll give Jackorice some good money coming in.

"Yeah you really have been thinking about it. Sounds good t'me." I could tell he was impressed.

"Do you see any static at London Airport?"

"At Heathrow? Nah, they are more interested in ripping-off from the baggage than looking for dope."

At the time, Heathrow was known as 'Thiefrow' because of the stuff that went missing. In many cases, whole lorry loads of goods went out the back door.

"Do it, to it, man. Do what you gotta do."

"Sweet! Let's make some money man." I was inspired! Here was the opportunity to put some of my lessons into practice. All I needed was some bravado and a whole lot of bottle. I felt elated I felt I could now do anything, I was untouchable. Not only that but if trouble came along Dale would buy me out of it.

That was my reasoning at the time. I'd had enough of being on the bus with Timus, Kakey, Charley, Glynis, Black Bob. Adventure and money beckoned, so I'd decided that we'd be leaving the bus and going our own way and throwing in with Dale's firm. I'd learned a few things and I wasn't content to just drive round a busload of hippies, and then run out of money, especially when one of them drove me to distraction!

By the time I'd laid it all out to Dale he was as enthusiastic as I. "It's a good plan. Perhaps you and Isobel and the kids ought to move into my place, there's loads of empty rooms, man. You'll be right on hand to see stuff's done right."

"Nah, I think we'll keep the house, it'll be a sanctuary where no business is done. Doesn't mean I can't stay over for as long as needed, on occasion." I didn't tell him that

Isobel couldn't stand him! I guess the drugs, the partying and the heat, must have affected my judgement. I look back now, on what happened next, and shudder at what could have happened.

We had partied hard since being in Goa and the money was now getting low. The need to keep Isobel, me and the kids fed, was beginning to loom large on the horizon. I had to do something and to my slightly unbalanced view at the time, going back to England with the best part of a litre of hash oil in condoms, in my stomach, seemed a good idea and full of adventure!

I had another night of passion and lust, but in the daylight we got back to the business of travelling back home to Goa.

We pulled off down the road and the atmosphere was a bit more relaxed. I heard from Hank that Dale and Rita spent the night together and the bus springs were getting a good workout.

I drove all day without stopping. I felt like I was now separate from the others it was just me and the bus. Eventually I had to stop for diesel and we had a meal at the chai stall next door. We all draped ourselves round a big, black-top, table. As we all sat down at the table, the black top, took off with a horrible buzzing sound. The black top was in fact, flies! So many that you couldn't see the real colour of the table! I got the owner to wash the top down. We had created a little stir in the chai stop and a few of the locals were watching us. What they made of us I can only guess but they smiled at us and were very welcoming.

The fact that we spent what they normally take in a month, didn't escape me. I tried to see it from their eyes. These tall, white, weird looking, strangers arrive in their own bus. They buy Coca-Cola for the same amount that most people get for a day's work. We even left a tip the same size as the bill!

"You bloody septics! You ruin it for us all wherever you go, being kind, I put it down to your generosity. But now these guys are going to expect this kind of money from the next lot of tourists."

"You know me, man. Let's ALL make money."

"Yep, agreed, but it does ruin it for the next guy. Of all the thirteen countries we travelled through to get here. India has been the most corrupt and a rip-off, at the drop of a hat. But for every rip-off, there has been moments of incredible kindness and giving."

"Yeah I kinda forget that you actually drove here. Crazy fuckin' limeys. Over the hour that we stopped, we spent money, smoked a chillum, laughed and even danced with the local kids. It was a nice break on the outskirts of a town called Ambala.

Off onto the main road again. As we left, a small crowd waved us off. It was good that they will remember, fondly, when a bunch of hippies descended on them.

Just about late afternoon a couple of hundred miles south of Ambala, we came across a road gang working on the roads. When we use the term 'road gang' we picture a bunch of burly la ds, in reflective jackets, shovels in hand, lots of machinery and 'bum cleavage'.

In India it was vastly different.

A road gang in India consisted of thousands of people who would live in vast, tented, areas and move as the road progressed. Roughly half would be women. The women would be in groups of around a hundred spaced along the road at about kilometre intervals. They would all be equipped with lump hammers. With these, they would squat and break rocks all day. The first gang broke down the large boulders. This material would then be transported by women with woven baskets, carried on their head, to the next group, who broke it down smaller. This went on all down the road until the last group had beaten it down to a suitable size to be used on the roads.

I had slowed right down. It was fascinating to watch hundreds of people working with cans of molten tarmac. Spreading the tarmac and then rolling the small chippings into it. They'd do about a kilometre a day. Slow going compared to a Barber-Green tarmac laying machine, often seen on UK motorways re-surfacing. But a Barber-Green cost a couple of hundred thousand pounds. Why lay out all that money when labour was so cheap? Around one and a half rupees a day. Suddenly I heard a *clump, clump*, coming from the back wheel. I'd heard that sound before. It was the sound of a large stone trapped between the double wheels at the rear of the bus.

"I'm gonna have to stop!" I shouted over my shoulder to nobody in particular. There would be no arguments over this. It had to be got out now or the stone could shred the tyres.

When I got up from the driver's seat, I found I'd been talking to myself as they were all asleep. "Was'up, man?" Dale struggled into yawning consciousness.

"I've picked up a rock between the rear tyres. I'll have to get it out or it'll rip the tyres up."

"How yu' gonna do that?"

"I don't know but I'll think of something."

"Need any help?"

"Yes I will. Let's have a look at it shall we?"

We'd pulled over to the side of the road and were beginning to attract attention from the road workers.

"What I need is a long..." Just as I said that, as if written in a script (cue man with pinch-bar, please), round the corner comes an old-ish Indian dude wearing nothing but a loin cloth, turban, and flip flops! He was skinny and sunburned with a long grey beard. He smiled a big smile when he saw us. But most importantly, over his shoulder he was carrying a long heavy pinch bar, exactly what I needed. The guy didn't speak any English, just smiled a lot. We shook hands and I beckoned him to come with me to the rear axle of the bus. He must have wondered what this odd tourist was doing, dragging him under a bus, but he got down with me. As soon as he saw the rock between the tyres he understood completely. Without further a-do, he shoved the bar under the rock, using the axle as a fulcrum, with the far end of the bar against the road. He indicated that he'd keep an eye on it if I would drive the bus forward, so that the bar grounded and the forward movement would dislodge the rock. This I did and sure enough the rock came out with a 'crump' sound.

The old guy jumped for joy, waving his hands and grinning. By this time the girls had made some coffee, so we invited bar man to have a cup with us. He came on board, his eyes were wide, looking at everything. We finished the coffee and the old guy got up to go back to work. He smiled a lot and put his hand together as if praying, which is a respectful greeting or farewell.

Dale and I walked with him back to his camp. The other workers were surprised to see him with a couple of strange tourists. I took out a hundred rupee note and tried to give it to him discreetly. He looked at the note then back at me with utter surprise and delight. I'd just given him two weeks wages.

"Hey man, what happened to not spoiling'm?"

"Yes but it would've cost a lot more than that for a set of new tyres."

On we went into the heat of the afternoon when nothing else moved and anyone sensible would be sitting in the shade of a banyan tree, but 'Mad dogs and Englishmen, go out in the midday, out in the midday, sun!' As the heat was wearing me thin, and Indian road signage being what it was, we got lost. Much to my annoyance!

Of course everybody had an opinion as to where we went wrong and where we should go from there, and all of them different! We were slap bang in the middle of nowhere and no mistake. The road was just a patchwork tarmac that was now just one truck's width. I pulled over underneath some mango trees, it was nice and shady. "I'm going to walk down into that village and see if I can find out where the fuck on this planet we are."

That was greeted with all the enthusiasm of a tooth extraction. As I went out the door I could feel them all drifting back to sleep in the heat. That pissed me off for some reason. It's not as if they could have done anything more but some moral support might have been nice. I wandered down through mango groves and palm leaves to the small road that went over a bridge into the village. I was still feeling exasperated. As I got closer to the bridge I noticed an elderly man leaning against the parapet. He was dressed like Gandhi except this guy had a long beard and combed back hair. The only human being I'd come across for many miles. "And I bet you won't even speak English, either, what a great day this is," I spoke directly to him with frustration dripping off every word.

"As a matter of fact, I do, sahib."

"Whaaaa...?" Was all I could come out with. I felt so small and rude!

"I'm so sorry, Baba, I didn't mean to be rude. It's just that we are lost. Then I walk here, to a village in the middle of India and meet someone who speaks my language, fluently. Where did you learn?"

"When the Raj were ruling India, we were all taught English by the village elders. They said it would be good for our futures."

"It's wonderful to just talk normally without emphasising words and speaking slowly."

"Thank you sahib."

"No really, it's excellent English with hardly a trace of accent. How many Indian languages do you speak?" There were about thirteen main languages in India.

"I speak Gujarati, Konkani, Marharti, Punjabi, and Hindi. Everybody speaks English, in India it is a sign of status. Just as you will see many people here who are fat. It is a sign of affluence! So it is with English. It is a sign of education and is a very precious status."

"Do you know? I suddenly understand why two Indians will struggle along in English and I think to myself, why don't they just revert to their own language? Now I understand."

"Actually sahib I live most of the time in Bombay. I am an accountant. I have a flat and car. I'm here visiting my parents for a few days."

"Ah I understand. Slumming it, for a few days with the folks."

"Exactly, sahib exactly." We laughed and I sat with him for an hour or so, swapping stories from our lives.

He was a successful accountant in Bombay and sent a large piece of his earnings back to his folks and the village. He spent most of his time dressed in a business suit.

"I suppose I'd better get back to my bus. I have passengers waiting."

"You have a bus sahib? An English bus?"

"Yes I drove it out here from England."

"Well I never. That was a long drive."

"Oh yes it was an adventure. Something to tell the

grandchildren, I guess."

"How do you find it, sahib?"

"Phwarr, immense richness, intense poverty. Ancient knowledge, history and stunning architecture from ancient history. Countryside and jungle, mountains and scenery like I've never seen before. But the effect here and here, touching my heart and head, is what I find stunning." I suddenly realised that I'd gone right into it, and was in danger of babbling.

"Do not go any further down this road. It will not be good for the bus. You must turn around and go back."

"Yes I'm looking for the NH7 to Belgaum and then into Goa."

"You will find the NH7 a few miles back toward the last village. It is about ten miles, sahib. Have a good journey, you are welcome in my country."

"Thank you very much. It's been a pleasure to meet you, and I must apologise again, for my bad manners."

I wandered back still heat haze everywhere. It felt that if it got any hotter it would ignite the dry grass around me. I got back to the bus to find it had been tidied up and cleaned out.

"Bus looks great, thanks, whoever did it."

"It was the girls," said Pete. Why didn't that surprise me?

"Yah! But I did der dishes," chimed in Hank. Dale was grinning and keeping quiet.

"What did 'is nibbs, do?" I asked, jerking my thumb at him.

"'Is nibbs? What the fuck is that?" asked Pete.

"It means someone who thinks they are more important than they actually are. 'His Nibbs' and 'His

Highness' are the same put down.

"Fuckin' limeys," Dale put in.

"This fuckin' limey is now gonna drive us to Goa, you lucky colonials."

"Yeah let's get back. I just want to get some beach time and see the Mrs and littl'uns."

"Vy is dat, Alun? Not gettin' enough?" asked Hank with obvious 'shit-stirring' in his intent.

I glanced at Lilliana. She was looking at me and her body language said, "Fuck all of you. I sleep with who I want." She held her head up in a typical Latino female stance.

Dale obviously found it amusing. When everyone looked at him for his reaction, he just grinned. "Ain't no buisness'a mine, who sleeps with who." This was not the reaction that Lilliana wanted from Dale. She leaned down to his face.

"We no'a do much'a sleeping, huh?" Her eyes flicked to me as she turned and walked down the back of the bus. I felt like a million dollars! Dale, Pete, and Hank were doing their best not to splutter with laughter and cast exaggerated, admiring glances at me. I thought it diplomatic to slide into the driver's seat and attend to something really important!

"Right you bloody colonials, that doesn't include you Hank, you're just a damn foreigner, hocht verrdomma!"

"Ja, just drive der fuckin' bus, Englander swinehund!"

"Don't be like that," I said, as sarcastically as I could, and hit the 'play' button on the cassette recorder. On came Lou Reed, 'Rock 'n' Roll Animal' and we all waited till the really rhythmic section of the intro track, when as one, right on the beat, we burst into air guitar and dancing like loonies, until the bus springs squeaked! I, of course, was in the drumming seat.

We fell about laughing. Eventually I got myself together and fired up the engine. I let it warm up a bit then pulled onto the road in the opposite direction.

We did shameful amounts of coke and I drove like one possessed. Not dangerously fast but steady and aware of everything around me. The coke helped with concentration and stamina and mammoth drives were part of the story. I drove through several lines of latitude as we headed back to Goa. I took the Western Ghats in my stride, in the dark! Even the local truck drivers thought I was loony. As dawn came up, we were dropping down to the plains where we would cross into Goa. But that crossing was still five hundred miles through forest, rice fields and outright jungle.

I pulled into a chai stop. The truck drivers were just stirring. Wrapped in shawls against the morning chill they huddled around a brasserie while the chai stall opened up for business. I thought I'd have some of that chai and a warm round the brasserie. Funny to think that in two hours' time, it would be crippling heat! I was still wearing 'Goa clothes' and I was feeling the cold as well. I threw on the embroidered shawl I'd bought in Delhi. It was first made into a hood, then the end was flipped over the shoulder. I joined the drivers around the fire and got a few nods and, "Good morning sahib," from those that spoke English. I took my steaming cup of 'special chai' and sat at one of the tables under the banyan tree, looking like a boxer taking a break during his training. I even felt as if I was steaming! Probably due to the raised temperature from the tiredness and the coke in my system.

I was engaged in filling a chillum, when Lilliana sat down beside me. "Lilliana I... I'm sorry about earlier."

"Not worry. I no sorry. It was wonderful night." She squeezed my arm.

"It will stay with me all my life," was the simple and

honest answer from me.

We shared the chillum and just sat there watching the sun come up. After a while I got myself together for the last leg of the journey. "I guess we'd better get back to going home, back to my Isobel and the little'uns." I smiled and turned and walked back to the bus. I started the engine and let it idle while everyone got back on.

"I'll drive till it gets too hot. I'll take a couple of hours sleep in the shade then we can drive all night, in the cooler time. We should get to Anjuna about nine in the morning. That sound good for everyone?"

"Yeah man, let's do it, to it," said Dale, already settling down to some heavy sleeping. Rita was semi-conscious beside him.

I pulled back onto the road, waving to a few drivers as we passed. They waved back enthusiastically. I'd see them again down the road. Sure enough, several hours later the sun was blazing down. I was feeling like I could sleep a few hours and the state line for Goa was only three hundred and fifty miles away, now.

I pulled over to a chai stop. It had two big banyan trees and many outside tables. I parked in the shade and looking at the direction of the sun, would be in the shade for many hours.

In most chai stops there would be a couple of cots around the back, in the shade. Truck drivers would use these cots to sleep as long as they spent some money in the chai shop. Seeing as we were spending about a week's takings for the shop, in a few hours, we were more than welcome to use the beds. They were very basic of course, just plated rope slats, more like a hammock with a turned and painted frame. If you could stick the odd rat running around the legs as you slept then they were quite comfortable. Provided that the monkeys didn't pelt you with nuts or fruit from the mango trees. Whatever you did you must not forge t to stand the legs of the bed in buckets of water. It stopped the scorpions and other insects from crawling up the bed legs as you slept! There were always stocks of empty, catering-sized tins for that purpose.

During the day, the chai shops were quieter, and you could get a few hours sleep in the midday and afternoon heat, and that's exactly what I did. I left instructions on the bus that it was not to be left alone under any circumstances. I was to be woken in four hours' time.

"I suggest y'all get some shut eye as we'll be driving all night, non-stop to Anjuna."

"I can't fuckin' wait, man. I need to wash the city and road, outta me," said Dale.

Sleep soon overcame the residue of drugs in my system. I awoke a few hours later in exactly the same position as that when I went to sleep. When I got on the bus they weren't sleeping, they were partying. Big surprise!

I checked the engine oil and radiator. All was well. We had a full tank of diesel so one more tank after this would see us home. I fired up the engine and let it warm up gently. I was excited to think I'd be seeing Isobel and the kids.

I eased the bus into gear and let off the handbrake. As of now, I would go into my own head space as I hunkered down to a long drive. I must remember that we were carrying a lot of hash. It was well stashed and British tourists were never hassled. As soon as we came to a state line I'd usually lean out the driver's window and yell, "Tourist!" The barrier would be raised and we'd be waved through, past all the waiting buses and trucks.

On and on we went, I didn't want to stop. Sundown came with long red rays and shadows a mile long. On came the headlights. I just kept driving and got annoyed when toilet stops were requested. The road went on hour after hour, with every hazard you can think of lurking in the dark, to get me. A broken down truck, just left in the road where it broke, while the driver took the broken part to the local mechanic's shop for repair, even if it was an engine, gearbox or axle. An overloaded ox cart with broken axle, stopped just round the bend, its load spread all over the carriageway. All these things were bad enough but then add the appalling state of the roads. We arrived at the Goa state line, at about six in the morning – it was still getting light. They waved us straight through. We'd be home around ten or eleven. I filled up with diesel at the first filling station over the state line.

I drove on and on. Around ten o'clock we arrived home. I dropped Dale and the others at his house and I drove on to Anjuna and parked in the same place, overlooking the beach. I sat there for a while. There was nobody else around, they were all on the beach or shopping.

I suddenly realised that Isobel and the kids were down there swimming and sunbathing. I could see the kids playing with their friends and their mum and dad nearby. Then I realised that the other couple laying naked and sunbathing, were Isobel and a guy I didn't recognise. They were laying close together. So what I'd heard from other friends that had come to Bombay, from Goa after we left, was true. They were telling me they'd seen Isobel with another man friend.

I watched them for a while and it became more obvious that they were in some kind of relationship. Oh well, I guess when the cat's away, etc., etc.

I blew the horn. Isobel looked around. Her face lit up. She grabbed a towel, which didn't cover her very much. She called the kids over and pointed up to the bus. They just ran up the cliff path to me. Isobel struggled to keep the towel in place and was losing the fight.

I hugged the kids as they came onto the bus. They were telling me everything that had happened to them while I'd been away. Isobel came aboard, still grappling with the towel. She just let it fall and hugged me close and tight. By now the kids, satisfied that I wasn't going off again, were making their way down to the beach, and their friends, but only after promising them we'd go to Tito's restaurant tonight and have a good meal together. Tito's did a stuffed tuna that the kids loved, me too. Not only that but they had ice cream too. One of the only fridges on Anjuna beach. Most of the restaurants were pretty makeshift. No electricity, no gas, no storage. Everything cooked in them was less than four hours old. We tumbled onto the bunk and all the missing, and wanting, and substitutes were washed away.

Afterwards, I lay back on the bunk with Isobel laying against me.

"So who was that you were sunbathing with?"

"Oh that's Eric off of Sten's bus. You remember him don't you? English, comes from Barnett."

"How long has he been hanging around? All the time I've been away, I'll bet."

"No. Not all the time."

"Have you been sleeping with him?" There was a long pause.

"Do I take it that the answer to that is 'yes'?"

"It's been really difficult to..."

"Isobel. Have you or have you not, been sleeping with him?"

"Yes, but not very often."

"How did that happen then?" I found I was a bit jealous but compared to what I'd been up to, she had been quite good.

"Oh you know, those full moon parties. The kids were sleeping over with their friends and I just fancied seeing a few people."

"Yes it can get boring even in paradise I suppose."

"Anyway you know how dark it is coming back through the trees. Well, we'd been all talking and smoking round the little fire we'd made on the beach. We had a couple of smoochie dances, y'know nothing much."

"And?" I asked, a bit sharply.

"If you are going to get all territorial about it, I'm not talking about it anymore."

"Sorry. I didn't mean to, I'm not down on you. We both have had good time. I ain't been a saint."

"Really? You do surprise me. I bet you've been shagging that Lilliana, type." She must have noted the look on my face. "Yes I thought so. I noticed the way she was looking at you."

"Nice bit of deflection, off subject, there. Let's get back to walking you home, in the dark."

"Well he walked me back home 'cos it was early in the morning. He asked if he could stay with me. I was missing you big time, you know how I get in the heat. I didn't have the strength to tell him to go."

"Was that the only time?"

"No. There were a couple of other times, and not always him."

"Oh you've taken multiple lovers then?"

"No. But you know what these house parties are like, around here. There were a couple of times when I took what was offered. Tell you the truth I can't remember who was who, but it was just partying, y'know."

"Yah I guess so. But you remember, and were hanging

out with, Eric."

"Yes we spent a lot of time together because the parents of the kids' friends, are friends of his. The kids were never there when Eric stayed. I made that clear. You were away anyway what was I supposed to do?"

"It's cool don't worry, as long as I know, I'm OK with it."

"What about you. You've been partying, I bet."

"Yes that's true we did party a lot."

"So who?"

"Well you were right about Lilliana, but like you, it was just company for a night. Plus she wanted to get back at Dale for shagging a couple of young Indian whores."

"You been with whores?" she said, startled.

"No I didn't! What do you think I am? I like to put it about maybe, but these girls were young and I've never paid for it in my life. I slept outside on the beach, to get away from it. Then Lilliana came out because she was so upset. I told her to sleep with me tonight, meaning she should stay away from the partying on the bus. She took it that I was trying to seduce her so she stayed. Simple as that."

"Was she the only one?"

"No there was Pillipe. That was just a one night thing, as well. Hank had loads of coke an' y'know what I'm like when I've had a line."

"Yes I do. You mean that French tart?"

"She's alright actually but it was just a body. Like you, it was just company."

"As long as you're back now. Don't go shagging any of them while you're home."

"That goes for you too," I said.

"Why would I need them when you are here?"

"Just what I was going to say about you."

Just then Black Bob walked on the bus and came straight to our bunk. "Hey Al, how's it goin', man?"

"Cool Bob, what about you?"

"Really cool. I'm in love, man! Just as he said that, Caroline, his girlfriend from Sten's bus, came aboard.

"I suppose we'd better get up and put some clothes on, then," I said.

"Nah don't bother, I'm enjoying the view," joked Bob with a leer and a playful slap round the head from Caroline.

We got dressed and made some coffee, while I brought everyone up to date. "Timus and Cathy are living on the beach most of the time. They'll be glad the bus is back," said Bob.

"It looks like we've all gone our separate ways. Maybe it's time for us to leave as well."

"I ain't surprised. You'n Charlie are at war."

"I just can't put up with the guy. He's just nutty as far as I'm concerned, and if we stay on the bus I'm going to end up clocking him again. I don't want my kids seeing that."

"The rest of them are going to be pissed off, losing their driver," said Bob.

"The time has come to move on Bob. We've had a great adventure, driving out here but I think it's best for all of us if I leave you to it."

"That's a real shame. There won't be many of us left 'cos me 'n' Caroline are going up to Poona, to check out the Rajneesh Ashram."

"Yeah I've heard one or two things about that place."

We went to Bobby's chai shop and had a chai and a smoke. Several people, hearing the bus was back, had called in to say hello. There were many more people coming to Goa, now that Christmas was near. The rich ones just got on a plane and came out for a few weeks. Full moon parties were even more mental. All the top quality drugs of all kinds came into Goa during the Christmas period.

"How is the house? Are Anne and Regine still there?"

"Regine is away at the moment. She'll be back on Monday. Annie's still here," said Isobel with a smile and a raise of the eyebrows.

"Oh yes, why did you say that with a smirk?"

"Well you know how Annie is. We had a little cuddle when things got really lonely. And before you drool all over me, no we didn't do anything. Just a little comforting and massage."

"Back massage?" I asked, getting more and more interested as time went by.

"Now don't get carried away. No, not just my back, all over. And before you ask, it was wonderful."

"I ain't gonna get any jealousy here am I?"

"Get on. You know what Annie's like. She fancies you just as much as me. She as much as admitted it to me."

I was very flattered and I will admit that my imagination went wild at the possibilities.

"OK so I guess we'll move all our stuff off the bus and live in the house." That night, to be on our own, Isobel and I slept out under the stars and palm trees. We lit loads of candles. It was wonderful, just the two of us, and the stars and the sea.

The sea put on a show for us. In the full moon, the waves contained phosphorus and really sparkled like an electric fire show, when they broke on the shore. The sea was one silver carpet below us, reflecting the light from the full moon. All this backed up by some really wonderful music coming from the full moon party, further down the beach.

It was spectacular and perfect, like something out of a romance novel. Something millions of bored husbands and housewives dreamt about doing. We were actually doing it.

We'd brought our double sleeping bag and a few cushions. We'd lit a fire just as the sun went down. We lay there under the stars as the balmy night made it too warm for being in a sleeping bag. I was reminded how sleeping with someone you actually love is a totally different experience, than just lust.

The romance and passion of that night under the stars, still has the power to move me even now. I also realised that our relationship had come through a bit of a test by the fact that, here we were in a tropical paradise with complete freedom to do as we pleased. Any drug, any sexual partner(s), complete freedom to do as we pleased. We came easily through it.

Goa was hedonistic. It had that effect. We both took full advantage of that situation, alone and together. We had been, and still were, partying hard. I must give credit to Isobel during these wanton times. She always put the children first. Nothing, not sex 'n' drugs nor rock 'n' roll, swayed her from her responsibilities to them. It was because of her, that I was able to go off to Bombay without them. I know she'd give her life to protect them and would always take the sensible approach to things, where the kids were concerned. She may not have given birth to them but they were as close as if she had done and they love each other very much, which was a big comfort to me.

Total freedom of that kind, effected people in different

ways. There was a certain type of person that couldn't take that freedom and it freaked them out. They'd wander around in a daze. They would come and sit next to you in a chai shop and start to babble in whatever language they spoke. Or they would say nothing, and just act in a loony way. For instance, start to take the food off your plate. We called them Goa casualties. The truth of the matter was that a lot of them had just run out of money and were living, 'wild' and affecting being a 'loveable' loonies.

One German girl I remember vividly, would come and sit in the chai shop with us. She would be completely naked, just sitting there, quietly. We all wore nothing on the beach. Maybe the females would be topless in the chai shop but to be completely naked, with the body of a goddess, was startling, and even in this 'peace and love' atmosphere, dangerous for her. In the end Isobel and Annie took hold of her, dressed her and found some sympathetic German couples who took her to the German Embassy in Bombay.

In the next few days we moved everything into the house. I was sad to see the bus go out of my life, especially as we'd driven a few memorable roads together. The prospect of life without Charlie and not having to scrimp and save, was attractive. I now had a way of making large amounts of money. So what if I was putting myself in danger? I was untouchable, invincible, or so I thought.

We spent Christmas day 1975, on the beach. Most of Sten's bus joined us and we had a massive cook up organised. It was from Tito's restaurant. He'd sent his Goanese chef to us and arranged for him to cook a Goa style Christmas dinner.

It was the first time we were all together since I'd returned from Bombay. These were all the friends we'd made while on an epic trip.

Alun Person

"Hi Alun 'ows it goin'?"

"Eric, right? Yeah I'm good man, you?"

"Good to see you again... I a..." He shuffled around a little.

"It's OK man, Isobel told me everything, I'm cool with it." You won't believe what happened to me on the road, but it stays on the road. That's my philosophy, Isobel's as well."

"Yeah Isobel said you'd be OK. I'm real glad man." He stuck out his hand and I took it. He turned out to be a really nice guy, I could see why Isobel would be attracted to him. We all ended up spending many days just lying in the sun together.

A couple of guys that I didn't know came over to say hi to Isobel and the kids. I guessed they were her other 'friends'. They certainly looked as if they knew each other well, and she was a little sheepish, casting glances at me all the time. When Christmas was over, many of the travellers either left for home or Kathmandu and numbers thinned out a little. I recruited the Goanese guy next door who was a carpenter. In the end, the guy made twenty-five tea chests, each one contained a nice piece of Indian art or souvenir. Down the frame I'd got the carpenter to drill a one and three-quarter inch diameter hole down each piece of wood that made up the frame of the chest.

Into these I inserted as much Thai weed as I could ram in there. When I had done this the carpenter made the frame up into a sizeable chest. We took it into Panjim to the freight handling company. We had a guy who works there. He used to come and party with us sometimes.

In the end we sent out the twenty-five crates, by airmail, all over the world. Much to my surprise and delight, every one of them got through! We made forty thousand US dollars!

The carpenter went from living in a rented Portuguese bungalow, to owning his own business and well on the way to owning his own house! The guy at the freight company opened another office and bought a big truck for his business.

We went even more wild, partying, hiring Jeeps and living it up. We'd hire whole restaurants and hotels. We'd fly up and down to Bombay to pick up money from Thomas Cooks, who unknowingly at the time, existed mainly to transfer smugglers money back into India. I lost count of the number of people that would be hanging around Bombay, 'waiting for money'. It was a time honoured tradition. Booking telephone calls to back home, we'd often bump into friends at the PTT office, around midnight! The phone lines were lousy and sometimes you had to shout. It went like this: "'Ello, 'ello? Pete. PETE! C'n you 'ear me Pete…? Did you get my parcel Pete? PETE CAN YOU HEAR ME PETE? PETE! DID YOU GET MY PARCEL? YOU DID! Ahem. You did? Wicked man… Yeah! The fat lady is singin'er fuckin' 'ed off."

You would emerge from the booth, soaked in sweat from the concentration and hot city night, with a big grin on your face. All we had to do was visit Thomas Cooks every day till the money arrived, hop on a plane and fly back down to Goa.

For me it meant money for living and making sure we had plenty of everything. When the stress of making sure that your family has a home and plenty to eat is taken away, then you can start to relax and enjoy, fully, what's going on.

Goa at this time of the year was fairly deserted. Only people who lived there, and worked from there, remained behind. As time went on, the heat became intense and the wells got low and paddy fields began to dry up. There was dust, scorched earth and burnt dry grass, everywhere. It was about this time that I decided it was time for me to fly home for a couple of weeks and take a few kilos with me. I look back now, at what I was about to do next, from the safety of time passed. I shudder at the risks I took. The stupid things I did. Like I said before, I felt invincible and full of bravado. I could handle anything.

Isobel, of course nearly packed up and flew home when I laid it out to her. I had made a deal with Dale that should anything go wrong, he would make sure Isobel and the kids were taken care of and put on a plane for home. We never did come to terms on this one. I begged her not to go home. He swore on his life that he'd take care of them which comforted me as I'd found him to be a man of his word. And I knew he had the money to do as I asked, as well.

"Anything happens, man. They'll want for nothing. I'll bring them home myself."

"Thanks, man. That means a lot."

I left Isobel with enough money to last several months, though I only expected to be away about three weeks.

"You expecting any static at Heathrow?" asked Dale one night as we were preparing for me to go.

"Nah man, it'll be simple. I'll look just like any tourist coming home with a few trinkets. I'm going to buy a few clothes and have a good haircut. They won't even look at me!"

Back in those days, H.M. Revenue & Customs were in turmoil and at odds with the government over pay and working conditions. They were underpaid and demoralised. Nowhere near the sophisticated service that they are now. When threats like terrorism and Semtex, cheap heroin and people smuggling came along, HMRC got really serious, with things like x-rays, sniffer dogs, and intelligence-led operations. But, in those days, they were more interested in whether you'd paid duty on your cigarettes and perfume! I'd decided I would take a kilo or so of oil, wrapped in condoms and swallowed.

I know! I know! I don't know what the fuck I was thinking at the time. Definitely a very stupid thing to do. I knew that nobody had ever died from an overdose of cannabis. It was just not possible for the human body to ingest enough cannabis to kill you. It would take several sack-fuls to do any damage. The only time anybody was hurt by cannabis was when a half-ton bale fell off the truck and broke the driver's leg!

So I said goodbye to Isobel and the kids and told them I'd be back in a couple of weeks.

Annie had moved out of the house and was now with an Italian guy just down the beach, which was a shame as it had been wonderful sharing a bedroom with her!

Regine was also due to move out as well. She fancied seeing Kathmandu and was going to fly up. Come the day for departure, Hank drove us all in the Jeep to the airport at Panjim. He, Isobel and the kids were going to do some shopping in town and then drive back to Anjuna. Rita, the Kiwi girl, and Dale's number one wife, wanted to go to Bombay. So he asked if I'd take her on the ferry that goes to Bombay as she didn't want to fly. It was a two day sailing but what the hell, could be a laugh. "Don't you go shagging her," was Isobel's parting advice.

"To be honest, I just don't fancy her. She's nice enough and a good bod, but not my type." Isobel relaxed. She knew we tell each other everything, and I would have no reason to lie to her.

It was a good trip. The ferry stopped a few times on the way, for a small row boat to bring out passengers to the grossly overloaded ship. The only place to sleep was on deck. The cabins smelled badly of vomit and urine. We slung out our sleeping bags on the top deck. We'd brought some of our own food and water, so all we'd need to buy was a hot cup of chai.

We needed that hot chai as well. Up on the top deck temperatures first thing in the morning dropped right down. We cuddled up together to keep warm. It was nice to feel her body against mine, and I got the impression that if I'd made a try for her, right in that moment, I'd be welcomed, but that was it, I didn't try. We just slept all night cuddled up together.

The boat pulled into the dock in Bombay, just down the road from the Gateway to India. Rita and I checked into separate rooms in Stiffles Hotel, just along from the Taj Mahal Hotel in Colaba. I crashed out immediately the boat ride had worn me out.

The next day Rita and I went to see Paeso, Dale's rich Indian friend. He lived in a plush tower block with his family and servants. It was a massive place and overlooked the bay.

"So you are flying back to England, then Alun. Won't it be a bit cold right now?"

"Too right it will. I shan't be staying there long, I'll be back in a couple of weeks."

He glanced at Rita, then back to me. "I'll come over to your hotel room tonight Alun, we'll go into the Taj Hotel and have a few, beers."

"Uh, yeah OK that'd be nice." I wasn't sure why he wanted to talk to me. We spent the afternoon booking my ticket. A single ticket was needed as I didn't know how long I'd need to sell all the hash oil. I had decided to take oil with me as it could be sold by the gram. That way would be best to maximise return. I'd already filled and wrapped the oil and it was all ready for swallowing. I'd figured that your average Christmas dinner must weigh the best part of a kilo, so it should be OK... I did say that I don't know what I was thinking at the time!

BEYOND THE 'BUT' *A Long Road to India*

That evening Paeso came over and took Rita and I to a really plush hotel and restaurant where they had every kind of food you could think of. All the waiters were in white livery, with turbans and peacock feathers. The cabaret was a beautiful Arabian belly dancer, but it wasn't her belly that was swaying in time with the music it was her unrestrained thru'penny bits!

It struck me how Indira Ghandi, the prime minister of India at the time, had applied a massive import tax on foreign goods. She wanted Indian-made goods only, to be available for sale. This meant very sub-standard and generally, badly made, goods. With all the excesses of the advertising trade, unleashed. You could still make any claim for your products. No Trade Descriptions Act or advertising standards, then. The upshot of this policy was of course, if you had money you could get around this legislation, and like all prohibitions the world over, was a charter for smugglers.

We ate and drank well into the night several of Paeso's friends including some beautiful Indian models, had come to join us. They kept disappearing into the Toilets. Paeso saw me notice this and tapped his nose and raised his eyebrows at me. I nodded imperceptibly and fell in behind him as we went to my room. The model types were racking out lines of coke on a huge mirror. "Ah Alun vy don't you have a line."

Hmm, I've known this girl for less than two hours and already she's using my first name. Why is a stunning Indian girl, who's way out of my league, being so friendly?

I was a little suspicious.

"How do you like my friend Rieeza, she's very beautiful, no?"

"She certainly is. An absolute stunner."

"Yes she is the daughter of an industrialist. Her parents

live on their yacht in Monte Carlo this time of year. She has the house, the cars and Daddy's wallet, while they are away. The parents think that the long time, trusted servants are looking after her, and they are. But what the parents don't know is that she got the dirt on each one of them and is buying their silence, on threat of exposure and dismissal.

"Wow! Devious little bitch," I said half admiringly.

"Who's a devious little bitch?" She had fallen across Paeso and I. Obviously enjoying the coke.

"Well from what I hear of it, you are. But I admire you going for what you want and making it happen. I think you are probably very good at that."

"You have been talking to Paeso too much." She slapped him playfully on the face then kissed him there.

"No. I'm just going by what I see."

"Oh and what do you see Mr Englishman?" Her frankness and beauty were intoxicating and I couldn't take my eyes off her.

"I see a young lady who knows what she wants and gets it by any means she can."

"Like what, Mr Englishman?"

"Like your stunning beauty and your incredibly beautiful figure. But you know that already don't you. You know full well, what effect you have on mere men like me."

The line that I'd snorted earlier was just coming on. It made me eloquent and I decided to be brazen.

"And what effect am I having on you then?" she teased, and moved in a little closer.

"Well if you asked, 'is that a gun in your pocket or are you just pleased to see me?' The answer wouldn't be a gun, know what I mean, toots?" I said, in best Bogart imitation.

That made her laugh and we were getting on well.

"Well it's been lovely meeting you Rieeza. I hope you have a good party, I wish I didn't have a meeting with Paeso. I'd like to talk a bit longer. I guess you'll be going soon, huh?"

"No I'm staying at the hotel tonight, with you." I naturally, assumed she meant Paeso and all of us. I took Paeso in the other room.

"I'm sorry mate but I don't want to talk in front of the girls, or anyone come to that. What did you have in mind?"

"Well I have some kilos of black Kashmir, I'd like to move on.

I thought about that for a minute. "What's the deal?" I asked.

"Fifty-fifty."

On an impulse I agreed to take ten kilos from him. I was thinking that I might as well be hung for a sheep as well as a lamb. My flight departed at four in the morning from Bombay airport so that left me tonight and all day tomorrow to get myself ready. If I was just going to load my suitcases then there would be no point in swallowing the oil. I'd just pack it with the rest.

"OK Guys I gotta go, I'm all in," said Paeso. Rita also went to her own room. They had all shuffled out the apartment door when the bathroom door opened and out came Rieeza with a smile on her face she turned and flipped the lock on the door. As she walked toward me she was undoing the buttons on her shirt...

I woke in the morning feeling like we'd been at it all night.

"Rieeza what a wonderful, unexpected night. Why did you want to stay with me?"

"Well I've never slept with an Englishman, Mr Englishman, besides Paeso asked me If I'd look after you."

"Ah you did it as a favour to Paeso."

"Partly. Does that bother you?"

"Not at all. I didn't think you did it 'cos you are madly in love with me." I flung back the covers. "I did it because of this beautiful body." I slightly regretted that action because I couldn't tear myself away from that beautiful sight.

An hour later, we decided to get out of bed.

I went to the bathroom and turned on the shower. I stepped in and felt the warm water all over me – a real luxury after cold water showers. A few moments later, in walked Rieeza. She came right in the shower with me. That was another hour gone!

Eventually she decided it was time to go. She finished dressing and said that she hoped she'd see me when I got back. I said I'd certainly try. We kissed and she was out the door.

I was in shock. She was a real Indian beauty with a body to die for. *Thank you Paeso.* She was real eye candy and a wonderful diversion for a night. I just hope Isobel wasn't having as much fun as I was!

It was all part of Paeso's plan to butter me up for his scam. I didn't tell him that as she walked toward me, unbuttoning her top, I would've sold my own mother!

Time was getting on and so far no sign of Paeso or his dope. *What's going on? Is he just another un-together, disorganised Indian?* I decided that if I didn't see him before six in the evening, I'd go ahead and swallow the oil. I had to be at the airport at two thirty in the morning, to catch the British Airways, four o'clock flight out to London. In those days it was a fifteen hour flight with stops at Tehran and Frankfurt. I wasn't going to miss this flight and want ed to get to the airport in plenty of time.

Five o'clock came and went. Rita had joined me a couple of hours ago and we waited out in the afternoon sunshine, on the balcony.

"Sod it! I'm swallowing the oil now. I ain't waiting anymore."

I got a couple of bottles of very expensive Perrier water from the hotel bar and, over the next couple of hours, swallowed the oil, all pre-packed into about fifteen grams per pack, and wrapped in three condoms. Of course, as soon as I finished swallowing the oil, in breezed Paeso with a bag with ten kilos in it!

"Where the fuck have you been? I'm really not into making arrangements only to end up being fucked around just when I don't need it. Because you are a couple of hours late I've swallowed the oil."

"I'm sorry so, so sorry. I had trouble picking up the hash. But it's completely ready, wrapped and everything, OK?"

"Yeah, I guess so, I'll pack it in my bags, now."

"When you've finished come down to the bar and we'll have a drink with my friends."

"I don't think I should be drinking, do you?"

"Well you can just have a fruit juice or mineral water. It will dilute the acid in your stomach. You must not eat on the plane but drink more fluid."

That was good advice actually so I packed the ten kilos in the two suitcases and went down with Rita to have a drink at the bar.

"Hey Alun! Over here, man." I saw Paeso sat with a bunch of Indian guys and six or more European-looking men and women. They were drinking and being very loud. I sat and talked with them for a couple of hours. They were getting more and more out of order and even louder.

They were English as well.

Around midnight I started to say my good nights to everyone.

"Where are you going Alun?" asked one of the English guys.

"I'm flying home tomorrow morning, I've got to be at the airport soon, so I'd better get myself together."

"Is that British Airways?"

"Yes."

"Ah don't worry then, you've got plenty of time."

"How do you know? Are you catching it as well?"

"Well yes you could say that. We're flying it! We're the flight and cabin crew of British Airways flight seven thirty one, to Heathrow," he said with a grin.

"No shit." I was gob-smacked. I looked around at them they were all drinking, including the stewardesses.

"But you're all drinking."

"Not all of us actually. See that older guy over there? He's on tonic water. He has over thirty thousand hours in his log-book. They don't come much more experienced than him."

"Thank God for that," I replied. The captain may be sober but the others were far from it. That filled me with confidence and no mistake.

"Hey Al, I'll call a taxi and ride to the airport with you," called out Paeso.

"Yeah I'm ready to go, almost."

I checked that I had my passport and money, paid my bill at the hotel, and grabbed my suitcases. Paeso had a cab ticking over outside. I gave Rita a kiss on the cheek and asked her to give my love to Isobel when she got back to

Anjuna.

"And don't take any shit from Dale, either."

"No fuckin' worries! Good luck Alun," she said with conviction.

We arrived at the airport. It was very big and noisy and so modern that it felt out of place here in Bombay. I said goodbye to Paeso and from then on, I was on my own. I checked in my suitcases. As I did so I realised I'd just put the ten kilos out of my control!

I waited in the departure lounge and had a couple of bottles of water. The time came to board the 747. I was amazed how big they were inside.

I settled into my seat and felt very comfortable. I was hoping for a trouble and hassle free flight. I'd probably get off for the hour and a half stop, in Frankfurt, just to stretch the legs.

We rumbled along the taxiway to the main runway, The captain was still waiting for take-off clearance, winding up the engines and holding the plane on its brakes. Suddenly he got clearance and let the brakes go. The acceleration was fantastic. Within seconds we were hurtling down the runway at a hundred knots. Take off speed was reached and up came the nose. There was whirring and bumping sounds as the gear came up and off we went. *Wow! What a rush!*

We climbed to cruise altitude and they brought round breakfast for us. None of which I wanted, just some orange juice. The cabin crew looked haggard and smiled a knowing smile at me. I dropped off for an hour or two. The captain announced that we'd be overflying a lightning and thunderstorm in the middle of the Indian ocean. He turned the cabin lights out and the show was spectacular. It broke up the longest leg of the flight, and was certainly better than the in-flight movie.

The turbulence from the storm was frightening. When the captain tells the cabin crew to sit down and buckle up, then you know it's going to get rough. The bit I didn't like was seeing the wings of the Jumbo Jet, actually flapping up and down and the engines vibrating from side to side!

I wondered how the rest of the flight crew were feeling right then! I remember thinking about the ground below and how it had taken us months to get to India. Now those same roads were flashing by. A journey across Asia that had taken us months, would now be done in some fifteen hours. It was awe inspiring!

We landed at Tehran and parked for half an hour and took on more passengers. We took off again and headed up to Frankfurt. A few hours and a film later, we were about to land in Frankfurt. The captain announced that we would be swapping planes for 'operational' reasons.

That received a groan of annoyance but when we landed everybody filed off with their bags. We had to pick up our hold baggage and then re-check in for another flight, for the last leg into Heathrow. My suitcases were some of the last to come round, and by the time I grabbed them, most of the other passengers had disappeared into the transit lounge. I set off with suitcases in hand. I didn't really have a clue where I was going but it didn't matter as I could always ask someone. Except that there was nobody in sight. I wandered down a few corridors trying to find the transit lounge or at least someone to ask.

Suddenly some automatic doors opened in front of me and there was the outside of the airport! There were buses and taxis waiting. I could've gone out into Germany and sold it all there and probably got more money for it. But no, all my contacts were at home. I decided to turn round and go back into the airport. I'd just plead ignorance.

As it happened, the only time I was challenged was entering the transit lounge. I had to show my boarding pass and passport but I'd inadvertently found a loophole in their security and walked right through and back again. *Let's hope it's that easy in Heathrow.*

We eventually took off again headed for London and were arriving in an hour's time. I was now getting a little nervous, but up to then it had been a relaxed flight. At one time the stewardess asked if I was alright as I had refused all the meals. I replied that I had picked up a stomach bug and couldn't eat.

Chapter 12

England

An hour or so later we dropped out of the March clouds about a thousand feet above the river Thames. We followed the river west. The 747 touched down. This was it. *In the next thirty minutes I'll know if I'm spending the next couple of years in the nick or if I'll be with my family tonight.*

I waited around for my bags. They came fairly soon and when I had picked them off the carousel, I looked around for the exit. Over in the far corner were the red and green exit channels. *Oh well*, I thought. *This is it!*

I walked steadily and with my head up, towards the green exit. As I came round the corner, there were two people who had been stopped for a check. *Shit!* There were a couple of other officers just stood around watching passengers come through, *I bet they'll stop me!*

Sure enough, as I approached the exit to the outside an officer started walking my way, Just as I thought he was going to stop me, he went for the couple behind me! Jesus Christ! If that officer knew how close he had come to busting ten kilos of hash, he would be kicking himself. I just kept going and looked as if I had seen people waiting for me at the barrier.

Then, I WAS THROUGH! I found myself in a busy concourse with my two suitcases. I felt elated and just stood there for a moment savouring the feeling.

"Right! Pull yourself together." The adrenaline was coursing through me, what a rush! I still had to get to Bristol and then home. Still some one hundred miles away. Still, I had plenty of time. It was just mid-morning. I stepped out of the airport building towards the Taxi rank. The fresh cold air was a big change. There were new cars, trucks, and buses after the patched up wreaks of trucks and old English-style cars of India. The air smelled crisp and there was a chill in the air, but the sun, albeit weak and watery, was out. I found it hard to believe that it was the same sun that, just hours before, was creasingly hot.

I felt more and more elated, I'd done it. All I'd need to do was sell it and I'd be on the plane back to India. *OK let's get home*, I thought. I needed to get to Victoria coach station to catch the bus to Bristol and then a bus to my home. I walked up to the first taxi in the rank. The driver was out of his car, cleaning his rear window.

"Victoria coach station, please driver."

"Sure pal, no problem but see that bus over there? 'E'll be going there right now and 'e'll be a quarter of the price."

"OK thanks," I said but thought to myself, *Why the fuck couldn't he do as he was told?*

The guy was just trying to be helpful, and he was

waiting for the more long distance work, but he unknowingly picked the wrong time. I'd have paid double just to get far away from that fucking airport. I knew that sometimes customs officers would mingle with the crowds to see what they could pick up. Also they liked to let a suitcase through that they knew contained contraband. They would then follow the person and wait to see if he was being met by anyone. They would arrest all those who turned up.

I just spun on my heel and nonchalantly, and sauntered over to the waiting coach.

I was the last one aboard. I paid the fare and stuffed my bags in the front luggage space. I sat where I could see my cases. I didn't want anybody taking mine by mistake. What a shock they would have got on opening mine! I arrived at Victoria coach station. I figured that the hash oil would be moving out of my stomach and into my gut by now, so perhaps I could have a sandwich as I was now very hungry.

The bus came into its stand and the driver was checking our tickets and stuffing the suitcases into the boot. I chose a seat halfway down the bus. We pulled out of the station and made our way through the West London traffic. It wasn't too long before we were passing Hammersmith Flyover on the elevated section of the M4 motorway. *That's it! I can relax now. Nobody following me. I'm totally invisible.* I felt on top of the world and the feeling that I could do anything had returned, tenfold. My god! How the pride went before the fall!

The motorway flashed by. We approached Membury service area and I can remember seeing the tall TV mast just beside the service area and thinking, *Ah Membury. Won't be long now.* I wished I was back in Anjuna. *They are so far away from me. Still I'll be back with them next week or so I'll have a swim in that sparkling sea... OH FUCK!*

I suddenly realised that I had drifted off into thought and had been staring intently at the back of the seat in front, while my mind had wandered back to Anjuna.

OH FUCKING NO! I'm getting stoned! But I haven't had a smoke since leaving the hotel in Bombay! That could only mean one thing! A condom full of un-cut, concentrated, top quality Kashmiri hash oil, had leaked and was now hitting my system!

OH MY FUCKING GOD! WHAT THE FUCK AM I GONNA DO?

All the realisation and questions and downright bowel-loosening fear went through my brain in a microsecond. I almost succumbed to blind panic, right there.

I could feel the effect getting stronger and stronger. *What the fuck am I gonna do?*

None of the other passengers would have seen anything of the turmoil going on inside me. They may have perhaps seen the very slight physical jerk, as I sat upright when I realised what was happening. I was getting more and more stoned, my eyes were now bloodshot and half open, my heart was thumping and I was feeling very flaky. *What if one condom has broken on some obstacle in my gut, and when the next package comes along, it'll break as well?* That thought drove me to the very edge of panic.

By the time we pulled into Bristol bus station, I was almost out of control, on rubber legs and a neck that wouldn't quite support my head without tremendous effort. To focus my bloodshot eyes was equally difficult. To cap it all, my mouth was as dry as the Gobi desert!

I've got to get to a hospital or I'm going to die. I struggled out of my seat and stumbled off the bus. I remembered that Bristol Royal Infirmary was right next door so I headed off in that direction.

FUCK, FUCK, FUCK! MY CASES!

I turned around and swayed unsteadily back toward the bus. It had left the stand and was reversing prior to pulling out of the station. Its next stop was Exeter!

I just jumped in front of the bus and put my arms up. The effort nearly made me pass out.

"Wassup?" demanded a well irritated driver.

"I'm real s- s- sorry pal, I've just come back from India and I've got a bad stomach bug. I needed to get to the hospital, but forgot my bags." I didn't need to act! He could see from my bloodshot eyes and my panting, white face.

His attitude changed completely.

"Oh alright, M'son. Don't you worry, we'll get 'm out, right here."

"Thanks so much drive." He held up several coaches as he got my bags out of the boot. He put them on the kerb for me.

"Hope you're better soon, son."

"Thanks again, driver."

He drove on and all the buses exited the station. I was left there with two bags. And about to pass out! Then, an inspiration came from somewhere. The left luggage office!

The last thing I needed was to pass out, holding the bags. The police would notice that kind of thing and they'd only have to ask me to open my bags, and the games up. I struggled over and filled out the form with shaky hand. I paid the money to the lady behind the counter.

"Are you alright?" she asked.

"No I'm not. I just came in from India and on the way home this food poisoning came on. I've got to get to the hospital before I pass out."

"Don't you worry. Just tuck that ticket in your pocket. Them bags'll be safe here. Now don't you worry, go an' get yerself seen to. You be able to get to hospital OK?"

"Yeah I'll make it, no need to bother anybody. Thanks so much, love."

I staggered to the emergency entrance of the hospital, through the doors and straight up to a young-ish, bespectacled, sister.

"Sister I have some hash oil, in condoms, in my stomach and one of them's burst!" I didn't follow it up, just stood there swaying a bit.

She looked at me with a mix of shock and disgust. "What?"

I took a shaky breath and started again.

"No don't bother. I don't want to know. Wait in that cubicle over there. Doctor will be with you as soon as he can."

"Will it be long, Sister? Because I think it's going to make me pass out, soon."

"Should have thought of that before swallowing that stuff. Doctor will be there as soon as he can." The curtains swished shut and I was left there alone.

I lay on the bed, my mind in complete turmoil. I was convinced I was going to die, no ifs or buts. I'd never see my family again. Did I tell them that I loved them, before I left? I wasn't thinking clearly of course and I was worried about their safety, but the kids were with Isobel. If my thinking had been clear, I knew she could handle anything that came along, without breaking a sweat.

There was a conversation going on next door. It was surreal. About somebody breaking a leg skiing, or something. The sound wrapped around, along with the room. Suddenly I sat up with a start! What the hell was I complaining about? I'd always said I wanted to go out, stoned. *So here you are. What's the problem?*

It was like a slap in the face. I just sat there on the edge of the bed completely calm and, in my mind, waited to die. I don't know how long I sat there in my death trance. It was eventually broken by a smiling, young, face in a white coat, with stethoscope over his shoulder.

"Eye, eye. Wha've you been up to?" He asked with a grin.

"I've just flown in from India and I've got about a kilo of hash oil in my stomach, in condoms and one of them's broke."

Without a flicker, he asked, "How much in each condom?"

"About fifteen or twenty grams each."

"Well you certainly don't look as if it's all hit your system. Do you smoke a lot, normally?"

"Yes. I guess you'd call me a chronic user. I've smoked it all my adult life." I then quickly, related the tale of the 'elephant' in Quetta.

"Well it's your high consumption that has saved you this time. Your system is used to dealing with it. Go to the canteen and get the sweetest doughnut you can find, buy some chocolate as well, it'll help to cancel the effects of the massive THC dose."

I suddenly realised I hadn't got any worse. My heart was still thumping. I still felt like a wrung out flannel. Still sounded as if I was hearing everything as if down a long corridor. The room, that I viewed through heavily bloodshot eyes, wasn't staying still, but no worse!

"Take these tablets now. Then use this suppository. The tablets will irritate your gut so much that it won't absorb any more. The suppository will work instantly, and remove anything from your bowel, so be by a toilet! How was India? I was there last year for three months. Got shit-faced every night in Srinagar."

"Oh, up in Kashmir?" I said.

"Yeah, loved it. Stayed at my Indian friend's house. We were at uni together. OK! Use that suppository and come back here, we'll see how you are by then," and he was already looking at his next case.

"Thanks Doc."

I took the suppository and headed for the toilet. As I stepped out into the annex, I saw two uniformed police officers talking to the sister that I'd spoken to first.

They were between me and the toilet. I had to pass right by them. My guts dropped but it was too late to turn round. I brazened it out and walked right past them.

I got into the toilet, it was empty, thankfully. I went inside a booth, shoved the suppository up my arse, sat on the toilet and waited. It was instant alright. A steel hand gripped my guts. Eventually I was looking down at two condoms in the toilet pan. *What do I do? Wash them off and put them in my pocket and possibly get busted by the Old Bill, waiting outside?* Or flush them? That way I'd have nothing on me, and I could deny everything. I chose the latter. Goodbye expensive and pure smoke. It really went against the grain but had to be done.

I came out of the toilet and again walked the gauntlet back to the cubical. This time one of the policeman turned to look at me but turned back to the sister, who was still talking with them. I went and sat on the bed again, still feeling like a trashed ragdoll. And now very paranoid. They could come and arrest me any time. Eventually the doctor turned up with a few more of the coarse brown tablets he'd given me before.

"Take these over the next few days but stay near a toilet. Oh, and don't do anything so bloody stupid again, do you fully realise how close you came?"

"Doc I can't thank you enough but I reckon that sister

has grassed me up to the Old Bill."

"I doubt it very much. The police are here on another matter. Go home. Take the tablets and get some rest, bye."

"Bye Doc. Thanks again." He cast a smile back over his shoulder and was gone.

I walked out into the annex again. Sure enough there was no sign of the sister or the police. Talk about relief. I had, in my mind, without any shadow of a doubt, just escaped death by the smallest margin. I had been totally and one hundred per cent, certain that I was about to die.

The feeling of being reborn was remarkable. It even penetrated through the drug haze. I stumbled back toward the bus station. I had to think of a way to get my suitcases out, without a ticket. I'd destroyed my ticket. Thinking that I was about to pass out. I didn't want anything connecting me with ten kilos of hash! By some miracle of chance, the office was still open with the same woman behind the counter.

"Oh it's you again. You sure you're OK? You look like shit."

I slumped down in the chair by the counter. "I've been up the hospital and they gave me some pills. It's just a real bad stomach bug. You wanna see the colour of the tablets they gave me. The only trouble is in all the confusion, I've lost my ticket. I've still got my passport and it'll be the same name on the ticket."

"That's alright, you'll recognise your own cases?"

"Yeah, no problem."

"OK that'll save me searching all the labels. Come with me."

We went back to an area of high steel, racking.

"There they are. On the second level." The effort of getting the suitcases down, made me almost pass out again and I sat down a bit quickly on a nearby crate.

"Alright I'll fill out a lost ticket form. I should get yourself home if I was you."

"Thank you so much for your help. I think I'll go and get a taxi."

I took my cases and walked down to the taxi rank. I went to the first car. "Can you take me to Chilcompton? It's down by Radstock. I might fall asleep on the way. I've just come down from Heathrow on the bus. I flew in from India this morning and I've got a real bad stomach bug."

"Dun't thee worry, m'son, I'll get 'e 'ome."

"Thanks so much." I settled into the back seat. My head was clearing a little but still well flaky. I realised what a trial I'd just been through. I was lucky I'd got away with it. It could have been so different if I'd been caught. Isobel would have had to come home with the kids and I'd probably be in the nick for a few years. Our wonderful adventure would have come to a bad end. I realised how stupid and thoughtless I'd been. I had no trouble with the breaking the law bit. Even back then the corruption and graft by big companies and the greed of the banks with politicians in their pocket. As for the police, well they were more corrupt than anyone.

Of course it's easy to rationalise any action or thought but in my mind you either take a shafting and say thank you to them for keeping you down, or you quit your moaning and take control of your own life. We pulled up outside my parents' home in Chilcompton. It was dark now and the lights were on inside. The taxi drove off with my grateful thanks and a good tip. I stood there in the middle of a small village in the West of England. Not twenty-four hours ago I was in the sun with Isobel and the kids. I was now missing them big time. The culture shock was strong. I'd already phoned home as soon as I'd landed so they knew I was coming. But that was a lifetime ago, or so it seemed, so intense were the last few hours. Time to pull myself together. I was going to face a barrage of well-meaning questions as to why I'd come home without Isobel and the kids. They'd naturally want a full report. I'd be as honest as possible about why I was home.

It was great to see everyone again. My brother and his wife had come over as well. They all remarked on how crappy I was looking but I had the stomach bug story ready for that. I had just come from India, after all. I made it to bed early the old body clock was all over the place. Thank goodness Mum and Dad were both still working, Mum, part time. Dad, full time in a petrol station, so I had the house to myself. I spent the time sitting in my room with a bucket! By the time nature had taken its course, it turned out that between twenty and thirty grams had leaked into my system. How the hell had I come out of that alive?

OK, a couple of days to recover and I'll be fine. I made a phone call to my most trusted contact and told him what I had. He got really excited and came over right away. By this time I'd unpacked all the hash and oil. The oil, which was the most difficult stuff in the universe to deal with, due to its intensely sticky nature. It was more sticky than molten pitch. The only effective way to deal with it, was to freeze it. It could then be chipped off in grams or multiples thereof, in between some cigarette papers. In this way nothing gets wasted. Put it in any other container and it stuck to it like the proverbial 'shit to a blanket', and some would always get wasted. But you could always smoke the cigarette papers when all the oil had been used.

Phill, my contact and old friend, came over. I opened the door to him just a crack. "Alright Phill? That you, mate?" I opened the door a little more.

"Fuck man, you look like shit. Where's Isobel and the rugrats?" I held up my hand.

"Dial it back a bit will yu' Phill. I'm really, really, fragile at the moment. I'll fill you in, in a while but business first. Let's go up to my room."

We walked in and I threw back the blanket that I'd covered it all with, on top of the bed.

"Jesus H. Christ. Woow will you look at that?"

"It's black Kashmir hash of the finest quality. This kind of stuff never makes it over here. You won't believe how strong it is. Have you had a smoke of anything, yet?"

"Ahhh, no, I ahh, not yet." He was mesmerised by the dope on the bed.

"It's un-cut Kasmiri hash oil as well. It's really kick arse stuff. I can vouch for that! Let's get some coffee and you can skin one up and test the strength, but I warn you go slowly and carefully."

My warning served only to excite him more and his eyes sparkled. Of all the people I knew, Phill loved a good smoke and he could keep up with me. Just! I smiled at him.

"It's really that good Phill. You are in for such a treat. He rolled a single one up and I started to tell him the story of what had just happened to me.

He listened with growing disbelief. His jaw was literally dropping.

"Stop! For fuck's sake! I can't take this in. The dope! This shit!" He waved his hand toward me. "What the fuck are you telling me? It's like some dreadful nightmare. Fuck, man fuuuuuck! This is some wicked shit, fuckin' hell." He actually put the spliff down and let it go out. He was only a quarter of the way down it!

"Phill I swear that's exactly what happened, no bull."

"Fuck man, that is some kick arse, shit, what's the deal? Quick before I pass out." He laughed.

"OK, this is it. You take a small sample and you see your people and you handle it all. I can't do it up front, they are going to have to trust you and pay you without seeing any of it Just what you give them to smoke. The other thing is I want you to sell it by the ounce."

"You're kiddin' me."

"No I ain't. Think about it. You've got this shit, the like of which comes along every blue moon. It's going to fly off the shelves. You'll be limiting how many ounces you sell to each person. Don't do any discount for quantity. Even if you charge them double the market rate, they'll buy, because the quality is exceptional. It's not as if we're ripping anyone off, it IS top quality."

"Yeah you're right I guess."

"Yeah, and I gotta do it quick. I'm hoping to fly back to India next week."

"Shit! Al, that ain't a lot of time. I don't know about that. I couldn't promise that."

"What do I hear? Am I hearing this from you? A legend in your own lunch time? You have as many contacts as me, you know as many people as me, probably more, and you love the weed, just like me. There were a couple of others I could call but I thought you'd like first crack at it. You can make a lot of money on this, but that's how it's got to be done. I know it ain't the way we normally work, but this is exceptional, especially when you think of what I've been through to get this here."

"No shit on that one. I can do it. I'll rope the Mrs into it."

"I'll stay by the phone and you can come round when you need to, about this time of day when it's quiet, but call me only this time of day I don't want the phone going off all the time. From here mate, it's full speed ahead, you up for it?"

"Fuckin' right pal," he grinned. We hung out for a few hours and I caught him up on the trip so far. He got fairly wasted and enjoyed and appreciated the smoke, but, and this is why I called him first, when it was time to go to work he did it, and lived it, till it was done. I spent a relaxed evening with Mum and Dad. They both listened closely and Dad was fascinated to hear how Pakistan had become. He was stationed in Rawalpindi before and during the war. Mum wanted to know everything that we'd done, and especially the kids. She didn't want me to take the kids away in the first place.

Next morning the phone went.

"Fuckin' 'ell man! I need to come over."

"Yeah. All quiet at the moment Phill. Been a long night?"

"You ain't gonna believe it. See you in a minute." The line went dead. Phill swooped in with the March wind. He was carrying a brown Hessian carrier bag.

"Look at this." He pulled the towel off the top of the bag. It was full of cash!

"Fuck me! Went down a treat, then." He looked how I felt.

"There's enough for three kilos there, in ounces of course. They loved it. The only question I get asked is, 'how much can I have?' I'd tell them they could only buy it by the ounce. They weren't impressed with that. But, you were right, the quality overcomes all that. One guy bought a kilo at ounce prices."

We got busy and counted all the money into different piles, fives, tens, and twenties. There were so many piles, you couldn't see the carpet clearly. We weighed it all out and away went Phill again with the bag under his arm.

During the week, Phill came and went each day, carrying that brown bag. In the end we had almost twenty grand and still had a kilo and most of the oil, yet to sell. I'd managed to send a telegram to Dale telling him that I'd had some problems but that all being well, I'd be back by next weekend. That didn't happen because of the hash oil. Oil is not the easiest thing to sell but eventually the quality of it was so good that I sold it all in one go. I had to cut it a bit to make up for what I'd lost. It took nearly another week. I booked a ticket back with Air India, and told Mum and Dad I'd be back in a month or so, with Isobel and the kids.

Phil came round that evening before I left, and we got wasted together. "You've done a magnificent job mate. How much did you make? I don't mean exactly , but ball park, must be around six or seven."

"Just under ten actually. We're going to put it down on our own place."

"Brilliant! Not bad for a few days' work eh? Bet 'she who must be obeyed' is happy with that."

"'Appy ain't the word. Your name is hallowed in our gaff. If I brought her over she'd give you a blowjob." I did a coffee-down-the-nose job.

"Leave it out! Anyway, I'm off to London tomorrow and catching the early flight back to Bombay the day after, so perhaps she could save it till next time."

We laughed. It felt good to think that I'd done Phill some good. He'd always been straight with me and we'd had some wild times together. I also know that he'd put even more, onto each ounce.

"How are you going to get the cash out?"

"I thought I'd pack it into a cornflake box and a big pack of tea bags, or something that can't be bought in India."

"I should have those kind of problems."

"Truth is, that if you've got a British passport nobody looks at you. German, French, Italian, they all get a look, now and again. But I've never heard of a Brit, getting bothered. It's a hangover from the Raj days."

I got up next day and spent most of the day sorting the money. I put ten grand in the bank, took two grand for spending money, and divided the rest up between Dale and Paeso. I bound all the money in plastic bags and wrapped them in parcel tape. I carefully opened a giant pack of cornflakes and stuffed the money in. There wasn't much room for cornflakes but at least in those days they didn't have x-ray machines and very very few sniffer dogs.

I checked in at Heathrow and as the bags went off, I remembered the nickname that Heathrow had at the time, 'Thiefrow'. It made me a little uncomfortable. I could claim for missing cases but claiming for the money would be right out of the question. Even so, I still felt like 'Jack the Lad', buying presents for the kids and Isobel, newspapers, a Canon SLR camera, spare telephoto lens, also boxes of film for it.

The flight was long and boring. I ordered a bottle of wine with the appallingly plastic in-flight, meal. It sent me to sleep, and I caught up on some of the sleep I'd missed out on in the last couple of weeks. I fell asleep thinking how I'd soon see Isobel and the kids. I can remember thinking I hoped that Eric hadn't been substituted too often, but realised that wasn't realistic. After all, they would be in an empty house together.

Chapter 13

India

We landed at Bombay airport at four in the morning. As I stepped out of the air-conditioned plane, the full heat and 90 per cent humidity hit me like walking into a hot shower. The smell of India was in the air. Completely different background smell to London.

Paeso was there to meet me and had a car waiting. We drove through the suburbs of Bombay to his palatial flat. As I counted out his money from the cornflakes box he laid a bomb on me. "Hollywood Pete was here yesterday. He said Isobel wasn't very well. He thought she had hepatitis."

"Oh Jesus I've got to get back to Anjuna. Paeso. Can your driver take me back to the airport?"

"Sure but the flight's not until midday, at least have

some breakfast. I'll get my cook to put something together."

"Yeah OK. Fucking hepatitis! Shit that's not good."

"I expect it was from the water. The wells get low just before monsoon and that's where it comes from."

I went straight back to the airport and waited for the flight to Goa, now worried sick. It was a rotten journey. The taxi ride from the airport was horrendous. It involved a ferry that was little more than a raft with a spluttering outboard and enough room for 4 cars! Eventually I ended up outside the house in Anjuna. It was dark but I could see a few candles flickering. When I got inside, poor Isobel was laying in the bed looking yellow in colour and very ill. She had managed to drag herself to the hospital along with the kids and been treated. The Goanese lady, Maria, next door, had looked after her and the kids. She and Eric had helped look after the kids and cook for them and Isobel. Eric had to move on with Sten's bus so Maria took over completely. She also told the kids that if they didn't behave, Isobel could die! Can you believe that shit? They were Catholics after all, who believe in hell-fire and damnation for any transgression. But I was a bit angry about that. Typical Catholic medieval, reaction. I also really didn't like the way they would tie Joseph's hands to his feet and sit him out in the midday sun, as a punishment! Either way I paid her well for her help with Isobel while I was away.

Maria had called in the herbalist lady, Mrs DeSilva. She made up some herbal remedies, one of which was a banana cut along its length with some herbs sprinkled along it. Isobel had had a hard time getting herself to hospital and being really ill, I just dropped everything and concentrated on getting her back to health. The very next day I called in a taxi and got him to take us to the best doctor in Goa. I told the driver, "Money, no problem. You understand?" He did, and took us to a university Professor of Medicine. This guy was called upon, by various embassies when visiting dignitaries got ill. He was a wonderfully eccentric old gentleman. Rather reminded me of the character 'Catweazle', beloved by children.

He gave Isobel a thorough examination and prescribed some injections that Isobel had to do herself. He allowed that because of Isobel's nursing background, otherwise she would have either to attend his surgery every day or he would have to visit every day. She assured him she was fully capable of injecting herself. This she did for a week. I just felt so guilty, buggering off to England on a high risk venture. If I'd have done what I did from home, it would've been different. Gradually bit by bit I told Isobel what had happened. We spent many a hot afternoon in the shade of our front porch. It ran the whole length of the house and was wonderfully cool in the afternoons.

"I think this may have taken a lot out of you physically. I think it might be time we went home for a while. It just isn't possible to get the high protein stuff you should be having. Unless we go to Bombay for recuperation."

During the next couple of weeks I worked at Dale's house and started a few more projects, winging round the world.

"Dale I think it's time for me and the family to go home."

"Man you're kiddin' me. And we've got such a good thing going here." He was right. With Dale's knowledge and experience, I'd learned a lot. His money and my practical skills had made us a good amount of money. Dale was holding ten thousand pounds of mine, which true to his word, I eventually got when I asked for it. That was another thing I liked about this loud, Willie Nelson look-alike. He may have been every Englishman's stereotype of a typical loud-mouthed, done-everything-been-everywhere Yank, but he was honourable.

He didn't have the money now. As I had spent lots of money getting Isobel treatment, I was fast coming to the point where I'd have only enough money with me to pay for the tickets home. So I faced the choice of getting more money sent out. That meant more time hanging around Bombay. and complicated arrangements for my bank to send cash. Or I could fly us all back home for a while so that Isobel could have everything that we couldn't get here. I wasn't going to risk a relapse. "I just can't risk it, mate. Anyway it ain't just that. I've learned things since we've been travelling. Much of it from the journey and the people we've met along the way, including you. You've shown me that provided you don't hurt anyone, you can do as you please. Thanks for the food hampers, by the way."

"My pleasure. She wouldn't let me take her to the hospital, though."

I learned that Dale had gone up in Isobel's estimation as he had called in weekly, with baskets of provisions and fruit. She still didn't have much time for him, but he was no longer "That gobshite on legs." She could be stingingly cruel, could Isobel, if crossed.

"What I want to do is go back and buy another bus. I'm going to bring tourists here for Christmas. Paying passengers. And I reckon between you and this house, with all its Goanese charm and empty rooms, we could make loads of money, while still, discreetly in the background, working on little projects around the world, as we've been doing. Oh! And I think you should buy Nelson's Bar, over there. It would be a great place for tourists to hang out. Goa is going to be a big tourist attraction in years to come. I know that's not what we want but it's going to happen. Either way, we could have a sweet little earner, while living in paradise."

"Goddamn limeys, what the fuck's an earner?"

"Fuckin' septics. You earn at it. Y'know. Make money. It's a nice little earner."

"So how long're y'gonna be gettin' back here with another bus?"

"I reckon just about three months. Maybe less, depending on how Isobel recovers."

"Your bus has gone. Did you know that?"

"Yeah they came to see me the other day, well at least. Timus and Kakey did. They got some guy to drive them up to Kathmandu and he is going to teach Charlie to drive the bus. I'll miss that old bus, it was a good, strong one."

"Yeah but you c'n buy another, right?"

"Yeah, now I've got the wonga."

"Fuckin' speak English, m'thafucka!"

"So sorry, old boy. One can now purchase with ease, another omnibus or Charabanc."

"I'm gonna miss this shit."

"Yeah, stick with me, and I'll teach you how to speak correct English. 'England and America. The only two countries separated by the same language' as Oscar Wilde once said."

"Wasn't that guy a screamin' fag?"

It was only recently when I was contacted by Glynis on Facebook, after thirty odd years, that I learned the rest of the story and what happened to the bus after we left. Charlie had apparently taken over the driving of the bus but fell out with everybody he came across. His attitude and treatment of Glynis became physically abusive on his part. He and Glynis and Syd, who left the bus in Tehran and who they met again on the way through Kabul city, had started to drive back toward the UK. They got as far as Greece, where Charlie had an accident and totalled a car and put the driver and his family in hospital.

Being unable to meet the compensation payment to the Greek family he'd trashed, they took the only thing of value that he had. The bus! Glynis told me how Charlie had to do it properly. They made him telex London to get a certificate stating that the Carnet de Passage would be null and void and permanent export status to the Greek government would be registered on the vehicles records at DVLC. This meant that should it turn up in England and apply for road tax, it would be refused, as that vehicle was shown as permanently exported.

Glynis said it was a paperwork nightmare that lasted weeks. Charlie was detained while it was sorted. She also told me that after this, she and Charlie broke up. She couldn't handle his extreme ways and the physical abuse. I wasn't surprised when I heard this. Charlie still spends six months of the year in Goa, apparently.

It was intensely hot and dry just before the monsoon broke. The humidity was unbearable at night. I would light a chillum at night time and the effort of coughing would break me out in a sea of sweat. You just couldn't we ar anything around the house, it would be drenched in a matter of minutes.

We decided to travel up to Bombay on the 'luxury' bus. That was a laugh. I inspected the double tyres on the back of the bus. It had obviously had an explosive blow-out that had badly damaged the wall of the tyre. Rather than discard a tyre that still had a bit of tread, someone had cut out a part of a side wall from another tyre and bolted, yes, I did say 'bolted', with large-diameter washers and coach bolts with their rounded heads positioned inwards so that the bolts didn't pierce the inner tube! Unbelievable! If they thought I was getting on a bus like that and put my family's life at risk. I told the operator that if I turned up in the morning and they put us on a bus with tyres like that, I'd report him to the police and the tourist board.

"Oh, sahib don't vorry it is safe."

"You may get away with that, with other tourists, but I'm a heavy vehicle mechanic and I know how dangerous that is. You have refused to give me my money back, so be ready tomorrow." I was full of righteous indignation. How could they put people's lives at risk like that. How many buses did I pass, upside-down in the ditch, or nose down, in some field? How many times did some local newspaper have screaming headlines, "Bus runs off road! twenty passengers killed and forty injured!" How many were there on that bus?

We all got shamefully wasted that evening and night. Except for Isobel, who was holding court with all her friends, who hadn't seen her since she became ill. I learnt later, that she had sent them all away, including Eric, when it was confirmed that she had hepatitis and was highly infectious. She was still looking washed out. Well, as washed out as you can look with a deep, all over tan! But she certainly looked like she'd been through, not just physical pain, but severe mental strain as well. We'd both been through an ordeal that had pushed us to our limits! We'd both come through it. Scarred, but through it.

I got the feeling that Isobel felt that, even though she had been seriously ill, the children had come first, every time. It had made her feel good with herself, deservedly. As far as I was concerned, when the chips were down, when reality smacks you in the face, you do the right thing. My opinion and love for her could not have been stronger at this point. I would have given my life for her, in a heartbeat.

It goes without saying that gratitude and love is even stronger as I write this some thirty years later.

We flung the suitcases in the taxi. Everyone waved us off and we drove to Mapusa bus station. We sat in the chai shop opposite, while the roof-rack was packed with everything including, chicken, a goat and huge billowing sheets stuffed with belongings and tied at the corners. This was all being tied down by bus station wallahs and porters, while being loudly cajoled and instructed from the ground by the relevant passengers. In short, it was chaos and pandemonium with the loud knob full on! It seemed that the operators didn't want to deal with the police, or risk the wrath of the tourist board, which was run by local traders, in the form of a British style 'Lions Club'. All the tyres were in good condition!

The rains had started a few days ago. There was a freshness in the air. It was not the Monsoon proper, but the first few rains followed about a week or so later by massive downpours, which even in rainy England, we had not seen the likes of.

The pre-rains caused wonderful plants and flowers to spring from the ground, virtually, overnight. It also caused the dangerous snakes including the deadly cobra to become active. The wells and rice fields overflowed with fresh water and everything seemed fresher. We had a fairly uneventful ride in the bus, at least that's by Indian standards. We lost one young lad passenger who was riding with his goat on the long roof rack on top of the bus. We went round a corner a little too quickly and too close to a tree. He got knocked in the head and had to be taken to the nearest hospital. We passed three buses like ours, with their wheels in the air with accompanying scenes of carnage. I was never so glad to pull into a bus station in my life!

We caught a taxi round to Stiffles Hotel, Just behind The Taj Mahal Hotel on Colaba seafront. We rested for a day helped by the Black Kashmir that I bought from one of the back-street traders for ten rupees. It was like horse tranquiliser. Sometimes it was all I could do to get out from underneath the overhead fan. It was all I could do to lift my head.

I managed to book us all tickets home. We'd be flying in a couple of days' time. We took the time to look around the centre of Bombay and visited the Prince of Wales Museum, a magnificent building in the style of Wren, that the British had built. The museum was full of exquisitely and intricately carved ivory, accompanied by photographs of the pride of the British Raj standing in front of rows and rows of dead animals that they'd shot. It was sickening. The ivory was bad enough. Each exhibit in the ivory and the silver and gold exhibit had a little card stating it was owned by Sir Ratan Tata. Head of the Tata Industrial Dynasty that is now a global company. Owning amongst, other things as Jaguar cars and Land Rover. Most of the trucks in India at that time, were Tata copies of Mercedes Benz.

I spent the rest of our waiting time getting a slab of Black Kashmir dope to stuff down my pants and walk through Heathrow Airport. (I wasn't going to swallow anything this time!) We were all excited about going home and seeing everybody. The kids drew pictures to show Nanny and Grampy what it was like here. The morning came and we got to the airport for the four o'clock British Airways to London. Exactly the same route that I'd taken before. Though I didn't drink in the bar with the flight crew the night before! Isobel and the kids were excited, though a little scared as none of them had flown before. I'd done it a couple of times, now.

We read, slept, ate, watched some corny film, smoked and wandered down to the toilets just to stretch our legs. The pilots voice came over the speaker, "Ladies and gentlemen, boys and girls, we've started our decent into Tehran and because I have had an indicator light come on on the panel, I'll get it checked out on the ground. It's a very minor fault and I anticipate it will be fixed quickly. We will be on the ground a little longer than usual so we are going to disembark everyone to the transit lounge.

Your wait will be more acceptable there. Temperature on the ground is ninety, Fahrenheit. There are lavish toilet facilities and a duty free shop."

There were moans and mutters until the captain added, "There's also a bar."

The huge glass windows over our waiting plane were letting in fierce afternoon sunshine. The temperature was in the nineties outside. We waited and waited. I stupidly managed to break off a small piece of hash and went out to the toilets. I made up a 'Farsi' and blew the smoke out of the window. When someone came in, I shot into a cubical. The smell must have hung around but I just didn't think or worry about it. Very silly indeed.

As I came out of the toilet a fully armed policeman grabbed my arm. *Oh Christ*, I thought. *Someone has grassed me up to him*. He leaned in close to my ear.

"Mister! You can buy two carton 'vinniston cigarette, at Duty Free, for me. No possible for me. Big trouble with my capitan, you understand?"

"Yeah. No problem, Agahar;" I took the two one thousand rial notes with relief, and bought the cigarettes for him.

"Thank you mister, thank you."

The P.A. went off.

"Will all passengers on British Airways, flight seven, three, one, to London, please board the plane through gate nineteen." That caused us all to move toward the gate.

I thought it a bit strange that the engines didn't start after we'd all got on board. Next thing you know the captain told us that our take-off slot had been taken because of the time lost on the fault. That meant we had to sit on the tarmac without engines running, therefore no air conditioning. It got so stifling on board that the captain ordered all the doors open and a cabin crew member to be stationed at every door to stop people accidentally falling out. Eventually the captain 'accidentally' left his P.A. microphone switched on while he spoke to the tower.

"Tehran. This is Speedbird seven, thirty, one, papa, delta. Now come on. What's going on? Sort this out please. I have three hundred and twenty seven souls aboard and I still don't have engine start clearance. It's hotter than hell here."

We didn't hear the reply but it must have been positive, as very soon after, I heard the engines start to 'spool up'. The captain came over the P.A. again. "Sorry to keep you waiting. We now have a take-off slot but unfortunately the take-off direction will be over the city. I'll then turn one hundred and eighty degrees and head north for London. The other thing is that taking off over the city will be very bumpy because of the heat coming up from the city. Don't worry. This is perfectly normal and easily within the capability of the seven four seven, but as I say, it will get a bit bumpy. If I have any further information for you, I'll speak to you again when we reach cruising height. So make sure your seat belts are done up. As soon as I get final clearance we'll be off. Thank you."

A few moments later we got clearance and we hurtled off down the runway. It seemed to take ages to reach take off speed. Just when it seemed we'd run out of runway, up came the nose and we started to climb. I noticed that the cabin crew were still strapped in when usually by this time they'd be busy with whatever it is they do.

Then we started to shake. Then we started to shake violently and, as the climb went on, I felt the plane start to drop. The engine throttle was opened and the power started us climbing again. By this time the cutlery and equipment in the galley were vibrating noisily. Isobel, the kids and I, were sat in the four central seats and right in front of one of the movie screens. As the plane banked round to the north, all hell let loose as the plane at one moment had wind beneath its wings and the next moment, none! And it would make bowel emptying, drops for a hundred feet or so, till the wind came back under the wings and we climbed on. Overhead lockers were falling open and a few oxygen masks came down in error. This did nothing to calm the passengers.

Isobel was watching the plastic mouldings around the movie screen all move in different directions. "Is that meant to move like that?" she asked, nodding toward the mouldings but not letting the kids see how worried she was. None of them had flown before. As the plane hit another low pressure trough, I assured her that this was normal.

"They always move around like this when there's turbulence. It's designed to move like this." This I knew to be bullshit but it was comforting to her. If I wasn't worried, she would not be. I couldn't let on that I was as scared as they were.

Eventually we left Tehran airspace and crossed the mountains. It was no was smooth as a motorway and we were about thirty eight thousand feet up at cruise altitude. The stop in Frankfurt was much shorter than last time and, what seemed all of a sudden, the captain announced he was starting our decent into Heathrow.

Chapter 14

England

We were getting excited now. We'd be seeing Nanny and Grampy and all the cousins. We'd be landing late afternoon at Heathrow. The captain came on again to tell us that the shuttle bus drivers were on strike and there would be temporary buses laid on, but as they were extremely busy, we'd probably have to wait hours to go into central London.

"In short ladies and gentlemen, it's chaos down there. Be prepared for long delays. Welcome to Heathrow."

"This is it," I whispered to Isobel. "I'd better pull me underpants up tight. Don't want anything dropping out, do we!"

"Is this going to be alright?"

"Yeah. Our bags are clean. We don't have anything do

BEYOND THE 'BUT' *A Long Road to India*

we!" It always helped to forget you were carrying anything and put it out of your mind. It then showed in the confidence in your face. Look everybody in the eye. Sounds crazy, I know, but it works.

We retrieved our bags and made for the green channel to exit the airport. Just as we rounded the corner we were stopped by a very young customs officer. He had an older, grey-haired officer behind him who stood back silently and just observed. I got the impression that the young guy was under training.

We got all the usual questions and I smiled and looked them right in the eye. I answered as truthfully as possible. After going through my bag, they gave us the 'all clear' without touching Isobel's bag. How innocent it was in those days. No sniffer dogs. No machines that read, at the molecular level, swabs put into it, etc., etc.

The place was heaving with people waiting to get clear of the airport. We went to the first coffee bar we came to, and had a coffee while we decided what to do. I needed a light for my cigarette so I went back to the counter and asked for a box of matches.

"Sorry sir. We don't sell matches here but you can buy a pack of three Bic disposable lighters."

Just as he said that, a uniformed arm with a hand holding a lighter, appeared over my shoulder.

"Thanks," I said, turning to see the young customs officer that had searched my bag. I was surprised to see him.

"Oh by the way, we forgot to look in the kids' stuffed toys," he said with a grin and a wink.

"You forgot to look up my arse as well," I countered, brazenly.

"We ain't THAT interested." We laughed at that one.

"Thanks again for the light."

"All part of the service." He smiled, picked up his coffee and was gone.

"What did he want?"

I related word for word, what had been said. She shifted uncomfortably. "I think we might as well try and make our own way west. It's no good waiting for hours just to go the other direction, into Victoria or Paddington. It'll be crowded there at this time of day. Why don't we get a taxi from here to the slip road of the motorway, or even several junctions down west, and then thumb it from there?"

"That's going to be a hassle with the kids and cases," said Isobel.

"Well it's either that, or we may be here all night. We'll probably get a lift with the kids and all. Why don't you go and put a nice tight T-shirt on and stand in front of the hand drier so that your nipples stand out like organ stops? We'll get a lift soon enough!" I got a dig in the ribs for that.

The taxi dropped us at the slipway for the western carriageway. I'd already phoned home to say we were on our way, but that there was a strike the airport and we'd decided to thumb a lift. I asked my brother if he'd meet us at the roundabout at the top of the Bath junction.

We'd been thumbing for about half an hour when a lad in a Ford Cortina pulled up. He was a Welsh kid on his way home to Cardiff.

"Bloody perfect. I will of course pay for your coffees and a sticky bun, should you care to stop." I smiled.

"Well, we'll see how it goes boyo, eh. So where have you come from?" he asked as we pulled onto the motorway.

"India!" I said dramatically.

"Go on. You're kiddin' me."

"No. We landed an hour ago. We've been out East about a year." He was fascinated and listened to a few tales from our travels. He flicked his eyes to the rear view mirror. Seeing that the kids were asleep and Isobel was nodding, he leaned in close.

"Did you get to smoke any good hash. Is it as good as they say?"

"Fuck man! It's mind blowing. Toxic substance."

"Wow!" he said excitedly.

"Like a smoke then, you taffs?"

"Oh aye man, but we don't get much good stuff down at the end of the M4. It's mainly 'home grown'."

Genetically altered 'skunk' had yet to appear. All home grown was very rarely in flower when picked. The leaves were dried and smoked. It was considered better than nothing, at the time. "Oh yes I'd love to try it to see what it's like."

"Funny you should say that," I said, and removed the plaque of shiny black hash from down my pants.

"You didn't bring some back did you boyo?" his eyes going very wide when he caught sight of the hash. Oh bugger me. Will you look at that beautiful sight, now, Bach."

"Got any skins?"

"In the glove box."

I rolled up a normal English-style joint, lit it and passed it to him. The fragrance was sweet and pungent. I hadn't had a smoke since Tehran and it was relaxing me nicely. We drove in silence for quite a while and I was just congratulating myself on a good decision to hitch. The young lad suddenly jerked into speech.

"Would you mind talking to me. I can't feel my legs, or anything below my waist." He decided to tell me this in the fast lane, at seventy miles an hour! Very confidence-building!

"It's OK. Just relax and pull over, I'll do some driving while you relax and get it together, if you like."

"Man that is the best shit I've ever smoked. I could actually feel it creeping up the back of my neck and it's made my teeth itch!"

"Yeah cool stuff, huh? Look! Six miles to Membury services. Pull in there will you, Taff. We need to get some sugar into your bloodstream. Have a sticky bun and a sweet coffee, That'll bring you round."

"Aye no problem. I could do with a pee anyway. What the fuck is that stuff?"

"It's Black Kashmiri. It comes from high up in the foothills of the Himalayas. Legend has it that the atmosphere is so rare up there, that the plant has to secrete extra strong resin to protect its leaves from the intense sunlight. The plant has uninterrupted sunlight from sun-up to sun-down. It's said that at high noon with the sun directly overhead, the resin stands out like dew drops and the perfume of the female flowers is pungent on the air."

I had his full attention and he was lapping it up! All in all, a very successful diversion away from the strange feelings he was having. So I went for the coup d'état.

"Then there's the village girls and the flowering ceremony," I teased.

"What about them?"

"Well, and this is only what I've heard and things I've seen, the girls run naked through the fields of flowering plants, just at the most fragrant, pungent and stickiest time. The young men then come along to rub off the resin deposited on the girls skin as they ran through the shoulder high and very sticky, plants."

"Wowwwww, man. Fuck, woooowwwww," he said, articulately. I noticed his eyes flicked to the rear view mirror, now and again. He was in full control.

"How are the legs now?"

He shuffled round in the seat a bit. "I can feel them now, but a bit pins and needles you know, boyo. That's some heavy shit, and no mistake."

He went silent for most of the rest of the way to Membury services, except for the occasional, "Fuck man! Naked through the plants..."

He was running his own version of the pictures I'd conjured up with my story. I'd entertained him with bullshit but the story would be repeated until it attained legendary status. He would dine out on the story for years... "I was coming down from London and I gave this guy a lift. He had some amazing hash! You wanna hear how he got it?"

"Here's the services." We decelerated down the slip road, that woke up Isobel, who very unusually, had dropped off.

"Where are we?" she asked with a stretch.

"Membury," I replied and I sat staring at the red navigation lights on the TV mast next to the service area. I was thinking about the last time I had seen that mast. I had been heading for a very traumatic experience. I gave a little shudder.

"Wha's up?" Isobel noticed that shudder. I told her how that mast was the last thing I remember before realising that I was in trouble. The last thing I remember seeing before being convinced I was going to die!

"I guess that mast will always remind me of a nightmare time."

Sure enough even now, every time I go past Membury,

and that mast. I remember, and I bless whatever kept me together! We wandered with bleary-eyed kids, one walking, one being carried, into the services. They needed the toilet and were hoping for some sweets. I made a call to home to say we were at Membury services so we wouldn't be long to junction eighteen. We had coffee and a sugary bun for Taff, who was looking a little less pale by now. I was looking around at how fashions had changed since we'd been away. The seventies were known for dodgy fashions. All flares and lace shirts with medallions on chains and lots of hairy chests on display. And that was just the women!

"This is it then. We're an hour or so from the end of our journey."

"'I bin reminded lately, what a long strange trip it's been'." Isobel quoted a line from an old Grateful Dead song.

"Fuck! You can say that again, young'un! Shall we push on? C'mon littl'uns only an hour or so, and we'll see Nanny and Grampy." That got them gleefully jumping up and down.

We arrived at junction eighteen and Taff dropped us on the roundabout. I had quietly broken a piece of the hash off, and pressed it into his hand. His eyes lit up. There was enough for a week's smoking.

"Thanks Taff. You made the last part of our journey a gas."

"It's been a bloody adventure, boyo!" He grinned and stuck his hand out the window. I shook it.

"Cheers Taff, be lucky!" His rear lights disappeared down the slip road. I could see my brother's car over in the lay-by and we headed for it. There was a big welcome for us and we jabbered like crazy on the drive home.

"Thanks for picking us up," I said to him and Maureen, his wife, who'd come along for the ride.

"Can I give you something for the petrol?"

"Nah. It's OK," said Donald, my brother.

By the time we got to the house it was way dark and late. That didn't dampen the enthusiasm that the kids felt on seeing Nanny and Grampy again. "Oh! Look how you've grown. Proper grown up children now." Mum was in tears and squeezing the life out of them. They were running between Nanny and Grampy and getting the stuffing hugged out of them. Their cousins Raquel and Tracey, were there and we spent a couple of hours catching up and drinking tea with fresh MILK!

There was a telegram waiting for me. It was from Dale.

"HAVE TEN STOP WHEN YOU – QUESTION STOP" (I have your money. When are you coming back?)

I smiled to myself at that news. He must have sent it as we left. Mellony fell asleep on Nanny's lap and Alun Jnr. was hanging. We carried them up to beautifully made, soft and warm beds. They were deep in sleep before we left the room.

"It's so lovely to see them. We missed them so much. I'm so glad you are all back safe." Mum began to cry again.

We were back down stairs now with the others. I gave mum a big hug and a kiss on the cheek.

"OK. So now you can have them for as long as you like for at least a couple of weeks as I've got a really busy time, next week."

"Oh how lovely." Both she and Dad were delighted with that news. "What are you going to be doing then?" asked my brother Donald, with mock suspicion.

"Why! I have to go and see a man about a bus!" I grinned.

Printed in Great Britain
by Amazon.co.uk, Ltd.,
Marston Gate.